Albion's Fatal Tree

Albion's Fatal Tree

Crime and Society in

Eighteenth-Century England

Douglas Hay
Peter Linebaugh
John G. Rule
E. P. Thompson
Cal Winslow

PANTHEON BOOKS A Division of Random House
New York

Library of Congress Cataloging in Publication Data
Main entry under title:

Albion's Fatal Tree.

  Includes bibliographical references and index.
  1. Crime and criminals—England—History—
Addresses, essays, lectures. I. Hay, Douglas.
HV6943.A54   1975   364'.942   75-23256
ISBN 0-394-47120-2
ISBN 0-394-73085-2 pbk.

Manufactured in the United States of America

Illustrations

(between pages 64 and 65)

Maps

Abbreviations

Brit. Mus. Add. MSS
  British Museum, Additional Manuscripts

C (H) MSS
  Cholmondeley (Houghton) Manuscripts, Cambridge University Library

CJ
  Commons' Journals

DNB
  Dictionary of National Biography

GLCRO (Mddx Div.)
  Greater London Council Record Office (Middlesex Division)

HLRO
  House of Lords Record Office

HMC
  Historical Manuscripts Commission

Lond. Corp. RO
  London Corporation Record Office
  [All other record offices as (County) RO]

LG
  London Gazette

LJ
  Lords' Journals

The Ordinary's *Account*
  The Ordinary of Newgate, His Account of the Behaviour, Confession, and Dying Words, of the Malefactors who were Executed at Tyburn

PP
  Parliamentary Papers

The Proceedings
  The Whole Proceedings upon the King's Commission of Oyer and Terminer and Gaol Delivery for the City of London and also the Gaol Delivery for the County of Middlesex

Abbreviations

PRO   Public Record Office
   Adm   Admiralty
   Assi   Assizes
   Customs   Board of Customs and Excise
   HCA   High Court of Admiralty
   HO   Home Office
   KB   Court of King's Bench
   PC   Privy Council
   SP   State Papers, Domestic
   T   Treasury
   TS   Treasury Solicitor
   WO   War Office

Radzinowicz
   Sir Leon Radzinowicz, *A History of English Criminal Law and its Administration from 1750*, 4 vols., 1948–68

RCP
   The library of the Royal College of Physicians

RCS
   The library of the Royal College of Surgeons

Suss. Arch. Coll.
   Sussex Archaeological Collections

WSL
   William Salt Library, Stafford

In footnotes the place of publication is London unless otherwise given. Wherever possible we give dates as New Style.

What are these golden Builders doing
Near Mournful ever-weeping Paddington
Standing above that mighty Ruin
Where Satan the first victory won.

Where Albion slept beneath the Fatal Tree
And the Druids golden Knife
Rioted in human gore,
In Offerings of Human Life

They groan'd aloud on London Stone
They groan'd aloud on Tyburns Brook
Albion gave his deadly groan,
And all the Atlantic Mountains Shook.

WILLIAM BLAKE

Preface

All the contributors to this book have been associated at one time in the Centre for the Study of Social History at the University of Warwick. We were all concerned with the social history of eighteenth-century England. And we were all centrally concerned with the law, both as ideology and as actuality and with that century's definition of crime. We were equally concerned with criminality itself, the offences, the offenders and the popular myths of offenders (such as highwaymen and smugglers) as part-hero, part dreadful moral exemplars.

These questions, we became convinced, were central to unlocking the meanings of eighteenth-century social history. From one aspect it appears as if 'crime' multiplied in this century. The statistics are still not fully established and they present difficulties in interpretation. Contributors to this volume (notably Douglas Hay and Peter Linebaugh) are still engaged in their own investigation of these figures; and we have all benefited from the findings and advice of Professor J. M. Beattie of Toronto who has carried this investigation furthest. From another aspect it appears as if it is not just a matter of 'crime' enlarging but equally of a property-conscious oligarchy redefining, through its legislative power, activities, use-rights in common or woods, perquisites in industry, as thefts or offences. For as offences appear to multiply so also do statutes – often imposing the sanction of death – which define hitherto innocent or venial activities (such as some forms of poaching, wood-theft, anonymous letter-writing) as crimes. And the ideology of the ruling oligarchy, which places a supreme value upon property, finds its visible and material embodiment above all in the ideology and practice of the law. Tyburn Tree, as William Blake well understood, stood at the heart of this ideology; and its cere-monies were at the heart of the popular culture also.

This book begins to unlock these meanings; but we do not propose it as offering more than a partial disclosure. In one particular the book has not come out as we had planned it. It is rather easy, when taking a superficial view of eighteenth-century evidence, to propose two distinct kinds of offence and offenders. There are 'good' criminals, who are premature revolutionaries or reformers, forerunners of popular movements – all kinds of rioters, smugglers, poachers, primitive rebels in industry. This appears as 'social crime'. And there then are those who commit crime without qualification: thieves, robbers, highwaymen, forgers, arsonists and murderers. (Around the thieves of all degrees, with their necessary concomitant organization of receivers, informers, the drink and sex trades, it is deceptively easy to borrow contemporary criminological terms of 'deviance' and 'sub-culture'.)

As it turned out, this book appears to draw heavily upon evidence from the first kind of offender. But this is in part accidental. Two or three contributors fell out, and we hope will publish their work subsequently in other places. Existing contributors found some of their materials (of the second sort) unmanageable within the confines of an essay and will be publishing their findings independently. Thus Peter Linebaugh is engaged upon exhaustive research into London criminality in the first half of the eighteenth century; Douglas Hay into Midlands evidence; while Edward Thompson's first submission to this book, on the origins of the Black Act of 1723 and the subsequent history of the act, grew to book-length and is being published as *Whigs and Hunters*.

As a result this book became more weighted towards 'social crime' than we had intended. But we should say that in our researches into legal archives and into the actual offences and offenders it became less possible to sustain any tidy notion of a distinction between these two kinds of crime. There is a real difference in emphasis at each pole: certainly the community (and its culture) was more likely to give shelter to some 'social' offenders (smugglers or rioters in popular causes) than to thieves or sheep-stealers. Yet in many cases we found little evidence of a morally endorsed popular culture here and a deviant sub-culture there. Several of the contributors have raised this question in the context of their own studies, and their conclusions differ in emphasis. In London it appears that the same kind of men and women, with the same kinds of life history, found their way to the gallows for both kinds of offence. In rural parishes, perhaps the more constricted horizon of village life sharpened the definitions about what was, and was not, crime, while certain communities were dependent upon certain products for their livelihood (for example, sheep or cloth) and united against offenders. On the other hand, the same kind of community, in west Yorkshire, appears to have tolerated or sheltered coiners. These distinctions (and our ignorance of popular attitudes in this area is only slowly shifting) were not, however, based on inhibitions upon violence. Poachers and smugglers punished informers and threatened life and property as readily as the Tyburn rioter. And in all spheres of popular culture informers and law-enforcers often lived in a symbiotic relationship upon the structures of taking and receiving by which the poor redistributed some small part of the wealth of England.

This dimension of our examination, then, still needs further exploration. And several of the contributors, with others who helped in this book, continue to explore it. The book has been at every stage a collective work and the product of repeated discussions among a larger group, although Douglas Hay, Peter Linebaugh and Edward Thompson have taken responsibility for its editorial presentation. We have gained very much from other members of this group, and in particular from Malcolm Thomas, whose extensive bibliographical knowledge has been placed at our disposal; Pamela James, who has typed and assisted us in several secretarial ways; Jeanette Neeson, Michael Sonenscher, Victor Bailey, Julian Harber, Bernice Clifton, Robin Clifton, John Merrington, Hugh Blackman, Dorothy Thompson and Richard Andrews. In addition Professor Royden Harrison, the present Director of the Centre at Warwick, read and advised on several drafts, and we gained from discussions with other members of the staff of the History Department at Warwick and from seminars and discussions with the staff and graduates of the Centre; Professor David Montgomery and Professor Melvyn Dubofsky, both visiting lecturers in American labour and social history, took a close interest in the work.

We all acknowledge gratefully help from the staffs of the Public Record Office, the British Museum and the Library of Warwick University (where Jolyon Hall helped all of us in many ways). In addition, each contributor wishes to acknowledge particular assistance: Douglas Hay to Professor J. M. Beattie for advice and encouragement, Mr F. B. Stitt and his staff at the Staffordshire Record Office and William Salt Library for much help, the Marquess of Anglesey for permission to use papers deposited at Stafford and others held at Plas Newydd, and the Earl of Harrowby for quotations from papers at Sandon Hall. Acknowledgement is also made to the Countess of Sutherland, to the Lord Hatherton, and to the Hatherton trustees for short quotations from manuscripts deposited at Stafford; Cal Winslow to the Archivists and staff at the West Sussex and East Sussex Record Offices; the Goodwood MSS (the papers of Charles Lennox, the second Duke of Richmond) were used by courtesy of His Grace the Duke of Richmond and Gordon, with acknowledgements to the West Sussex Record Office; and the Cholmondeley (Houghton) MSS were drawn upon by courtesy of the Marquess of Cholmondeley, with acknowledgements to the Librarian of Cambridge University Library. John Rule wishes to thank members of seminars at the University of Southampton and at St Antony's College, Oxford, for their criticisms.

Peter Linebaugh wishes to thank the staffs of the library of Lincoln's Inn, the London Library, the library of the Royal College of Surgeons, the library of the Royal College of Physicians and the Bodleian Library. The Archivists of the Middlesex Division of the Greater London Record Office and of the London Corporation Record Office assisted him in many particular ways. Edward Thompson wishes to thank E. E. Dodd for much patient help in collecting letters from the *London Gazette* and John Walsh, Alfred Peacock, Michael Carter, Robert Malcolmson, Julian Harber and James Epstein for contributing other anonymous letters. Transcripts of Crown-copyright records in the Public Record Office appear by permission of the Controller of H.M. Stationery Office. All these, from all of us, are expressions of appreciation for particular kinds of help. Other colleagues and other institutions have assisted us, and we apologize for our inability to mention each one.

Note: In quotations from contemporary sources the original spelling and punctuation has in general been preserved.

[1] DOUGLAS HAY

Property, Authority and
the Criminal Law

I

The rulers of eighteenth-century England cherished the death sentence. The oratory we remember now is the parliamentary speech, the Roman periods of Fox or Burke, that stirred the gentry and the merchants. But outside Parliament were the labouring poor, and twice a year, in most counties in England, the scarlet-robed judge of assize put the black cap of death on top of his full-bottomed wig to expound the law of the propertied, and to execute their will. 'Methinks I see him,' wrote Martin Madan in 1785,

with a countenance of solemn sorrow, adjusting the cap of judgement on his head. . . His Lordship then, deeply affected by the melancholy part of his office, which he is now about to fulfill, embraces this golden opportunity to do most exemplary good – He addresses, in the most pathetic terms, the consciences of the trembling criminals . . . shows them how just and necessary it is, that there should be laws to remove out of society those, who instead of contributing their honest industry to the public good and welfare, have exerted every art, that the blackest villainy can suggest, to destroy both . . . He then vindicates the *mercy*, as well as the *severity* of the law, in making such examples, as shall not only protect the innocent from outrage and violence, but also deter others from bringing themselves to the same fatal and ignominious end. . . He acquaints them with the certainty of speedy death, and consequently with the necessity of speedy repentance – and on this theme he may so deliver himself, as not only to melt the wretches at the bar into contrition, but the whole auditory into the deepest concern – Tears express their feelings – and many of the most thoughtless among them may, for the rest of their lives, be preserved from thinking lightly of the first steps to vice, which they now see will lead them to destruction. The dreadful sentence is now pronounced – every heart shakes with

terror – the almost fainting criminals are taken from the bar – the crowd retires –
each to his several home, and carries the mournful story to his friends and neighbours; – the day of execution arrives – the wretches are led forth to suffer, and
exhibit a spectacle to the beholders, too aweful and solemn for description.[1]

This was the climactic moment in a system of criminal law based on
terror: 'if we diminish the terror of house-breakers,' wrote Justice Christian of Ely in 1819, 'the terror of the innocent inhabitants must be increased, and the comforts of domestic life must be greatly destroyed'. He
himself had dogs, firearms, lights and bells at his own country home, and
took a brace of double-barrelled pistols to bed with him every night.[2]
But his peace of mind mostly rested on the knowledge that the death
sentence hung over anyone who broke in to steal his silver plate. A regular
police force did not exist, and the gentry would not tolerate even the idea
of one. They remembered the pretensions of the Stuarts and the days of
the Commonwealth, and they saw close at hand how the French monarchy
controlled its subjects with spies and informers. In place of police, however, propertied Englishmen had a fat and swelling sheaf of laws which
threatened thieves with death. The most recent account suggests that the
number of capital statutes grew from about 50 to over 200 between the
years 1688 and 1820.[3] Almost all of them concerned offences against
property.

This flood of legislation is one of the great facts of the eighteenth
century, and it occurred in the period when peers and gentry held power
with least hindrance from Crown or people. The Glorious Revolution of
1688 established the freedom not of men, but of men of property. Its
apologist, John Locke, distorted the oldest arguments of natural law to
justify the liberation of wealth from all political or moral controls; he
concluded that the unfettered accumulation of money, goods and land
was sanctioned by Nature and, implicitly, by God. Henceforth among
triumphant Whigs, and indeed all men on the right side of the great gulf
between rich and poor, there was little pretence that civil society was
concerned primarily with peace or justice or charity. Even interests of
state and the Divine Will had disappeared. Property had swallowed them
all: 'Government,' declared Locke, 'has no other end but the preservation
of property.'[4] Most later writers accepted the claim uncritically. William

1. Martin Madan, *Thoughts on Executive Justice with Respect to our Criminal Laws,
particularly on the Circuit*, 1785, pp. 26–30.
2. Edward Christian, *Charges delivered to Grand Juries in the Isle of Ely*, 1819, pp. 259,
260n; see below, p. 53, n. 1.
3. Sir Leon Radzinowicz, *A History of English Criminal Law and its Administration
from 1750*, 4 vols., 1948–68, vol. 1, p. 4.
4. *The Second Treatise of Government*, 1690, sections 85 and 94. Locke sometimes
defines property to mean 'life and liberty' as well as 'estates', but his argument assumes

Blackstone, the most famous eighteenth-century writer on the law and constitution, declared it self-evident that 'there is nothing which so generally strikes the imagination, and engages the affections of mankind, as the right of property; or that sole and despotic dominion which one man claims and exercises over the external things of the world, in total exclusion of the right of any other individual in the universe.'[1] The common and statute law, it seems, extended throughout not only England but the cosmos. When Christian edited the twelfth edition of Blackstone's *Commentaries on the Laws of England* in 1793, he reduced the claim only a little, to 'that law of property, which nature herself has written upon the hearts of all mankind'.[2]

Once property had been officially deified, it became the measure of all things. Even human life was weighed in the scales of wealth and status: 'the execution of a needy decrepit assassin,' wrote Blackstone, 'is a poor satisfaction for the murder of a nobleman in the bloom of his youth, and full enjoyment of his friends, his honours, and his fortune.'[3] Again and again the voices of money and power declared the sacredness of property in terms hitherto reserved for human life. Banks were credited with souls, and the circulation of gold likened to that of blood. Forgers, for example, were almost invariably hanged, and gentlemen knew why: 'Forgery is a stab to commerce, and only to be tolerated in a commercial nation when the foul crime of murder is pardoned.'[4] In a mood of unrivalled assurance and complacency, Parliament over the century created one of the bloodiest criminal codes in Europe. Few of the new penalties were the product of hysteria, or ferocious reaction; they were part of the conventional wisdom of England's governors. Locke himself defined political power as the right to create the penalty of death, and hence all lesser ones.[5] And Shaftesbury, the enlightened rationalist who attacked both Hobbes and the Church for making fear the cement of the social order, at the same time accepted that the 'mere Vulgar of Mankind' might perhaps 'often stand in need of such a rectifying Object as *the Gallows* before their Eyes'.[6]

Eighteenth-century lawyers were well aware that never before had the

the paramount importance of landed and other wealth. See C. B. Macpherson, *The Political Theory of Possessive Individualism, Hobbes to Locke*, Oxford, 1962, pp. 199ff.

1. William Blackstone, *Commentaries on the Laws of England* (12th edn by Edward Christian), 1793–5, vol. II, p. 2.

2. Christian's note, *Commentaries*, vol. II, p. 7.

3. ibid., vol. IV, p. 13.

4. John Holliday, *The Life of Lord Mansfield*, 1797, p. 149.

5. *The Second Treatise of Government*, section 3.

6. *Works* (1727 edn) vol. I, p. 127; quoted in Basil Willey, *The Eighteenth-Century Background*, 1972, p. 77.

legislature passed such a mass of new capital statutes so quickly. They floundered, however, when seeking for explanations. Many men, including learned ones, blamed the ever-increasing depravity of the people. In the 1730s Lord Chancellor Hardwicke blamed 'the degeneracy of human nature'; almost a century later, Justice Christian indicted 'the wicked inventions, and the licentious practices of modern times'.[1] He drew a picture of a besieged government gradually making harsh new penalties as outrages demonstrated the uselessness of the old. But other observers were aware that the larger changes of trade, commerce and manufacturing might have something to do with the increasing weight of the statute book. Justice Daines Barrington cited 'the increase of trade': the great circulation of new and valuable commodities made any comparison of England's laws with those of other states unsound, for 'till a country can be found, which contains equal property and riches, the conclusion cannot be a just one'.[2] In similar vein, the editor of the sixth edition of Hawkins's *Pleas of the Crown* wrote in 1788 that 'the increase of commerce, opulence, and luxury' since the first edition of 1715 'has introduced a variety of temptations to fraud and rapine, which the legislature has been forced to repel, by a multiplicity of occasional statutes, creating new offences and afflicting additional punishments'.[3]

Undoubtedly this is a more persuasive explanation than 'degeneracy'. The constant extension of inland and foreign trade from the late seventeenth century, the exploitation of new mines, the wealth of London and the spas and the growth of population all increased the opportunities for theft. The relationship of each of these factors to the level of crime is still uncertain; indeed, whether there was any increase in the amount of theft *per capita* is the subject of current research. What is certain is that Parliament did not often enact the new capital statutes as a matter of conscious public policy. Usually there was no debate, and most of the changes were related to specific, limited property interests, hitherto unprotected for one reason or another. Often they were the personal interest of a few members, and the Lords and Commons enacted them for the mere asking.

Three bills from mid-century illustrate the process. An act of 1753 prescribing hanging for stealing shipwrecked goods was brought in on behalf of the 'Merchants, Traders and Insurers of the City of London' whose profits were being diminished by the activities of wreckers; the

---

1. Brit. Mus. Add. MSS, 36, 115, fos. 75–88; Christian, *Charges*, pp. 233ff.
2. Daines Barrington, *Observations on the More Ancient Statutes*, 4th edn, 1775, pp. 482–8, 479.
3. William Hawkins, *A Treatise of the Pleas of the Crown* (6th edn, 1788), preface.

existing laws were declared to be too gentle.[1] In 1764 Parliament decreed that the death penalty would apply to those who broke into buildings to steal or destroy linen, or the tools to make it, or to cut it in bleaching-grounds. But the penalties were contained in an incidental clause in an act passed to incorporate the English Linen Company, whose proprietors included Lord Verney and the Right Honourable Charles Townshend; the death penalty was routinely added to protect their investments.[2] Finally, a law of 1769 suggests how the class that controlled Parliament was using the criminal sanction to enforce two of the radical redefinitions of property which gentlemen were making in their own interests during the eighteenth century. The food riot was an organized and often highly disciplined popular protest against the growing national and international market in foodstuffs, a market which alarmed the poor by moving grain from their parishes when it could compel a higher price elsewhere, and which depended on a growing corps of middlemen whom the rioters knew were breaking Tudor and Stuart legislation by wholesale trading in food. Country gentlemen often tolerated such a 'riot', or at least handled it sensibly, but Parliament was not prepared to let property suffer.[3] Some mills had been torn down in the nation-wide riots of 1766 and 1767, and the 1769 act plugged a gap in the law by making such destruction a capital offence. If death for food rioters was an excellent idea, so was transportation for enclosure rioters. Within three days the bill was enlarged so that gentlemen busy on the expropriation of common lands by Act of Parliament were as well protected as the millers. By the time the bill became law two weeks later, it had also become a transportable offence to meddle with the bridges and steam-engines used in the mines which were bringing ever-increasing revenues to the gentry and aristocracy.[4] As the decades passed, the maturing trade, commerce and industry of England spawned more laws to protect particular kinds of property. Perhaps the most dramatic change in the organizational structure of British capital was the growth of promissory notes on banks as a medium of exchange, and the increase in negotiable paper of all kinds. This new creation was exposed to fraud in many ways never foreseen by the ancient criminal law. The result was a rash of capital statutes against forgeries and frauds of all kinds, laws which multiplied towards the end of the century.

These, then, were the legal instruments which enforced the division of property by terror. They were not the largest parts of the law – much

1. 26 Geo. II.c. 19; *CJ*, 23 January to 15 May 1753.
2. 4 Geo. III c. 37.
3. E. P. Thompson, 'The Moral Economy of the English Crowd in the Eighteenth Century', *Past and Present*, no. 50, February 1971, pp. 76–136.
4. 9 Geo. III c. 29; *CJ*, 12 April to 1 May 1769.

more dealt with land, 'with its long and voluminous train of descents and conveyances, settlements, entails, and incumbrances', and commerce, for which the eighteenth-century judges at last created a coherent framework.[1] The financial details of the marriage settlement, so often the sacrament by which land allied itself with trade, provided the best lawyers with a good part of their fees. But if most of the law and the lawyers were concerned with the civil dealings which propertied men had with one another, most men, the unpropertied labouring poor, met the law as criminal sanction: the threat or the reality of whipping, transportation and hanging. Death had long been a punishment for theft in England, and several of the most important statutes were passed in Tudor times. But the gentry and merchants and peers who sat in Parliament in the eighteenth century set new standards of legislative industry, as they passed act after act to keep the capital sanction up to date, to protect every conceivable kind of property from theft or malicious damage.[2]

Yet two great questions hang over this remarkable code. The first concerns the actual number of executions. The available evidence suggests that, compared to some earlier periods, the eighteenth-century criminal law claimed few lives. At the beginning of the seventeenth century, for example, it appears that London and Middlesex saw four times as many executions as 150 years later.[3] Equally interesting is the fact that in spite of the growth in trade and population, the increasing number of convictions for theft, and the continual creation of new capital statutes throughout the eighteenth century, the number of executions for offences against property remained relatively stable, especially after 1750. The numbers of executions did not increase to match the number of convictions because of the increasing use of the royal pardon, by which transportation could be substituted for hanging, on the recommendation of the judges. Sir Leon

1. Blackstone, *Commentaries*, vol. I, p. 6.

2. The extension of benefit of clergy (the right to a lesser sentence of transportation on first conviction for the capital crime of grand larceny) made it increasingly possible to avoid the gallows. The development of clergy since the sixteenth century was countered in the eighteenth by many statutes removing it from particular kinds of larceny. Other capital statutes at the same time extended the death penalty to offences never punished so severely before.

3. The figures are inexact and inconsistent but it appears that the average number of executions per year was 140 in London and Middlesex in the years 1607–16, and 33 per year for the period 1749–99. The eighteenth-century figures vary from a low decadal average of 21 (1790–99) to a maximum of 53 (1780–89); Radzinowicz, vol. I, pp. 141, 147, citing Jeaffreson and the *Report* from the Select Committee on Criminal Laws, 1819. The numbers of executions in Devon between 1598 and 1639 were also as high as 74 a year; J. S. Cockburn, *A History of English Assizes, 1558–1714*, Cambridge, 1972, pp. 94–6.

Radzinowicz, in the most complete study of the subject, has shown that in London and Middlesex the proportion of death sentences commuted increased as the century progressed. He has argued that Parliament intended their legislation to be strictly enforced, and that the judges increasingly vitiated that intention by extending pardons freely.[1] But this is an unsatisfactory conclusion. A conflict of such magnitude between Parliament and the judiciary would have disrupted eighteenth-century politics, and nothing of the sort happened. With few exceptions, gentlemen congratulated themselves on living in a century when the bench was wise and incorruptible, one of the glories of the constitution. Secondly, we shall see that the men who controlled Parliament were precisely those who usually brought their influence to bear in requesting pardons for condemned convicts from the judges and the king. We have yet to explain the coexistence of bloodier laws and increased convictions with a declining proportion of death sentences that were actually carried out.

This first problem is related to a second one. Most historians and many contemporaries argued that the policy of terror was not working. More of those sentenced to death were pardoned than were hanged; thieves often escaped punishment through the absence of a police force, the leniency of prosecutors and juries, and the technicalities of the law; transported convicts were so little afraid that they often returned to England to pick pockets on hanging days; riot was endemic. The critics of the law argued that the gibbets and corpses paradoxically weakened the enforcement of the law: rather than terrifying criminals, the death penalty terrified prosecutors and juries, who feared committing judicial murder on the capital statutes. Sir Samuel Romilly and other reformers led a long and intelligent campaign for the repeal of some laws, arguing from statistics that convictions would become more numerous once that fear was removed. The reformers also used the arguments of Beccaria, who suggested in 1764 that gross and capricious terror should be replaced by a fixed and graduated scale of more lenient but more certain punishments. His ideas were widely canvassed in England, as well as on the continent. Even Blackstone, the high priest of the English legal system, looked forward

---

1. Radzinowicz, vol. I, pp. 151–9, 163–4. The 1819 figures, on which Radzinowicz bases his argument, do not in fact reveal a *constantly* increasing divergence between the numbers executed and the numbers sentenced. Assuming the comparability of London figures with those from London and Middlesex combined, the proportion of executions to death sentences fluctuates from about 35 per cent in 1710–14 to about 60 per cent in the 1750s, before gradually declining. Nor do Home Circuit figures show a gradual divergence. The change from 55 per cent at the beginning of the century to 35 per cent had largely occurred by mid-century; thereafter it remained steady, barring a few exceptional years; see my forthcoming article on the figures.

to changes on these lines. Yet Parliament resisted all reform. Not one capital statute was repealed until 1808, and real progress had to wait until the 1820s and 1830s.

Why the contradiction? If property was so important, and reform of the criminal law would help to protect it, why did gentlemen not embrace reform? Given the apparently fierce intentions of the legislature, why was the law not changed to make enforcement more certain? Historians searching for the roots of the modern criminal law and the modern police usually devote most of their attention to the triumph of reform in the nineteenth century. But the victors in the eighteenth century were the conservatives, the hangers and gibbeters, and they resolutely ignored over fifty years of cogent criticism. Two immediate explanations are commonly given. The gentry undoubtedly refused to create a regular police force, a necessary part of the Beccarian plan. Moreover, the lack of secondary punishments, and the unsatisfactory nature of those in use, such as transportation, made it seem desirable to keep the death penalty for the incorrigible rogue. Neither fact, however, explains why there was such unbending opposition to the repeal of even those capital statutes that were seldom used. This determination of Parliament to retain all the capital statutes, even when obsolete, and to continue to create new ones, even when they were stillborn, suggests that the explanation for the failure of reform lies deeper in the mental and social structure of eighteenth-century England. A few historians have attempted explanations, but they are usually vague or tautological: that the industrial revolution, as a time of social change, induced conservatism; that the French Revolution did the same; that legal reform in England is always, and inevitably, slow.[1] These explanations ignore the underlying assumptions of the governors of England, and do not show how the old criminal law matched that mental world. For it is difficult to believe that Parliament would have been so complacently conservative about the unreformed law unless they were convinced that it was serving their interests. And here the testimony of conservatives is more helpful than the claims of reformers.[2]

Timothy Nourse antedated Beccaria and Romilly by a good half-century, but he expressed an enduring belief of the gentry when he declared that many of the common people were 'very rough and savage in

1. See Radzinowicz, vol. I, pp. 40, 351–4, for a summary.

2. Historians have accepted the assumptions of the reformers, which are also those of modern criminology: that the criminal law and the police are no more and no less than a set of instruments to manage something called crime. Effective detection, certain prosecution and enlightened rehabilitation will accomplish this practical task. (Radzinowicz, *Ideology and Crime*, 1966.) Criminology has been disinfested of grand theory and class purpose. Much of it has thereby become ideology.

their Dispositions, being of levelling Principles, and refractory to Government, insolent and tumultuous'. Civility only made them saucy.

The best way therefore will be to bridle them, and to make them feel the spur too, when they begin to play their Tricks, and kick. The Saying of an *English* gentleman was much to the purpose, That three things ought always to be kept under, our Mastiff-Dog, a Stone-Horse, and a Clown: And really I think a snarling, cross-grained Clown to be the most unlucky Beast of the three. Such Men then are to be look'd upon as trashy Weeds or Nettles, growing usually upon Dunghills, which if touch'd gently will sting, but being squeez'd hard will never hurt us.

The instruments to deal with such 'stubborn, cross-grain'd rogues' were at hand: '*Beadles, Catchpoles, Gaolers, Hangmen*, . . . such like Engines of Humanity are the fittest Tools in the World for a Magistrate to work with in the Reformation of an obdurate Rogue, all which, I say, may be so used and managed by him as not to endanger his own Fingers, or discompose his thoughts.'[1] This is language far removed from Romilly's cool calculation of rates of conviction, or even Justice Christian's hysterical talk of alarms, watch-dogs and double-barrelled pistols. Nourse knew instinctively that the criminal law is as much concerned with authority as it is with property. For wealth does not exist outside a social context, theft is given definition only within a set of social relations, and the connections between property, power and authority are close and crucial. The criminal law was critically important in maintaining bonds of obedience and deference, in legitimizing the status quo, in constantly recreating the structure of authority which arose from property and in turn protected its interests.

But terror alone could never have accomplished those ends. It was the raw material of authority, but class interest and the structure of the law itself shaped it into a much more effective instrument of power. Almost a century after Nourse, another defender of the unreformed system described the other side of authority: 'Could we view our own species from a distance, or regard mankind with the same sort of observation with which we read the natural history, or remark the *manners*, of any other animal,' he wrote in 1785,

there is nothing in the human character which would more surprise us, than the almost universal subjugation of strength to weakness – than to see many millions of robust men, in the complete use and exercise of their faculties, and without any defect of courage, waiting upon the will of a child, a woman, a driveller, or a lunatic. And although . . . we suppose perhaps an extreme case; yet in all cases, even in the most popular forms of civil government, *the physical strength lies in the governed.* In what manner opinion thus prevails over strength, or how power,

1. Timothy Nourse, *Campania Foelix* (2nd edn, 1706), pp. 15–16, 273–4.

which naturally belongs to superior force, is maintained in opposition to it; in other words, by what motives the many are induced to submit to the few, becomes an inquiry which lies at the root of almost every political speculation. . . Let civil governors learn hence to respect their subjects; let them be admonished, that the physical strength resides in the governed; that this strength wants only to be felt and roused, to lay prostrate the most ancient and confirmed dominion; that civil authority is founded in opinion; that general opinion therefore ought always to be treated with deference, and managed with delicacy and circumspection.[1]

These are the words of Archdeacon Paley, and they were published a few years after the Gordon Riots. Paley is not usually quoted as an exponent of 'delicacy and circumspection', but as the most eloquent defender of the old criminal law as a system of selective terror. He was cited by almost every subsequent opponent of reform, and has often been considered by later writers as little more than an ingenious apologist or uncritical conservative. But he was in fact an acute observer of the bases of power in eighteenth-century England, and although he did not make the connection explicit, the criminal law was extremely important in ensuring, in his words, that 'opinion' prevailed over 'physical strength'. The opinion was that of the ruling class; the law was one of their chief ideological instruments.[2] It combined the terror worshipped by Nourse with the discretion stressed by Paley, and used both to mould the consciousness by which the many submitted to the few. Moreover, its effectiveness in doing so depended in large part on the very weaknesses and inconsistencies condemned by reformers and liberal historians. In considering the criminal law as an ideological system, we must look at how it combined imagery and force, ideals and practice, and try to see how it manifested itself to the mass of unpropertied Englishmen. We can distinguish three aspects of the law as ideology: majesty, justice and mercy. Understanding them will help us to explain the divergence between bloody legislation and declining executions, and the resistance to reform of any kind.

II

Majesty

If we are to believe an undated couplet from Staffordshire, at first sight the majesty of the law did not always impress:[3]

1. William Paley, *Principles of Moral and Political Philosophy*, 1785, Book VI, ch. 2.
2. By ideology I mean 'a specific set of ideas designed to vindicate or disguise class interest . . .'; A. Gerschenkron, *Continuity in History and other Essays*, Cambridge, Mass., 1968, p. 65.
3. Dudley Wilks, *Fragments of Stafford's Past*, Stafford, 1932, p. 32.

COUNTRYMAN: What mummery is this, 'tis fit only for guisers!

TOWNSMAN: No mummery Sir, 'tis the Stafford Assizes,

for coupled with wealth, a considered use of imagery, eloquent speech, and the power of death, the antics surrounding the twice-yearly visits of the high-court judges had considerable psychic force. They were accorded far greater importance by contemporaries than by most historians, who have been concerned more with county government, particularly at Quarter Sessions, than with the majesty of the law. The assizes were a formidable spectacle in a country town, the most visible and elaborate manifestation of state power to be seen in the countryside, apart from the presence of a regiment. The town was crowded, not only with barristers and jurors, but with the cream of county society, attending the assize ball and county meetings, which were often held in the same week. Tradesmen and labourers journeyed in to enjoy the spectacle, meet friends, attend the court and watch the executions. And the court arrived in town with traditional, and calculated, panoply: 'The judges,' wrote a French observer,

upon their approach are received by the sheriff, and often by a great part of the wealthiest inhabitants of the county; the latter come in person to meet them, or send their carriages, with their richest liveries, to serve as an escort, and increase the splendour of the occasion.

They enter the town with bells ringing and trumpets playing, preceded by the sheriff's men, to the number of twelve or twenty, in full dress, armed with javelins. The trumpeters and javelin-men remain in attendance on them during the time of their stay, and escort them every day to the assize-hall, and back again to their apartments.[1]

In the court room the judges' every action was governed by the importance of spectacle. Blackstone asserted that 'the novelty and very parade of ... [their] appearance have no small influence upon the multitude':[2] scarlet robes lined with ermine and full-bottomed wigs in the seventeenth-century style, which evoked scorn from Hogarth but awe from ordinary men. The powers of light and darkness were summoned into the court with the black cap which was donned to pronounce sentence of death, and the spotless white gloves worn at the end of a 'maiden assize' when no prisoners were to be left for execution.

Within this elaborate ritual of the irrational, judge and counsel displayed their learning with an eloquence that often rivalled that of leading

1. Charles Cottu, *The Administration of Criminal Justice in England*, 1822, p. 43. Cottu, a judge, came to England on behalf of the French government to study the English legal system, with a view to suggesting reforms for France.

2. Blackstone, *Commentaries*, vol. III, p. 356.

statesmen. There was an acute consciousness that the courts were platforms for addressing 'the multitude'. Two stages in the proceedings especially were tests of the rhetorical power of the bench. The first, the charge to the grand jury, was ostensibly directed to the country gentry. Judges gave close attention to content and to delivery. Frequently charges were a statement of central policy, as well as a summary of the state of the law and the duties of gentlemen. Earlier in the century they castigated Jacobitism; and in the 1720s the judges used them to denounce 'unfounded and seditious' criticisms of government policy on the South Sea Bubble. Tone was important: before he went on circuit in 1754, Sir Dudley Ryder reminded himself, 'When I would speak to [the] Grand Jury I should mean to persuade them to do their duty, I should therefore speak to them as I would to a number of my tenants whom I would instruct and persuade, and therefore make them fully acquainted with everything necessary to that end, or as I would to my son.'[1] The flavour of paternalism was important, for usually the charge was also directed at the wider audience in the court room. It was often a secular sermon on the goodness of whichever Hanoverian chanced to be on the throne, the virtues of authority and obedience, the fitness of the social order:

> It is the king's *earnest Desire*, as well as his *truest Intent*, that all his subjects be easy and happy. In this he places his greatest Security & Glory; and in the preservation of the Laws of the Kingdom, & of ye liberties of his People, the Chief support of his title & Government... Without order [continued Hardwicke in this charge to Somerset Assizes], how miserable must be the condition of the People? Instead of a regular observance and a due execution of the laws, every man's lust, his avarice, his revenge, or his ambition would become a law to himself, and the rule of his dealing with his neighbour.[2]

The second rhetorical test for the judge demanded not the accents of paternalism, but the power and passion of righteous vengeance. The death sentence, we have suggested, was the climactic emotional point of the criminal law – the moment of terror around which the system revolved. As the cases came before judge and jury at assizes, the convicted were remanded for sentencing on the last day; and on that day the judgements were given in ascending order of severity, reserving the most awful for the last. Before passing sentence of death, the judge spoke about the crimes and the criminals. 'A wise and conscientious judge', wrote Thomas Gisborne,

> will never neglect so favourable an occasion of inculcating the enormity of vice, and the fatal consequences to which it leads. He will point out to his hearers the

1. Harrowby MSS, vol. 430, S/H, doc. 27, part 4b, p. 61.
2. Brit. Mus. Add. MSS, 36, 115, fos. 75–88.

several causes, when they are sufficiently marked to admit of description and application, which have conducted step by step the wretched object before them through the several shades and degrees of guilt to a transgression unpardonable on earth. He will dwell with peculiar force on such of those causes as appear to him the most likely, either from the general principles of human nature, or from local circumstances, to exert their contagious influence on the persons whom he addresses.[1]

Most published sentences come up to Gisborne's standard.[2] The aim was to move the court, to impress the onlookers by word and gesture, to fuse terror and argument into the amalgam of legitimate power in their minds. For execution was a fate decreed not by men, but by God and Justice. The judge might deepen the effect when visibly moved himself. In 1754 at Chelmsford the Chief Justice condemned a girl to hanging and dissection for murdering her baby. He had pressured the jury to bring in a simple verdict of guilty (at first they found her insane); but having exacted justice, he then expressed the helplessness of men before it: 'Before I pronounced the sentence,' he confided to his diary, 'I made a very proper speech extempore and pronounced it with dignity, in which I was so affected that the tears were gushing out several times against my will. It was discerned by all the company – which was large – and a lady gave me her handkerchief dipped in lavender water to help me.'[3]

In its ritual, its judgements and its channelling of emotion the criminal law echoed many of the most powerful psychic components of religion. The judge might, as at Chelmsford, emulate the priest in his role of human agent, helpless but submissive before the demands of his deity. But the judge could play the role of deity as well, both the god of wrath and the merciful arbiter of men's fates. For the righteous accents of the death sentence were made even more impressive by the contrast with the treatment of the accused up to the moment of conviction. The judges' paternal concern for their prisoners was remarked upon by foreign visitors, and deepened the analogy with the Christian God of justice and mercy. Moreover, there is some reason to believe that the secular sermons of the criminal law had become more important than those of the Church by the eighteenth century. Too many Englishmen had forgotten the smell of brimstone, and the clergy – lazy, absentee and dominated by material

1. Thomas Gisborne, *An Enquiry into the Duties of Men in the Higher and Middle Classes of Society in Great Britain*, 1794, p. 270.

2. Even Madan, who thought the ideal sentence too seldom achieved, admired the speech of the judge at Surrey summer Assizes in the year of his pamphlet. 'I felt ready to sink with horror,' he was pleased to report. Fifteen capital convicts were condemned with 'solemnity, and heart-felt awe . . .' (*Thoughts on Executive Justice*, p. 88.)

3. Harrowby MSS, vol. 1129, doc. 19(f), p. 5.

ambition – were not the men to remind them. The diminished effectiveness of damnation to compel obedience was accentuated by the decline
of the ecclesiastical courts since early Stuart times to mere arbiters of
wills and marriages and occasional cases of slander.[1] In sharp contrast,
the sanctions of the criminal law had not lost their bite: 'The government
has wisely provided corporal and pecuniary punishments, and Ministers
of Justice for the execution of them,' Sir James Astry told his juries;
'for the punishment of the Pocket, or a sound Whipping to some, is more
effectual Rhetorick, than the preaching of Divine vengeance from the
Pulpit; for such lewd Wretches has a sordid notion, that Preaching is only
a Trade, and to the ministers of gospel, Godliness is great gain. . .'[2]
Timothy Nourse was more succinct: 'a good strong pair of Stocks, and
a Whipping-post, will work a greater Reformation than Forty Doctrines
and Uses.'[3] Religion still had a place within the ritual of the law: a clergyman gave the assize sermon, and others attended the condemned men on
the scaffold. But we suspect that the men of God derived more prestige
from the occasion than they conferred upon it. A suggestion of this can
be seen in an evangelical pamphlet published in 1795. In the metaphors of
power, judges usually had been likened to God, deriving their authority
from divine authority, mediated through the Crown. But the author
reversed the metaphor in his attempt to resurrect religion: he likened
the deity to an English high court justice, and called the Day of Judgement
the 'Grand Assizes, or General Gaol Delivery'.[4] The secular mysteries
of the courts had burned deep into the popular consciousness, and perhaps
the labouring poor knew more of the terrors of the law than those of
religion. When they did hear of hell, it was often from a judge. Sentencing
a murderer at Gloucester in 1772, Justice Nares reminded him that his
gibbeted bones would never enjoy Christian burial, but would hang 'as a
dreadful spectacle of horror and detestation, to caution and deter the rest
of mankind'. But he reminded him that he also had an immortal soul,
and exhorted him to seek salvation: 'Then, although your sins are as
scarlet, they may be white as snow, – 'tho they be as crimson, they shall be
as wool.'

The assizes were staged twice a year in most counties. Quarter Sessions,
held twice as often, could not match them as spectacles, but as courts of

1. The strength of Church discipline as coercion under the early Stuarts was weak,
but its ideological importance was undoubtedly greater than in the eighteenth century;
see R. A. Marchant, *The Church under the Law*, Cambridge, 1969, p. 228.

2. James Astry, *A General Charge to All Grand Juries, and Other Juries* (2nd edn, 1725),
p. 40.

3. Nourse, op. cit., p. 102.

4. *The Grand Assizes; or General Gaol Delivery* (Cheap Repository, n.d.).

law they derived some of their impressiveness by association. The magistrates on the county bench had visited and dined with the circuit judges a few months before; the wealthier J Ps had entertained their lordships at their homes, spoken familiarly with them in court. Indeed, their wives and daughters sometimes turned the assizes to their own purposes, giving a competitive display of charm before the assize ball: 'By a condescension sufficiently extraordinary,' wrote a bemused Frenchman, 'the judge permits his Bench to be invaded by a throng of spectators, and thus finds himself surrounded by the prettiest women of the county – the sisters, wives or daughters of grand jurors. . . They are attired in the most elegant négligé; and it is a spectacle not a little curious to see the judge's venerable head, loaded with a large wig, peering among the youthful female heads.'[1] To most of those in the court-room, the spectacle was less amusing and more serious than the foreign barrister found it: it was a reminder of the close relationship between law, property and power.

For certain offences, the full majesty of the criminal law could be summoned outside assize times, and when Quarter Sessions were not sitting. The court of King's Bench would allow prosecution by information for serious misdemeanours, including riot, aggravated assaults and some game offences. The offender was usually tried at the next assizes, but he could be compelled to appear at Westminster, tried in the most awesome surroundings, and pilloried or whipped among the crowds of the metropolis. It was said to be a popular belief that one could be 'put into the Crown Office' for any offence, at any time. It happened just often enough to give colour to the story. Finally, on a great many occasions throughout the century the full panoply of the law was sent into the counties in the form of a Special Commission to try a particular, dangerous offence. The Special Commission was used when exemplary hangings or at least exemplary trials were deemed necessary for the public peace. Gentlemen often petitioned for them when riot in their counties was becoming too serious, or when the violence associated with popular crimes (such as smuggling) verged on insurrection against their authority. The assize judges descended from London, the sermon was preached in the nearest cathedral, and the breach in the social and moral order was healed with the rituals of justice: speeches, fear and the sacrifice of lives on the gallows. As at the regular assizes, at least in the provinces, those executed at Special Commissions were mostly local men, with neighbours, parents, brothers and sisters in the watching crowd.

1. Cottu, op. cit., pp. 103–4; Nares's sentence in *Aris's Birmingham Gazette*, 30 March 1772.

Justice

'Justice' was an evocative word in the eighteenth century, and with good reason. The constitutional struggles of the seventeenth had helped to establish the principles of the rule of law: that offences should be fixed, not indeterminate; that rules of evidence should be carefully observed; that the law should be administered by a bench that was both learned and honest. These achievements were essential for the protection of the gentry from royal greed and royal tyranny, and for the regulation, in the civil side of the courts, of the details of conveyancing, entailing, contracting, devising, suing and releasing. Since the same judges administered the criminal law at its highest levels, on the same principles, even the poorest man was guaranteed justice in the high courts. Visitors remarked on the extreme solicitude of judges for the rights of the accused, a sharp distinction from the usual practice of continental benches. It was considered to be good grounds for requesting a royal pardon if the judge 'did (contrary to the usual custom) lean against the prisoner'.[1] The assize judge's attention to the rights of the prisoner did much to mitigate the prohibition against legal counsel in felonies. It was a tradition which permeated the courts, and it was sustained too by the public nature of trials. Sir John Hawkins, chairman of Middlesex Quarter Sessions, complained,

... in courts of justice, the regard shown to offenders falls little short of respect ... Those whose duty it is to conduct the evidence, fearing the censure that others have incurred by a contrary treatment of prisoners, are restrained from enforcing it; and, as it is an exercise of compassion that costs nothing, and is sure to gain the applause of vulgar hearers, every one interests himself on the side of the prisoner, and hopes, by his zeal in his behalf, to be distinguished as a man of more than ordinary humanity.[2]

Equally important were the strict procedural rules which were enforced in the high courts and at assizes, especially in capital cases. Moreover, most penal statutes were interpreted by the judges in an extremely narrow and formalistic fashion. In part this was based on seventeenth-century practice, but as more capital statutes were passed in the eighteenth century the bench reacted with an increasingly narrow interpretation.[3] Many prosecutions founded on excellent evidence and conducted at considerable expense failed on minor errors of form in the indictment,

1. Sir Cecil Wray in behalf of Edward Cooper, PRO, HO 42/11, fo. 43; cf. Cottu, op. cit., pp. 90–91, 103.
2. John Hawkins, *Life of Samuel Johnson*, 1787, p. 522.
3. Radzinowicz, vol. I, pp. 25–8, 83–91, 97–103.

the written charge. If a name or date was incorrect, or if the accused was described as a 'farmer' rather than the approved term 'yeoman', the prosecution could fail. The courts held that such defects were conclusive, and gentlemen attending trials as spectators sometimes stood up in court and brought errors to the attention of the judge. These formalisms in the criminal law seemed ridiculous to contemporary critics, and to many later historians. Their argument was (and is) that the criminal law, to be effective, must be known and determinate, instead of capricious and obscure. Prosecutors resented the waste of their time and money lost on a technicality; thieves were said to mock courts which allowed them to escape through so many verbal loopholes. But it seems likely that the mass of Englishmen drew other conclusions from the practice. The punctilious attention to forms, the dispassionate and legalistic exchanges between counsel and the judge, argued that those administering and using the laws submitted to its rules. The law thereby became something more than the creature of a ruling class – it became a power with its own claims, higher than those of prosecutor, lawyers, and even the great scarlet-robed assize judge himself. To them, too, of course, the law was The Law. The fact that they reified it, that they shut their eyes to its daily enactment in Parliament by men of their own class, heightened the illusion. When the ruling class acquitted men on technicalities they helped instil a belief in the disembodied justice of the law in the minds of all who watched. In short, its very inefficiency, its absurd formalism, was part of its strength as ideology.

'Equality before the law' also implied that no man was exempt from it. It was part of the lore of politics that in England social class did not preserve a man even from the extreme sanction of death. This was not, of course, true. But the impression made by the execution of a man of property or position was very deep. As executions for forgery became increasingly common throughout the century, more such respectable villains went to the gallows. The crime was punished with unremitting severity even though it was often committed by impecunious lawyers of good family. This rigour was distressing to many middling men: the agitation led by Johnson against the execution of the Reverend Dr Dodd, a former Royal Chaplain and Lord Chesterfield's old tutor, was enormous.[1] Dodd died at Tyburn in 1777 but he lived in popular culture for a long time, his case persuasive evidence that the law treated rich and poor alike. The occasional sentence of transportation or death passed on gentlemen with unusual sexual tastes or guilty of homicide, cases widely reported in the *Newgate Calendar* and other versions, similarly served to justify the law. Undoubtedly the most useful victim in this respect was Lawrence

1. Gerald Howson, *The Macaroni Parson*, 1973.

Shirley, Lord Ferrers, who killed his steward, was captured by his tenantry, tried in the House of Lords, sentenced to death, executed at Tyburn, and dissected 'like a common criminal' as the publicists never tired of repeating. He was hanged in his silver brocade wedding-suit, on a scaffold equipped with black silk cushions for the mourners. But hanging is hanging, the defenders of the law repeated enthusiastically. An enormous literature surrounded his execution in 1760, much of it devoted to celebrating the law. Later in the century the event was often recalled as an irrefutable proof of the justice of English society. An anti-Jacobin in the 1790s advised his 'brother artificers':

> We have long enjoyed that Liberty and Equality which the French have been struggling for: in England, ALL MEN ARE EQUAL; all who commit the same offences are liable to the same punishment. If the *very poorest and meanest man* commits murder, he is hanged with a hempen halter, and his body dissected. If the *Richest Nobleman* commits a murder, *he* is hanged with a hempen halter, and his body dissected – *all are equal here*.[1]

Hannah More used the same argument in her anti-Jacobin pamphlets for the poor; Ferrers became one of the best-known villains of the century. In some counties the story of the wicked aristocrat who met a just end on the scaffold was told at popular festivities until well into the 1800s.

In the parlour of the Justice of the Peace, *stare decisis* and due process were not always so much in evidence as in the high courts. Many justices convicted on flimsy evidence, particularly when they were subservient to a local magnate, and when they were enforcing the game laws. It was perfectly possible to combine arbitrary powers with an obeisance to the rules, however, and it appears that most JPs made an effort to appear, at least, to be acting legally. Moreover, even at the level of the justice the rules of law could be used effectively on behalf of a labouring man. It was not unknown for labourers caught deer-stealing to make an ingenious use of the contradictory statutes protecting informers to escape punishment.[2] The occasional success of such ruses, and the attempts to use them, probably helped sustain the belief that the integrity of the law was a reality and not merely the rhetoric of judges and gentlemen. Perhaps even more important in this respect were the frequent prosecutions brought by common informers, where the poor could go before a JP and use the law in their own interests. Prosecutions under the excise, game and turnpike acts – often against farmers and tradesmen who on most other occasions were those who used the courts – occasionally allowed the powerless to make the law their servant, whether for personal

1. *Job Nott's Advice*, Staffs. RO, D1778, bdl. 57.
2. See below, Chapter 5, 'Poaching and the Game Laws on Cannock Chase', p. 198.

revenge or the sake of the reward. Moreover, Justices of the Peace some-times intervened in the administration of the poor laws, prosecuting callous overseers who forced paupers to marry to remove them from the rates, or who dumped them over parish boundaries to die at the expense of their neighbours. Every county saw trials for such cruelties every few years, and the gentlemen who brought them clothed the issue in the language of constitutionalism. An extremely pervasive rhetorical tradi-tion, with deep historical roots, was invoked and strengthened on all such occasions. The law was held to be the guardian of Englishmen, of all Englishmen. Gentlemen held this as an unquestionable belief: that belief, too, gave the ideology of justice an integrity which no self-conscious manipulation could alone sustain. The real guarantees of the law were, moreover, confirmed in several celebrated political trials: Lord Mans-field's finding against general warrants in 1765, the Middlesex jury's acquittals of the leaders of the London Corresponding Society in 1794. In the latter case the striking contrast with the Scottish trials under Braxfield the year before was treated as an object lesson in the superiority of the English courts and bench.

Yet the idea of justice was always dangerous, straining the narrow definitions of the lawyers and the judges. It was easy to claim equal justice for murderers of all classes, where a universal moral sanction was more likely to be found, or in political cases, the necessary price of a constitution ruled by law. The trick was to extend that communal sanction to a criminal law that was nine-tenths concerned with upholding a radical division of property. Though Justice seemed impartial in crimes against the person, wrote Mandeville,

> Yet, it was thought, the sword she bore
> Check'd but the Desp'rate and the Poor;
> That, urged by mere Necessity,
> Were tied up to the wretched Tree
> For Crimes, which not deserv'd that Fate
> But to secure the Rich, and Great.[1]

In times of dearth, when the rulers of England were faced with food riots by men desperate with hunger and convinced of the rights of their case, the contradiction could become acute. At such times two conceptions of justice stood in sharp opposition: an older, Christian version of natural rights, which guaranteed even the poorest man at least life; and the justice of the law of property, sanctioned by the settlements of the seventeenth century. Keith Thomas has suggested that the erosion of the moral sanctions surrounding charity, and the ambiguity accompanying the birth

---

1. *The Fable of the Bees*, 1705.

of a more rationalized and less indulgent attitude to poverty, produced strong conflicts of guilt and blame, with seventeenth-century witch trials as their partial expression.[1] A century later, the ambiguities had still not been altogether resolved in the law, which in its ideological role had to reconcile popular ideas of justice with the absolute claims of property. From time to time writers in jurisprudence took up with distaste the ancient civil doctrine that a starving man had the right to steal enough food to keep himself for a week. Hale had written in the seventeenth century that the rule had long been disused in England. Blackstone argued that in this, as in all things, English law was founded on the highest reason, 'for men's properties would be under a strange insecurity, if liable to be invaded according to the wants of others; of which wants no man can possibly be an adequate judge, but the party himself who pleads them.'[2] The judges agreed, for it was impossible to admit poverty as a legal defence without wholly eroding the property statute. Rather than acknowledge an archaic, alien and dangerous legal doctrine, the bench stressed their deep concern for the little personal property that the ordinary Englishman did have. From time to time they passed harsh sentences for certain crimes, such as the theft of clothes, which they proclaimed in court to be particular misfortunes of the poor. A great many words were lavished also on particular statutes for the same reason. An act of 1713 punished with death any housebreaker who stole goods worth forty shillings or more. Opposing repeal in a major debate in 1811, Lord Eldon declared 'that the property of the industrious cottager should be protected, who is often obliged to leave his cottage, and his little hoard of perhaps not more than 40s deposited in a tin-box in a corner of a room'.[3]

It is difficult to assess the weight such arguments had with the mass of Englishmen. Eldon's was jejune: few cottagers had savings of £2, the wages of a month or more, in the harsh year 1811. Equally few cottagers could afford to go to law to recover stolen goods. Ideologies do not rest on realities, however, but on appearances, and there were enough prosecutions on behalf of poor men to give colour to the Lord Chancellor's claims. Usually such cases were begun or paid for by employers, landlords

1. Keith Thomas, *Religion and the Decline of Magic*, 1971, p. 561.
2. Blackstone, *Commentaries*, vol. IV, pp. 31-2. Perhaps Blackstone sensed that the claims of poverty were not extinguished, for he resorted to chauvinist humbug. Theft might be justified on the continent, 'where the parsimonious industry of the natives orders everyone to work or starve', but it had no place in England, 'where charity is reduced to a system, and interwoven in our very constitution'. Many other writers also wrestled with the problem.
3. Quoted in Christian, *Charges*, p. 308. The Statute (12 Anne c. 7) was passed to punish thieving servants, and was usually used for that purpose. The judges agreed; see Radzinowicz, vol. I, p. 117.

or local associations for the prosecution of felons. The motives for men of property to assist the poor to prosecute were a tangle of self-interest and paternalism. Some gentlemen simply believed that the law was the birthright of every Englishman, and most were anxious to convict a thief who might prey on them as well. The consequence was that more poor men were able to use the law than the system of legal fees would otherwise have allowed. The poor suffer from theft as well as the rich, and in eighteenth-century England probably far more poor men lost goods to thieves, if only because the rich were few and their property more secure. In recognizing that fact, and extending its protection, however imperfectly, to ordinary men, the criminal law did much to justify itself and the gentlemen who administered it. Defending the constitution in the 1790s, Hannah More's ploughman sings,

> British laws for my guard,
> My cottage is barr'd,
> 'Tis safe in the light or the dark, Sir;
> If the Squire should oppress,
> I get instant redress:
> My orchard's as safe as his park, Sir.[1]

The justice of English law was thus a powerful ideological weapon in the arsenal of conservatives during the French Revolution. Wicked Lord Ferrers, juries and *habeas corpus* were leading themes in anti-Jacobin popular literature. They were usually contrasted with tyrannical French aristocrats, the inquisitorial system of law and *lettres de cachet*. In countering the influence of Tom Paine, the conservatives repeatedly emphasized the central place of law in the English constitution. Gillray caught the spirit of the argument perfectly in a print of 1801. He drew two trees. One, the blasted and rotten stump of Opposition, was surmounted by a French cap of Liberty, and on its few remaining branches hung the withered fruits of Blasphemy, Sedition, Anarchy, Democracy. The other tree, flourishing and green, he gave roots of Kings, Lords and Commons, sweet apples of Peace, Happiness and Prosperity, and he labelled its massive trunk JUSTICE.[2] It is important, however, to distinguish the argument against Paine from the wider ideological use of justice throughout the century. The author of *The Rights of Man* was in a peculiar position with respect to the law. As one of 'the middling sort' he was a man of moderate property, and he thought like one. He was not a critic of the

---

1. Hannah More, *Works*, 11 vols., 1830, vol. II, p. 76.
2. 'The Tree of Liberty, with the Devil tempting John Bull', no. 9214, *Catalogue of Political and Personal Satires*, ed. M. D. George, British Museum, Department of Prints and Drawings, 1942, vol. VII, p. 449.

institutions of the law. Indeed, Paine claimed that Quarter Sessions and assizes, as bodies of local administration, were two of the few organs of proper self-government. Nor did he criticize the law's tenderness for property.[1] The only effective answer to the Tory position would have been a thoroughly egalitarian critique and this Paine was unwilling to begin. An egalitarian on the subject of hereditary monarchy and corrupt aristocracy and landed wealth, he was no leveller of all property distinctions. Hence he had to suffer the conservatives' encomiums of justice in silence.[2]

Although Paine never lent his pen to the task, the institutions of the law were in fact exceedingly open to radical criticism. The conservatives based their defence on comparisons with French tyranny, the occasional punishment of a great man, the limited protection the law gave to the poor. They did not dare to attempt a reasoned examination of the whole legal system for the edification of the mob. All men of property knew that judges, justices and juries had to be chosen from their own ranks. The jury, the supposed guarantee that an Englishman would be tried by his equals, had a sharp property qualification. The reason, simply put, was that the common Englishman could not be trusted to share in the operation of the law. A panel of the poor would not convict a labourer who stole wood from a lord's park, a sheep from a farmer's fold, or corn from a merchant's yard. As Gisborne pointed out, even as witnesses 'many of the common people . . . are found to make use of a very blameable latitude in their interpretation of the ninth commandment; and think that they are guilty of no breach of it in deviating, though upon oath, from strict truth, *in favour* of the party accused'.[3] The cottager who appeared in court charged with theft had no illusions about being tried by 'his equals and neighbours', whatever the writers of law books claimed.[4] The twelve men sitting opposite him were employers, overseers of the poor, propertied men. In most cases they were the equals and neighbours of the prose-

1. Paine saw nothing objectionable in hanging men for forgery and counterfeiting, and his criticisms of the game and excise laws were the received wisdom of all men of his class. His only other comments on the substantive law were to the effect that the statutes were disordered and vague and sometimes tyrannical, but he never made more than passing reference to the subject.

2. The one exception is his trenchant criticism of special juries. By an act of 1729, civil suits and misdemeanours could be tried by a jury with a special property qualification; it ensured that gentry and aristocracy could always pack a jury with friends and neighbours if the occasion required. Paine reflected acidly, in print, on the advantages of special juries to the Government when it prosecuted *The Rights of Man* as seditious libel. But this is virtually his only criticism of criminal procedure; he accepts the property qualification for ordinary juries as a matter of course.

3. Gisborne, op. cit., p. 284 note b.

4. Blackstone, *Commentaries*, vol. IV, p. 350.

cutor, not the accused, and this was especially true in cases of theft. The point is not that such juries convicted against the evidence, but rather that a more democratic jury might not have convicted at all. In the constitutional struggles of the seventeenth century, 'middling men' of moderate property had wanted the widest possible extension of trial by jury; the Crown had tried to restrict it because juries shielded sedition. There was another small group, however, who had also wanted to control juries. Winstanley and the Diggers repudiated them as protectors of property against the rights of the poor. There were no Diggers in the eighteenth century, but cottagers and labourers were undoubtedly aware that English justice was still the creature of judges and juries.[1]

Eighteenth-century 'justice' was not, however, a nonsense. It remained a powerful and evocative word, even if it bore a much more limited meaning than a twentieth-century (or seventeenth-century) egalitarian would give it. In a society radically divided between rich and poor, the powerful and the powerless, the occasional victory of a cottager in the courts or the rare spectacle of a titled villain on the gallows made a sharp impression. Moreover, it would be wrong to suggest that the law had to be wholly consistent to persuade men of its legitimacy. 'Justice', in the sense of rational, bureaucratic decisions made in the common interest, is a peculiarly modern conception. It was gaining ground in the eighteenth century. Most reformers worked to bring about such law, and of all such schemes Jeremy Bentham's was the logical conclusion. Yet his plan for a criminal code that was precise, consistent and wholly enforced was alien to the thought of most eighteenth-century Englishmen. They tended to think of justice in personal terms, and were more struck by understanding of individual cases than by the delights of abstract schemes. Where authority is embodied in direct personal relationships, men will often accept power, even enormous, despotic power, when it comes from the 'good King', the father of his people, who tempers justice with mercy. A form of this powerful psychic configuration was one of the most distinctive aspects of the unreformed criminal law. Bentham could not understand it, but it was the law's greatest strength as an ideological system, especially among the poor, and in the countryside.

---

1. The class function of juries was also reflected in the fact that two important kinds of offences were removed from their jurisdiction. In neither game cases nor excise prosecutions could juries of 'middling men' be trusted to convict. (On poaching and juries, see below, p. 211; on smuggling, p. 138.) They felt the law to be unjust, a denial of the rights of property. Hence both offences were punishable on summary conviction by justices and excise commissioners acting without a jury. For all other property offences, tradesmen and farmers would not decide against the evidence.

Mercy

The prerogative of mercy ran throughout the administration of the criminal law, from the lowest to the highest level. At the top sat the high court judges, and their free use of the royal pardon became a crucial argument in the arsenal of conservatives opposing reform. At the lowest jurisdiction, that of the Justice of the Peace, the same discretion allowed the magistrate to make decisions that sometimes escaped legal categories altogether. Although he frequently made obeisance to the rules when convicting, as we have seen, he could dispense with them when pardoning, and the absence of a jury made it even easier for him to do so. Latitude in the direction of mercy caused some critics to complain that many justices, partly from laziness or carelessness 'but frequently from benevolent views improperly indulged', judged cases 'partly or entirely by their own unauthorized ideas of equity'.[1] This element of discretion impressed Weber when he examined the office of JP. He compared it to Arabic 'khadi justice' – a formalistic administration of law that was nevertheless based on ethical or practical judgements rather than on a fixed, 'rational' set of rules. It could combine rigid tradition with 'a sphere of free discretion and grace of the ruler'.[2] Thus it allowed the paternalist JP to compose quarrels, intervene with prosecutors on behalf of culprits, and in the final instance to dismiss a case entirely. The right of the pardon was not limited, however, to high court judges and Justices of the Peace. The mode of prosecution, the manner of trial and the treatment of condemned convicts gave some of the same power to all men of property. 'Irrationality', in the sense used by Weber, and the 'grace of the ruler' which grew from it pervaded the entire administration of the law.

Almost all prosecutions were initiated by private persons, at their discretion, and conducted in accordance with their wishes. Accustomed to organized state police and rigorous state prosecution, French visitors were inclined to marvel at this peculiar English institution. Charles Cottu, a French judge who toured the Northern Circuit in the early nineteenth century, exclaimed,

The English [that is, state officials] appear to attach no importance to a discovery of the causes which may have induced the prisoner to commit the crime:

1. Gisborne, op. cit., p. 28.
2. *From Max Weber*, ed. H. H. Gerth and C. Wright Mills, 1970, pp. 216–21. Brougham anticipated Weber in 1828, declaring 'there is not a worse-constituted tribunal on the face of the earth, not even that of the Turkish Cadi, than that at which summary convictions on the Game Laws constantly take place; I mean a bench or a brace of sporting justices': see J. L. and Barbara Hammond, *The Village Labourer* (1911), 1966, p. 188.

they scarcely even affix any to the establishment of his guilt. I am ignorant whether this temper of mind arises from their fear of augmenting the already excessive number of public offenders, or whether it proceeds from their natural humanity; it is however an undoubted fact, that they make no effort to obtain proofs of the crime, confiding its punishment entirely to the hatred or resentment of the injured party; careless too, about the conviction of the accused, whether his victim shall yield to feelings of compassion, or give way to indolence.[1]

Cottu did not appear to have heard, or understood, the traditional arguments of English gentlemen against a constabulary and state prosecution: that it could lead to despotism, a political police serving the Crown. He did understand, however, the consequences of private prosecution. The victim of the crime could decide himself upon the severity of the prosecution, either enforcing the letter of the law, or reducing the charge. He could even pardon the offence completely by not going to court. The reformers' objections to this system are well known. Private prosecution was capricious and uncertain, and too often rogues escaped due to the distaste, compassion or fear of their victims. But reformers failed to acknowledge the great power this conferred on the prosecutor to make the law serve his own purposes. In Cottu's words, the accuser became 'the arbitrator of the culprit's fate', and the law became an expression of his will. In short, it was in the hands of the gentleman who went to law to evoke gratitude as well as fear in the maintenance of deference.

In a rural parish with a relatively settled population there were many alternatives to a rigorous prosecution. The accused man could be made to post a bond not to offend again, or be given the choice of leaving the neighbourhood. The threat of prosecution could be held over his head to ensure his future good behaviour. He might also be allowed to escape the law by making compensation for his crime, and the negotiations between Richard Ainsworth and his master Nicholas Blundell in 1709 were repeated in all parts of England, throughout the century. Ainsworth was caught stealing, begged Blundell repeatedly not to prosecute, and entered into negotiations to work on one of his master's houses in return for forgiveness.[2] Other accused men simply appealed to the merciful feelings of the man who held them in his power. The wretched thief begging on his knees for forgiveness is not a literary conceit, but a reality described in many legal depositions. Critics of the law objected, however, that many prosecutions were dropped through fear as well as compassion. Certainly it is true that feeling against some prosecutors ran so high that they went in fear of their lives from popular opinion, or felt obliged to

1. Cottu, op. cit., p. 37.
2. Nicholas Blundell, *Blundell's Diary and Letter Book, 1702–1728*, ed. Margaret Blundell, Liverpool, 1952, pp. 109–11.

defend their actions in the press. Yet where certainty of enforcement had to be sacrificed to public opinion, even then graciously granted mercy could produce gratifying deference. Especially where the prosecutor was a landed gentleman, acts of mercy helped create the mental structure of paternalism. The papers of any large landed proprietor are peppered with appeals for pardons, and earnest thanks for them – pardons for poachers, for stealers of holly, for embezzlers of coal. 'I hope his Lordship will not insist upon your acquainting my Master of it,' wrote one poacher to a steward, 'as it would be productive of very great injury to me ... we are afraid the crime is so great that it will not admit of any excuse and therefore all we can say is that our future good behaviour shall be such that his Lordship will not repent of his Lenity and goodness in forgiving us.'[1] The phrases of benevolence constantly recur on the other side: 'it may so happen that my Good Lord Stafford may be inclined (as he generally is) to pardon the offenders...'[2] Such acts were personal ties, not the distant decisions of bureaucracies. They also bridged great vertical distances in the social order: in this case, between some day labourers caught pilfering, and the Lord Lieutenant of the county. We cannot, of course, infer gratitude from begging letters, but there is enough evidence to suggest that much of it was genuine. Many prosecutors, peers included, made the most of their mercy by requiring the pardoned man to sign a letter of apology and gratitude, which was printed in the county newspaper.

The nature of the criminal trial gave enormous discretion to men of property other than the prosecutor. Because the law did not allow those accused of felony to employ an attorney to address the jury, a poor man's defence was often a halting, confused statement. If he had a clear alibi he was lucky: to establish innocence in more complicated cases might be very difficult, even when the judge was sympathetic. Character witnesses were thus extremely important, and very frequently used. It was not uncommon for a man accused of sheep-stealing, a capital offence, to bring a dozen acquaintances to court to testify to his honesty. If the jury did convict, such favourable testimony might still induce the judge to pass a lesser sentence, or recommend a pardon. Yet in character testimony too, the word of a man of property had the greatest weight. Judges respected the evidence of employers, respectable farmers and neighbouring gentlemen, not mere neighbours and friends. A labourer accused of a serious crime learned again his enormous dependence on the power of property to help him, or abandon him, as it chose: 'I am now going to

1. Staffs. RO, D593/L/1/15/10, Worsey to Howard, 15 October 1780.
2. Staffs. RO, D593/M/2/1/8, letter of Thomas Heath, 5 November 1798.

take a dredful tryal and god nose but my poor Life may Lay at Stake,'
William Sheffield wrote to his masters a month before the assizes,

therefore I hope Both of you will stand my frend this time jest to Come and give
me a Careckter for the time that I Lived with you and I hope you will do that
for me the judg I am told will Look Upon that as a great thing in my Behaff. . .
So pray my dear mastters Consider my Unhappy state this time for gods sake
and stand my frend and if plees god it should Ever Laye in my power I will
neaver think nothing two much to make you amends Eaver to Lay my selfe at
your feet if I can be of haney serviss to you for your passt goodness to me in so
doing. . .[1]

If respectable character witnesses did not succeed in convincing the jury
to acquit, their support was the first step in influencing the judge to
consider a pardon. A free or conditional pardon from the king was the
hope of almost every capital convict in the eighteenth century, and many
men under lighter sentences also struggled to obtain it. For the historian
it epitomizes the discretionary element of the law, and the use of mercy
in justifying the social order.

Pardons were very common. Roughly half of those condemned to death
during the eighteenth century did not go to the gallows, but were transported to the colonies or imprisoned. In many cases the judge made the
decision before he left the assize town, but if he did not intend to recommend mercy, it was still possible to petition the king, through the Secretary
of State, up to the moment of execution. The grounds for mercy were
ostensibly that the offence was minor, or that the convict was of good
character, or that the crime he had committed was not common enough in
that county to require an exemplary hanging. The judges also used the
pardon when necessary to meet the requests of local gentry or to propitiate
popular feelings of justice. The bench could ultimately decide whom to
recommend for mercy and whom to leave to hang, but they were not
usually willing to antagonize a body of respectable feeling. Justice Ashurst,
asked to endorse a pardon for a horse-stealer from Cambridge, reported
to the king, 'I had whilst on Circuit received such favourable Accounts
of him as induced me to reprieve him & had those accounts remain'd
uncontradicted I should have thought there could be no objection . . . for
a free Pardon. . . But I have this day received a letter from some Gentlemen of the University desiring to retract their former applications for
mercy. . .'[2] The judges were well aware that the gentry of the county
were charged with government and criminal justice between assize times,

---

1. William Sheffield to Evans, Hinds and Best, *re* his trial at Aylesbury, Lent 1787;
PRO, HO 47/6. Sheffield's employers found it inconvenient to attend; he was condemned, although Best wrote on his behalf.
2. Report of Justice Ashurst, 10 April 1787, *re* John Higgins; PRO, HO 47/6.

and hence usually gave their opinions a serious hearing. The pardon could be used, however, to show mercy when the death penalty seemed too severe, and this discretion became part of the explicit justification of the law to the poor. In passing sentence of death on a prosperous sheep-stealer in 1787, Sir Beaumont Hotham argued that the law understood the trials of the poor and properly held the rich rogue to stricter account. 'He noted the difference between a poor wretch in distress committing such a crime, and a man of seeming reputation; – that the latter, under the mask of a fair and upright character, was enabled to make depreda-tions on his neighbours and the public, without being suspected, therefore was not to be guarded against, and consequently, in his eye, was much more culpable than the poor man, who commits such acts from real want.'[1] Since most death sentences were pronounced for theft, the most recent historian of the pardon concludes that it moderated the barbarity of the criminal law in the interests of humanity. It was erratic and capri-cious, but a useful palliative until Parliament reformed the law in the nineteenth century.[2]

Such an analysis stresses the narrowly legal use of the pardon, but ignores its social significance, the crucial point that interests us here. As in so many other areas of the law, custom and procedure allowed wholly extra-judicial considerations great influence. The pardon allowed the bench to recognize poverty, when necessary, as an excuse, even though the law itself did not. But the manner in which a pardon was obtained made it an important element in eighteenth-century social relations in three other ways. In the first place, the claims of class saved far more men who had been left to hang by the assize judge than did the claims of humanity. Again and again in petitions the magic words recur: 'his parents are respectable persons in Denbighshire'; his father is 'a respect-able farmer'; his brother is 'a builder of character and eminence in Lon-don'.[3] There are very few petitions that plead what one in 1787 called 'the common excuse for larceny, poverty and distress'.[4] It may have been the common excuse, but those requesting pardons knew it held little weight –

1. *An Account of the Life, Trial, and Behaviour of William Bagnall* (WSL, Broad-sheets 2).

2. Radzinowicz, vol. 1, pp. 116, 137.

3. Justice Perryn's report, 3 December 1787, on John Knott, and letter of the Bishop of Salisbury (n.d.), *re* Joseph Moreland, PRO, HO 47/6. Moreland's petition is endorsed, 'family and connection respectable'. Cf. Justice Cardil's recommendation of mercy for John Jepson, a highway robber: he was young, and 'I find that his Mother and Relations live very reputably, *which are Considerations that will have their due weight with your Majesty in favour of this unhappy young man*'. (Emphasis in original; PRO, SP 36/111 fos. 46–7.)

4. John Eden on behalf of Smith, PRO, HO 42/12 fo. 157 (1787).

only two of the hundreds of petitions that year bothered to mention it. In contrast, the excuse of respectability was pleaded *in extenso*. Even need, rarely admitted as a legitimate excuse for a poor man, could become a compelling reason to forgive a richer one. When an officer returned from India was caught stealing silver from inns as he travelled by sedan chair through Oxfordshire, Lord McCartney testified to his valour in imperial wars, and urged that he must have been distressed. This evidence and the support of a 'very reputable' family procured a full pardon.[1] Similar considerations that would never have saved a labourer from the gallows worked in favour of the respectable. When the son of a secretary of the London Foundling Hospital was condemned for a serious burglary, he was saved from execution out of consideration for his mother, and 'Seven unmarried Sisters and a Brother' who would 'unavoidably Share the Ignominy due only to his Crimes'.[2] John Say's case was similar: he came from 'an exceedingly Worthy & respectable family who will feel the disgrace of a Public Execution beyond expression, his Young Sister also now at Boarding School will be irreparably Injured by a disgrace which no time can Obliterate & which will greatly affect her future Interests thro' Life.'[3] The future interests of the sisters of condemned labourers were never mentioned in petitions, because they had no prospects. When the families of poor convicts were taken into consideration, it was usually through fear that execution would create too many orphans to be supported on the parish rates.

The pardon thus served to save a good many respectable villains. It was all very well to hang Dr Dodd and Lord Ferrers, but to hang every errant son of the rich who tried his hand at highway robbery to pay gambling debts would have made too great a carnage in the better circles. Pardons also favoured those with connections for another reason: mercy was part of the currency of patronage. Petitions were most effective from great men, and the common course was for a plea to be passed up through increasingly higher levels of the social scale, between men bound together by the links of patronage and obligation. The bald language of place-seekers recurs here too; trading in life and death became part of the game of interest. 'If anything can be done in consequence of the inclosed letter,' wrote Lord Viscount Hinchingbrooke, 'I shall be very thankful for it – as

---

1. Report of Burton and letter of Lord Macartney *re* William Ludlane, PRO, HO 47/6.

2. John Jones, alias Collingwood, tried Essex Lent Assizes 1787 and transported for life on application of the Duke of Leeds, without further report (letter of his father, affidavit of father's position, report of Justice Thomson, 31 March 1787, PRO, HO 47/6).

3. Letter of Philip Slater, PRO, HO 42/11 fo. 39.

the writer of it is a particular friend of mine in the county of Huntingdon.'[1]
Sir George Yonge forwarded another application for mercy from 'Sir
John Pole, a Neighbour of mine and a gentleman of Family, and Considerable Property in Devonshire and Dorsetshire – If there is occasion for it,
Humanity as well as regard to the application from such a respectable
Quarter make me wish to interfere with success.'[2] Often a long chain of
interest and connection had to rattle before the judges and the king
listened. In one case, not untypical, the condemned man pleaded with the
gaoler and chaplain, the chaplain wrote to a more important London cleric,
the latter appealed to William Wilberforce, and the evangelical MP asked
the Home Secretary to consider the case. This pressure, plus the active
intervention of Lord Ludlow, finally resulted in a pardon.[3] It was the
greatest good fortune to get the attention of a sympathetic peer. In a
system which gave first weight to those with most power, their influence
was naturally greatest. Even the domestic politics of a great house could
count for more than the organized pressure of a whole county of lesser
men. Lord Montagu asked the Secretary of State to pardon the man who
stole his curtains rather than leave him to be hanged, for 'if he is I had as
good be hanged with him, for the Ladys of my family give me as little
rest to save him from being hanged as I do you. . .'[4] In petty cases a peer's
word was law, and judges would agree to cut sentences and even advise
the king to grant free pardons at a mere request. In very outrageous cases,
where property had been so abused that only extraordinary influence
could prevail, there was often a conscious weighing up of the *avoirdupois*
of class. After an attorney had been condemned for forgery at Oxford,
the Lord Chancellor forwarded to the Secretary of State a plea for mercy
from the Bishop of Oxford: 'I apprehend that the King had rejected the
Duke of Marlborough's application, which was made by the Duke of
Bedford; and if the affair is quite over, I have nothing to say. If it is not
quite over, the Bishop's letter may be thrown into the scale.'[5] The ability
to obtain a pardon was recognized as a mark of importance among the
great and the propertied. A landowner who could not obtain one in a
reasonable case was well aware that his prestige could suffer – and this
fact itself was advanced sometimes as a good reason for granting the boon.

Beyond class favouritism and games of influence, the pardon had an
equally important role to play in the ideology of mercy. The poor did not

1. Hinchingbrooke to Townshend, 31 October 1787, PRO, HO 42/12.
2. Yonge to Nepean, 24 October 1787, PRO, HO 42/12 fo. 130.
3. Report of Justice Ashurst, 22 March 1792, Ludlow to Grenville, Tattershall to
Coke and to Grenville, Wilberforce to Dundas in the case of Philip Huckle; PRO,
HO 44/14.
4. PRO, SP 36/5 fo. 218 (1728).
5. Brit. Mus. Add. MSS, 32,719 fo. 50 (1749).

see the elaborate ramifications of interest and connection. Although the convolutions of the patronage system at the lowest level were known to every man who wished to become a tidewaiter, the law was set apart, and no gentleman wished to admit too openly that justice itself was but another part of the system. Moreover, pardon-dealing went on at the highest levels only, well concealed from the eyes of the poor. Therefore the royal prerogative of mercy could be presented as something altogether more mysterious, more sacred and more absolute in its determinations. Pardons were presented as acts of grace rather than as favours to interests. At the lowest levels, within the immediate experience of the poor, pardons were indeed part of the tissue of paternalism, expressed in the most personal terms. The great majority of petitions for mercy were written by gentlemen on behalf of labourers. It was an important self-justification of the ruling class that once the poor had been chastised sufficiently to protect property, it was the duty of a gentleman to protect 'his' people. Thus William Trumbull of Berkshire struggled to save a youth from the gallows when he discovered that the boy's father had been a servant to his own father, the Secretary of State, many years before.[1] A Norfolk gentleman asked for mercy on the grounds that 'all this man's family live in the neighbourhood near Norwich and are employed occasionally by me.'[2] And the Duke of Richmond obtained a pardon for a man who claimed to have once saved the life of the Duke's father.[3] Men facing imminent death tried to exploit some improbably remote connections. The son of Lord Courtenay's former butler appealed to Sir George Yonge on behalf of another relative, on the grounds that Yonge had known the butler years before: 'for Sir George it is in your power to save him from death if Sir George you will be so kind. . .'[4] These were not empty or exaggerated words. Influence in pardons, though rarely the only factor considered, was extremely important. A convicted labourer, even in a rural parish, was likely to know only a few men of property well enough to ask for their help, and if they were feeling more vengeful than merciful, death was a pretty sure thing. John Wilkes of Staffordshire had a sister who worked for the Reverend John Fletcher, the saintly Vicar of Madeley, and she tried to get the cleric to help save her condemned brother. Fletcher wrote Wilkes that his crimes were too serious, and that he suspected him of

1. Brit. Mus. Add. MSS, 32,732 fo. 479 (1753).
2. PRO, HO 42/12 fo. 137.
3. Brit. Mus. Add. MSS, 33,732, Richmond to Newcastle, Strasbourg, 21 October 1753.
4. PRO, HO 32/12 fo. 88 (1787). John Dennis demanded that the Pelhams should help him 'and never be ashamed to hear yourselves named to a free and accepted Mason'. Brit. Mus. Add. MSS, 32,734 fo. 182 (1754).

robbing one of Fletcher's own houses. 'If you committed that robbery, I desire you to confess it before you leave this world . . . ,' he wrote him, and rather than write a petition prepared Wilkes a prayer. It ended, 'Let the hands of human justice push me into the arms of divine mercy.'[1]

Petitions for pardons were occasionally opposed, but usually by determined prosecutors. Where a prosecutor had second thoughts or wished to indulge his humanity after exacting terror and recovering his property, he sometimes was the first to add his name to a plea for mercy – and thereby gave it greater weight. Most successful petitions, however, were begun by other men of respectable position, with good connections, and their activity on behalf of the condemned could only enhance their reputations as men of compassion and magnanimity. To the poor, the intercession of a local gentleman was proof of his power to approach the throne. He took no blame if the petition failed, for an unanswered plea was attributed to the determination of the king, who was popularly believed to sign all death warrants. A successful outcome was attributed to mercy at the same exalted height – and Blackstone argued that 'these repeated acts of goodness coming immediately from his own hand, endear the sovereign to his subjects, and contribute more than anything to root in their hearts that filial affection, and personal loyalty, which are the sure establishment of a prince'.[2] And all the chaplains, country gentlemen and peers who had helped to obtain a pardon shared somewhat in the reflected glory of the merciful ruler.

The pardon is important because it often put the principal instrument of legal terror – the gallows – directly in the hands of those who held power. In this it was simply the clearest example of the prevailing custom at all levels of criminal justice. Here was the peculiar genius of the law. It allowed the rulers of England to make the courts a selective instrument of class justice, yet simultaneously to proclaim the law's incorruptible impartiality, and absolute determinacy. Their political and social power was reinforced daily by bonds of obligation on one side and condescension on the other, as prosecutors, gentlemen and peers decided to invoke the law or agreed to show mercy. Discretion allowed a prosecutor to terrorize the petty thief and then command his gratitude, or at least the approval of his neighbourhood as a man of compassion. It allowed the class that

1. Fletcher himself sought more worldly profit by publishing a pamphlet, from which this account is taken: *The Penitent Thief, or a narrative of two women fearing God, who visited in prison a highway-man, executed at Stafford, April the 3d, 1773, with a Letter to a condemned malefactor: and a penitential office for either a true churchman or a dying criminal. By a country clergyman* (2nd edn, 1773).

2. Blackstone, *Commentaries*, vol. IV, p. 397. Blackstone explicitly repudiates Beccaria on this crucial question.

passed one of the bloodiest penal codes in Europe to congratulate itself
on its humanity. It encouraged loyalty to the king and the state:

> And Earthly Power doth then show likest God's
> When mercy seasons justice.

And in the countryside the power of gentlemen and peers to punish or
forgive worked in the same way to maintain the fabric of obedience,
gratitude and deference. The law was important as gross coercion; it was
equally important as ideology. Its majesty, justice and mercy helped to
create the spirit of consent and submission, the 'mind-forged manacles',
which Blake saw binding the English poor. But consent, in Archdeacon
Paley's phrase, must be managed 'with delicacy and circumspection'.
To understand fully the social functions of the eighteenth-century
criminal law, we must understand how it embodied those virtues too.

Delicacy and circumspection

Deference in eighteenth-century England, although pervasive, was not
complete. The gentry managed to maintain order without anything
resembling the political police used by the French, but it was order that
often seemed to rest on precarious foundations. The common Englishman
was renowned for his riots, and also for his dislike of standing armies.
Although the ideology of justice could be used by gentlemen to quiet a
mob, and with success, words sometimes lost their magic. Then the discretion embodied in the law allowed the authorities to use terror with
great flexibility. Examples of this delicate adjustment of state power are
legion, especially in decisions about executions, the most emotive act in
civil government. In 1756 Justice Willes was holding the Warwick Assizes
when food riots broke out in the county. He announced his intention of
trying and executing immediately all rioters brought before him, adjourn-
ing the court from week to week until order had been restored. Within
days he convicted four,

> And, when I passed Sentence upon Them, I said a good deal to show the
> heinous nature of their crime, and the great folly of the attempt. . . And I
> ordered the captain and another notorious offender to be executed on Wednesday
> next; and told . . . the others . . . that I would adjourn 'till Monday s'en night,
> and that then, if the insurrection was quite at end, I would apply to his Majesty
> to pardon them; but if not, I would immediately execute the two other persons
> that were convicted.

No one thought it strange to hang some men for crimes committed by
others. The Secretary of State wrote to Willes to congratulate him, and

49

expressed the hope that other judges would follow his example in similar cases. 'The King, the Duke, the whole court, are full of Commendation, & the general voice is, that these Insolent Rioters could not have fallen into better Hands.'[1]

Gentlemen were very sensitive to opinion in their neighbourhoods, for there might be serious consequences if the show of force was either not quite impressive enough, or so brutal that it outraged men and destroyed the mystique of justice. Lord Hardwicke, when Chief Justice, ordered a Cornish rioter's body to hang in chains, a refinement of capital punishment that added infamy to death. He agreed to respite that part of the sentence, however, when the local gentry informed him that

in the present circumstances of affairs it would be more advisable not to do it, for tho' his crimes, as your Lordship says, demand the most terrifying Example yet there must be the greatest regard had for the Peace of our Country, which we were apprehensive might be again disturbed if that measure was pursued. It is undoubtedly in theory right and would be extremely necessary in most parts of the Kingdom, but in this there has been such an unaccountable run in his favour, that if any of his particular Friends should cut Him down, which would be a fresh insult upon Authority, The Rabble would call it the last blow, and the spirit might revive. . . We are in hopes that the examples are carried far enough to work upon the Fears of his friends, without giving them the opportunity of any new Triumph.[2]

Edmund Burke used the same argument a half-century later in the case of the Gordon rioters. A week of looting, arson and unchecked defiance of authority severely shook the foundations of order. Burke therefore advised the government to limit the number of executions in spite of the gravity of the offence: 'If I understand the temper of the publick at this moment, a very great part of the lower, and some of the middling people of this city, are in a very critical disposition, and such as ought to be managed with *firmness and delicacy*.' He continued, 'In general they rather approve than blame the principles of the rioters . . . This keeps their minds in a suspended and anxious state, which may very easily be exasperated, by an injudicious severity, into desperate resolutions; or by weak measures, on the part of the Government, it may be encouraged to the pursuit of courses, which may be of the most dangerous consequences to the public. . .' His recommendation was for six executions with maximum publicity, a calculated blend of terror and mercy under the strict rule of law.[3]

1. Brit. Mus. Add. MSS, 32,867 fos. 3–4, 8–11, 94.
2. Brit. Mus. Add. MSS, 35,585 fos. 299–303.
3. 'Some Thoughts on the Approaching Executions', *Works*, 1812, vol. IX, pp. 268–71. My emphasis.

The rulers of eighteenth-century England spent much time gauging opinion in this way. The façade of power had to be kept undamaged. The gentry were acutely aware that their security depended on *belief* – belief in the justice of their rule, and in its adamantine strength. Hence, punishment at times had to be waived or mitigated to meet popular ideas of justice, and to prevent popular outrage from going too far and thereby realizing its own strength. The aim above all was to avoid exposing the law and authority either to ridicule or to too close scrutiny. Contempt of court was therefore punished severely: the convict who heard the death sentence with no sign of repentance, and who instead damned the judge, could hope for no pardon. It was also important for those administering and using the law to be circumspect, discreet – to leave unsaid anything that might mar the illusion of power. Hence a gentleman who trifled with the mob or called into question the ultimate justice of the law was execrated by his fellows as a knave and a fool. Lord George Gordon did both. The impotence of England's governors in the face of disorder, and the measure of their contempt for class traitors, was epitomized by a curious scene in the House of Commons in June 1780. As Gordon's supporters raged outside and threatened to break in upon the Honourable Members, several MPs followed him about the House with their hands on their swords, vowing to run him through if the mob broke in. When Gordon continued his wayward career a few years later by publishing a protest of the convicts of Newgate against capital punishment for theft, he was committed to prison as a libeller of justice. Most gentlemen thought him mad.

Discretion was necessary in thousands of small things, too. It permeated the operations of the law. The decisions that moved the levers of fear and mercy were decisions of propertied men, and they made them privately, among themselves. At the most informal level, before Justices of the Peace – country gentlemen – the operation of the law was often the result of an agreement on tactics between the JP and the prosecutor, especially when the latter was a friend or powerful neighbour. At the level of prosecution, the gentry particularly were likely to allow the offender to escape if they were not completely sure of a conviction: it was better to feign mercy rather than reveal impotence. Since the legal process was largely a secret between landowner and magistrate, nothing was easier to arrange. Where a JP wished to chastise, but found to his chagrin that the legislature had somehow failed to pass the right law, he was advised to use others:

Complaints are made to magistrates, with respect to a thousand immoral and wicked actions, over which they have no jurisdiction whatever. In such cases, *it will be prudence to conceal the infirmity of their authority*: but they will frequently find that [the statute against swearing] has been violated by one or both parties. I should then recommend, that they should exert their full authority in the punishment of *this* offence; and to dismiss the parties, with an admonition or a reprimand, where the law has given them no power to act.[1]

The opacity of the law also made it possible for the rulers of England to act in concert in managing hangings, arranging backstage the precise moment of the emotional climax. This was crucial not only at times of disorder; it was part of the routine administration of the law. The Hanoverians themselves sometimes took seriously their legal prerogatives in this respect. Shortly after he came to the throne, George III agreed to the routine mitigation of the death sentence to one of transportation in the case of a highway robber. He gave instructions, however, that

as his Majesty hopes so to terrify this unhappy Man, on the present occasion that he may not hereafter be guilty of the like offense; it is the King's intention that *he should not be acquainted of his Majesty's having extended his royal mercy towards him, 'till he comes to the place of execution.* It will be proper therefore, that you give orders to the sheriffs, for this purpose, so that he be carried with the others, who are to suffer; to the place of execution, and that he be informed, then, and not before then, of the reprieve. . .[2]

'Circumspection' is a euphemism in such circumstances. The private manipulation of the law by the wealthy and powerful was in truth a ruling-class conspiracy, in the most exact meaning of the word. The king, judges, magistrates and gentry used private, extra-legal dealings among themselves to bend the statute and common law to their own purposes. The legal definition of conspiracy does not require explicit agreement; those party to it need not even all know one another, provided they are working together for the same ends. In this case, the common assumptions of the conspirators lay so deep that they were never questioned, and rarely made explicit.[3]

It is important to recognize this fact, for it raises some important methodological questions for the student of authority and the law. There is a danger, which perhaps this essay has not avoided, of giving the impression that a system of authority is *something*, rather than the actions of

1. Christian, *Charges*, p. 291 (my emphasis, followed by Christian's).

2. C. Jenkinson to Recorder of London, 22 May 1761; PRO, SP 44/87, fos. 19 and 20 (my emphasis).

3. The legal definition requires that the purpose should be unlawful, not simply 'extra-legal'. But here the law falls into a 'vagueness [which] renders it possible for judges to treat all combinations to effect any purpose which happens to be distasteful to them as indictable crimes, by declaring this purpose to be "unlawful" '. (*Kenny's Outlines of Criminal Law*, 19th edn, 1966, p. 430). Many eighteenth-century Englishmen would have found private agreements by the powerful to manipulate the law not only distasteful but deceitful and dangerous. But only judges and legislators can make matters of taste also matters of law.

living men. The invisible hand of Adam Smith's political economy was metaphor, shorthand for an effect rather than a cause; it was a description of recurrent patterns of useful behaviour forged out of the energy, conflicts and greed of thousands of individuals in a capitalist market. In a somewhat similar way, much of the ideological structure surrounding the criminal law was the product of countless short-term decisions. It was often a question of intuition, and of trial and error. In handling a mob it was useful to appeal to ideals of English justice: but that was a lesson that was slowly learned over many generations, and rarely raised to the level of theory. The necessity of gauging reactions to executions was an immediate problem of public order, not a plot worked out by eighteenth-century experts in public relations for a fee. The difficulty for the historian of the law is twofold. He must make explicit convictions that were often unspoken, for if left unspoken we cannot understand the actions of the men who held them.[1] Yet in describing how convictions and actions moulded the administration of justice, he must never forget that history is made by men, not by the Cunning of Reason or the Cunning of System. The course of history is the result of a complex of human actions – purposive, accidental, sometimes determined – and it cannot be reduced to one transcendent purpose. The cunning of a ruling class is a more substantial concept, however, for such a group of men is agreed on ultimate ends. However much they believed in justice (and they did); however sacred they held property (and they worshipped it); however merciful they were to the poor (and many were); the gentlemen of England knew that their duty was, above all, to rule. On that depended everything. They acted accordingly.

Seen in this light, much of the historical literature on the eighteenth-century ruling class seems misconceived. Their attitudes to the law are often made a test of their moral worth. Romilly and the other reformers usually have received alphas, as the forerunners of the armies of liberal enlightenment and humanitarianism, and as the 'winners'. But in praising the reformers we caricature the conservatives. Descriptions of a ruling class in terms of abstract moral judgement have contradictory results, because they are profoundly unhistorical. The substantial literature on the

---

1. Those who describe beliefs that are widely held but seldom expressed are often unrepresentative figures. Nourse was an Anglican cleric who converted to Roman Catholicism and literature, Madan another eccentric clergyman whose call for more hangings was repudiated by the judges. The Evangelicals (More, Gisborne) were often embarrassingly direct in their social prescriptions, Cottu was a foreigner, and Christian was a long-winded, egotistical bore. For these reasons they sometimes raised in argument points that more conventional men thought banal or indiscreet, or did not think consciously of at all.

county magistrate is another case in point. Historians have reached divergent conclusions, although the present consensus seems to be that their rule was 'in general upright and humane'.[1] Still, pessimists (to borrow the terms of another moral debate) can find evidence that many JPs were 'pretty great tyrants', and at least one optimistic historian has hailed them as the finest governors the world has ever known. These peculiarly idealist explanations, which count or weigh the number of good acts against the number of bad, then judge whether or not to admit the eighteenth-century ruling class into the heavenly kingdom of twentieth-century respectability, hinder rather than aid understanding. Nor does it help to take a relativist moral tack, and assert that the rulers of England were about as humane as the society that they lived in, some a bit better, some a bit worse. Humanity and inhumanity are real dispositions, rooted in individuals, and more or less general, perhaps, in groups of men with similar experiences. But conscious dispositions can be shaped by much deeper social imperatives, justifications are not always the same as motives, and even the sincerest convictions and most authentic emotional responses may be called forth, or subdued, or even at times reversed, by the patterns of power within a culture or a class. Men were merciful and merciless in the eighteenth century: the historian's task is to answer the questions when, and why. It is not something we can judge in the light of eternity. Rather, we should be content to know why Lord Montagu was able to please his ladies by saving a man's life, and why a Midlands cleric was prepared to use the gallows to help his parishioner find God.

The second question raised by a discussion of the law as ideology is evidential: how can we prove that it worked? Much of the evidence cited here comes from the avowed intentions and observations of the rulers, not the ruled. Perhaps much of what the gentry interpreted as the deference and gratitude of the poor was in fact conscious deception. Perhaps the ordinary Englishman played the role assigned to him, but was never convinced by the play. The eighteenth century produced much genteel cant about justice, but it also produced a large popular literature marked by cynicism and disrespect for the law. And there were many more forceful demonstrations of incredulity, including riots at executions, and rogues who mocked their judges.

Much research remains to be done before we can give confident answers to some of these questions. But two general points may be made. In the first place, most of the evidence that we have of loud popular disrespect for the law comes from London, and London differed in important ways from the rest of eighteenth-century English society. It had a highly transient population, and a large body of disorderly and parasitic poor,

1. G. E. Mingay, *English Landed Society in the Eighteenth Century*, 1963, p. 119.

living on the gathered wealth of commerce, the port and the disorderly and parasitic rich. In sharp contrast to the provinces, the men hanged at Tyburn were mostly born in distant places. They had come to London from the country, and in doing so left behind the close and persisting personal relationships that still characterized much of English society. And it was in such intimate dealings of fear and gratitude that much of the ideology of justice was realized. Some historians have suggested that 'urban alienation' accounts for London disorder and crime in the eighteenth century. It may be more correct to say that the instruments of control there were weaker, in part because the class relationships that fostered deference were. Resistance to the law, disrespect for its majesty, scorn for its justice were greater. Equally, judicial mercy in London was more often a bureaucratic lottery than a convincing expression of paternalism.

The provinces too erupted in disorder: food riots, militia riots, excise riots, turnpike riots, gang poaching, endemic and often violent smuggling. The hegemony of the law was never complete and unbroken, even in the most deeply rural, most traditional counties. The fabric of authority was torn and reknit constantly. The important fact remains, however, that it was reknit readily. The closer mesh of economic and social ties in rural society, the public nature of those relationships compared to the complexity and obscurity of much of metropolitan life, allowed the creation of an ideology that was much more pervasive than in London. When it was momentarily challenged in a county riot or by a defiant labourer, no serious harm resulted; the prevailing code was, in fact, usually strengthened. An ideology endures not by being wholly enforced and rigidly defined. Its effectiveness lies first in its very elasticity, the fact that men are not required to make it a credo, that it seems to them the product of their own minds and their own experience. And the law did not enforce uniform obedience, did not seek total control; indeed, it sacrificed punishment when necessary to preserve the belief in justice. The courts dealt in terror, pain and death, but also in moral ideals, control of arbitrary power, mercy for the weak. In doing so they made it possible to disguise much of the class interest of the law. The second strength of an ideology is its generality. Provided that its depths are not explored too often or by too many, it remains a reservoir of belief throughout the society and flows into the gaps made by individual acts of protest. Therefore, those using it are concerned above all with surface appearances. Undoubtedly the gentleman accepting an apology from the man in his power, the thief or the rioter, would have been gratified to know that the contrition was absolute, from the soul. But provided that the act of contrition was public and convincing, that it served to sustain general belief in the justice of the social order, it sufficed. It became part of the untested general idea, the ideology which made it possible to stigmatize dissent as acts of individuals, of rogues and criminals and madmen.

The hypothesis presented here is that the criminal law, more than any other social institution, made it possible to govern eighteenth-century England without a police force and without a large army. The ideology of the law was crucial in sustaining the hegemony of the English ruling class. This argument, if sound, helps us to explain their resistance to suggestions for drastic legal reform. It also casts some light on the membership of that ruling class, and the character of their society.

III

The long resistance to reform of the criminal law has perplexed later writers. The conservatives who opposed reform have been generally criticized, but historians have failed adequately to explain the growth in numbers of capital statutes and the simultaneous extension of the pardon. When the criminal law is seen not simply as a coercive instrument to punish crime, however, both problems seem largely resolved.

The post-revolution Parliaments passed more and more capital statutes in order to make *every* kind of theft, malicious damage or rebellion an act punishable by death. Although most executions took place under Tudor statutes rather than these fresh-minted ones, the new legislation gave the power to make terrible examples when necessary. Sometimes the new laws merely re-created the death penalty for offences which had been affected by the development of benefit of clergy; more often they added it to newly defined offences, including some not foreseen by the lawmakers of Elizabeth's time, such as the forging of banknotes. But if gentlemen in Parliament were willing to hang a proportion of offenders every year in order to stage the moral drama of the gallows, it is extremely doubtful that they ever believed that the capital statutes should be strictly enforced.[1] The impact of sentencing and hanging could only be diminished if it became too common: 'It is certain,' wrote Burke, 'that a great havock among criminals hardens, rather than subdues, the minds of people inclined to the same crimes; and therefore fails of answering its purpose

1. This is Paley's doctrine, embraced by every subsequent conservative apologist. Radzinowicz explicitly rejects it on the grounds that the divergence between the law and its administration was increasing (Radzinowicz, vol. 1, p. 164, n. 59). His argument ignores the probability that Parliament passed many laws in part *because* they knew they would not be rigorously enforced; that is, that they legislated on the basis of their experience. On the evidence for divergence, see above, p. 23, n. 1.

as an example.'[1] Equally important, a return to the severities of the Tudors and early Stuarts probably would not have been tolerated by the people. At that period and earlier the gentry and the great houses usually had small armies of their own with which local disaffection could be crushed when necessary. But from the later seventeenth century the importance of managing opinion had made nuance, discretion and less obvious coercion a necessary part of the art of ruling. If London rioted at Tyburn, how much worse would disorder be if the executions were four times as numerous? In the counties, three or six hangings in each, twice a year, afforded splendid occasion for lessons in justice and power; but scores of victims would have revolted the people. Although some gentlemen in Parliament did pen bloody new laws in the heat of anger and an uncompromising spirit of revenge, they saw the wisdom of pardons when confronted with long gaol calendars and the spectre of county towns festooned with corpses.

Considerations such as these probably influenced the judges most in determining their general policy over the century. For although it is asserted that after 1750 a constantly declining proportion of death sentences was actually carried out, this is only true in London. In the home counties the proportion of condemned who were executed remained fairly steady over the same period.[2] But the common element in both jurisdictions was the effect of the differing policies on the absolute numbers hanged. In both cases, the number of the condemned who actually died on the gallows was relatively constant over much of the century. The law made enough examples to inculcate fear, but not so many as to harden or repel a populace that had to assent, in some measure at least, to the rule of property.

The second great paradox about the old criminal law, the delay in reform long after a good case had been made that capital statutes allowed theft to increase by making prosecutions uncertain, may also be resolved. Romilly and Eden and the other reformers proposed to replace capital punishment with lesser penalties, and the model which they followed implicitly and sometimes used publicly was that of Beccaria: 'a fixed code of laws, which must be observed to the letter.'[3] But Beccaria's plan made no provision for the needs of government. The conservative gentlemen of England balked not only at the 'unconstitutional' police that such plans required: they instinctively rejected rational plans as pernicious. A complete rationalization of the criminal law would remove those very elements

1. 'Some Thoughts on the Approaching Executions', *Works*, vol. IX, p. 270.
2. See above p. 23, n. 1.
3. Cesare Beccaria, *On Crimes and Punishments*, trans. Henry Paolucci, New York, 1963, ch. 4, p. 16.

of discretion, such as the pardon, which contributed so much to the maintenance of order and deference. Beccaria's thought, as Venturi has pointed out, was no mere *mélange* of humanitarianism and reason. His machine-like system of judgement and punishment would work only where differences of power between men did not exist, where the 'perhaps unnecessary right of property' had disappeared. His principal European opponents seized on this fact: his ideas, they claimed, spelt the end of all authority.[1]

In England the opposition was muffled, since the rhetoric of Whiggism denied that arbitrary measures existed and claimed that the criminal law was *already* fixed and determinate. Most of the opponents of reform therefore argued only that it was impossible to create a schedule of crimes and punishments complete enough to do 'justice' to the subtle differences between cases. But there were hints even in England of the deeper fears for authority. In 1817 Christian, always a frank defender of the unreformed law, recalled Livy's description of the fixed laws enacted after the expulsion of the Roman kings:

> The King was a man from whom you might obtain by petition, what was right, and even what was wrong: with him there was room for favour and for kindness: he had the power of showing his displeasure, and of granting a pardon; he knew how to discriminate between a friend and an enemy. The laws were a thing deaf and inexorable, more favourable and advantageous to the weak than to the powerful: they admitted of no relaxation or indulgence, if you exceeded their limits.

'He knew how to discriminate between a friend and an enemy' – no criminal code could do that, in Christian's opinion. And had not the French Revolution shown that rigid laws could favour the poor rather than the propertied? With such reforms, the judge concluded, 'we should all be involved in republican gloom, melancholy, and sadness'.[2]

Throughout the period we have been considering, the importance of the law as an instrument of authority and a breeder of values remained paramount. The English ruling class entered the eighteenth century with some of its strongest ideological weapons greatly weakened. The Divine Right of Kings had been jettisoned in the interests of gentry power, but the monarchy lost as a consequence much of its potency as a source of authority, and so too did religion. At the same time control had flowed away from the executive in the extreme decentralization of government

---

1. Franco Venturi, *Utopia and Reform in the Enlightenment*, Cambridge, 1971, p. 101, quoting Beccaria, ch. 30. On this statement compare Paolucci on Beccaria, op. cit., p. 74, n. 39.
2. Christian, *Charges*, pp. 278–9.

which characterized the century. With Stuarts plotting in Europe, Jacobitism suspected everywhere at home, and a lumpily unattractive German prince on the throne, English justice became a more important focus of beliefs about the nation and the social order. Perhaps some of the tension abated after the last Jacobite attempt in 1745, which may help to account for Blackstone's relatively favourable attitude to reform in mid-century. But within a few decades renewed assaults on the structure of authority – the riots of 1766 and 1780, Wilkes and the French Revolution – determined the English ruling class to repel any attacks on the mystery and majesty of the law.

In doing so they apparently sacrificed some security of property. Romilly and the rest of the reformers were undoubtedly right that convictions in the courts were uncertain, and that the occasional terror of the gallows would always be less effective than sure detection of crime and moderate punishments. Yet the argument had little weight with the gentry and aristocracy. In the first place they had large numbers of personal servants to guard their plate and their wives. Their problem was not attack from without but disloyalty within their houses. No code of laws or police force would protect them there. Their own judgement of character and the fair treatment of servants within the family were the only real guarantees they could have. Nor did the technicalities of the law bother country gentlemen when they did come to try pilferers of their woods and gardens. For as MPs they passed a mass of legislation that allowed them, as JPs, to convict offenders without the trouble of legalistic indictments or tender-minded juries. In cases involving grain, wood, trees, garden produce, fruit, turnips, dogs, cattle, horses, the hedges of parks and game, summary proceedings usually yielded a speedy and simple conviction.[1] The other crime from which the gentry commonly suffered was sabotage: arson, cattle-maiming, the destruction of trees. Although all these offences were punished by death, few offenders were ever caught. Here too gentlemen knew that a reform of the capital statutes would not increase the certainty of a conviction. Moreover, sabotage was primarily an attack on their authority rather than their property. Their greatest protection against such assaults was acquiescence in their right to rule: the belief in their neighbourhoods that they were kind and just landlords and magistrates. In one area alone were they exposed to the danger of great financial loss from theft. Their largest possession was land. The only way it could be taken from them illegally was by forgery – and it is significant that forgery

---

1. The growth of this body of legislation was remarked by lawyers, who sometimes argued that it threatened trial by jury; its expansion paralleled the growth in capital statutes.

was punished with unmitigated severity throughout the century, by death.[1]

Lower down the social scale, the property of men in trade and manufacturing and farming was much less secure. In the eighteenth century very few of the offences from which such men suffered were punishable on summary conviction. Instead, to recover embezzled banknotes or shoplifted calico or stolen sheep, it was necessary to go to the expense and trouble of a full criminal trial. Its outcome was always uncertain: the technicalities of indictment or the misplaced sympathies of juries allowed many thieves to escape. After the trial came the misplaced sympathies of petitioners for pardons. Martin Madan, anxious to see property secured by a more rigorous execution of the laws, argued that 'the outside influences of great supporters' had too great effect on the prerogative of mercy. The result was that the great indulged their humanity at the expense of lesser men's property.[2]

There was, therefore, a division of interest among propertied Englishmen about the purpose of the criminal law. The reformers' campaign spoke to humanitarians of all classes, men revolted by the public agonies of the condemned at the gallows. But their argument that capital punishment should be replaced by a more certain protection of property appealed mostly to that great body of 'middling men', almost half the nation, who earned from £25 to £150 a year at mid-century, and created more than half England's wealth.[3] Although they could use the discretionary elements of the law to a limited degree, their property was the prey of thieves undeterred by terror. Their complaints did not impress a tiny but powerful ruling class, whose immense personal property in land was secure, who could afford to protect their other goods without public support, and who in any case were most concerned with the law as an instrument of authority.

It is in such terms that we must work toward a definition of the ruling

1. 'Forgery is also punished capitally, and nobody complains that this punishment is too severe, because when contracts sustain action property can never be secure unless the forging of false ones be restrained.' Adam Smith, *Lectures on Justice, Police, Revenue and Arms* (1763), ed. Edwin Cannan, 1896, p. 150.

2. Madan, op. cit., pp. 55ff.

3. Derived from the estimates of Joseph Massie in 1760, the figures can be trusted only as general estimates (Peter Mathias, 'The Social Structure in the Eighteenth Century: A Calculation by Joseph Massie', *Economic History Review*, 2nd ser., x, 1957, pp. 30–45). According to Massie, families with this range of income accounted for 48 per cent of the population and 57 per cent of the total of all families' 'annual income and expenses'. Above them, with incomes of more than £200, were the landed gentry, great merchants and aristocracy. The merchants, 1·6 per cent of the population, accounted for another 8·9 per cent of total income, and the landed classes (1·2 per cent of the population) over 14 per cent.

class of eighteenth-century England. Far from being the property of
Marxist or *marxisant* historians, the term is a leitmotiv in studies of the
period.[1] Partly this is due to the testimony of the sources: gentry and
aristocracy claimed the title with complete assurance. Its historical usage,
however, remains imprecise. Usually it has been defined in terms of
income or status: the rents of the great landed estate, or the exact meaning
contemporaries gave to the word 'gentleman'. Class, however, is a social
relationship, not simply an aggregate of individuals. As a relationship
based upon differences of power and wealth, it must be sought in the
life of the institutions that men create and within which they meet. The
law defined and maintained the bounds of power and wealth, and when
we ask who controlled the criminal law, we see a familiar constellation:
monarchy, aristocracy, gentry and, to a lesser extent, the great merchants.
In numbers they were no more than 3 per cent of the population. But
their discretionary use of the law maintained their rule and moulded
social consciousness. An operational definition of the ruling class – asking
who controlled a critical institution like the law, and how they manipulated it – is a more useful approach than drawing horizontal lines in
Blackstone's list of forty status levels. For it is necessary to define in
detail what it means to rule.

Many historians, confronted with the hegemony of the eighteenth-
century ruling class, have described it in terms of absolute control and
paternal benevolence. Max Beloff argued that after the Restoration they
enjoyed an unparalleled sense of security which explained 'the leniency
with which isolated disturbances were on the whole treated, when compared with the ferocity shown by the same class towards their social
inferiors in the times of the Tudors and early Stuarts'.[2] It seems more
likely that the relative insecurity of England's governors, their crucial

1. Max Beloff, *Public Order and Popular Disturbances 1660-1714*, 1938, p. 154,
discussed the 'social thinking' of the Restoration ruling class; David Mathew in *The
Social Structure in Caroline England*, Oxford, 1948, p. 8, asserted that 'within the
general social structure the diverse elements were being moulded which would in time
form themselves into a ruling class'; W. R. Brock wrote that country life taught 'a code
of behaviour and first lessons in public life' to the eighteenth-century ruling class
(*New Cambridge Modern History*, vol. VII, 1957, p. 243); Esther Moir referred to the
landowners as 'the backbone of the traditional ruling class' in *The Justice of the Peace*,
Harmondsworth, 1969. Latterly a certain embarrassment occasionally has attached to
the term. Peter Laslett, in *The World We Have Lost*, 1965, discussed at length why the
governors of eighteenth-century England constituted the only class, but avoided joining
the evocative words: England had one class, but they were a 'ruling segment'. Harold
Perkin, however, with a similar interpretation of the dynamics of the society, readmitted
the term: *The Origin of Modern English Society*, 1969, p. 56.
2. Beloff, op. cit., p. 154.

dependence on the deference of the governed, compelled them to moderate that ferocity. More recent writing has stressed the importance of patronage; Harold Perkin has argued that this was the central bond of eighteenth-century society. Patronage created vertical chains of loyalty; it was, in fact, 'the module of which the social structure was built'. Powerful men bound less powerful ones to them through paternalism, controlling the income, even the 'life-chances' of the dependent client or tenant or labourer. Such ties, repeated endlessly, formed a 'mesh of vertical loyalties'. Social control in the eighteenth century seems a gentle yoke from this perspective: a spontaneous, uncalculated and peaceful relationship of gratitude and gifts. The system is ultimately a self-adjusting one of shared moral values, values which are not contrived but autonomous. At one point the author concedes that insubordination was 'ruthlessly suppressed'. But mostly social solidarity grew quietly: 'those who lived within its embrace . . . [called it] friendship.'[1] Coercion was an exceptional act, to handle exceptional deviance.

Yet it is difficult to understand how those loyalties endured when patronage was uneven, interrupted, often capricious. Many contemporaries testified to the fickleness of wealth: disappointed office-seekers, unemployed labourers or weavers, paupers dumped over parish boundaries. Riot was a commonplace; so too were hangings. Benevolence, in short, was not a simple positive act: it contained within it the ever-present threat of malice. In economic relations a landlord keeping his rents low was benevolent because he could, with impunity, raise them. A justice giving charity to a wandering beggar was benevolent because he could whip him instead. Benevolence, all patronage, was given meaning by its contingency. It was the obverse of coercion, terror's conspiracy of silence. When patronage failed, force could be invoked; but when coercion inflamed men's minds, at the crucial moment mercy could calm them.

A ruling class organizes its power in the state. The sanction of the state is force, but it is force that is legitimized, however imperfectly, and therefore the state deals also in ideologies. Loyalties do not grow simply in complex societies: they are twisted, invoked and often consciously created. Eighteenth-century England was not a free market of patronage relations. It was a society with a bloody penal code, an astute ruling class

1. Perkin, op. cit., pp. 32–49, a sustained historical use of the idea of 'social control' currently orthodox in the sociological literature. The origins of the concept lie at least as far back as Durkheim's 'social conscience', and it has a marked ideological history of its own. Its increasingly common usage in historical writing, often with little critical examination, therefore bears watching. Its assumption of the relative autonomy of normative sanctions seems dubious, particularly in descriptions of the power of the state.

who manipulated it to their advantage, and a people schooled in the lessons of Justice, Terror and Mercy. The benevolence of rich men to poor, and all the ramifications of patronage, were upheld by the sanction of the gallows and the rhetoric of the death sentence.

1. Hogarth's painting of *The
Bench*. The central figure is Sir
John Willes, lecher, Chief
Justice, and scourge of rioters:
'And, when I passed sentence
upon Them, I said a good deal
to show the heinous nature of
their crime, and the great folly
of the attempt.... And I
ordered the captain and another
notorious offender to be
executed on Wednesday next....'

2. Wreckers on the Cornish coast,
after Rowlandson.

3. Smugglers breaking open the Custom House at Poole, 7 October 1747.

4. The murder of the excise officer Chater. This and the attack in Plate 3 earned the Sussex smugglers a place in most editions of the *Newgate Calendar*.

5 and 6. Equality before the
Law: mock 'tickets' to hangings.
The equation of corruption
among the great with that of
criminal London inspired much
satire.
Below: To the chagrin of some
stockholders, the offence of the
South Sea Company directors
was not capital.
Right: Jonathan Wild was less
fortunate and was hanged in
1725 under a statute written to
break his empire of receiving
and betrayal.

JONATHAN WILD THIEF-TAKER GENERAL OF GREAT BRITTAIN & IRELAND

To all the Thieves,
Whores, Pick-pockets,
Family Fellons &c.
in Great Brittain & Ireland
Gentlemen & Ladies.
You are hereby desir'd to
accompany y.ᵉ worthy friend y.ᵉ
Pious Mᵣ. I— W—d from his
Seat at Whittingtons Colledge
to y.ᵉ Tripple Tree, where he's
to make his last Exit
on   , and his
Corps to be carry'd from thence
to be decently Interr'd a=
=mongst his Ancestors.

Pray bring this Ticket with you

7. Equality before the Law: the execution of Lord Ferrers was a better illustration of the principle.

8 *(opposite above)*. A convict about to be hanged in his shroud. The ideal dying speech was a full confession, and a warning to youth.

9 *(opposite below)*. Hanging in chains: pirates sketched by Rowlandson on the Isle of Dogs.

10 *(left). The Idle 'Prentice Executed at Tyburn*, Industry and Idleness XI, by Hogarth.

11 *(right)*. 'Back view or scetch of Tyburn. Taken October 14 1767 the day that Guest, the Bankers Clark, was hanged. It was the custom of Lamplighters in those days to erect their Ladders together for persons to mount them at 2d and 3d each to see the Executions. Some of their partys frequently pulled down the ladders to get fresh customers to mount.'

Behold the Villain's dire disgrace!
Not Death itself can end.
He finds no peaceful Burial Place:
His breathless Corse, no friend.

Torn from the Root, that wicked Tongue,
Which daily swore and curst!
Those Eyeballs from their Sockets wrung,
That glow'd with lawless Lust!

His Heart expos'd to prying Eyes,
To Pity has no Claim:
But dreadful from his Bones shall rise,
His Monument of Shame.

12. *The Reward of Cruelty,*
Hogarth's view of Surgeon's Hall.

13. John Smith was cut down from the gallows after a late reprieve and entered execution folklore as 'Half-hanged Smith'.

14. The body of a murderer exposed for dissection at the Surgeon's Hall, Old Bailey.

15. A cautionary tale from *Select Trials*. The pickpocket turns highwayman, but is arrested, condemned, and executed.

The Tyburn Riot
Against the Surgeons

Poor Brother Tom had an Accident this time Twelvemonth, and so clever a made fellow he was, that I could not save him from those fleaing Rascals the Surgeons; and now, poor Man, he is among the Otamys at Surgeons Hall.

JOHN GAY, The Beggar's Opera

Our penal laws punish with death the man who steals a few pounds; but to take by violence or trepan a man is no such heinous offense.

MARY WOLLSTONECRAFT, Vindication of the Rights of Man

I

'O yes! O yes! O yes! My Lords, the King's Justices, strictly charge and command all manner of persons to keep silence while sentence of death is passing on the prisoners at the bar, on pain of imprisonment.' The court room thus silenced by the crier, one of the king's justices arose from his seat and regarded the prisoner directly, his view unobstructed by the nosegays placed on the bench to sweeten the air otherwise fouled by the stench of the criminal. He then spoke the terrible words, 'The law is, that thou shalt return from hence, to the Place whence thou camest, and from thence to the Place of Execution, where thou shalt hang by the Neck, till the body be dead! dead! dead! and the Lord have Mercy upon thy Soul.' The prisoner, shackled, sometimes close to expiring from gaol-contracted typhus, occasionally with spirit enough to damn his prosecutor and the jury, was returned to the condemned cell in Newgate there to bide the time until the next hanging took place upon the gallows some three miles west of Newgate across London at Tyburn. There he was hanged, *in terrorem*, testimony to the Majesty of the Law, a Dreadful and Awful Example to Others, a Sacrifice to his Country's Justice.[1]

1. The hanging sentence is quoted in Martin Madan, *Thoughts on Executive Justice with respect to our Criminal Laws*, 2nd edn, 1785, p. 26.

65

Or at least this was the hope. While terror, majesty, dread and some pity (as provided by the Ordinary of Newgate's last ministrations to the condemned) were the emotions that the state sought to arouse in the multitudes witnessing the hanging, the low slang and canting dictionaries that have survived to record the speech of the eighteenth-century London poor give us a different picture. In contrast to the solemn abstractions of the law the speech of the labouring class described the hanging with irreverence, humour and defiance.

The hanging words uttered by the king's justice were 'cramp words'. A hanging day was a 'hanging match', a 'collar day', the 'Sheriff's Ball', a 'hanging fair' or the 'Paddington Fair'. To hang, like a dance, was 'to swing', to 'dance the Paddington frisk', 'to morris'. It was 'to go west', 'to ride up Holborn hill', 'to dangle in the Sheriff's picture frame', 'to cry cockles'. After a trap door in the scaffold was introduced to replace the horse and cart which formerly had drawn away the support beneath the felon's feet, to hang was 'to go up the ladder to rest'; it was 'to go off with the fall of a leaf'. To be hanged was to be jammed, frummagemmed, collared, noozed, scragged, twisted, nubbed, backed, stretched, trined, cheated, crapped, tucked up or turned off. Awe, majesty and dread were riddled to their proper meaning, death by hanging. What was to dance at Beilby's Hall where the Sheriff plays the music? What was to ride a horse foaled by an acorn? It was to hang. Such a death was not pretty. Hanging was to have a wry mouth and a pissen pair of breeches; it was to loll out one's tongue at the company. A man hanged will piss when he cannot whistle.[1]

The engine as much as the fact of the state's ultimate power became the theme of scores of proverbs, riddles, words and descriptions bearing evidence to the facts that London, as an older historian put it, was a 'city of the gallows', and that its people both recognized this and accommodated themselves to it, but upon their own terms.[2] The scaffold consisted of three posts, ten or twelve feet high, held apart by three connecting crossbars at the top. It stood at Tyburn from the early Tudor period until 1783 when a new scaffold was constructed in Newgate. Tyburn was St Tyburn, the three-legged mare, the three-legged stool. As it bore fruit the whole year round it was the deadly nevergreen. It was the trining cheat, the

1. The most comprehensive eighteenth-century canting dictionaries are Anon., *A New Canting Dictionary*, 1725, and Francis Grose, *A Classical Dictionary of the Vulgar Tongue*, 1785, but see also George Parker, *A View of Society and Manners in High and Low Life*, vol. II, 1781, and Charles Hitchin, *The Regulator*, 1718. Eric Partridge's private edition of Grose's dictionary notes more than a hundred different cant denominations for the gallows. Only the number of names for money exceeded that for the gallows.

2. Alexander Andrews, 'The Eighteenth Century; Or Illustrations of the Manners and Customs of our Grandfathers', *The New Monthly Magazine*, 105 (1855), p. 370.

topping cheat, the nubbing cheat, the cramping cheat, or simply, the cheat.

Death by hanging, like most kinds of death in the eighteenth century, was public. Not isolated from the community or concealed as an embarrassment to it, the execution of the death sentence was made known to every part of the metropolis and the surrounding villages. On the morning of a hanging day the bells of the churches of London were rung buffeted. The cries of hawkers selling ballads and 'Last Dying Speeches' filled the streets. The last preparations for death in the chapel at Newgate were open to those able to pay the gaoler his fee. The malefactor's chains were struck off in the press yard in front of friends and relations, the curious, the gaping and onlookers at the prison gate. The route of the hanging procession crossed the busiest axis of the town at Smithfield, passed through one of the most heavily populated districts in St Giles's and St Andrew's, Holborn, and followed the most-trafficked road, Tyburn Road, to the gallows. There the assembled people on foot, upon horseback, in coaches, crowding near-by houses, filling the adjoining roads, climbing ladders, sitting on the wall enclosing Hyde Park and standing in its contiguous cow pastures gathered to witness the hanging. By the eighteenth century this crowd had become so unruly that the 'hanging match' became well known to foreign visitors and English alike as both a principal attraction of the town and a periodic occasion of disturbance.

The efficacy of public punishment depends upon a rough agreement between those who wield the law and those ruled by it. Whipping, ducking and the pillory, like public hangings, depended upon the public infliction of ignominy, execration and shame. As hangings were attended with disruptions, threatened rescues, disorders, brawls and riot, by the time of the eighteenth century order at them rested less upon community consensus in the justice of the sentence or in the manner of its execution than by the force of arms and the spectacular terror in the panoply of a state hanging. The fracture in conceptions of justice did not heal. In 1783 it was more firmly separated and the dangers to the body politic of this rupture were reduced by the removal of the site of execution to the safer confines of the prison walls in Newgate. Hangings were still public but, in the abolition of the procession to the gallows, a step had been taken towards privately inflicted punishment and a major source of disorder at hangings had been removed.[1]

'All grandeur, all power, all subordination rests on the executioner: he is the horror and the bond of human association. Remove this incomprehensible agent from the world, and at that very moment order gives way to chaos, thrones topple, and society disappears'; so wrote de Maistre at

1. James Heath, *Eighteenth Century Penal Policy*, 1963, develops this theme.

the end of the eighteenth century. While his conception of state power had clearly become obsolete in the conditions of nineteenth-century England, very few of those concerned with grandeur, power and subordination in eighteenth-century England would have found in his formulation much to disagree with. Defoe recommended solitary confinement of the condemned in the days before hanging – no drink, no visitors, no light and the simplest food. Bernard de Mandeville writing in 1725 was equally distressed by the discord and chaos of hangings and recommended that a greater contingent of municipal and military officers should be present in the procession and at the hangings. Henry Fielding found in the disorders at the hanging one of the causes of the increase of robbery at mid-century. He advocated removing hangings from public view: 'a Murder behind the Scenes, if the Poet knows how to manage it, will affect the Audience with greater Terror than if it was acted before their Eyes.' After mid-century, criticism of the management of hangings became commonplace. That of Francis Place, while not important in his own day, is perhaps the most frequently quoted by historians. The public's support of the condemned, the felon's behaviour, the carnival atmosphere and the ineffectuality to deter criminals are indiscriminately mixed together in a sustained and curiously embittered attack upon the Tyburn hangings. 'No solemn procession, it was just the contrary; it was a low-lived, black-guard merry-making.' In a judgement uncritically accepted by several generations of historians he wrote of the people comprising the crowd at Tyburn: 'the whole vagabond population of London, all the thieves, and all the prostitutes, all those who were evil-minded, and some, a comparatively few curious people made up the mob on those brutalizing occasions.'[1]

Few history-books of eighteenth-century England fail to mention the spectacle of public hangings at Tyburn. Indeed, so often is it, as a symbol of all that is bestial, violent and brutal in eighteenth-century society, counterposed to the architecture, taste, music and literature of genteel civilization that it has lost whatever accurate connotations it once may have had and has now entered the ranks of the historical cliché. A passing reference to the 'harshness of the criminal code', the 'brutal spectacle of public hangings' or the 'love of aggression of the London mob' and we are brought back to the civility of life in well-landscaped gardens, the Good Sense of the Hanoverian compromise, and the quiet accumulation quantified in account-books of London and Bristol merhants. Undis-

1. Daniel Defoe, *Street Robberies Considered*, 1728, pp. 52–4; Bernard de Mandeville, *An Enquiry into the Causes of the Frequent Executions at Tyburn*, 1725, pp. 23–4; Henry Fielding, *An Enquiry into the Causes of the Late Increase of Robbers &c.*, 2nd edn, 1751, p. 189; Brit. Mus. Add. MSS 27,826 (Place Collection, 'Grossness'), fo. 107.

turbed except by these minor shoals, eighteenth-century English history, slowly, inevitably, meanders on, a broad river spreading peace and bounty to adjoining fields, carrying forward those mighty vessels, 'Trade and Commerce' and the 'Constitution'.

It is, certainly, a pleasant scene and one which we would be reluctant to upset were it not for the fact that amidst all the outcry, denunciations and arguments for the reform of public hangings nowhere are we told exactly why, year after year (there were as many as eight hanging days in one year), they were disrupted by brawls, disorders and tumults. The three-mile procession through the metropolis from Newgate Gaol to the gallows and the rather maladroit rituals of state hanging performed before sometimes thousands of people not only caused inconveniences to the commercial traffic into London, or nuisance to the Whig and Tory building speculators laying out the Augustan squares of the West End; the hangings also presented an increasingly intolerable irritation to the order of the City and the dignity of the Law.

The surgeons and physicians, their beadles and porters, were the most common targets in these disorders. By the beginning of the eighteenth century, at the gallows standing at the conjunction of the Tyburn and Edgware roads, we find that the history of the London poor and the history of English science intersect. Advances in one branch of medicine, anatomy, depended as much upon eighteenth-century penal practices as it did upon the idealist transmission of knowledge. (One historian ascribes the medical 'revolution' of the early eighteenth century to the scientific 'revolution' of the late seventeenth century, itself the product of the philosophical 'revolution' of the early seventeenth century.)[1] The law passed judgement in sable garments and executed sentence with the red towel of the dissecting room. A main cause of disturbances at hanging days lay in the relations between the judges sitting at the Old Bailey and the physicians and surgeons around the corner in Warwick Lane and Cripplegate. On the other hand, it appears as though a precondition of progress in anatomy depended upon the ability of the surgeons to snatch the bodies of those hanged at Tyburn.

II

An emphasis upon teaching and clinical experience characterized British anatomy in the eighteenth century. It was not the Royal College of Physicians and the Company of Barber–Surgeons, two corporations

1. Peter Gay, *The Enlightenment: An Interpretation*, vol. II, *The Science of Freedom*, 1969, pp. 12–13.

chartered in the sixteenth century to train doctors and surgeons, which took the lead in the promulgation of these new methods. Advances in the understanding of morphology, pathology and therapeutics upon which rested the pre-eminence of British anatomy in the eighteenth century grew out of the patient work conducted by anatomists at the private teaching schools and the hospitals of London, both of which had to proceed against the jealousies of the College of Physicians and the Company of Barber–Surgeons. At the beginning of the century the doctors of St Thomas's, St Bartholomew's and St George's hospitals began to train their own students and conduct their own dissections. The foundation of other hospitals (Westminster in 1719, London in 1740 and Middlesex in 1745) extended the teaching of anatomy to an even larger extent and, perforce, added to the demand for corpses.[1]

William Hunter, the most important anatomist of eighteenth-century Britain, recalled his schooling at Guy's Hospital during the 1730s when the new methods of teaching were still unorthodox (and expensive): 'I attended as diligently as the generality of students do, one of the most reputable courses of anatomy in Europe. There I learned a good deal by my ears, but almost nothing by my eyes, and therefore hardly anything to the purpose. The defect was that the professor was obliged to demonstrate all the parts of the body upon one dead body.'[2] To attend a dissection cost five guineas and to perform a dissection cost seven. By the middle of the 1740s empirical experience in the dissection of corpses had become conventional practice in surgical training. A guide to trades and professions described the surgeon in terms which a generation earlier would have been unthinkable. 'The young Surgeon must be an accurate Anatomist, not only a speculative but practical Anatomist; without which he must turn out a mere Bungler. It is not sufficient for him to attend Anatomical Lectures, and see two or three Subjects cursorily dissected; but he must put his Hand to it himself, and be able to dissect every Part, with the same Accuracy that the Professor performs.'[3]

Owing then to both the changed methods of teaching anatomy and the creation of additional schools, the demand for corpses increased suddenly in the early eighteenth century. The Royal College of Physicians, by letters patent granted by Queen Elizabeth and renewed by Charles II, was allowed 'the Bodies of One or Six Persons condemned to Death

1. Richard H. Shyrock, *The Development of Modern Medicine: An Interpretation of the Social and Scientific Factors Involved*, 1948, and K. F. Russell, *British Anatomy 1525–1800: A Bibliography*, 1963.

2. Quoted in Samuel Wilks and G. T. Bettany, *A Biographical History of Guy's Hospital*, 1892, pp. 87–8.

3. R. S. Campbell, *The London Tradesman*, 1747, p. 50.

within London, Middlesex, or Surrey for anatomical Dissection. . .' and a royal grant permitted the Company of Barber–Surgeons the bodies of four executed felons a year.[1] These were the only authorized sources for getting corpses in London, and they permitted a maximum of ten corpses a year. The hospitals and private schools to whom the corpses were most necessary had therefore to rely upon illegal and hazardous methods. They either robbed graves or competed with the agents of the Physicians and Surgeons for the bodies of hanged malefactors.

In 1723, a year in which corpses were especially costly to obtain, a body-snatcher in Southwark was sentenced at Guildford Assizes to be whipped. The parish officers of the Savoy risked the violence of the mob when they returned the body of a condemned man to the surgeons after the Tyburn mob had put it in their graveyard. The Riot Act was read against 'several People' who assembled in St Giles's churchyard 'upon the Reasons they had to suspect some inhuman Practises with regard to dead Bodies, which it seems were no sooner interr'd than dug up and sold to Anatomists'. In 1736 the grave-digger of St Dunstan's, Stepney, who sold bodies to a private surgeon, felt the full fury of the courts' sentence upon him:

> Sentence was executed upon him very severely by John Hooper, the then common Executioner; and on the Day appointed for him to be whipped; there was, perhaps, the greatest Concourse of People that ever was known. A Mob of Sailors and Chimney Sweepers rendevouz'd in Stepney Church-yard, and when [the] poor Culprit was ty'd to the Cart, they led the Horses so slow, that he received some Hundreds of Lashes, the Hangman being encouraged by the Mob (who gave him a good deal of Money) not to favour the Delinquent, but to do his Duty.

Only a few months earlier the same hangman had to appear before the Court of Aldermen to answer charges that he sold the bodies of condemned criminals to private surgeons.[2]

Agents from the hospitals and private surgeons, we know, also loitered about Newgate prison on the morning of hanging days offering to buy the bodies of the condemned. John Wilkins, a veteran of the battle of Fontenoy, inquired after 'a Surgeon to purchase his Body' so that he could pay his expenses in prison. In 1752 William Signal sold his body to the surgeons in order to buy decent clothes to hang in, 'for, by G—d, he was resolved to die game'. John Hill lay in Newgate in 1744. On the morning of his hanging 'after Prayers was over, as he was going out of Chapel,

---

1. Petition of the President of the Royal College of Physicians, 5 February 1723-4. *CJ*, xx, p. 253; and Sidney Young, *The Annals of the Barber–Surgeons of London*, 1890.
2. See Anon., *A Genuine Narrative of the Sacriligious Impiety of John Lamb*, 1747, p. 6; *Worcester Journal*, 9 November 1723; *British Journal*, 9 February 1723; GLCRO (Mddx Div.), 'Confession of Thomas Jenkins, 9 April 1736', *Sessions Papers*, MJ/SP 58.

ask'd a Gentleman, why he looked at him, do you know me? No, Friend, replied the Gentleman. I suppose, says Hill, you are some Surgeon, and if I had a knife in my Hand, I would slit you down the Nose.' A private surgeon in 1738 acquired the body of Isaac Mortished just after he was cut down from the gallows. In 1741 Elizabeth Fox hanged for a small theft was taken to St Thomas's hospital by the agents of their surgeons. That a considerable private trade in dead bodies existed is suggested by the fact that when Lavater, a Swiss anatomist, lectured at the Ashmolean Museum in 1710 he was able to obtain corpses from London without much trouble. The commerce in dead bodies was a dark, shoddy business and while the evidence for it must necessarily be scattered and indirect the study of anatomy in the eighteenth century could not have been done without it.[1]

With the advance in understanding of anatomy and the corresponding development of private trade in corpses, we can find in the early eighteenth century a significant change in attitude towards the dead human body. The corpse becomes a commodity with all the attributes of a property. It could be owned privately. It could be bought and sold. A value not measured by the grace of heaven nor the fires of hell but quantifiably expressed in the magic of the price list was placed upon the corpse. As a factor in the production of scientific knowledge, the accumulated rituals and habits of centuries of religion and superstition were swept aside. Bernard de Mandeville, himself trained as a physician, but known mainly for demonstrating that 'private vices are public virtues' in *The Fable of the Bees*, wrote a series of articles for the *British Journal* in the months before Jonathan Wild was hanged in 1725. Addressed to 'men of business', they provide the first utilitarian defence in eighteenth-century England of the dissection of condemned criminals.

I have no Design that savours of Cruelty or even Indecency, towards a human Body; but shall endeavor to demonstrate that a superstitious Reverence of the Vulgur for a Corpse, even of a Malefactor, and the strong Aversion they have against dissecting them, are prejudicial to the Publick; For as Health and sound Limbs are the most desirable of all Temporal Blessings, so we ought to encourage the Improvements of Physick and Surgery...

However, even if the relatives of the dead felt themselves or their dead relation defiled by this procedure 'the Dishonour would seldom reach beyond the Scum of the People'. Mandeville wondered why the thieves who injured the public were not grateful for this opportunity of making

1. The Ordinary's *Account*, 21 January 1747; ibid., 13 July 1752; ibid., 24 December 1744; ibid., 8 March 1738; *Daily Post*, 19 March 1741; and T. Hearne, *Remarks and Collections 1705-1735*, Oxford Historical Society, 1884-1918, vol. VIII, p. 156.

a useful restitution to it. By the end of the century some writers combined arguments of scientific utility with the language of political economy and wrote of the 'supply and demand' of dead bodies. Such arguments of scientific utility were still rare in the early eighteenth century and typically were mixed with the frank expression of class hatred. In retrospect we know that any justification utilitarian arguments may have had applied only to the practices of the private schools and the teaching hospitals, the sites of progress in anatomical knowledge.[1]

Neither the Crown (which granted the bodies of condemned felons to the Physicians and the Surgeons) nor the legislature (which strengthened by law the royal grants) regarded the dissection of felons from the standpoint of science; far from it. They were motivated less by the hope of causing 'Health and sound Limbs' than by the anticipation of dishonour to the 'Scum of the People'. The Crown and Parliament were assisted in their punitive views by the backward, if not reactionary, attitude towards teaching maintained by the College of Physicians and the Company of Barber–Surgeons. In contrast to the empirical teaching methods of the private schools and the teaching hospitals, they taught their students by disputation and demonstration. The Company of Barber–Surgeons held four public lectures a year, each lasting three days, during which time a corpse was dissected. Lectures concluded with a banquet whose cost was the largest single item in the annual budget. Unaffected by the new teaching and research methods, both institutions nevertheless faced difficulties by the beginning of the eighteenth century in getting their bodies from Tyburn, difficulties caused in part by the increasing competition at the gallows from the agents of the private surgeons and the hospitals.[2]

In 1694 it cost the beadle of the Royal College more than thirteen shillings to get a body at Tyburn, twelve shillings to pay two men to help carry it away in a coach, six shillings for the coach, and another four shillings of miscellaneous expenses, thirty-five shillings all told. Twenty years later it cost the College twenty shillings just to pay the Sheriff to sign the warrant granting the College the body of the hanged felon. The College found that if it did not pay the Sheriffs' officers enough, the private hospitals would pay more and take possession of the bodies. In

1. Mandeville, op. cit.; William Rowley, *On the Absolute Necessity of Encouraging ... the Study of Anatomy*, 1795, and Edward G. Wakefield, *Facts Relating to the Punishment of Death in the Metropolis*, 2nd edn, 1832, p. 207; Charles Singer and S. W. F. Holloway, 'Early Medical Education in England', *Medical History*, vol. IV, January 1960.

2. The Barber–Surgeons' Company, *Audit Book 1715–1785*, Guildhall Library, MSS 5255, vol. III; and N. Goodman, 'The Supply of Bodies for Dissection: A Historical Review', *Arris and Gale Lecture*, 1944, MSS at the RCS.

1720 the President of the College 'acquainted the College with the difficulty of getting bodies from the gallows for publick dissection' and
ordered a petition be drawn up to Parliament. After reviewing the Letters
Patent of 7 Elizabeth and 15 Charles II, the petition went on to complain
that

the felons and other Malefactors condemned to be executed in and about this
City through the dread & fear which they generally have from an apprehension
of their body's being dissected after their execution do very often prevail on
their Confederates & other disorderly people to take & carry away the executed
bodys in defiance of all legal authority in a forcible & violent manner whereby
great dangers & mischief frequently happen to the persons who attend to have &
take an executed body for your petitioners & the Sheriff's Officers who attend
such executions sometimes pretend that they are not obliged or at least not
able to assist your petitioners therein By which means your petitioners are
deprived of the privileges granted them by the said Royal Charters & prevented
from having such bodys for the publick use aforesaid and Malefactors are in
some measure encouraged by assurance of having their body's rescued from a
dissection which to some renders the Sentence of the Laws more terrible.

Apparently nothing came of their petition and three years later the President proposed that the College should attempt to obtain an Act of
Parliament 'for securing executed Bodys'.[1] In December 1723 a draft of a
bill was prepared and in February 1724 it was read for the first time in the
House of Commons. In April the bill was read in committee of the House
of Lords: 'The next Clause, Enacting a Confirmation of Powers formerly
granted by Charles for the College of Physicians to take certain Bodies
Executed for Felony & other Offences, for Anatomies, Read. After
Debate, the same was agreed to be Left out, as were likewise the rest of
the Clauses in the Bill the same relating to the Matter of Executed Bodies
for Anatomies.'[2] This appears to have been the last attempt by the Royal
College to assure to itself 'executed Bodys'; their *Annals* for the rest of
the century contain no mention, at any rate, of attempts to do so.

Similar problems of mounting opposition at the gallows, escalating
costs for obtaining bodies, and more frequent complaints to Parliament
characterized the history of the Barber–Surgeons' Company during the
first two decades of the eighteenth century. Unlike the Physicians,
however, the Barber–Surgeons persisted at least into the 1750s in their

1. Envelope 45a., MSS Box 4, RCP Library; 'Cash Book 1664–1726' and 'Cash Book
1726–1778', RCP Library; *Annals*, vol. VIII (1710–21), p. 233, RCP Library; 'Petition
to the House of Commons', Envelope 179, MSS Box 9, RCP Library.
2. *CJ*, vol. XX, 24 February, 10 March, 13 March, 17 April 1724. HLRO, MS of
Proceedings (*Minute Book*), vol. LXX, pp. 207–10; also HLRO, 'Main Papers', 31 March
1724.

attempts to obtain corpses from Tyburn. At the beginning of the century they customarily paid the hangman a Christmas box worth two and a half shillings; by the 1720s its value increased fourfold. The Company also paid a customary fee to the Sheriff's officers when a body was delivered successfully to the Company Hall. The beadles of the Company in addition to their regular salary were given encouragement of £2 for each body they seized at Tyburn. In 1718 'My Lord Chief Justice Parker's Tipstaff' was paid £1 'for taking up severall persons who rescued the Dead Body from the Beadles'. On several occasions the Barber–Surgeons prosecuted those who attempted to rescue the bodies from them, each time the costs of prosecution exceeded £15. If the condemned man's clothes were torn or lost after he was cut down from the gallows, the hangman (for whom the clothing of condemned felons was an important perquisite of office) had to be compensated for the loss. In 1724 hackney coachmen were paid £4 13s. od. 'for Damages done to their Coaches this year in fetching Body's from Tyburn'. Witnesses to the Tyburn riots had to be paid to testify in court. The cost of printing the Court of Alderman's orders permitting the Company dead bodies sometimes amounted to £5. Windows broken during rioting were replaced at the Company's cost. Constables had to be paid to protect the surgeons and their Hall during the four annual lectures.[1]

At the time that the Physicians petitioned Parliament, the Barber–Surgeons at a cost of £20 petitioned the Secretary of State:

That within few years last past great Numbers of Disorderly and riotous persons have frequently assembled themselves at the Place of Execution and with open Violence forced away the dead bodyes from your Petitioners Beadle tho' assisted by the Sheriff of the County in obtaining your Petitioners right and particularly at the Past Publick Execution several of Your Majesty's Guards surrounded the Gallows and threatened the life of your Petitioner's Officer in case he offered to carry away any of the said Dead bodys but who such persons were or to what Regiment they belonged Your Petitioners have not as yet been able to discover. That your Petitioners have prosecuted Sundry of the said Rioters at Law from time to time But it is so very Difficult for your Petitioners to find out the names and places of abode of the persons who thus Interrupt them and such Prosecutions are attended with so much Expense to your Petitioners that your Petitioners cannot hope to Suppress this growing Evil effectively by any method within their own Power.

The Surgeons then reminded the Secretary of State of their usefulness to the Royal Navy (whose surgeons they examined) before concluding:

1. The Barber–Surgeons' Company, *Audit Book 1715–1785*, vol. III, Guildhall Library, MSS 5255; and Company of Surgeons, *Minute Book of the Court of Assistants 1745–1800*, vol. I, RCS Library.

'Your Petitioners Do most humbly Pray that your Majesty will be most Graciously pleased to permit and direct that a File or two of Your Majesty's Foot Guards shall upon your Petitioner's application to the Commanding Officer attend the Publick Executions from time to time to see that no Interruption be given to your Petitioner's Beadle in the taking away so many Dead Bodies yearly as are granted. . .'[1] The Foot Guards were often deployed in 'A File or Two' at Tyburn thereafter, but did not do much good. During the 1730s and 1740s the Barber–Surgeons frequently complained to the Court of Aldermen about the 'great Numbers of loose and disorderly persons [who] often assemble at the place and times of Execution'. The Court responded by ordering the attendance of both Sheriffs of London, by arousing the civil officers of Middlesex to guard the crowds at the hangings, and by providing arms to the sergeants and yeomen of the City compters who also attended as guards.[2]

The Christmas boxes to the hangmen, the petition to the Secretary of State, the bribes to the constabulary, the application to the War Office, the specially hired beadles' assistants, the stream of complaints to the Aldermen, none of these policies secured a cheap and regular supply of bodies to the Surgeons. The cost of obtaining corpses was still high: in the period 1715–50 the Company disbursed over £465 for the purpose, an amount which averaged (assuming the Company got four a year) at £3 7s. od. a corpse. The account-books of the Court of Assistants of the Company supply us with the evidence to measure the difficulties the Barber–Surgeons faced at the gallows. The startling drop of costs in the period following the late 1740s, as illustrated in the graph (p. 77), reveals a deep change in the conditions of getting the bodies of executed men and women. Owing to the results of the Penlez Riots of 1749 and 'An Act for Preventing the horrid Crime of Murder' (usually called the 'Murder Act') passed in 1752, the balance of forces at the gallows shifted in favour of the friends of the condemned while the Surgeons won new legislation which partially removed the obstacles to obtaining bodies.

Except for a minority of surgeons and sympathetic observers, dissection was considered less as a necessary method for enlarging the understanding of *homo corpus* than as a mutilation of the dead person, a form of aggravating capital punishment. The preamble to the 'Murder Act' (25 Geo. II, c. 37) stated, 'it is become necessary that some further Terror and peculiar

1. PRO, SP 35/19/57. 'The humble Petition of the Masters or Governours and Assistants Livery and Freemen of the Company of Barbers and Surgeons of London.' See also Christopher Lloyd and Jack L. S. Coulter, *Medicine and the Navy*, 1961, vol. III.
2. Lond. Corp. RO. *Repertories of the Court of Aldermen*, CXI 83, CXXXIII 172, CXXXIX 264–5, CXL 377, CXLIV 311.

Mark of Infamy be added to the Punishment.'[1] And so dissection by the Surgeons and public exposure of the corpse was added to the punishment of death by hanging. Although the Parliament's sole interest in the law

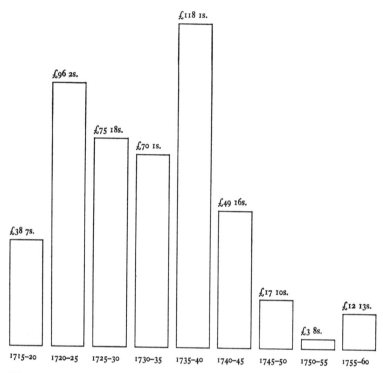

The cost to the Barber–Surgeons' Company of getting corpses at Tyburn (five-year totals, 1715–60).[2]

was in making the death sentence terrifying, the Company of Surgeons, happy at this coincidence between the interests of criminal deterrence and its own, immediately appointed a committee to aid the legislature in its intentions. In addition to the reasons for criminal deterrence, the Ordinary of Newgate culled his scriptures to find in Genesis 6: 5–6 (where

1. For an account of the provisions of the Act and the circumstances of its passage, see Radzinowicz, vol. I, pp. 208 *et seq.*

2. The figures used to make this graph were compiled from two sources: the Barber–Surgeons' Company, *Audit Book 1715–1785*, vol. III, Guildhall Library, MSS 5255, and for the period following 1745 (after the surgeons and barbers split company), the Company of Surgeons, *Minute Book of the Court of Assistants 1745–1800*, vol. I, RCS Library.

God grieves at the wickedness of man and repents of having made him) divine vindication of the act. A provision denying Christian burial to murderers is singled out for particular praise 'lest the Earth should again be filled with Violence'. Finally the Ordinary brings to bear the dreadful prophecy of Revelation: 'But the fearful, and unbelieving, and the abominable, and murderers, and whoremongers, and sorcerers, and idolaters, and all liars, shall have their part in the lake which burneth with fire and brimstone: which is the second death.' Thomas Wilford, a one-handed workhouse orphan, saved twelve shillings and married a fruit-seller of St Giles-in-the-Fields. One evening in Dyot Street in a drunken fit of jealousy he killed her. After the court pronounced the new sentence upon him he 'was taken from the bar weeping and in great agonies, lamenting his sad fate'. He was the act's first victim.[1]

In the first half of the eighteenth century empirical discoveries advanced the science of anatomy and established British predominance in the field. The private surgeons working in their own schools or in hospitals, without the help of the College of Physicians or the Surgeons' Company, made these discoveries. Their needs led to an enormous increase in the demand for corpses. Their struggle to obtain bodies from the gallows threatened the ancient privileges of the College of Physicians and the Barber-Surgeons' Company. This conflict, however, lay concealed beneath a far more serious antagonism. The combined demands of the Physicians and the Surgeons on one hand and the surgeons of the schools and the hospitals on the other produced an intolerable situation to the 'loose and disorderly Persons' gathered beneath the gallows' tree, whose violence against all types of surgeons intensified.

Such were the factors causing the disturbances at Tyburn. The relative peace which settled at the gallows after mid-century resulted from the partial satisfaction of the interests of all parties. The Physicians, as appears from their records, ceased to obtain bodies from Tyburn by the third decade of the century. After 1752 the Company of Surgeons received a regular supply of them. The private surgeons got corpses from parish graveyards and from those of their own hospitals, but not from the gallows. This unsteady settlement arose not from arguments with the 'Scum of the People' but from their own protracted struggles.

1. *Minute Book of the Court of Assistants of the Company of Surgeons*, vol. I, p. 50, RCS Library; The Ordinary's *Account*, 2 July 1752; *London Magazine*, vol. XXI, July 1752, p. 333; *British Weekly Journal*, 9 July 1752.

III

The surgeons and physicians called their opponents at the gallows 'loose
and disorderly Persons'. To Mandeville they were the 'Scum of the
People'. To the newspapers that reported the disturbances they were
simply the 'Mob'. In the case of some of the disturbances, direct evidence
survives which enables us to know much more about the members of the
Tyburn crowd; but in the majority of instances we must infer their
backgrounds from the type of appeals which the condemned felons often
made to those they hoped would protect them from the surgeons. Those
to whom the felons appealed for help and those actually initiating the
battle for possession of the corpse can conveniently be described by five
kinds of solidarities – the family, the personal friends, fellow workers, the
Irish and sailors – though (as we shall see) these particular divisions were
often transcended in the general passion of struggle.

Felons appealed first to their families. Martin Gray got into trouble
when he violated his apprenticeship indenture to a Thames fisherman
by marrying before his time was up. He became a pickpocket, was caught,
and sentenced to transportation. He returned early from America, was
caught again, and hanged in 1721. He said 'he was greatly frighted lest
his Body should be cut, and torn, and mangled after Death'. He sent his
wife to his uncle, a country grazier of some substance, who arranged the
protection of Gray's body and secured its decent burial.[1] In the same year
John Casey rode with his brother in the tumbril to the gallows, and
successfully led the fight against the surgeons. James Caldcough had an
incompleted apprenticeship as a shoemaker and five years as a common
soldier in the second regiment of Guards behind him before he was
hanged in 1739 for a highway robbery. The little money he had at the end
was paid to a Newgate scrivener who wrote letters to his father asking him
to attend the hanging and save his body.[2] Married to a house carpenter
to whom she bore ten children, Sarah Wilmshurst was hanged for the
murder of a bastard infant. 'How her Body was to be dispos'd off' was her
only worry on the morning of her execution. She was assured on the
route to her hanging that her 'Father & Brother would look after her Body,
and have it decently interr'd in a Christian Manner'.[3]

One of the most striking demographic characteristics of the London
population was its high proportion of the young, the geographically
mobile and the unmarried. The migration to London of young town and

1. The Ordinary's *Account*, 3 April 1721, and *The Proceedings*, 4–7 December 1719.
2. The Ordinary's *Account*, 2 July 1739.
3. ibid., 18 May 1743.

79

country dwellers caused its growth, a tendency reflected in the fact that among those hanged two thirds were born outside London.[1] Family ties were often loose but not necessarily weak. For those sentenced to death, the last hours of life were often passed in locating and gathering them together. William Seston, 'not thinking his Pay sufficient' as a soldier, became a highwayman. He was hanged in 1728. His wife, whom he had not seen for three years, came down from Lancashire to protect his body at the hanging.[2] Matthew Lee, a shoemaker, was hanged for stealing a silver watch. His brother and sister travelled from Lincoln to guard his body and give it a Christian burial.[3] Oliver White's father came down from Carlisle to protect his son's body from the surgeons and to watch over his grave at night.[4] Samuel Curlis and his father were both tailors in Malden. In 1727 the son walked to London to find journeyman's work. He arrived in the summer ('cucumber time' as the tailors called this, their dull time of year) and not finding work he enlisted as a soldier. Four years later he was hanged for stealing a brown mare. His father left off work and walked the thirty-odd miles to London to see the hanging of his son. Beneath the gallows he took possession of his son's corpse and returned it to his home for Christian burial.[5]

Considering the distances travelled, the work forsaken at home, the cost of the way, and the dangers meeting them at Tyburn, substantial sacrifices by brothers, uncles, fathers, mothers and wives were made for the sake of this last union at the gallows. Indeed the surgeons sometimes found it simpler to get bodies if their agents masqueraded as the parents of the dead rather than try to insist upon their prerogatives by force of arms. Nevertheless, few of the total number of felons hanged were able to have their families with them; to secure a decent burial, to prevent the surgeons from taking their bodies, the condemned malefactors had to rely on others to perform this family office.

Samuel Richardson writing in 1740 described a Tyburn riot:

1. E. A. Wrigley, 'A Simple Model of London's Importance in Changing English Society and Economy 1650–1750', *Past and Present*, 37, July 1967, and D. V. Glass, 'Socio-economic Status and Occupations in the City of London at the End of the Seventeenth Century', *Studies in London History*, ed. A. E. J. Hollaender and William Kellaway, 1969, pp. 385–7, contain material on migration to London in the early eighteenth century. The figure of two thirds is based upon my own findings (as yet unpublished).

2. The Ordinary's *Account*, 20 May 1728, and *London Journal*, 25 May 1728.

3. The Ordinary's *Account*, 11 October 1752, and *Worcester Journal*, 19 October 1752.

4. *The True and Genuine Confession . . . of all the Malefactors that were Executed at Guildford*, 16–21 March 1738.

5. The Ordinary's *Account*, 16 June 1731. The Ordinary writes that Curtis was born in Malden, Sussex: I have been unable to trace this place, and assume he meant Maldon in Essex, but there was a Malden near Maidstone in Kent and another in Surrey.

As soon as the poor creatures were half-dead, I was much surprised before such a number of peace-officers, to see the populace fall to hauling and pulling the carcasses with so much earnestness, as to occasion several warm rencounters, and broken heads. These were the friends of the persons executed . . . and some persons sent by private surgeons to obtain bodies for dissection. The contests between these were fierce and bloody, and frightful to look at.[1]

James Clough, a Clare market vintner, murdered a fellow servant, Mary Green, whom he had been courting. When the tumbril passed their shop in Holborn on the way to Tyburn, Clough had it stopped, called for a pint of wine, and stated his innocence. His friends mobilized at Tyburn and defeated the surgeons. They buried him in St Andrew's graveyard.[2] Vincent Davis pleaded in court that he might be hanged in chains, not because he liked the idea of his corpse exhibited to travellers passing into London, but because even this humiliation he thought preferable to dissection by the surgeons. In prison he 'not only sent many Letters to all his former Friends and Acquaintances to form a Company and prevent the Surgeons in their Designs upon his Body; but at the Chapel strove to conceal his looks from those whom he suspected to be such'. His friends stood by his request; they buried him in Clerkenwell.[3] Lot Cavenagh had survived service in the French and British armies, three tours at sea, and ten years of highway robbing around London and the southern counties of England before he was betrayed, caught, condemned, and hanged in 1743 for robbing a butcher. Dorothy Rowland wrote to him in Newgate,

Lot Cavenagh, you do very well know that I have been very much deceived by you; I need not tell you the Particulars for you know them right well; and notwithstanding that, I have endeavour'd to assist you to the uttermost of my Power to do that THING which you requested of me, touching the saving of your Body from the Surgeons; you speak threatning Words to me, telling me, that if you can, you will trouble me after you are dead.[4]

Friends included mistresses and lovers, comrades and neighbours. Included too were cohorts in crime, or 'fellow men' as they were called in the thieves' canting talk.

> But if our Friends will stand by us,
> Six and Eight-pence for to pay;

1. *Familiar Letters on Important Occasions*, 1928 edn, p. 219.
2. *Select Trials*, vol. III (1742), pp. 122–34.
3. The Ordinary's *Account*, 30 April 1725; *Select Trials*, vol. II (1742), p. 194; and Robert Hovenden, ed., *A True Register of all the Marriages, Christenings and Burials of St. James, Clerkenwell*, vol. VI (1720–54), The Harleian Society, 1893.
4. The Ordinary's *Account*, 13 April 1743.

> He takes his Cheve and cheves us down,
> And they carry our Bodies away.[1]

The surgeons could pay the hangman much more than 'six and eight-pence' to cut down and deliver the corpse. The drinking-song expresses the fellowship that existed among the London poor, but it scarcely reflects the realities and risks that the friendship could entail. John Miller was captured and incarcerated in Clerkenwell New Prison for attempting to rescue the body of his friend George Ward from the surgeons. John Clark lost his life for trying to save the body of his friend. 'I had been to Tyburn,' he said, 'to assist in carrying off the Body of my Friend, Joseph Parker from the Surgeons, and was seen by the Prosecutor.'[2]

The third type of solidarity expressed between the condemned and the Tyburn crowd, that of common experience in work, warns us against making too facile a separation between the criminal and the working class. Charles Connor was born, schooled and bred a sawyer in Shoreditch. After some years of service aboard a man-of-war in the Baltic and Mediterranean he returned to Shoreditch, and did journeyman's work for a Mr Blizard near Hoxton Square. He was hanged in 1735 for murdering his wife. From Newgate he wrote to his former master, '. . . and I begg of all Love that you would desire all such Friends, that shall come to see me Dye, that they will be so good as not to let the Surgeons have my Body, but to give me their Assistance, for my Brothers and other Friends have promised me so to do, which I hope in God they will, for my Desire is to lay by my Wife if possible I can. . .'[3] Henry Bosworway, another sawyer, was hanged for killing one of his fellow journeymen during a fist fight at their lunch break in the Clerkenwell workshop. From Newgate he wrote to a fellow sawyer pleading with him to intercede with their master, 'I desire you'll go to Mr. Poregar and put him in mind, for he has promised to get a coch and some help to save my Body from the Surgeons and I hope the rest of my Fellow-Sarvents will be ther to assist.'[4] Richard Tobin, a drawer, was hanged for stealing a peruke (valued at seven shillings) from a gentleman in the street. He wrote to his former master, the keeper of the Globe Tavern in Hatton Garden,

... take some Pity on me ... for my Friends is very Poor, and my Mother is very sick, and I am to die next Wednesday Morning, so I hope you will be so

1. Anon., *Villany Exploded: Or, the Mistery of Iniquity laid open*, 1728, contains the complete text of this ballad.
2. The Ordinary's *Account*, 6 August 1740; ibid., 24 May 1736; *Reade's Weekly Journal*, 29 May 1736.
3. The Ordinary's *Account*, 22 September 1735.
4. ibid., 29 June 1737.

good as to give my Friends a small Trifill of Money to pay for a Coffin and a Sroud, for to take my Body a way from the Tree in that I am to die on . . . and dont be faint Hearted . . . so I hope you will take it into Consideration of my poor Body, consedar if it was your own Cace, you would be willing to have your Body saved from the Surgeons. . .[1]

In the cooper's yard, the sawyer's pit, the apothecary's shop or brewer's house, master and man, if not doing the same job of work, cooperated to make the same product. In the paternalism characteristic of the period of manufacture, Capital and Labour did not oppose each other in inexorable contradiction. The sudden destitution which so often led to highway robbery or house-breaking came about as easily from the insecurities of credit and the vagaries of the market as it did from lay-offs or wage reductions. Catastrophe came to the master and his journeyman alike. Often they joined together in the Friendly Society, Benefit Society or 'Box Club' to defend themselves against a precarious existence. By the 1740s these clubs were common in London. The pennies set aside each month during the working years as dues to the club provided a sum which would alleviate the hardships of sickness or provide some relief to the widows and orphans of members. Mainly the money ensured members of a 'decent funeral'. The Friendly Society and the struggles against the surgeons were two forms of working-class cooperation in the face of death.[2]

When brick-makers came out to defend the bodies of two felons with several years of good standing in the trade against the surgeons, when bargemen came down from Reading to guard one of their own at his hanging, when the Hackney coachmen rallied to keep the body of a fellow coachman 'from being carried off by Violence', or when the small cottagers and market people of Shoreditch surrounded the tumbril of Thomas Pinks their neighbour in the village, 'declaring they had no other Intention, than to take Care of the Body for Christian burial', the evidence (while not allowing us to see the obligations of the Friendly Society at work) shows the depth of the mutuality of the poor, their solidarity in the face of personal disaster. Such evidence reminds us to be on guard against those glib explanations of urban crime of the eighteenth-century London poor which refer so easily to the anonymity of city life or that atomization of individuals accompanying the 'Process of Urbanization'.

Many of the labouring poor could not rely on the specific duties of the Friendly Society or the closely knit ties of workshop, but drew instead

1. ibid., 30 May 1739. His plea was successful and Tobin was buried. *Register of Burials*, St Andrew's Holborn, 1726–39, Guildhall Library, MSS 6673/9.

2. M. D. George, *London Life in the Eighteenth Century*, 1965, pp. 292–5, contains a discussion of Friendly Societies in London.

upon quite different sources of defence. The Irish, who supplied 16 per cent of the casualties at Tyburn in the first half of the eighteenth century, appealed to one another. George Ward, a carpenter from Dublin, was hanged in May 1736 for robbing a Clerkenwell watchmaker's house. After he was cut down, the surgeons moved in for his body. 'A terrible Battle ensued', and Ward's Irish friends beat off the surgeons. Edward Row, a fellow Dubliner, was one of them. He was hanged six months later, but the surgeons then triumphed.[1] William Rine, a veteran of ten years' service in the Irish Regiment in France, was hanged in December 1736 for robbing an innkeeper. The surgeons paid the Sheriff's officers £9 for their support against the Irish who had come to protect Rine. They paid another £2 to hire men to guard their Hall against a mob of Irish when his body was dissected.[2] While James Timms was in Newgate, he received a letter from a friend,

Dear Jamey –

I am sorry you take us all to be so ungrateful, as not minding that there was a Petition given in Behalf of you; but to no Purpose. I have been there very often and could not get to speak to you; we shall take Care of your Body. Dear Jamey, as you are a Dying Man, for the small Time you have to live, Mind your Soul.

All from your sincere Friend,
John Barry

P. S. I shall write to you To-morrow and bring you a Cap.

Some time later, on St Patrick's Day, 1741, James Timms and other Irishmen failed in an attempt to break out of Newgate. The next day, escorted across London by musketeers, Light Horse, and about 'forty of the Foot', he was hanged and his body taken by the surgeons.[3]

Michael MacGennis, born in Ireland, came to London and sold milk about the streets. 'He had been used to attend Executions and been often seen there, and to his Cost went there once too often: And, indeed, Pity it is, that such Numbers to the Neglect of all Business, should be so fond of flocking together at these Times, or that there should be so frequent Occasions of giving them Opportunity. But to come to the Point.' At the hanging of 11 November 1751 a sailor from Waterford, two Dublin publicans, and a Dublin calico-printer were hanged. MacGennis and 'forty or fifty' other Irish were there to protect the corpses:

1. The Ordinary's *Account*, 24 May 1736, and *Reade's Weekly Journal*, 29 May 1736.
2. The Ordinary's *Account*, 27 September 1736; *London Post & Daily Advertiser*, 27 September 1736; Barber–Surgeons' Company, *Audit Book 1715–1785*, Guildhall Library, MSS 5235.
3. The Ordinary's *Account*, part 1, 18 March 1741.

They came unprovided with any Vehicle for that Purpose, and when the Bodies were cut down, the Friends scarce had thought of the Matter how to convey them away. The poor Fellow murdered had brought his Cart and Horses there as the Custom is to get a few Pence by letting People stand up in it to see the Execution. After it was over MacGennis and his Party, seeing the Cart near the Gallows, took it from the Driver by Force, and putting the Bodies into it, drove to Bayswater. There they staid drinking some Time. By and by they return'd towards Tyburn in Triumph, resolved against giving Way to any Opposition, and this unfortunate Man being as forward as any, has dearly paid for it. The Man was waiting, and upon their Return, for seizing hold of his Horse's Head, was treated very ill by several present; but being determined if possible, to recover his own Cart and Horse from them, would not let the Horses's Head go, tho' much threatened. This he persisted in, and upon that Account received a Blow with a Hanger, which did his Business.

MacGennis took the bodies across London to Tower Hill. There he was apprehended, and four months later he had 'his Business' done to him at Tyburn. Irishmen protected his body and gave it Christian burial.[1]

The Irish detonated several of the disturbances in the turbulent months of political and industrial struggle of 1768. Two of them, James Murphy and James Dogan, were found guilty of stabbing a sailor to death who was unloading coals in defiance of the all-river strike by the coal-heavers. They were hanged on 11 July. As the 1752 'Murder Act' was law they were also sentenced to be anatomized. Although the act provided a sentence of seven years' transportation for any person attempting to rescue the corpses as they were carted between the hanging at Tyburn and the dissection at Surgeons Hall, many must have intended to do this as the Sheriff thought it prudent to divert the carts from the normal route back to the City because it led through Irish territory in St Giles's. He circumvented the quarter by turning down to Grosvenor Square, Soho and Fleet Street to Surgeons' Hall. The Irish soon discovered the ruse and surrounded the Hall. A great number of Irish women assembled and prayed that 'their countrymen might live again'. The Foot Guards were ordered to disperse the crowd. A cry against the surgeons of 'Murder' became widespread.[2]

About a quarter of those hanged at Tyburn in the first half of the eighteenth century belonged to the 'deep-sea proletariat'. They had been to sea in the carrying trade to the East, the South Seas and North America or in the Royal Navy. The sailors who intervened at the gallows against the surgeons had many other reasons for hating the medical profession.

1. ibid., 11 November 1751; ibid., 23 March 1752; *The Proceedings*, part 2, 16–20 January 1752.
2. *Westminster Journal*, 16 July 1768.

For one, hospitals were used as crimping houses[1] and detention centres for impressed and runaway sailors. For another, the chief killer of seamen was neither combat nor the hazards of the ocean, but diseases ('black vomit', 'ague', 'ship fever' and 'the bloody flux') which were made worse by the tetanus and gangrene caused by the ships' surgeons. Tobias Smollett, who sailed as a surgeon's mate to the bloody action at Carthagena (1741), 'was much less surprised that people should die on board than that any sick person should recover'. In eighteenth-century sailors' slang the surgeon was called 'crocus', an elision of 'croak us', meaning to 'kill us'.[2] From about a dozen documented cases of gallows' riots initiated by seamen we will look at two.

James Buchanan, a Scot, ran away from school and boarded a ship at Newcastle which took him to Virginia and the American coastal trade. Years later, in October 1737, his ship, an East Indiaman, lay at anchor in the Wampoo River in China. Scottish sailors working another ship joined him in the evening to drink. Much later in the night the fourth mate, well known on board for his hot temper, ordered Buchanan to begin loading goods. He refused, they quarrelled, knives were drawn and the fourth mate slain. A year later Buchanan was tried by the High Court of Admiralty at the Old Bailey and sentenced to be hanged at Execution Dock in Wapping. The Admiralty expected trouble at the hanging; it ordered the Sheriff to mobilize a strong force and asked the parochial officers of Wapping to maintain order 'with a competent and sufficient Guard'. The weather was bitter on the day of the hanging: the wind came out of the north-east, snow had begun to stick on the warehouse gables and ice formed at the river's edge by the wharfs. A vast crowd of sailors assembled upon the quays and in wherries and lighters in the river. On the scaffold Buchanan usurped the prerogative of the Ordinary of Newgate. He conducted the service from the Presbyterian paraphrase and then led the throng in singing the twenty-third Psalm,

Yea, though I walk through the valley of the shadow of death, I will fear no evil: for thou art with me; thy rod and thy staff they comfort me.
Thou preparest a table before me in the presence of mine enemies: thou anointest my head with oil; my cup runneth over.

The Sheriffs, tipstaffs, watch and constabulary could not assure the delivery of his body to the surgeons; 'some sailors got on the Scaffold and

1. Crimping house: 'a house used for the decoying and confining of men in order to force them into the army, navy, or merchant service.' (OED).
2. Eric Partridge, *A Dictionary of the Underworld*, 3rd edn, 1968; Smollett describes his experiences as a surgeon's mate in *Roderick Random*; and see, too, Lloyd and Coulter, op. cit.

endeavour'd to cut him down; on which a scuffle ensu'd; but many other Sailors coming to the Assistance of those who first made the Attempt he was cut down . . . and his Body carry'd off with loud Acclamations of Joy, accompanied by a great many Sailors.' One of the assembled sailors had been in hiding afraid of being caught for a crime he had committed two years earlier. At the rescue of Buchanan's corpse he exposed himself to the presence of his enemies, was caught, and later hanged.[1]

John Lancaster was born in 1726 in Black Lion Yard, Whitechapel. The time of his youth was divided between an apprenticeship to a velvet-weaver and education at the newly founded Methodist charity school at the Foundry on one hand, and, on the other, gambling at the skittles' grounds and drinking at alehouses. One Bartholomew Fair time he robbed the Foundry of some pieces of velvet and for fear of being caught went to sea. Years later he returned to take up weaving work in Spitalfields with a small garret master. With another journeyman working looms in the same shop he robbed his master of nineteen yards of velvet and sold them to a Jewish fence in Houndsditch. He was caught, convicted and sentenced to be hanged.

In Newgate his former teacher, Sarah Peters, whom Wesley described as 'a lover of souls, a mother of Israel', visited him several times and super-vised his conversion. The procession of the ten condemned prisoners from Newgate to Tyburn was more like a revival meeting than a hanging match if we credit Wesley's account. Down Snow Hill, up High Holborn, and along Tyburn road, Lancaster stood in the tumbril exhorting the 'multi-tude' to prayer and leading the other malefactors in song,

> Lamb of God, whose bleeding love
> We still recall to mind,
> Send the answer from above,
> And let us mercy find.
>
> Think on us, who think on thee,
> And every struggling soul release!
> O remember Calvary,
> And let us go in peace.

At the tree 'a solemn awe overwhelmed the whole multitude', a fact to which a contingent of the Foot Guards who had been sent to reinforce the civil officers no doubt contributed. After the hanging Wesley detected signs of miraculous intervention in the fact that Lancaster's face was neither bloated nor otherwise disfigured. Disfigurement at the hands of

1. The Ordinary's *Account*, 22 December 1738; PRO, HCA 1/57 (*Examination Book*), fos. 27–31; *Reade's Weekly Journal*, 30 December 1738; *Craftsman*, 23 December 1738; *The Diary of Stephen Monteage*, vol. II, Guildhall Library, MSS 205.

the surgeons was prevented by a secular agency. 'A Company of eight sailors with truncheons in their Hands, looked up to the gallows with an angry countenance, the bodies having been cut down some minutes previous to their arrival. An old woman, who sold gin, observing them to grow violent, mildly said, "Gentlemen, I suppose you want the man the surgeons have got?" ' They did. She directed them to Paddington where the sailors overtook the surgeons' men and rescued Lancaster. They carried his body in triumph across London, through Islington, Shoreditch and Coverele's Fields where they left his body with his mother, who gave him fitting burial two days later. The sailors had known Lancaster perhaps from Bart's Fair or the Moorfields skittles' ground. Perhaps they had been to sea together. Or perhaps they only heard his song across London,

> O remember Calvary,
> And let us go in peace.[1]

In part because the evidence for each case is so sparse and in part for convenience's sake, we have described the people who fought against the surgeons at the gallows in five separate groupings. No doubt the procedure is arbitrary. The Irish for example had friends, families, comrades at work and of course had been to sea. They might (had the evidence permitted) have been as justly discussed in other contexts. But whether they acted at Tyburn in precisely the social groupings that we have identified or in others, these were the 'Scum of the People': a tailor from Essex, a country grazier, a London house carpenter, lost country relatives, sawyers, mistresses, innkeepers, market folk, weavers, sailors and soldiers, the Irish, coal-heavers and 'fellow men'. They were, as far as we can tell, of a piece with the London labouring poor as a whole, heterogeneous and defying a simple classification between the criminal class and the working class. For most of the period their struggles against the surgeons were noted only in passing by the press, by the Ordinary of Newgate's *Accounts*, and by the Barber–Surgeons and Physicians. Rarely was their fight dangerous enough to attract serious attention. When it was, as in 1749, other issues came to play. Nevertheless, the conclusion of the Penlez Riots seriously and permanently altered the balance of forces at Tyburn.

1. John Wesley, *Journals*, Everyman edn, vol. II, pp. 83–90; Silas Told, *The Life of Silas Told*, 3rd edn, 1796, pp. 63 *et seq.*; the Ordinary's *Account*, 28 October 1748; *The Proceedings*, 7–10 September 1748; Arthur Griffiths, *The Chronicles of Newgate*, 1884, vol. II, p. 116.

IV

The Penlez Riots of July 1749 began at a time of widespread unemployment in London. During the year preceding, more than 40,000 men were demobilized following the conclusion of hostilities of the War of Jenkins' Ear. Smollett noted one consequence: 'rapine and robbery . . . domineered without intermission ever since the return of peace.' In what is perhaps the first statistical study of the relation of crime to war and peace, Stephen Theodore Janssen found that the annual average number of persons condemned at the Old Bailey doubled after peace was declared. Indictments for felony in Middlesex were higher in 1749 than they had ever been in the century. Of the forty-four men and women hanged in London that year, more than half had been to sea. The discharged seaman arrived on shore flush with wages and eager to seek some relief from the months at sea in drink, gaming and sex. He found landspeople ready to help him: bum bailiffs, sharpers, panders and bawds. The riots began against these parasites.[1]

On the death of his father, an Exeter clergyman, Bosavern Penlez came to London in 1747. He worked for sixteen months as a journeyman barber and peruke-maker. In April 1749, he left this work to become a gentleman's servant, taking up lodgings in Wych Street, only a few steps from the Strand where the riots of which he was to be the only casualty started. Penlez had nothing to do with the riots until they had almost run their course.[2]

On Friday evening, 30 June 1749, two sailors complained to one Owen, the keeper of The Crown, that they had been robbed of thirty guineas, two moidores (Portuguese coins) and their watches. Instead of receiving satisfaction from the bawdy-house-keeper they were given 'foul Language and Blows'. Accordingly, 'the honest Tar denounc'd Vengeance to his House, and repair'd immediately to his Shipmates and brother Sailors'. On Saturday evening their shipmates from the *Grafton* man-of-war invaded The Crown, and removed its furniture, bedding and pillows into the Strand to build a bonfire. They 'suffer'd no Injury to be done to the poor Damsels'. After the demolition of the contents of the first house was completed, General Campbell, at Somerset House a few hundred yards away, summoned the troops who 'loiter'd about, rang'd themselves

1. Tobias Smollett, *The History of England from the Revolution to the Death of George the Second*, 1804, vol. III, p. 294; Janssen, *Tables of Death Sentences*, 1772; and GLCRO (Mddx Div.), *Calendar of Indictments*, vols. II–V, MJ/CJ.

2. Short biographies of Penlez are contained in the Ordinary's *Account*, 18 October 1749, and *Select Trials*, 1764, vol. IV, pp. 272 *et seq*.

on both Sides the Street, or stood very compos'd round the Remains of the Bonfire, as if that had been what they were sent to Guard, and not the Bawdy-Houses'. Other troops from the Tilt Yard were called in time to prevent the sailors from burning down another bawdy-house, The Bunch of Grapes, owned by Lord Stanhope. By three in the morning the sailors were dispersed.[1]

On Sunday, 2 July, at nine o'clock in the evening, 400 sailors again assembled at Temple Bar and with hand bells ringing swung down the Strand 'threatening that they would pull down all Bawdy-Houses'. Lord Stanhope 'had Reason to fear that the said Mob would come and demolish his House', as the High Constable of Holborn Division, Saunders Welsh, later testified. The fear was justified; by midnight The Bunch of Grapes was burnt to the ground. The sailors then turned to The Star off the Strand in Devereux Court, only a few yards from Temple Bar. Its previous keeper had been hanged for a highway robbery; and its present keeper for six years, Peter Wood, was held in ill fame by the parish. Several informations had been laid against him as a disorderly house-keeper, and he had paid at least once a £20 fine for retailing liquors without a licence. By early morning the crowd had attracted several landsmen, mostly neighbours like Bosavern Penlez who lived across the street from The Star, but others were said to have been there too. A nameless 'gentlemen', it was said, inspired and paid the mob to take apart The Star, whose windows, shutters, panes, sashes, furniture, pillows, bedding and curtains were either smashed or fired. A woollen-draper and burgess of the City of Westminster, Mr Wilson, applied to Saunders Welsh for troops from the Tilt Yard, and they arrived, drums beating, to disperse the mob late in the night of 2–3 July.

On Monday morning, the third day of disorders, the crowds began to

1. 'A Gentleman not Concern'd', *The Case of the Unfortunate Bosavern Penlez*, 2nd edn, 1750, pp. 17–22. I have relied most heavily on this pamphlet for a narrative of the riots. It is an attack on the frankly polemical and self-interested account of Henry Fielding, *A True State of the Case of Bosavern Penlez*, 1749, which however remains invaluable because it reprints the examinations and depositions that Fielding took on 4 July. *Remembrancer*, 8 July 1749, *London Evening Post*, 1–4 July 1749, and *Worcester Journal*, 6 July 1749, have relatively detailed accounts. Written evidence submitted for the trials at the Old Bailey in the eighteenth century survives only in patches, and the summer and autumn 1749 unfortunately is not one of them. See GLCRO (Mddx Div.), *Westminster Sessions Papers*, WJ/SP (1749), and *Middlesex Sessions Papers*, MJ/SP (1749); and also Lond. Corp. RO, *Sessions Papers* (1749). Although the trial was conducted at the expense of the Crown (see Bedford's letter to Sharpe, 6 July 1749, PRO, SP 44/185 fol. 152), the Treasury Solicitor's papers which usually comprise Crown briefs contain nothing on the case. The muster lists for *The Duke of Grafton* are missing for the summer of 1749; see PRO, Adm. 33/350–83.

assemble again in the Strand, and at the same time Henry Fielding, the Chairman of the Westminster Quarter Sessions, returned to London from a short absence to a difficult situation. Not only had a slight incident been allowed to develop to a point where only the military could suppress the disorder, and this owing in part to the absence of early, decisive action by the magistracy, but by Monday morning attacks began against the constabulary, too. The authorities had only exacerbated the situation, so on Monday the bawdy-house-keepers took unilateral action: 'Great Diligence was used all Monday in removing the Goods &c. of certain Houses in Covent Garden, Bridges Street, some courts in Fleet Street, Gun-Powder Alley, King's Head Court, Shoe Lane & Old Bailey for fear of their being made the scenes of succeeding Representations.' Nevertheless, the mobs at the Old Bailey, mainly sailors, broke the windows and attempted to fire the bawdy-houses in the neighbourhood of the court. The beadle of the liberty of the Duchy of Lancaster had the windows of his house broken and his life threatened by sailors who attempted to rescue a rioter whom he had taken during the previous day. At Fielding's office in Bow Street a mob assembled 'in a riotous and tumultuous Manner' and rescued one prisoner. The constable of St George the Martyr deposed that despite an armed escort it was with 'the utmost Difficulty that the . . . Prisoners were conveyed in Coaches through the Streets, the Mob . . . crowding towards the Coach Doors'. On hearing that the sailors planned to continue 'their Work' that night, Fielding sent Welsh to the Secretary of War for troops. By noon a detachment of sixty stood ready at Temple Bar, and others patrolled the Strand during the day.

Fielding's decision to continue the policy of suppressing the disorders by recourse to the military was ill-judged and showed evident signs of panic in a situation where moderate action, such as the effective mobilization of the civil officers of neighbouring parishes (as would happen in October) or the exemplary punishment of a bawdy-house-keeper (as would happen in August), would have served his purpose at least as well. His pamphlet, published in November, took pains to show that the situation had deteriorated sufficiently to justify this decision, but the evidence adduced fails to do this. Saunders Welsh convinced Fielding that the house of the bankers, Snow and Denne, standing adjacent to The Star, was in danger; but whether the danger issued from the flames next door or from the designs of the sailors in the Strand, Welsh did not say. Fielding drew his own conclusion:

What *must have been* the Consequence of exposing a Banker's Shop to the Greediness of the Rabble? Or what *might we have* reasonably apprehended from a Mob encouraged by such a Booty and made desperate by such atrocious Guilt? . . . The Cry against Bawdy-Houses *might have* been easily converted into an Out-cry of a very different Nature, and Goldsmiths *might have been* considered to be as great a Nuisance to the Public as Whores [italics added].

'The Clamour against Bawdy-Houses was . . . a bare Pretence only,' he wrote. The mob consisted of 'Thieves under the Pretence of Reformation'.[1] No other evidence, not even the examinations that Fielding publishes in his pamphlet, corroborates these assertions. All other accounts say that sailors comprised the majority of the crowds. One observer went to considerable length to refute Fielding's view. He stressed the single-mindedness of purpose of the sailors.

A boy who stole a gilt cage from The Crown was discovered carrying it off and the sailors took it from him to throw on the fire. 'Nothing in short was imbezzled or diverted.' Certainly the actions of the parishioners of St Clement Danes belie Fielding's picture of thieves out to pillage and loot. The matron of a cheesemonger's shop clapped her hands as The Bunch of Grapes was razed. 'A Gentleman not Concern'd 'directly contradicts Fielding's view:

> As to the Neighbours, who were at their Doors and Windows, seeing the Whole without the least Concern or Alarm, there was not probably one of them who, though as good and as loyal Subjects as any his Majesty has, and as well affected to the Peace and Quiet of his Government, imagin'd or dream'd there was any Spirit of Sedition or riotous Designs, in all these Proceedings, beyond the open and expressed Intention of destroying those obnoxious Houses.

One observer in St Clement Danes was quoted as saying that 'he hop'd to see [the sailors] all hang'd at *Tyburn*; *for G—d Z—ds* who knows whose House they may call a Bawdy-House next, and down with it', but he 'lay under Suspicion of keeping no better a House than he should do'.[2] For a time on Monday Fielding believed that 400 sailors had gathered at Tower Hill to raid the armoury in preparation to launching an insurrection. It is true that on Tuesday sailors assembled in Lemon Street, Goodman's Fields, to break the windows and to burn down reputed bawdy-houses; but they were dispersed without calling on the military.[3] The only troops deployed at that end of town were a detachment of grenadiers sent to the Navy Pay Office, off Tower Hill, to guard a convoy carrying 'His Majesty's Treasure' to Portsmouth.[4] Neither the course of events nor the evidence of

1. Fielding, op. cit., pp. 48-50. Radzinowicz, vol. 1, p. 400, accepts Fielding's characterization of the rioters without criticism: they were, he writes, 'an unruly mob always ready to take advantage of any incident to create disorder and endanger public safety'.

2. 'A Gentleman not Concern'd', op. cit., pp. 19-23.

3. *Penny Post; Or, the Morning Advertiser*, 5-7 July 1749, and *Worcester Journal*, 13 July 1749.

4. PRO, WO 4/46 (Secretary at War, *Outletters*), fo. 256.

other sources bears on general pillage or insurrection. Fielding sought some justification for at least the former point in his policy to the arrested rioters, one of whom was caught with stolen property from The Star. An energetic prosecution of this case would make some amends for Fielding's precipitous actions by seeming to confirm the criminal intentions of the rioters.

On Monday morning two watchmen, one a shoemaker of the Liberty of the Rolls, the other a labourer of St Dunstan-in-the-West, apprehended Bosavern Penlez asleep in Bell Yard (off Carey Street and some distance from The Star) and found stuffed under his shirt ten lace caps, four lace handkerchiefs, three pairs of lace ruffles, two lace clouts, five plain handkerchiefs, five plain and one laced apron. Bosavern Penlez was taken to the Watch house where the constable of the Liberty of the Rolls was not able to find a witness to swear against him, so the following morning (Tuesday) Penlez was taken to Bow Street to be examined by Justice Fielding.

Peter Wood, the landlord of The Star, claimed at this examination and again subsequently in September at the trial that Penlez had stolen the linen during the gutting of The Star. Wood's oath did not mean much. John Nixon, the collector of the scavenger's rate in the parish, said of Wood and his wife, 'For my own Part I would not hang a Cat or a Dog upon their Evidence.' One of the officers apprehending Penlez claimed that he took the linen only after having been himself robbed of fifteen shillings in the house. By all accounts Penlez was drunk. He began drinking early in the morning and had wandered from one tavern to another along Temple Bar, the Strand and Somerset Stairs, until late on Sunday night he fell in with the mob at The Star. By his own account he could not remember how the linen got into his hands. At any rate he was one of seven arrested during the riots. One of these escaped, one died in prison, the indictments of two were found *ignoramus*, one was acquitted, one pardoned and Penlez himself hanged.[1] John Wilson and Penlez were tried under the Riot Act for 'being feloniously and riotously assembled to the Disturbance of the public Peace', despite the fact that there remains considerable doubt as to whether the act was ever read, as by law it had to be if prosecutions were to ensue under it. The jury found them guilty on 14 September, and the justices pronounced sentence of death. Nevertheless the court, at the jury's instigation, 'recommended [them] to mercy'.

Hundreds petitioned the King to pardon the two prisoners. The twelve jurors of Middlesex who had found Penlez guilty, themselves petitioned, not just upon grounds of 'Humanity and Compassion', but also on the

---

1. PRO, SP 44/85 (*Entry Books*), fo. 152, in which the Secretary of State, the Duke of Bedford, directs Sharpe to prosecute them under the Riot Act.

grounds that Peter Wood's testimony at the trial was untrustworthy, as later became clear by 'universal Representation'. Only the 'fatal Neglect' of the Court or of the defence to produce witnesses contradicting Wood's evidence had led them to their verdict.[1] In the first week of October, eighty-seven of the parishioners of St Clement Danes petitioned the Duke of Newcastle to intercede for a pardon. A week later 600 petitioners from St Paul's, Covent Garden, the Savoy and St Mary-le-Strand begged the King to demonstrate his royal clemency. At about this time 'several Gentlemen of Rank and Credit, accompany'd by a Reverend Divine, went in a decent solemn Procession, all drest in Black, to deprecate the Execution of the Sentence'. On the eve of the hanging other gentlemen waited on His Majesty at Kensington to petition for a respite of sentence. Partial success greeted these appeals. Wilson's sentence was respited on the evening before he was to have hanged, although, according to Fielding, it was not the pressure of many petitions which caused this but the intercession of 'a noble Person in great Power'. Penlez was not pardoned, and in Fielding's opinion the decisive fact for applying the rigour of the law to Penlez was that he, unlike all the others, was taken with stolen goods in his possession.

> Of 400 Persons concerned in the same
> Attempt he only suffer'd
> Tho' neither Principal nor Contriver.

Such were the lines that concluded an inscription which the parishioners of St Clement's proposed to place on his tomb.[2] Deep parochial opposition to the hanging of Penlez arose not only because his role in the riots was incidental, but also because widespread sympathy existed for the object of the sailors' attack. A month after the riots concluded the Middlesex Quarter Sessions sentenced a woman to be whipped at the cart's tail along the Strand and back for keeping a disorderly house there. St Clement Danes had at one time a reputation for vigilance against such houses, and the government only a few years earlier had caused Petty Sessions to be held in order to suppress them.

In the days before the rioting began Fielding's own work as a magistrate concerned the suppression of bawdy-houses and the reduction of the 'profligate Lewdness' which he thought characterized his age. Later he would be accused of complicity with bawds 'by laying them under annual or casual contributions'. An author of a letter to the *London Magazine* thought the accusation was confirmed by the fact that in *An Enquiry into the Causes of the Late Increases of Robbers* (1751) Fielding failed to mention

1. PRO, SP 35/29, part II, fo. 52.
2. *Gentleman's Magazine*, October 1749.

prostitution or brothel-house-keeping as a cause of crime in London.[1] Certainly both some of those preceding and some following him in this office made tidy sums from these kinds of peculation and extortion. Only a few months after Penlez was hanged the Middlesex bench petitioned the Lord Chancellor against a justice in the east end of the city for keeping disreputable houses in Goodman's Fields.[2] Thomas Hurnall, one of the City's marshalls (1746–58), who took a prominent position in the procession carrying Penlez to his hanging, was discharged from office for extorting victuallers.[3] There is, however, no reason to believe that Fielding added to his income by accepting 'the dirtiest money on earth'. Indeed, he suffered because he had not done so.[4] His behaviour on 3 July was not influenced, therefore, by a material connection with Strand victuallers, or bawdy-house-keepers.

Nine days before the Penlez Riots Fielding took the lead in a case similar to the sort which touched off the rioting. He took evidence from John Lambert

who being upon Oath Says that between eight and Nine of the Clock last Night he was pickt up by a person now present who calls herself Ann Baldwin . . . in Drum Alley in Drury Lane who Carryed him into a house where they had some Liquor, Says that Baldwin . . . asked this Informt. what it was a Clock, Upon which he pulled out his Watch in order to tell her, at which time she feloniously and forcibly Snatched it out of his hand and run away with the Same. . .[5]

Only two days before the riots began, Fielding, as Chairman of the Westminster Sessions, delivered a charge to the Grand Jury in which he called their attention to several misdemeanours (which it was their duty to present) and 'particularly of such as do in a more especial Manner infest the Public at this Time'. To the first of these, 'profligate Lewdness', he devoted more than half of his attention. Profligacy, he argued, debilitates the body, endangers the soul and wastes livelihoods. It corrupts youth, destroys marriages and threatens future generations. He cited the legal authorities, Coke, Lambard, Pulton and Popham, to prove that it was a crime and recalled 'the exceeding Wrath of God against the Children of Israel for their Fornication with the Daughters of Moab' to prove it a sin. In a note of caution he reminded the Grand Jury that 'to eradicate this Vice [bawdy-houses] out of Society, however it may be the Wish of sober

1. *London Magazine*, March 1751.
2. W. J. Hardy and W. Le Hardy, eds., *A Calendar of the Middlesex Sessions Books and Orders of Court 1639–1751* (mimeograph, 1921), vol. XII, pp. 110, 123, 130–36.
3. Lond. Corp. RO, 'History of the City Marshalls', MSS 134–5, fol. 169.
4. See his introduction to *The Journal of a Voyage to Lisbon*, 1754.
5. GLCRO (Mddx Div.), 'The Information of John Lambert, 22 June 1749', *Sessions Papers*, MJ/SP/128.

and good Men, is, perhaps, an impossible Attempt; but to check its Progress, and to suppress the open and more profligate Practice of it, is with the Power of the Magistrate, and it is his Duty.'[1] Fielding may have been reluctant to have recalled these words during the course of the next few days. Certainly when he came to write of the riots in November, the martial spirit replaces the reformer's; and we hear less of the dangers of 'profligate Lewdness' than of the possibilities of insurrection and general rapine. It appeared that the magistrate's duty lay less in bringing down bawdy-houses than in keeping them standing. Indeed, where in July he quotes Coke against adultery and fornication, in November he quotes Hale to argue that the pulling down of bawdy-houses is high treason. In July Fielding had nothing to lose, but in November not only did he have his own actions to defend but these and the case of Bosavern Penlez had become an issue in the Westminster election. The incident and Fielding's handling of it threatened to combine the grievances of the Opposition against the standing army, corruption and the Riot Act.

One person who failed to support the mounting campaign to pardon Penlez was a Member of Parliament for Westminster, Lord Trentham. When he was appointed a Commissioner of the Admiralty later in the summer he was obliged to re-submit his candidacy to the 'independent' scot-and-lot electors of Westminster.[2] During the polling, which began on 22 November (more than a month after Penlez was hanged), 'Penley's Ghost' came back to haunt Trentham, the government's candidate, in the form of nightly candle-lit processions winding through the streets of St Clements led by 'Penlez' shrouded in his coffin.[3] Opposition propaganda produced acrostics signed by Penlez, suggested that Peter Wood campaigned for Trentham, and claimed that Penlez rose from the dead to vote for Sir George Vandeput, the Opposition's candidate. It parodied

1. *A Charge Delivered to the Grand Jury at the Sessions of the Peace Held for the City and Liberty of Westminster*, 1749, p. 49. This was not the only cause of embarrassment to the inexperienced magistrate (he entered the commission in December 1748), for it was at about this time that four well-known house-breakers robbed a merchant whose shop stood opposite Fielding's office in Bow Street; see GLCRO (Mddx Div.), 'The Information of John Bonen, 20 July 1749', *Sessions Papers*, MJ/SP/131.

2. Smollett, op. cit., pp. 289 *et seq*. The definitive social analysis of the voting and a suggestive reconstruction of Westminster politics is found in Nicholas Rogers, 'Aristocratic Clientage, Trade and Independency'; *Past and Present*, 61, November 1973. There is a briefer account of the election in George Rudé, *Hanoverian London 1714-1804*, 1971, pp. 159-61.

3. Sir Thomas Robinson wrote to the Duke of Richmond (owner of several Westminster properties), 4 December 1749, 'Penley's Ghost (wch they have carried about in Triumph & surely a high insult on Government) has raised more People to vote for St. Clems. than there are Houses in the Parish.' West Sussex RO, Goodwood MSS, 51, fo. 60.

Trentham's role during the campaign for a pardon in '*Peg Trim Tram's* Sorrowful LAMENTATION':

> Poor Penlez I might have saved,
>   But I did refuse the same
> Tho' it were so justly craved,
>   By great Numbers of good Fame.
> But, alas! it is too late, Sirs,
>   And I can't recall the Time,
> Which has almost craz'd my Pate, Sirs,
>   For I own it a great Crime.
> Mark the People, how they're rouzed,
>   Like to Lions in their Dens;
> Mostly to Sir *George* espoused,
>   And asperse me with their Pens.[1]

Trentham sought to deny these accusations in a handbill saying that he had no role in the *prosecution* of Penlez. Trentham's brother-in-law, the Duke of Bedford, the largest landholder of Covent Garden, printed about a quarter of a million squibs, broadsides and handbills in support of the Government's candidate.[2] As Secretary of State (1748–51), the Duke of Bedford might easily have prevented Penlez from receiving a pardon.

The election was said to have been one of the most expensive that the Government had experienced. The electoral management of the Duke of Bedford and Trentham ('bribery, threats and compulsions') was thought to have been especially 'scandalous and base' even by those without a direct interest in the election.[3] Ninety per cent of the Opposition voters were tradesmen and shopkeepers in the victualling, provisioning and out-fitting trades. These were concentrated especially along the Strand. On the other hand, more than nine tenths (seventy-six out of eighty-three) of the magistrates polled voted for Trentham.[4] Fielding, who owed his seat on the Westminster bench to his friends in the Pelham administration, supported Trentham to the extent of taking depositions in Bow Street which attempted to discredit the allegations of Opposition propaganda. Fielding's energetic prosecution of Penlez and Trentham's failure to inter-cede to acquire a pardon for him clearly implicated the administration

1. Anon., *T—t—m and V—d—t. A Collection of the Advertisements and Hand-bills, Serious, Satyrical and Humourous Published on both Sides during the Election*, Dublin, 1749, p. 39.

2. Rogers, op. cit.

3. Grove to Grimston, 5 December 1749. HMC, *Ducane MSS*, 1905, pp. 203–4. See also Joseph Grego, *A History of Parliamentary Elections and Electioneering*, 1886, p. 121.

4. Rogers, op. cit.

in the sorry affair. Penlez was hanged for stealing the ruffles of a cock bawd. But he was also hanged so that the Government by the severity of its retribution could lend support to its characterization of the riot and to the decision to rely upon the military to suppress it, as if the seriousness of the punishment determined the gravity of the crime. As it happened the actual hanging demonstrated the opposite. Sheriff Janssen, in marked departure from the policy followed in July, showed that threatening crowds could be handled quite differently.

The 'Tyburn Fair' at which Penlez and fourteen others were hanged was fraught with danger. Rescues of rioters from the Bow Street Office had been attempted the previous July, and in one case had been successful. Crowds had gathered menacingly at the Old Bailey to protest at the imprisonment of other rioting sailors. In late September, three weeks before the hanging, some of the condemned prisoners sawed through their chains with tools smuggled into them by friends and attempted to break out. Less than a week before the hanging on 12 October it was reported 'that the Convicts under Sentence of Death in Newgate, having got a Quantity of Gunpowder, Chips and other Combustibles, convey'd to them, design'd to attempt an Escape, by Setting Fire to, or blowing up Part of the said Gaol'. The plan was discovered, and its perpetrators were placed under heavy guard and chained to the floor. All accounts of the unusually large crowd in the streets that day stress the prominence of sailors.[1] At the hanging gathered 'some thousands of sailors [appearing] armed with bludgeons and cutlasses', according to one observer. With the exception of Penlez all the fourteen men hanged were sailors; the one woman hanged that day was the daughter of a Rotherhithe publican and married to a seaman.[2] Attempts to rescue the condemned prisoners during the long, crowded procession were widely reported and feared. Order at the hangings in the year or so preceding that of Penlez was maintained by reliance upon contingents of the Foot and Horse Guards. In June 1748 a strong guard attended the execution. A party of Horse Guards was present at the hanging of October 1748 but did not (or could not) prevent the body of Lancaster from being rescued by some sailors. In March 1749

1. *Worcester Journal*, 28 September 1749 and 12 October 1749; *Remembrancer*, 23 September 1749; 'Philonomous', *The Right Method of Maintaining Security in Persons & Property to all Subjects of Great Britain*, 1751, p. 53.

2. The others hanged that day were (age and birthplace in parentheses) Philip Lacy (17, Mile End), John Graham (35, Londonderry), Thomas Hazard (24, Holborn), Thomas Mynott (24, Copenhagen), Thomas Arnold (40, Clerkenwell), Mary Dyman (22, Rotherhithe), John Collison (34, Maidstone), George Aldridge (19, Rumford), Thomas Robinson (22, Virginia), John Cross (25, Guinea), David Boyd (24, Northern Ireland), John Alford (27, Wiltshire), William Cavenagh (26, Dublin) and James M'Gennis (27, Dublin). The Ordinary's *Account*, 18 October 1749.

the sailors rescued from the surgeons the bodies of Holly and Burk. The Foot Guards attended the April 1749 hanging, and in August a troop of horse guarded the hanging of two smugglers associated with the Hawkhurst gang in order to prevent anticipated rescue attempts.[1]

Theodore Janssen, Alderman of Bread Street Ward, Member of Parliament for the City and Sheriff of London, was in this last capacity responsible in law for the execution of the death sentence. Unlike many of his predecessors in that office he took this responsibility seriously. By a combination of daring, massive deployment of the civil officers and concessions made to the sailors at a critical juncture he averted a dangerous situation. Janssen himself rode at the head of the procession. With him were the High Constables of the five divisions (Westminster, Holborn, Kensington, Finsbury and Tower Hamlets), who with their petty constables formed an armed body of 300 foot and horse. The City of London's Upper and Lower Marshalls with their attendants marched two by two. The wardens of the two London compters with their livery servants and the Middlesex Sheriff's officers marched next. With swords drawn or javelins in hand, they made an altogether imposing array of municipal strength that set out with the six tumbrils from Newgate. As they left the jurisdiction of the City at Holborn Bars a party of the Foot Guards attempted to join the procession, but Janssen with the golden chain of office around his neck and the Sheriff's white wand in his hand waved aside the military support offered by the Crown. A mile and a half farther on at Tyburn the mounted civil officers formed a large circle around the gallows while the petty constables and officers on foot formed a smaller circle within.[2] 'The multitude of spectators was infinite. Though a rescue had been threatened by many ... there yet was not the least disturbance, except during a moment at the gallows where a vast body of sailors, some of whom were armed with cutlasses and all with bludgeons, began to be very clamorous as the unhappy sufferer was going to be turned off.'[3] Order was kept but at a price. The Sheriff avoided a battle at the gallows by taking responsibility for the dead bodies, which he delivered to the friends of the hanged. The 'vast Body of Sailors ... assembled there to save the Bodies ... from the Surgeons' left Tyburn without having to fight against the surgeons. Penlez was buried in St Clement's burial ground whose parishioners had raised a subscription for this purpose.

Praise for Janssen's dismissal of the Guards was widespread and long

1. *Penny Post; Or, the Morning Advertiser*, 22-4 June 1748; *London Evening Post*, 21-3 June 1748; *Worcester Journal*, 10 August 1749; and the Ordinary's *Accounts*, 28 October 1748, 17 March, 26 April and 4 August 1749.

2. *London Magazine*, October 1749; 'A Gentleman not Concern'd', op. cit., pp. 54-5.

3. 'Philonomous', op. cit., p. 54.

remembered.[1] He was lauded for a tactical victory in preventing a rescue or major disturbance during the hanging, but with more significance his decision was praised for political and strategical reasons. Thus 'Philonomous' in a 'Letter to a Member of Parliament' published two years later took the incident as an occasion for an essay in praise of the Saxon conception of the Sheriff. The Normans brought to England the principle of military law and military force, which 'is not the proper aid, and can very rarely, if ever, be called to the assistance of the civil magistrate, without infringing the constitution, or endangering our liberties'. A 'Gentlemen not Concern'd' found in Janssen's decision a 'Demonstration of Fact, that nothing could be falser than the Imputation of a riotous seditious Humour being prevalent among the People' and of the 'Right and Sufficiency of the Magistracy to protect itself in the Execution of its Office'. Here was a gesture which showed 'the old *British* spirit' and which proved 'that his Majesty's Reign was that of the Laws, and not of the Sword'. Thus the contrast between Fielding's and Janssen's approach to situations of potential or actual riot assumed a political form, and became a matter of principle.

However, the use of the troops to aid the magistracy in their duties had occurred before and would again without causing political objections. In January 1749 two sergeants and twenty-four men from the Tower assisted the officers of the Surrey Quarter Sessions in the suppression of a disorderly house in Southwark. In 1744 the Middlesex bench thanked the government for 'the provision of His Majesty's Guards whenever required' which included their use in the apprehension of suspected criminals. On the day after Penlez was hanged a journalist was assured that 'some of the Guards will be quarter'd in the Towns around London which are to Patrole the Roads and Foot-Paths from Town to Town from Five in the Even 'till Eleven'. In February 1750 a detachment of the Guards left the Tower 'to disperse a Mob of upwards of three Hundred Sailors assembled in Bartholomew Lane'. In February 1751 Fielding and Saunders Welsh in an ironic alteration of their policy of 1749 called upon a detachment of the Guards to help them raid a disorderly house in the Strand where forty-five people were seized. A dozen years later at the height of another period of rapid demobilization in the summer of 1763, the Guards were called several times to repel mobbing sailors who in March and September tried to prevent the magistracy from committing prostitutes to prison. At least eight sailors lost their lives in these confrontations.[2]

1. For example by Francis Place in the 1820s, see Brit. Mus. Add. MSS 27,825, fol. 77.
2. PRO, WO 94/5 (*Garrison Papers*), fos. 111–12; W. J. Hardy and W. Le Hardy, eds., op. cit., vol. XX, pp. 37–42; *Worcester Journal*, 19 October 1749; *Reade's Weekly*

If Janssen's decision to dismiss the Guards did not result in a permanent shift in policy away from the use of the military in suppressing civil disorders, his decision at the gallows to reserve the condemned bodies for their friends had a more lasting effect. In the five or six years beginning in 1750 and from time to time after that, the municipal and county officials responsible for the execution of the death sentence used the authority and forces at their command to prevent the surgeons from appropriating the corpses of condemned felons. At the next Tyburn hanging all the 'proper Officers' were ordered to attend. At the hanging of 6 July 1750, we read that the felons were 'attended (as usual) by Mr. Sheriff Janssen with five High Constables, and their Petty Constables; and but a few of the London and Middlesex Officers . . . The Execution was over by a little after Ten O'Clock, and the Bodies being cut down by Order of the Sheriff, were delivered to their Friends.'[1]

For a time a degree of order and the semblance of solemnity so often called for by the critics of Tyburn hangings was maintained by the removal of the most frequent cause of disorder, the claims of the physicians and the surgeons. Whenever John Taylor or Steven Roe, the Ordinaries of Newgate, take note of the manner of disposal of the hanged corpses in the 1750s, they invariably report that their 'Bodies were all carry'd off by their Friends; nor was there any Disturbance'.[2]

Isolated from other sources of tension, the gallows' brawls against the surgeons never developed into the full-scale danger to metropolitan order that we find in the Sacheverell, Wilkes or Gordon riots. Instead they inflicted only a minor but frequent irritant to the city's stability. The rioters were neither dangerous enough to provoke decisive intervention by the Government nor so weak as to enable the surgeons to achieve a victory of their own. But the disturbances were always a potential flashpoint of full-scale riot. When combined, as they were in 1749, with the political issues of the Opposition and the general insecurities attendant on the sudden demobilization of the fleet, only the prudent action of Janssen prevented them from detonating a serious municipal explosion. Janssen capitulated to the surgeons' opponents. In the evening after Penlez was

---

Journal, 11 February 1751; *Annual Register*, 20 March, 6 September and 13 October 1763; *The Proceedings*, 14–20 September 1763.

1. *Penny Post; Or, the Morning Advertiser*, 7–9 February 1750 and 6–9 July 1750.

2. See the Ordinary's *Accounts* for 7 February, 26 March, 16 May, 8 August, 25 March 1750, 29 July 1751, 11 October 1752, 3 December 1753, 5 June 1754, 17 March and 12 November 1755. A search through a newspaper which otherwise regularly reported brawls against the surgeons reveals the same. See, for instance, *Berrow's Worcester Journal* for 6 July, 8 August 1750, 14 February, 31 October 1751, 19 October 1752, 4 October 1753, 20 November 1755, 26 May 1757, 20 October 1763, 5 January, 23 February, 15 March, 23 August 1764 and 21 February 1765.

hanged, there was no dissection in Warwick Lane; instead we read that 'Dr. Freake spoke the Herverian Oration before the President, Fellows, and the rest of the Royal College of Physicians ... after which they had an elegant Entertainment in the Hall'.[1] At Tyburn in the years following mid-century the surgeons could get on a regular basis only the bodies of felons sentenced to be dissected under the 1752 'Murder Act'. The days of constant tumult at the gallows were over.

V

Having described the arguments of the surgeons' advocates in favour of dissection, identified those who opposed them, and recounted the 1749 riot which altered the balance of forces at Tyburn, we now may try to evaluate the significance of the struggle against the surgeons to the labouring poor.

The high mortality rates of eighteenth-century London (sometimes standing to baptisms at a ratio of two to one) may, unless care is taken, suggest that death could not have mattered very much. Infant mortality was high in all classes of society. In hospitals, ships and prisons death was omnipresent. The plague had disappeared but the toll taken by other diseases was great. A bad harvest or severe winter even in the metropolis brought with it an immediate increase in mortalities. Under these conditions, with death so common, a daily and public event, a toughness, even an indifference to death might appear to have been the typical response. However, this was not the case to the people who were hanged and who went to hangings. Their behaviour if anything suggests the opposite – the supreme importance of death.

Their attitude to death (even to the death of the most lowly) was a compound of Christian and quasi-pagan beliefs. While we probably can never disentangle all of them, there are some elements which we can identify with certainty. Let us first consider 'resurrection'. Properly speaking this was not an attitude to death but the last chance of escaping it. Nevertheless its prevalence explains in part the hostility to the surgeons.

As we have seen, in 1768 when the bodies of Murphy and Dogan (two militants of the coal-heavers' strike) were taken to Surgeons' Hall to be dissected, a crowd of Irish women formed outside the Hall praying that their countrymen 'might live again'. Their hope was not necessarily superstitious, because at times it was reasonable to regard the surgeons, not the hangman, as the agent causing death. During the first half of the eighteenth century the cause of death at Tyburn was asphyxia, not dislocation of the

1. *London Evening Post*, 17–19 October 1749.

spine. A broken neck was decisive. Asphyxia, however, could result in temporary unconsciousness if the knot was tied, or the noose placed around the neck, in a particular fashion. The hangman was thus able to exercise discretion in carrying out his work; this was a well-known fact which gave rise to much negotiation and considerable interest in knot-lore. To take one of the more famous examples of the practice, the hangman was bribed to adjust the noose in the proper way at the hanging of Dr Dodd in 1777. In the event Dodd died, but incomplete hangings without fatal strangulation were common enough to sustain the hope that resuscitation ('resurrection' as it was called) would save the condemned. In the sixteenth century 'resurrections' were so frequent and the costs incidental to them so substantial that the Barber–Surgeons ruled that the expenses thus entailed should be borne by those who brought the body to the 'Thanatomistes'.[1] William Petty in the seventeenth century attained considerable notoriety when he began to anatomize Anne Green, a murderess, and found that she revived under his scalpel.[2]

The successful revival of hanged people occurred several times in the eighteenth century. In 1709 John Smith, a former packer, sailor and soldier was left dangling from Tyburn Tree for two hours after he had been 'turned off'. He was cut down, taken to a near-by house where 'he soon recovered in consequence of bleeding and other proper applications', and for the next ten years of his life he was known as 'Half-Hanged Smith'.[3] In August 1736 Thomas Reynolds was hanged for a Black Act violation in going about armed and in disguise while engaging in the destruction of a Herefordshire turnpike. The wife of another turnpike 'leveller' came to London to provide him with a coffin and a shroud: 'just as they had put him into his Coffin and were about to fasten it up, he thrust back the Lid, and to the great Astonishment of the Spectators, clapt his Hands on the Sides of the Coffin in order to raise himself up'. The hangman was about to string him up again, but was prevented from doing this by the 'mob', who carried the coffin to Paddington, where 'they put Sack and Brandy to his Mouth, and us'd other Means to recover him, and a Man

---

1. 'Yt ys agreed that yf any bodie which shall at anie tyme here after happen to be brought to o'r hall for the intent to be wrought upon by Thanatomistes of o'r Companie, shall revyve or come to lyfe agayne, as of late hathe been scene, the charge aboute the same bodie so revivinge, shall be borne, levied, and susteyned, by such person, or persons, who shall so happen to bringe home the bodie.' Minutes of the Court of Assistants (13 July 1587), quoted in Edward Wedlake Brayley, *Londiniana*, 1829, vol. II, pp. 33–4.

2. *Notes and Queries*, Second Series, vol. I (January–June 1856), vol. II (July 1856), edns., op. cit., vol. XX, pp. 37–42; *Worcester Journal*, 19 October 1749; *Reade's Weekly* p. 73; vol. XI (April 1861); Radzinowicz, vol. I, pp. 466–7; H. M. Sinclair and A. H. T. Robb-Smith, *A Short History of Anatomical Teaching in Oxford*, Oxford, 1750, pp. 12–13.

3. Alfred Marks, *Tyburn Tree; Its History and Annals*, 1908, pp. 221–2.

wrap'd him in his Coat to keep him Warm. . .' Reynolds expired while the 'mob' was returning him to town.[1] Three years later, after James Buchanan was rescued from the surgeons by the sailors following his hanging in Wapping, twelve affidavits were submitted to the High Court of Admiralty attesting to the fact that 'Buchanan is yet living'.[2] In November 1740 William Duell, aged seventeen, hung from Tyburn for half an hour before the surgeons took his body to their hall in Cripplegate. Richard Hoare, the Sheriff, reported:

just as they had taken him out of the coach, and laid him on a table at that place in order to make the necessary preparations for cutting him up, he was, to the great astonishment of the surgeons and assistants heard to groan; and upon examination, finding he had some other symptoms of life, some of the surgeons let him blood, after having taken several ounzes he began to stir, and in a short space of time was able to rear himself up, but could not immediately speak, so as to be heard articulately.

Duell was not hanged again, but sentenced to transportation for life.[3] In 1782 John Hayes revived after his hanging and remembered passing St Andrew's, Holborn, 'then I thought I was in a beautiful green field and that is all I remember till I found myself in the dissecting room'.[4] At about the same time, a private surgeon in Gough Square purchased for dissection the body of a man who had been hanged. He revived, and the surgeon paid his passage to America.[5]

Life after 'death' therefore had a quite practical reality for those sent to Tyburn to hang, and for many of them their time in Newgate before the hanging day was spent in preparation for such 'resurrections'. Thomas Hill, born in the 'other end of the Town', served out his apprenticeship to a playing-card-maker. He went to Holland on the completion of his apprenticeship, to have a die made in order to be able to counterfeit the duty stamp on playing-cards. He was hanged for this. In the days before his execution he spent his time in Newgate mobilizing his friends to arrange a *post mortem* revival. 'He was cut down and carried to the Talbot in Tyburn-road by Mistake, the Mob that took care of his Body, was to carry him to Benjamin Boswell's where a Surgeon waited on Purpose to bleed him.'[6] William Parsons served at sea in Jamaica and New-

1. The Ordinary's *Account*, 11 August 1736, and *Morning Post*, 23 August 1736.
2. See above, pp. 86–7.
3. *A Journal of the Shrievalty of Richard Hoare, Esquire, in the Years 1740–41* (privately printed, 1815), pp. 57–8; *Reade's Weekly Journal*, 30 December 1740; and *Craftsman*, 23 December 1740.
4. *Notes and Queries*, 5th series, vol. 1 (June 1874), p. 444.
5. *Memoirs of Joseph Brasbridge*, 1824, p. 224.
6. The Ordinary's *Account*, 17 February 1743–4.

foundland and as a lieutenant in the Grenadiers, but mainly, he lived off his father's credit, and was a rake, a gamester and a sharper. In 1748 he was transported for forging a note upon his father's bankers; he returned a couple of years later to rob the same bankers on Hounslow Heath. He was hanged in 1751. His friends organized a defence against the surgeons and carried him to Paddington where 'an Experiment was intended to be tried on him to bring him again to Live'.[1] Jack Sheppard escaped twice from the condemned cell in Newgate, it once having been rebuilt to contain him. A final effort to escape during the procession to Tyburn was detected. He 'earnestly desired some of his Acquaintance, that, after his Body was cut down, they would, as soon as possible, put it into a warm Bed, and try to let him Blood'. He hung from the gallows for fifteen minutes before a soldier cut him down. There were others at his execution, however, who wished to take possession of his body. The surgeon's man, a bailiff, acquired Sheppard's body by giving it out that another man, an undertaker whom the bailiff in fact had hired as a decoy, was the agent of the surgeons. Several 'gentlemen' interested in burying Sheppard themselves discovered the ruse, informed the crowd of it, and led them in riot against the bailiff in Long Acre where he had conveyed Sheppard preparatory to moving him to Surgeon's Hall. The crowd was not entirely convinced of the good intentions of these nameless 'gentlemen', and the Foot Guards had to be called to ensure that not the 'mob' but these gentlemen took possession of the corpse. The coach which took Sheppard to St Martin-in-the-Fields had to be protected by two files of the Foot Guards 'marching on each side of the Coach with bayonets fix'd at the Ends of their Muskets'. There Sheppard was buried. The surgeons were not able to dissect him nor his friends permitted to try to revive him.[2] The attempt in April 1736 to revive a smuggler following his hanging in Edinburgh was the first incident which led to the Porteous Riots of that autumn.[3]

Death by hanging in the eighteenth century was problematical. While infrequent, the possibility of revival following a poorly executed hanging was a real one and reminds us that the theme of supernatural resurrection which guides Southey's ballad, 'Robrecht the Robber', and scores of folk tales about the revival of the dead to redress grievances could have a basis in actuality.

1. Anon., *A Genuine and Authentick Account of the Life and Transactions of William Parsons, Esq.*, 1715, p. 10.

2. *Select Trials*, 1742, vol. II, p. 156; Rev. Mr Villette, *The Annals of Newgate*, 1776, vol. I, pp. 266 *et seq.*; *British Journal*, 16 November 1724.

3. See *Gentleman's Magazine*, September 1736; D. G. D. Isaac, 'A Study of Popular Disturbances in Britain 1714–1754', unpublished PhD thesis, University of Edinburgh, 1953, pp. 130–41.

'We therefore commit his body to the ground; earth to earth, ashes to ashes, dust to dust; in sure and certain hope of the Resurrection to eternal life, through our Lord Jesus Christ; who shall change our vile body, that it may be like unto his glorious body. . .' So, the office of burial of the Established Church. None hanged at Tyburn left testimony that they expected their 'vile body' to become 'like unto His glorious body', but we cannot for that reason exclude from consideration a literal faith in the Resurrection of the flesh. So obvious was the need for proper treatment of the dead for the peaceful departure to an afterlife that it hardly needed to be mentioned. Exceptional and unusual beliefs, however, required stating and do survive in the evidence. Some regarded the resurrection of the flesh in ways quite different from those of the Church of England. Lot Cavenagh's former mistress, it will be recalled, promised to take steps to prevent the surgeons from getting his body. She assured him that she would have done this without his speaking 'threatning Words to me, telling me, that if you can, you will trouble me after you are dead'. The belief that the dead possessed the power 'to come again' was the last revenge of the dead upon the living; as such, it provides us with indications not only about the popular conception of death but also of popular notions of justice.

Elizabeth Boile ('Betty the Cook') was hanged in 1714 for stealing two gold rings. One of her former friends refused to visit her in Newgate, so 'she swore she would haunt him after Death'. Again, 'having a Smock at Pawn in Holborn, she call'd at the Pawnbroker's as she rid by to Tyburn; but her refusing to give it her, she in a very great Passion swore she would plague him for it after she was hang'd'.[1] Thomas Saunders, a sailor, hanged for house-breaking in 1723, said 'if any Thing should happen either to her [his wife] or his Child he believed it would be impossible for his Body to rest under Ground'. Burnworth, hanged for killing a thief-taker in the Mint in 1726, told one of his guards at the gaol before the hanging procession set out 'that if he did not take Care to see his Body decently buried after Execution he would meet him in a dark Entry and pull his Nose off'.[2]

The threat 'to come again' or 'to be troublesome' after death was directed not just against those who refused to perform some last kindness before death or responsibility after death, but also against those who brought about the death in the first place, as when during the election of 1749 'Penley's Ghost' was paraded in the streets against Trentham, who had failed to obtain Penlez a pardon. Mary Green, debauched by a baronet

1. Alexander Smith, *A Compleat History of the Lives and Robberies of the Most Notorious Highway-Men, Footpads, Shop-Lifts, and Cheats*, 1719, vol. II, p. 319.
2. *Select Trials*, vol. II, pp. 23, 360.

early in the 1730s, bore him a child to whom a bawdy-house-keeper in the
Minories, Ann Girlie, became godmother. Mary Green was hanged in
1745 for stealing fifteen guineas from a sailor who had come to London
from Sheerness to collect his dead brother's back pay. Mary Green bore
several grievances against Ann Girlie: first, she took five shillings in the
pound from the earnings of her lodgers (not including rent); second, she
turned king's evidence at the trial when her own life was not endangered;
third, she did nothing to obtain a reprieve for Mary Green despite the
good connections she maintained with the people of fashion in St James's.
Mary Green therefore promised to haunt Ann Girlie and 'women of
quality [who] glory in the misery of others'.[1] William Stevens was seventeen years old when he was hanged in 1748 for stealing half a pound of
tobacco and six gallons of brandy from a shopkeeper's counter. He was
indicted under a statute of Queen Anne (12 Anne c. 7) which removed
benefit of clergy from the offence of larceny in a dwelling-house or shop
without breaking in if the value of the goods stolen was forty shillings or
more, thus making hanging the mandatory sentence. From the condemned
cell in Newgate he wrote to his prosecutor, 'We are sorry you valued your
Goods at three pounds, which an eminent Distiller says, were not worth
half the Money... So you will hear no more from us, till after our
Decease.'[2]

The principles which activated the spirits of the dead 'to trouble' mean
or retributive prosecutors also governed the behaviour of the living in
exacting a more material revenge. Cornelius Saunders, blind from birth,
came to London from Amsterdam at the age of ten in 1740. For years he
lived from hand to mouth in the outer eastern and northern parishes of
London. In the spring and summer he was casually employed by street
carters to call out vegetables and greens. He assisted the white coopers in
making wash-tubs during the winter and autumn months; not regular
work certainly, but it earned him a few pence and perhaps meals and drink.
Even a scratch-as-scratch-can existence if implanted in a network of
permanent acquaintances and membership in particular neighbourhoods
had its own kind of security. He lodged in Lamb Street, Spitalfields,
where he did domestic duties in the household of Mrs White, a victualler,
in return for a place to sleep and the important perquisite of the empty
wooden packing crates. These he supplied to the coopers in the Minories
who remade them into wash-tubs, bathing-tubs, casks and household
containers. In the summer of 1763, while fetching salmon kits from Mrs
White's basement he came across her cache of savings, some thirty

1. The Ordinary's *Account*, 4 April 1746, and *The Proceedings*, 11–14 September 1745.
2. The Ordinary's *Account*, 18 March 1748, and for a good treatment of the law of
larceny in dwelling-houses and shops see Radzinowicz, vol. I, pp. 41–9.

guineas hidden in a shoebox, and stole it. Blind Cornelius Saunders was
well known in the neighbourhood; so the next day when he paraded himself in Moorfields decked in a new suit of clothes and silver knee-buckles,
the constables sent out by Mrs White had no trouble in finding him and
recovering the money. We cannot get closer to the resentments bred of
thirteen years' service and dependence which led to this foolish theft, nor
to the venomous spite of his benefactress which seems to have informed
her day-to-day dealings with him. We do know that to the inhabitants of
Spitalfields, Aldgate and the Minories Mrs White's prosecution at the
Old Bailey was far more brutal than the case deserved, where a ducking
at the conduit or a thrashing in the street (an extra-judicial and commonly
administered direct punishment) would have been more usual. The
strength of feeling against this recourse to the justice of the Old Bailey
showed itself in the attempted rescue of Saunders on the way to Tyburn
(it came to nothing) and again after his body was cut down from the
gallows. 'The giddy multitude' protected his body from the surgeons and
then 'for the purpose of riot and misapplied revenge' carried it across
London to Spitalfields and Mrs White's house in Lamb Street. 'Great
numbers of people assembled', forced open her door, carried out all her
furniture and all her salmon tubs, and burnt them in the street before her
house. A guard of soldiers was called; but 'to prevent the guards from
extinguishing the flames, the populace pelted them with stones, and would
not disperse till the whole was consumed'.[1]

Similar episodes occurred in subsequent years. In 1764 a mob attempted
to burn down the house of the prosecutor of John Dixon, a sailor found
guilty of petty thievery. In 1774 the friends of two street robbers saved
their bodies from the surgeons and ran riot against the prosecutor's
house.[2] Those like Betty the Cook, Mary Green, Lot Cavenagh and
William Stevens who threatened to haunt the living were not perhaps able
to tap the wells of community feeling which brought out the men and
women of Spitalfields and the Minories against the prosecutors of
Cornelius Saunders and John Dixon. If the difference between efficacious
social action and superstition needs no emphasis, we should note that their
social functions in these cases were identical. Both the mobbing of prose-

1. The Ordinary's *Account*, 24 August 1763; *The Proceedings*, 6–11 July 1763;
Gentleman's Magazine, August 1763; *Berrow's Weekly Journal*, 1 September 1763;
*A Collection of Prints, Broadsheets, and Biographies Relating to Criminals Executed at
Tyburn*, London Museum, L52.1.
2. The Ordinary's *Account*, 11 June 1764; *The Proceedings*, part ii, 2–7 May 1764;
Berrow's Worcester Journal, 14 June 1764; *Gentleman's Magazine*, December 1774; and
Annual Register, December 1774; in this section I have found suggestive Keith Thomas,
Religion and the Decline of Magic, 1971, pp. 597–606.

cutors and the belief in ghosts were designed to bring 'bad fame' upon the prosecutor, to terrify the prosecutor to the end of her days, and to deter others from hanging a person for a trifling offence. No doubt in some circumstances it may have been as difficult to live with the public curse of a dying man as to rebuild a razed house.

No evidence has come to light to show that the Tyburn crowd thought that somehow the dissection of felons impaired the specific powers of the spirits of the dead to return to the living. However, a belief in life after death, especially in the forms which we have described, was connected with beliefs about justice, the law and the value of life. In these cases therefore the added humiliation of the surgeon's scalpel to the hangman's noose rendered the injustice of the law all the more loathsome.

Despite regional and class differences a single rule may be said to have governed the folklore, ritual and superstition surrounding death and burial; meticulous attention to the proper forms of burial was required to ensure the peaceful departure of the dead. When death was violent and moreover willed by society, as in deaths by hanging, something of a corollary to this rule existed. Believing that the corpse possessed thera-peutic powers, able to cure sickness and heal wounds, it appeared that even this most terrible of society's sanctions against wrongdoers was qualified in popular belief by the ability of the corpse to confer by magic some marvellous sign of health to society. In Dorset it was believed that touching the corpse of the hanged person would cure common skin com-plaints. A withered limb could be made whole by placing it upon the neck of a recently hanged man. It was believed in Somerset that any swelling would disperse by touching it with the dead hand of a man who had been publicly hanged. In the north of England a splinter from the gallows was thought to be a cure for the toothache. In Norfolk it was thought that the dead hand of the executed felon had the power to cure goitre or a bleeding tumour if applied to the affected part. In Wessex it was thought that ulcers and cancerous growths could be similarly cured. In the same place it was reported that sterile women went secretly to the gallows to be stroked by the dead hand in order to become fruitful.[1]

Similar beliefs were common in London. Nurses brought children to the gallows to be stroked by the hands of executed criminals as a general guarantee of good health. 'A Halter, wherewith anyone has been hanged, if tied about the Head, will cure the Headache' was another view. Wood chippings from the gallows worn in a bag around the neck were said to be

---

1. J. S. Udal, *Dorsetshire Folk-Lore*, 2nd edn, 1970, p. 186; Robert Hunt, *Popular Romances of the West of England*, 2nd edn, 1871, p. 378; William Henderson, *Notes on the Folk-Lore of the Northern Counties of England and the Borders*, 1879, p. 145; and Elizabeth Mary White, *Rustic Speech and Folk-Lore*, Oxford, 1913, p. 59.

an effective cure against the ague. John Morris, hanged in 1739 for robbing the Reading wagon, had his jawbone shot off during an earlier highway robbery. He saved the pieces and before he was hanged he distributed
them to the prisoners in Newgate as a token or charm. In 1767 a young
woman 'with a wen upon her neck was lifted up [to the gallows] and had
the wen rubbed with the dead man's hands'. In 1777 when Dr Dodd was
hanged 'a very decently dressed young Woman went up to the gallows in
order to have a Wen in her face stroked by the Doctor's hand; it being a
received opinion among the Vulgar that it is a certain Cure for such a
Disorder'.[1] Visitors to London remarked on these practices with as much
surprise as did later antiquarians. Meister, writing in 1789 about his tour in
England, 'remarked a young woman, with an appearance of beauty, all
pale and trembling, in the arms of the executioner, who submitted to have
her bosom uncovered, in the presence of thousands of spectators, and the
dead man's hand placed upon it'.[2] Twelve years earlier a French visitor
recorded, 'Des femmes crédules touchent la corde d'un ou deux pendus
croyant de se guérir de l'épilépcie ou de quelques autres maladies aussi
grandes.'[3] At a time when the monarchs of England allowed their thauma-
turgical powers to lapse and no longer 'touched' those inflicted with
scrofula, the 'death sweat' of executed malefactors was still held to possess
the power to cure this disease, 'the king's evil'. Just before the coal-
heaver, Murphy, 'was cut down at Tyburn a well dressed woman with a
child about three years old in her arms, was permitted to pass up to the
gallows, where she took the right hand of Murphy then hanging, and
stroked it thrice over the child's left hand, which had four holes in it with
the King's Evil'.[4]

The full significance of these gallows superstitions cannot be assessed
without a greater knowledge than we now possess; nevertheless, the
difference between them and surgical dissection is plain: where one
honours the powers of the felon's corpse, the other humiliates it. When
Mandeville defended the dissection of felons because it allows them to
'make a useful restitution to the Publick', he might with more justice have
described these superstitions, for it is in them that the living acknowledged

1. John Brand, *Observations on Popular Antiquities*, 2nd edn, 1813, vol. II, pp. 582–5;
The Ordinary's *Account*, 21 December 1739; *Gentleman's Magazine*, May 1767.

2. J. H. Meister, *Letters written during a Residence in England*, translated from the
French, 1799, p. 62.

3. F. Lacombe, *Observations sur Londres et ses Environs*, 1777, p. 186.

4. *Westminster Journal*, 11 July 1768. This aspect of the secularization of royal
authority in England is discussed in Marc Bloch, *Les Rois Thaumaturges* (Paris, 1924)
passim. For further instances of the healing powers at the execution see Gerald D.
Robin, 'The Executioner: His Place in English Society', *British Journal of Sociology*,
vol. XV (1964), pp. 234–53.

the special powers of those extirpated by the law. It is as though these beliefs were sustained by another; namely, that those killed by the community through its own sanctions should by virtue of their extraordinary death be given an extraordinary opportunity of bestowing some beneficence on the health of the living. The belief seems to appear again at another hanging custom, that of the 'gallows' wedding'.

The ceremonies, the customs, the traditional behaviour of the condemned malefactor on his procession from the condemned cells in Newgate through the metropolis to the final exit at Tyburn have been the subject of many descriptions in books of 'popular antiquities' and those representing an older kind of 'social' history.[1] The bell-ringing at St Sepulchre's, the nosegays tossed from the balconies to the prisoners on their last journey, the apparent rules of precedence in the tumbrils, are examples of details which, culled from the descriptions of different hangings, are used to evoke a composite picture deprived of any significance except curiosity in the quaint. As the evidence about gallows' customs is so meagre, the temptation to draw such a composite picture is great; but it is one that must be resisted in order to isolate those details which provide, however incompletely, some clues to the unelaborated beliefs about death of those hanged and of those witnessing the hanging.

The two-thousand-word article on the word 'gallows' in Wright's *English Dialect Dictionary* gives it eleven main meanings, at least three of which refer to various attitudes of behaviour – saucy, wild, mischievous, wanton – which have no connotations of wickedness. One of these denotes 'smart in appearance', a meaning which undoubtedly derived from the felon's great care (at many eighteenth-century hangings) to appear well dressed or 'flash' at his hanging. Nathaniel Hawes had a fine suit of clothes stolen in the days before he was to stand trial in 1721; 'unless they are returned,' he said, 'I will not plead for no one shall say that I was hanged in a dirty shirt and ragged coat.' The punishment, peine forte et dure, was applied: 250 pounds of weights were piled on his chest to force him to plead. He was found guilty and died in rags.[2] In 1753 Richard Broughton and James Hayes, two Irish highway robbers, refused to enter the tumbril at Newgate 'without a clean Shirt and Stockings to be hanged in'.[3] The friends of Russell Parnel gave him his proper dress in order to prevent him from confessing their part in his crimes.[4]

1. For example, John Laurence, *A History of Capital Punishment*, 1932; Gilbert Armitage, *The History of the Bow Street Runners*, 1932; Alfred Marks, *Tyburn Tree*, 1908; Christopher Hibbert, *The Roots of Evil: A Social History of Crime and Punishment*, 1963; and Patrick Pringle, *Hue and Cry: The Birth of the British Police*, 1955.

2. Arthur Griffiths, *The Chronicles of Newgate*, 1884, vol. I, p. 253.

3. *The Ordinary's Account*, 23 March 1753; *British Weekly Journal*, 26 March 1753.

4. *The Ordinary's Account*, 13 January 1752.

English and foreign visitors at Tyburn were struck by the fact that the condemned malefactors treated the days of their hanging as a wedding. 'He that is to be hang'd or otherwise executed,' wrote a Swiss visitor, 'first takes Care to get himself shav'd, and handsomely drest either in Mourning or in the Dress of a Bridegroom.' Defoe wrote that criminals 'go to [their] execution as neat and trim as if they were going to a Wedding.'[1] As has been mentioned, by the end of the century the hanging day was generally known as the 'hanging-match'. 'To be noozed' in canting talk meant either to be hanged or to be married. The guillotine in Halifax was called the 'maiden'. Suggestions of marriage often appeared in the dress of those to be hanged. Three smugglers of the Hawkhurst gang all dressed in white. Paul Lewis in 1763 went to his hanging in a white cloth coat, silver laced hat, white stockings and white silk breeches. George Anderson was hanged for stealing eight shillings' worth of silk ribbon. Both his wife and mistress were in Newgate on the day of his hanging. He wore a white linen waistcoat and breeches trimmed with black ferret. Henry Simms, 'Gentlemen Harry', was a hackney coachman and 'as famous a Thief as ever yet adorn'd the Gallows'. He hanged for stealing a silver watch. At his execution he was 'cleanly dress'd in a White Fustian Frock, White Stockings, and White Drawers'. At the age of twelve John Redmond went to sea. At the age of seventeen he went to Tyburn. He had written his aunt and uncle 'desiring they would sent him some white cloaths to appear in on the morning he was to suffer'. In the ballad, Mary Hamilton goes to her hanging in 'robes of white'.[2]

Others hanged at Tyburn made the comparison between a hanging and a wedding explicit. When John Weskett was hanged for stealing a gold repeating watch and three gold snuff-boxes from his master, the Earl of Harrington, he wore a white ribbon in his hat because, as he explained, 'I believe I am come to an untimely End, in order that my Soul might be saved; and I look upon this as my Wedding-Day.' Thomas Reynolds, an Irishman whose patron fell at Culloden, 'went to be hanged with as much Satisfaction as if he was going to be married'. Lawrence, the fourth Earl of Ferrers, was hanged for murdering his steward. He prepared for his hanging by dressing in his 'white wedding clothes, which were of a light colour, embroidered in silver, and he said he thought this, at least, as good an occasion of putting them on as that for which they were first made'. The combination of the nuptial clothing of the hanged felon with the

1. M. Misson, *Memoirs and Observations in his Travels over England*, 1719, p. 124; and Daniel Defoe, *Street Robberies Considered*, 1728, pp. 52–4.

2. *Remembrancer*, 29 April 1749; *Berrow's Worcester Journal*, 12 May 1763; The Ordinary's *Account*, 17 June 1747; ibid., 7 November 1750; ibid., 11 June 1764.

undercurrents of sexuality among the crowd at Tyburn opens Swift's ballad, 'Clever Tom Clinch Going to be Hanged':

> As clever Tom Clinch, while the Rabble was bawling,
> Rode stately through Holbourn to die in his Calling;
> He stopt at the George for a Bottle of Sack,
> And promis'd to pay for it when he'd come back.
> His Waistcoat and Stockings, and Breeches were white,
> His Cap had a new Cherry Ribbon to ty't.
> The Maids to the Doors and the Balconies ran,
> And said, lack-a-day! he's a proper young Man.
> But, as from the Windows the Ladies he spy'd,
> Like a Beau in the Box, he bow'd low on each Side.[1]

The only other kind of death which in the eighteenth century was treated as a type of wedding was the premature death of a virgin or childless woman. From reports of funeral customs from all over the country we know that the corpse was often dressed in white, that the pall-bearers were young women, and that white gloves, white bonnets, white silk shawls, scarfs and sashes were customarily worn. The white gloves appear again at Tyburn: 'on voit les criminels traverser la ville sur des charettes, parés de leur plus beaux habits, avec des gants blancs et des bouquets,' a French traveller noted.[2] And again in a ballad fragment that Francis Place recorded,

> Through the streets as our wheels slowly move
>   The toll of the death bell dismays us,
> With nosegays and gloves we are deck'd,
>   So trim and so gay they array us,
> The passage all crowded we see,
>   With maidens that move us with pity;
> Our air all admiring agree
>   Such lads are not left in the City.[3]

The particular tragedy of the death of a virgin was felt by the living in the loss not only of one life but in the loss of a future generation, in the failure of that life to reproduce itself. Consequently, the funeral marking such a death pays particular attention to that fact by extensive borrowings from wedding customs: the final rite of passage combines in itself customs

1. The Ordinary's *Account*, 11 June 1764; ibid., 7 November 1750; *The Life and Times of Selina Countess of Huntingdon*, vol. I, 1839, pp. 401–8; Harold Williams, ed., *The Poems of Jonathan Swift*, Oxford, 1937, vol. II, p. 399.

2. J. C. Atkinson, *Forty Years in a Moorland Parish*, 1891, p. 230; Mrs Gutch, ed., *Examples of Printed Folk-Lore concerning the East Riding of Yorkshire*, 1912, p. 136; Sidney Oldall Addy, *Household Tales with other Traditional Remains Collected in the Counties of York, Lincoln, Derby, and Nottingham*, 1895, p. 125.

3. Brit. Mus. Add. MSS, 27,825, fo. 155.

belonging to those that have not been carried out because of the untimely death. At Ophelia's funeral, she is 'allow'd her virgin crants,/Her maiden strewments'. Whether a similar sense of particular loss at the death of the condemned (who were usually in the full prime of manhood) was responsible for the marriage-like practices at some hangings would remain a matter of the imagination were it not for the survival of an unusual belief.

In 1602 John Manningham recorded in his diary, 'It is the custome (not the lawe) in Fraunce and Italy that yf anie notorious professed strumpet will begg for a husban a man which is going to execution, he shal be repreived, and she may obteine a pardon, and marry him . . . In England it hath bin vsed that yf a woman will beg a condemned person for her husband shee must come in his smocke onely, and a white rod in hir hand. . .'[1] This was certainly not customary practice at hangings in eighteenth-century Tyburn, although several acted as though it were. Eighteen maidens dressed in white petitioned the King to spare the life of Edward Skelton, condemned in 1686, on condition that one of them would marry him. In May 1722 John Hartley, called 'Pokey', was hanged. He was born in Shoreditch, schooled at the White Cross free school, and earned a living by serving the Honey Lane and Smithfield butchers and by robbing in the streets. His prosecutor refused to settle out of court or to reduce the charges ('he made his brags that he'd hang six of them, and get the money allow'd for taking them'). It was reported that 'seven young Women from that Neighbourhood [Honey Lane] having dressed themselves in White, and carrying white Wands in their Hands, went up to St. James's and presented a Petition to beg his Life; which if obtain'ed, one of them was to marry him under the Gallows'. In Newgate 'Pokey' 'much desired that the six Maidens . . . might be successful in their Undertakings'. They were not and he was hanged.[2] Three years later John Eades, a nineteen-year-old boy from Southwark, was condemned. 'A Great many young Women in White' petitioned the King that he should be repreived and sentenced to transportation, so that 'his Aged Father now in the Evening of his Days may not carry his Grey Hairs with Sorrow to the Grave'.[3] In 1749 another John Hartley and his comrade John South were condemned at a court martial for desertion and enlistment in the French service during the previous war. 'South's Sisters, who live in the Strand, with the intended Spouse of Hartley, and four other Maidens dress'd in White, with great Humility waited on his Majesty and others of the Royal Family with a Petition in Behalf of the Deceased.'

1. *Notes and Queries*, 4th series, vol. IV (1869), p. 417.
2. The Ordinary's *Account*, 4 May 1722, and *The Proceedings*, 4–6 April 1722; *Weekly Journal or Saturday Post*, 5 May 1722.
3. PRO, SP 44/81 (*Entry Books*), fo. 407, and SP 44/253, fo. 527.

It was unsuccessful, and with the full regiment out and drums beating Hartley and South were shot on Constitution Hill.[1]

These cases remind us that the treatment of the hanging as a wedding (even when the king's mercy no longer encompassed this ancient custom) was not entirely symbolic. In most cases, however, not even the faint hope of a gallows' wedding was present; and the 'flash' clothes signified anticipation of divine union or a proclamation of innocence before God and the Sheriffs. In other cases they perhaps indicated a flaunting, ostentatious display of opposition to the severities of the law and the austerities of prison. In the case of some of those hanged the nuptial clothing recalls the violent experience of conversion described by the early Methodists. Charles Wesley, John's brother, preached at a Wapping hanging, 'Well is the Spirit compared to a mighty rushing wind: we heard the sound of it now, and the flame was kindled. Many felt the pangs of the new birth. Behold, a cry; "The Bridegroom Cometh".'[2]

The possibilities of resuscitation after hanging, the widespread belief in the therapeutic powers of the malefactor's corpse, the view that the spirit of the dead could return to the living, and the treatment of a hanging as a wedding were some of the attitudes to death present among both the condemned and the Tyburn crowd. Suggesting as they do the complexity of plebeian conceptions of death and the gravity with which the fact of death was held, they contrast with the views presented by the surgeons and their advocates who mixed arguments of medical utility, traditional prerogative and penal retribution with attitudes of class hatred. In part they explain the hostility to the surgeons.

After all the complexities have been suggested (which perhaps can never be fully uncovered) we must finally return to what we most often find expressed by the condemned themselves: the simple, direct desire for a decent Christian burial, with its concern for order, propriety and the peaceful translation of the soul from this life to the next. Hanging removed a man by violence from this life. At least his soul should be allowed to enter the next in peace. This perhaps was the reason that Martin Gray 'was greatly frightened' by the thought of dissection. Sarah Wilmshurst wanted to be 'decently interr'd in a Christian Manner'. Thomas Pinks wanted 'Christian Burial'. Lot Cavenagh threatened his friends to make them do 'that THING' to save him from the surgeons'. Charles Connor

---

1. *Remembrancer*, 19 August 1749; *Worcester Journal*, 17 August 1749; PRO, WO 71/20 (*Court Martial Proceedings*), fos. 164–72. For some other cases of this practice see Hyder Edward Rollins, ed., *The Pepys Ballads*, Cambridge, Massachusetts, 1931, vol. III, pp. 248–54, and Narcissus Luttrell, *A Brief Historical Relation of State Affairs from September 1678 to April 1714*, Oxford, 1857, p. 168.

2. Charles Wesley, *The Journal*, 1849, vol. I, p. 215.

said he wanted 'to lay by my Wife'. Richard Tobin begged his master for 'A Coffin and a Shroud'. Hundreds of men and women rallied at Tyburn to provide the condemned with this last mark of humanity. The arguments of scientific utility that Mandeville directed to 'Men of Business' were never presented to those beneath the gallows who performed only what was decent, like Joseph of Arimathaea. 'The Hanging Song' (the Fifty-first Psalm) which the condemned and crowd alike sang at the gallows stressed the sacrificial aspect of the execution and enjoined them, 'Do good in thy good pleasure unto Zion: build thou the walls of Jerusalem.'

VI

One historian of the eighteenth century wrongly concluded (perhaps from the evidence of mortality rates) that 'a callous attitude to life induced an indifference to death'.[1] We have seen that the proper, respectful treatment of the dead was a profound and serious concern to the crowds attending Tyburn hangings. Why, with death so frequent, should this have been so? In general terms we can offer some suggestions.

The relation of age-specific mortality rates to the dominant social relations of production and family organization gave to death a far greater significance to the living than it has in our own time. So important is death to such types of societies that its effects upon the living have been called a 'death crisis'. When death strikes young, while men and women are fully engaged in family life and when the family as such performs a critical role in the social division of labour, a social vacuum is created whose effect was not one of sentimental loss only, but of deep moral and material consequence. More than three quarters of those hanged at Tyburn were between the ages of twenty and thirty. They died when the men were at the height of their strength and the women most fertile. This combination of broadly dispersed age-specific mortality and small productive units (often family-based) which characterized the life of the eighteenth-century London labouring poor provided the circumstances which made death such a shock to the social relations of the living. The violence of that shock was formalized and to a degree assuaged by an elaboration of funeral rites, burial customs and beliefs about death which, to an age like ours accustomed to the concealment of death and the privatization of bereavement, appear as bad taste or as superstition.[2] To

1. J. H. Plumb, *The First Four Georges*, 1957, p. 20.
2. These suggestions owe much to Robert Blauner, 'Death and the Social Structure', *Psychiatry*, vol. XXIX, 4 (November 1966), pp. 378–94.

the crisis that a death brought to the living was visited the additional ignominy of the law. The formalized customs of bereavement, depending as they often did upon the integrity of the corpse and the respect shown to it, were brutally violated by the practice of dissection. To the surgeons, their spokesmen, and the lords and squires sitting in Parliament, not only was humiliation at the death of one of the 'Scum of the People' a passing matter, but such further 'Marks of Infamy' as public dissection became a part of the policy of class discipline. Against that policy, with its shame and its disgrace, the men and women beneath the gallows' tree had to fight to provide decency for the dead and, like Antigone, to restore peace to the living in the bitterness of their loss.

Sussex Smugglers

I

Between 1740 and 1750 there was, in the words of Charles Fleet, an early historian of Sussex smuggling, '. . . a guerrilla war between the smugglers of Sussex and Kent and the officers of the government . . .' This war, he wrote, was marked by 'an organized resistance to the government, in which towns were besieged, battles fought, Customs Houses burnt down, and the greatest atrocities committed'. Fleet attributed this conflict, in particular its violence, to the class of smuggler involved. The smuggling of wool, the traditional commodity of Sussex smugglers, had been the custom, he believed, of 'men of substance, the landowners and farmers'. But, with the development of the illicit trade in tea, a 'lower class' of smuggler had come to predominate, and in the activities of these smugglers, a 'brutality showed itself'.[1]

Fleet's account of the class differences in smuggling was not strictly correct. There were 'men of substance' in the tea trade, just as there had been plebeian 'owlers', the contemporary name for wool-smugglers. Nevertheless, in the 1740s the authorities seemed especially preoccupied with the business of the 'poor' smugglers. Fleet's description of the 'guerrilla war' was right on the mark. And no visitor to eighteenth-century Sussex could overlook the bloody conflict. Daniel Defoe, touring the Sussex coast, 'perceived several dragoons, riding officers, and others armed and on horseback, riding always about as if they were huntsmen beating up their game. . .'[2] Some years later, Horace Walpole, travelling one night from Tunbridge to Battle, encountered armed camps of both smugglers and excise men, but 'as we were neutral powers, we passed

1. Charles Fleet, *Glimpses of Our Sussex Ancestors*, Lewes, 1878, vol. I, pp. 74–5.
2. Daniel Defoe, *A Tour Through the Whole Island of Great Britain*, Harmondsworth, 1971, p. 139.

safely through both armies'.[1] The conflict was widespread indeed, and often it was much like a war. In the violence that accompanied it, there was no shortage of brutality, though this was certainly not confined to the smugglers. In the last years of the 1740s alone, dozens of smugglers were hanged, while others were transported or sent to rot in the squalor of England's prisons.

Smuggling, of course, was not limited to Sussex, and neither was the conflict it produced. On one occasion, revenue officers in Cornwall, seeing a number of casks lying on the sand, turned their cutter towards the beach, only to have 'some shot ... fired at it from a battery on the shore...'[2] In Scotland in 1736, the execution of a well-known smuggler precipitated the famous Porteous riots in Edinburgh.[3]

Events such as these, when smuggling involved riot and the 'mob', inevitably led to the association of smuggling with the 'lower class' and the crimes were usually attributed to the poor. And while smuggling always remained something unique, it was commonly linked with other offences, primarily poaching and theft, but also with the crimes of protest, riot and forms of collective or popular action.[4] In 1734, for example, a Kentish Customs officer and six soldiers seized five hundredweight of tea and carried it to a public house in the parish of Sundbridge. But there 'they were followed by a great number of armed men who in a tumultuous and riotous manner threatened to pull down the house and to fire in upon the officers and the soldiers...'[5] And two years later, one of Sir Robert Walpole's informants wrote to him of the agitation against the Gin Act: 'It is evident that there are great disorders and murmurings throughout the mobbish part of town. The Gin Act and the Smuggling Act strike hard in the stomachs of the meaner sort of people...'[6] The result was

1. Quoted in Neville Williams, *Contraband Cargoes*, 1959, p. 120.
2. PRO, HO 42/20, 16 June 1792.
3. Newcastle Papers, Brit. Mus. Add. MSS, 33,049, fos. 17–117. For a recent reassessment, see H. T. Dickinson and K. Logue, 'The Porteus Riot, 1736', *History Today*, vol. XXII, no. 4, April 1972, pp. 272–81.
4. Critics of smuggling had no difficulty establishing the connection with other forms of crime. Dick Turpin, the famous highwayman, after an apprenticeship as a butcher, was first a smuggler and then a member of an Essex gang of house-breakers, before taking to the highway; see Christopher Hibbert, *Highwaymen*, 1967, p. 49. One Hawkhurst smuggler testified in 1747 that he had been sent by his master, a smuggler as well, '... to rob all the fish ponds round for several miles, that he had several men to assist him, and that they used to carry their fire-arms'. He also said that by these means his master had a 'vast quantity of fish brought him as well as fowls, hares, and venison, and that it was often impossible to eat it before it stunck'. John Taylor, *The Ordinary of Newgate*, 1747, pp. 30–31.
5. C(H) MSS 41/59.
6. ibid., 70/14; see also George Rudé, ' "Mother Gin" and the London Riots of 1736', in Rudé, *Paris and London in the 18th Century*, 1970, pp. 201–21.

that, as their trade and numbers grew, smugglers increasingly found their crimes adding to the swelling list of capital offences designed to protect the property and order of Georgian England.

The specific events which Charles Fleet called 'a guerrilla war' were possibly the most extraordinary chapter in the entire history of smuggling. And they provide exceptional material for a case study in social history, particularly of those people who smuggled. For while recent historical research has done something to establish the importance of smuggling in the development of commercial capitalism, knowledge of the smugglers themselves remains minimal. Though tens of thousands of people were involved, very little of them is known. Consequently smuggling has generally been left out of social history, and, unfortunately, out of the traditions of resistance, carried on by the poor, to the laws and institutions of their rulers. There have been exceptions, of course. Smugglers have at times been seen as a part of this resistance. But even here, they have been seen only on the fringe of the crowd, as, for example, when George Rudé, in *The Crowd in History*, writes that 'attempts to impose excise and to stop smuggling met with staunch resistance. . .' Rudé pointed to the hanging of Captain Porteous, but then concluded that 'such physical violence [was] quite exceptional'.[1] This is inexplicable, at least as a reference to smuggling. By placing smugglers in a more prominent position, we may correct the misconception (advanced by Mingay and others) that in the eighteenth century 'serious crime in the countryside was generally infrequent'.[2]

The best evidence for this period arises from several particularly brutal murders, and from the efforts of the authorities to capture and convict those responsible. Led personally by the Duke of Richmond, local and national authorities combined in an attempt to suppress the illicit trade once and for all, and in so doing they unleashed nothing less than a reign of terror on the smuggling communities of the south coast. Elaborate trials of dozens of smugglers were held at East Grinstead, Lewes and the Old Bailey, in addition to a Special Commission held at Chichester. These events provide a framework within which to begin the study of smuggling in Sussex.

II

John Collier was Surveyor-General of the Customs for Kent. In addition, he was the Duke of Newcastle's agent in East Sussex. His letter, written

1. George Rudé, *The Crowd in History*, New York, 1964, p. 35.
2. G. E. Mingay, *English Landed Society in the Eighteenth Century*, 1963, p. 252.

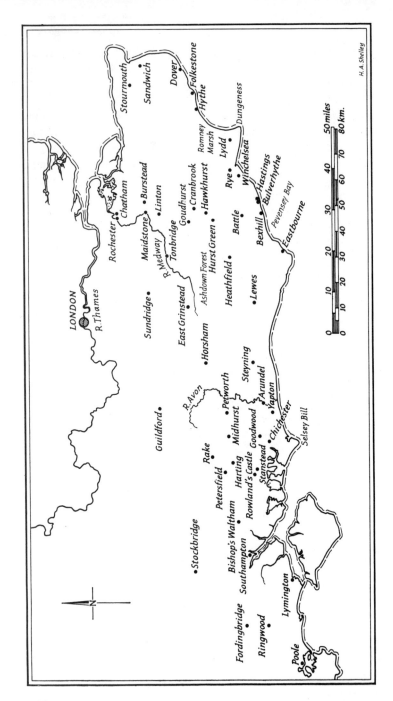

H.A. Shelley

LONDON

R. Thames
R. Thames

Rochester
Chatham
Stourmouth
Sandwich
Dover
Folkestone
Hythe
Dungeness
Romney Marsh
Lydd
Winchelsea
Hastings
Bulverhythe
Pevensey Bay
Eastbourne
Bexhill
Battle
Rye
Hawkhurst
Cranbrook
Goudhurst
Hurst Green
Ashdown Forest
Linton
Bursted
Maidstone
R. Medway
Tonbridge
Heathfield
Lewes
East Grinstead
Sundridge
Horsham
Guildford
R. Avon
Petworth
Steyning
Midhurst
Arundel
Goodwood
Yapton
Chichester
Selsey Bill
Rake
Harting
Petersfield
Stansted
Rowland's Castle
Stockbridge
Bishop's Waltham
Southampton
Fordingbridge
Ringwood
Lymington
Poole

N

50 miles
80 km.
40
30
70
60
50
40
30
20
10
20
30
20
10
0
0
10

on 11 December 1744 to Henry Simon, the Solicitor to the Commissioners of the Customs in London, provides a good introduction to smuggling in Sussex:

The smugglers are got to an amazing height on the Kentish and Sussex coasts, that it has for some time become a very serious thing, and highly worthy the consideration of the Senate, in regard to the vast quantities of goods clandestinely imported, and in a triumphant manner, and the insults, menaces, and abuses given not only to the Officers of the Revenue, but to any other persons that offer to speak against their detestable practices. The civil magistrates fully decline putting the laws in execution against them.

Perhaps Collier exaggerated, but probably not. He lived and worked in Hastings, and knew the world of smuggling well.

At any rate, Simon apparently shared Collier's concern, for his response, written four days later, expressed similar fear:

The insolence and outrageous behaviour of the smugglers in your parts has been, in my judgement, a public concern for some time, and calls loudly for a parliamentary redress. They are a standing army of desperadoes, who must pay themselves, and can subsist by no other means but public rapine and plunder, and if they cannot be broke, shut up Westminster Hall, and disband all your Officers of Justice as an expensive but useless incumbrance on the nation. I doubt not but that the terrour which they spread round your country makes Sussex a scene of horrour and confusion.[1]

Simon may have been carried away by his own pen here, but these views were held by many in the south-east.

Parliament did respond. The following year a hearing conducted by the Committee on Smuggling was held, the purpose of which was to 'enquire into the causes of the most infamous practice of smuggling and consider the most effectual methods to prevent the said practices'. The Committee's report told a great deal about the scope of smuggling.

Among the many witnesses was a Mr Samuel Wilson, a grocer, who formerly concerned himself in the running of tea. He testified that:

the vessels employed in running of goods do most of them belong to the subjects of this Kingdom, and are generally Folkestone cutters, from 15 to 40 tons burden; and that some are sent by the French and Dutch from Boulogne and Middleborough [Middelburg]: that these vessels are met, three or four miles from our coasts, by boats, which bring the goods ashore; and before the present act, he believes 20 or 30 cargoes were run in a week: that the smugglers buy their goods abroad with money, or wool; and that the principal commodity is tea.

1. East Sussex RO, Sayers MSS, 3871.

(*Opposite*) The South Coast, 1740–50

123

These smugglers, according to Wilson:

assemble together at Ports and places the most convenient for their purpose, particularly at Folkestone, where there is a great number; but their chief place of report is Hawkhurst in Kent: that they go armed; and although they are well known, people dare not venture to molest any of them; and if the soldiers are ordered to take them, they [the smugglers] have intelligence either from their agents, or perhaps from their relations or friends.

Another witness, Mr Abraham Walter, was a 'Dealer in Tea' who had also been a smuggler. He supported Wilson's estimate that there were more than 20,000 smugglers by trade, and added that:

it is extremely dangerous for Custom House Officers, or others, to attempt to seize goods in the coast counties; because smugglers are very numerous there, and can assemble to a great number whenever they have occasion; and that in particular at the village of Hawkhurst, Kent, 500 can get together, armed, in less than an hour: that not one person in ten in the country but would give them assistance, and do lend the smugglers their horses and teams to convey their goods. . .[1]

The Sussex coast was, of course, well placed for smuggling. Nathaniel Pigram, the Commander of the Customs sloop at Rye, wrote to the Duke of Newcastle in 1741, complaining that 'this station [Rye] is the most dangerous of any in England . . .'[2] Its long coastline was not heavily populated, it was often marshy, and it was both near London and yet remote, because of the notoriously muddy and dark Sussex lanes. Hawkhurst, easily the most famous of the smuggling villages in the 1740s, sat in the wooded hills on the south side of the Weald of Kent, adjacent to the main roads to London from both Hastings and Rye. With a strategic position and adventurous inhabitants, it was ideal for smuggling, but there were many villages like it. For the scale of eighteenth-century smuggling was immense. The witnesses to the Parliamentary Committee estimated that more than 3,000,000 pounds of tea were annually imported illegally in the years before Henry Pelham's reforms

1. *CJ*, vol. XXV (1745–50), pp. 101–5.
2. Brit. Mus. Add. MSS 32,697, fo. 19. Pigram went on to say that without a larger vessel 'it seems impossible to oppose the smugglers, which I occasioned to be transported and are returned again for which large rewards are offered for apprehending but as yet nobody has attempted to take them, they having a larger vessel well-armed and more men than these small sloops so they continue trading on this coast unmolested. . .' Pigram is referring to the group of smugglers often known as the Hastings Outlaws or the Transports, led by John Grayling. They were sentenced to seven years' transportation at the Winter Assizes in East Grinstead, 1737–8, but they returned and were prominent in the smuggling of the 1740s.

of 1745. That was more than three times the amount 'fairly' imported.[1]

The smuggled tea originally came from China; it was carried by ship to Europe. Most of the Sussex trade was with the Channel ports of France. Some Sussex smugglers went to Ostend and Holland, but most of the goods from the Northern European countries were smuggled across the North Sea, from Suffolk to Scotland. Generally English ships carried the tea and spirits across the Channel. One English merchant, 'having been several years at Boulogne in France', described the illegal brandy trade of that port in an anonymous report to Robert Walpole. 'The smugglers,' he wrote, 'which chiefly frequent this port are from Sussex and Kent.' 'I have observed,' he continued, 'in this harbour, many times from 10 to 18 smugglers. And I am informed, particularly from the houses that the smugglers lodge in, that they've many times brought in 3000 guineas in one week. . .'[2]

Wool was sometimes used in place of money, the export of English wool having long been outlawed. Richard Winter, a smuggler turned informer, told a Justice of the Peace that he:

two days after the first Green Fair, together with one John Allen of West Dean in Sussex, shopkeeper, Thomas Asten, farmer, Edward Edwards, alias Tall Boy, of Fiddlesworth, and a person called Jack-Come-Last of Burdshold in Clacton in Sussex bought of several persons in and about Fiddlesworth twelve packs of wool and packed up the same in order to send it to France, and in about a week's time after it was bought, they carried it from Fiddlesworth on a wagon to a wood near Hidower Mill in Sussex, where it lay for a week, then they carried it to Worthing and put it on board a boat which lay among the fishing boats, and John-Come-Last went with the wool to France and sold the same for £13 a pack. . .[3]

With the money received for the wool, tea or brandy could be purchased and brought back to Sussex.

Most of the time, however, smuggling seems to have been divided between those who carried the contraband goods across the water and those who received them on the shore. Small sloops, cutters and luggers would carry the tea, for instance, directly from France, or transfer it from larger ships in the Channel. Sometimes the tea was taken directly off British East Indiamen. On the shore, land smugglers would watch for a signal. Nicholas Hixon, a husbandman from Wickham in Southampton, testified that he saw 'near Steyning in the county of Sussex in company about seven or eight smugglers armed with fire-arms . . . looking out for

1. *CJ*, vol. xxv (1745–50), pp. 104–5.
2. C (H) MSS 41/35.
3. West Sussex RO, Goodwood MSS, 156/G 4.

a ship or cutter they expected there . . . intending to run goods. . . They waited on the sea coast at least four days for this purpose. . .' Hixon also testified that he bought tea from one of these smugglers, a William Cripps of Joe's Field near Steyning, '. . . at one time four bags containing one hundred and six pounds of run tea and at another time two bags containing fifty-three pounds of run tea. . .'[1] In the 1740s, smuggling in Sussex was still the business of provincial shopkeepers and smugglers. Contraband tea passed through many hands – the smuggler, the dealer, the innkeeper – generally remaining near where it was landed. It was only later in the century that smuggling became the business of the real 'men of substance', the London merchants.[2]

Nevertheless, in Sussex smuggling was becoming 'big business', particularly through the activities of the large gangs. Usually boats were unloaded at night, but as the trade increased this modesty was often foregone, as Samuel Grey, the Secretary to the Commissioners of the Excise, reported from Lydd in Romney Marsh:

> The smugglers pass and repass to and from the sea-side, forty and fifty in a gang in the day time loaded with teas, brandy and dry goods; that above two hundred mounted smugglers were seen one night upon the sea beach there waiting for the loading of six boats and above one hundred were seen to go off loaded with goods; that they march in a body from the beach about four miles into the country and then separate into small parties. . .[3]

These parties often went to London, where 'the run tea [was] . . . put into warehouses, under the care of agents'.[4] Stockwell, the 'smugglers' den' in Lambeth, was the chief depot of goods from Sussex. Mr Barnaby Bland, a Customs officer who testified before the Committee on Smuggling, reported that the smugglers 'came to London about two or three in the morning, and could sell to particular dealers from 1,000 to 2,000 pounds-weight, and be out of town again by six in the morning; and, by this quick return, they generally made a voyage every ten days. . .'[5] Or the smugglers might stay the night at places like the Nag's Head Inn, in Leather Lane, Holborn. This inn, according to Uriah Creed, a Hawkhurst smuggler, 'was at that time, a place of resort for the smugglers. When they had any goods to bring to town, there they generally first lodged,

1. ibid., G 18.

2. H. and L. Mui, 'Smuggling and the British Tea Trade', *American Historical Review*, vol. LXXIV (October 1968), p. 50: 'While the tea trade on the Continent had early been concentrated in the hands of affluent merchants who could purchase relatively large quantities of tea, smuggling into Britain before the 1760s was mostly dominated by many small-scale importers with little capital or credit.'

3. East Sussex RO, Sayer MSS, 269, October 1734.

4. *CJ*, vol. XXV (1745–50), p. 104.   5. ibid., p. 106.

and from thence sent out to their customers in parcels'.[1] The smugglers also sold their tea to persons called duffers, who 'go on foot, and have Coats in which they can quilt a quarter of a hundred weight of tea, and bring it to London in that manner, undiscovered; and that these duffers supply the hawkers, who carry it about the town, and sell it to the customers'.[2]

In ordinary circumstances, smuggling may have been fairly routine. Samuel Wilson believed that 'notwithstanding all the care of the Custom House officers, not one pound in twenty of run tea is seized'.[3] That which was seized, however, was often taken only after a considerable struggle. In the 1740s, the level of this struggle increased dramatically, and it is worth examining some of the cases which so alarmed men like Collier and Simon.

The first history of smuggling in Sussex in these years, written by

1. Taylor, op. cit., p. 61. Innkeepers in Sussex as well as in London were often involved in smuggling, as they were with highwaymen and other eighteenth-century offenders. Inns served as rendezvous, information points and centres for receiving. In 1739, for example, Charles Carkesse, the Secretary of the Board, wrote to Collier from the Custom House in London. 'The Commissioners observing that smuggling is grown to an excessive height and being satisfied the same could not be carried on in the manner it is at present unless the smugglers were harboured and concealed by the persons who keep public houses, especially near the coast, and this being the time of year for renewing licenses, the Commissioners have directed the several Collectors at the Out Ports where they have any proof of any house that the smugglers frequent and the owners know them to be such to wait on the Justices at their special sessions on the day appointed for renewing licenses and in their name to desire they will not renew the licenses of any persons keeping such disorderly houses. . .' Collier MS, Custom House Library, 327.

2. *CJ*, vol. xxv (1745–50), p. 104. There were of course many routes to London. One particularly detailed account described the efforts of a Richard Roote, a mariner from Chatham, and his companions who returned from Flushing with a cargo of 'about four hundred weight of tea'. They sailed up the 'river Thames as high as a place called Cliffe Marshes near Higham in Kent being about two or three miles below Gravesend to seaward and all the persons . . . did assist in unshipping and putting the tea out of the vessel and into a small boat taken out of the sloop . . . and landed the same into the marshes . . . the tea was put into linen bags covered with oilskins and canvas and carried about a mile on the land toward Higham and there laid up in hedges. . .' After that, the tea was divided among the four smugglers. Roote took his share, 'about one hundred and fifty pounds', on horses to Blackheath near Greenwich where he 'left the same with a person called by the name of Yorkshire Tom who then looked after the gardens belonging to the Duke of Montague's house on Blackheath . . .'. From there, Roote went to 'one Mr. Hunter's house near Nightingale's Lane and acquainted Mr. Hunter's wife . . .' of the tea. She agreed to purchase the tea, and 'appointed to meet [Roote] . . . in the night time at the Boote Ale House in Deptford'. Eventually Roote received ten shillings a pound for the tea, some of which Mrs Hunter and another woman, a Mrs Marryfield, 'carried away in the same bags tied under their pettycoats'. Kent RO, Q/SB 1728.

3. *CJ*, vol. xxv (1745–50), p. 104.

the 'Gentleman of Chichester', in 1749, described the period in this way:

The smugglers had reigned a long time uncontrolled; the officers of the Customs were too few to encounter them; they rode in troops to fetch their goods, and carried them off in triumph in daylight; nay, so audacious had they grown, that they were not afraid of the regular troops that were sent into the country to keep them in awe; of which we have several instances. If any of them happened to be taken, and the proof ever so clear against him, no magistrate in the country durst commit him to gaol; if he did he was sure to have his house or barns set on fire, or some other mischief done him, if he was so happy to escape with his life. . .[1]

The 'Gentleman' might have made an even stronger case. Here we will take a closer look at the activities of Sussex smugglers, and at the balance of forces in the county.

In 1740 an officer of the Customs, Thomas Carswell, was shot and killed in an affray with smugglers. One of the men involved, John Boxwell, who was taken up on the order of the Duke of Richmond nearly ten years later, gave the following account of the battle:

Between one and seven, in the morning of the 26th of December, 1740, it being then very moonlight . . . [he and several others] were aiding and assisting to each other in the clandestine running of a large parcel of tea, computed at about fifteen or sixteen hundred weight . . . at the shore between Hastings and Bulverhythe in Sussex and carried the same on about 13 or 14 horses to a barn near Hurst Green in the parish of Salehurst where they lodged it and went with their horses to the public houses at Hurst Green where they refreshed themselves and went to bed. . .

1. Anon. ('Gentleman of Chichester'), *A Full and Genuine History of the Inhuman and Unparalleled Murders of Mr. William Galley, a Custom House Officer and Mr. Daniel Chater, a Shoemaker, by Fourteen Notorious Smugglers, with the Trials and Execution of Seven of the Blood Criminals at Chichester*, n.d., *c*. 1749, p. 23. The 'Gentleman of Chichester' may have been the Duke of Richmond himself. Henry Simon wrote the following to Richmond, 1 May 1749: 'In obedience to Your Graces commands of yesterday, I have sent with this the draught of the trial. In three or four days after I last waited upon Your Grace at Whitehall, Sir Thomas Denison sent back the draught to me by his clerk Mr. Fenton with the obliterations and alterations which you find therein. And with his positive orders that no mention should be made, or the least intimation should be given, that he had perused it, or that the draught had been under his examination. This was a sufficient declaration to me, that the Judge of the Assize did not then think proper to license the publication, and if it had been published by order of the Commissioners of His Majesty's Customs only, I had good reason to know that in Westminster Hall this would have been thought an irregular and improper proceeding. The circumstances therefore were too nice for me to proceed one step further during Your Grace's absence.' West Sussex RO, MSS, 155/H 128.

The smugglers were soon awakened, however, with the news that they were pursued by a number of soldiers and revenue officers.

... before they [the smugglers] could get ready they saw the officers and soldiers pass them by at the public house and they imagined the officers and soldiers by the help of the moon would track their horses to the barn where the tea was lodged ... James Standford, John MacDonald, and John Apps went up to Hawkhurst and about that neighbourhood to procure fire-arms and other offensive weapons and people to assist in rescuing the tea which they imagined the officers by that time had seized...

Those who responded to the smugglers' call (a large number did, and quickly, though the accounts vary) were promised either twenty guineas or a hundredweight of tea. But by the time these recruits had returned with their firearms, the tea had been carried away, towards the King's warehouse in Hastings. At that point, according to another participant, Thomas Drury, 'all the persons assembled again on the green and armed themselves in the manner aforesaid, stript themselves to their shirts and drank brandy, wishing damnation might take him that returned before they had retaken the tea, then everyone of them being on horseback followed the wagon which they overtook at Silver Hill about half a mile from the green...' When the smugglers caught up with the soldiers and officers, Carswell (according to the testimony of the soldiers) ordered the dragoons to open fire. But in spite of this barrage, the smugglers managed to chase off the soldiers, wound 'one or two of their horses', recapture the tea, and kill Carswell in the process.[1]

Carswell was a Customs officer, and he was killed in the course of duty, yet even though a reward was offered for information against his killers, no person was taken until nearly ten years later when the Duke of Richmond took up the case. Similarly, when three dragoons were killed near Arundel by smugglers, there were no convictions, though the Secretary of War asked the Treasury to have armed vessels sent into the area.[2] In the next year, 1744, yet another dragoon was wounded in Sussex, and his company had three of their horses shot.

In another case, in November 1744, smugglers spared the life of the riding officer at Bexhill, though not, apparently, his dignity: '... a large gang of smugglers, at least sixty in number entered Bexhill armed with blunderbusses, carbines, and other offensive weapons ... [and] destroyed ... [Philip Bailly's] household goods and furniture and insulted his wife and family in a violent manner.' And the very next day, Edward Hurd,

1. West Sussex RO, Goodwood MSS 156/G 14 and G 17: depositions of John Boxwell (20 March 1749) and Thomas Drury (21 April 1749).
2. PRO, T 27/26 (J. Scrope to Treasury Commissioners, 24 January 1743).

the Collector of Customs at Eastbourne, after reporting the incident at Bexhill, informed the Lords of the Treasury that 'three large cutters had landed their goods in Pevensey Bay and there were by computation 5 or 6 hundred horse taking their goods ashore. . .'[1] Hurd did not connect the two events in his report, though they must have been related. While the smugglers may have been up to nothing more than settling an old score, the more plausible explanation is that they went to Bexhill to intimidate the revenue officers, thereby ensuring that the next day's work would not be interfered with.[2]

Sussex smugglers even went so far as to profit from the war with France – sometimes by carrying recruits for the Irish brigades across the Channel, and in at least one case by smuggling munitions. William Wood, the Secretary to the Commissioners of the Customs, wrote of this to Collier, informing him that 'the Commissioners [of the Customs] received information that the smugglers from Rye and Hastings have carried to France sixty or seventy swivel guns and that they openly carry over wool, the inhabitants not daring to oppose them. . .'[3]

The inability of the authorities to check activities such as these was credited by most contemporaries to the fact that the local population was largely intimidated. Whether or not this explanation was entirely true, there certainly was a campaign of intimidation on the part of the smugglers. In Samuel Grey's report from Lydd to the Commissioners, for example, he also wrote that 'between twelve and one o'clock in the day time the smugglers who were armed with blunderbusses waited above half an hour in sight of the whole town and declared they would be stopped by no body. . .'[4]

The fact that revenue officers, soldiers and the residents of the coastal towns and villages were openly intimidated by the smuggling gangs was in itself sufficient cause for concern, but the authorities in Sussex faced defiance of the law which went beyond even this. Just west of Sussex, in Hampshire, another gang of Sussex smugglers attacked and robbed the home of George Wakeford, a landowner, who turned to his neighbour the Duke of Richmond for help. The Duke in turn wrote of the robbery to Henry Pelham: '. . . Mr. Wakeford of Hampshire has lately been attacked,

1. PRO, T 11/23/112–13 (Customs book petition of Philip Bailly, who was given '£100 to encourage him in his duties').
2. For further evidence on the Carswell and Bailly affairs and on the role of the military, see Paul Muskett, 'Military Operations against Smuggling in Kent and Sussex, 1698–1750', *Journal of the Society for Army Historical Research*, vol. LII, no. 210, Summer 1974, pp. 89–110.
3. East Sussex RO, Sayer MSS, 348 (2 June 1747).
4. ibid., 269 (Grey to Collier, 1 October 1734).

his house broke open and plundered, by a set of these desparate villains. . .
He is afraid to move towards justice lest a greater evil should fall upon him
and dares not complain of it even to his neighbours. . .' Wakeford had
been awakened one night to find half the gang in his bedroom, and
Jeremiah Curtis, the well-known Hawkhurst smuggler, holding a carbine
to his head, demanding to know where his money was kept and threatening
to 'cut him to pieces'. The servants then watched helplessly as Wakeford
was pulled down the stairs, without his shoes or stockings, and finally
dragged 'part of the way upon the ground to the place where the horses
stood, where they afterwards left him, having threatened to murder him
if he made any noise'.[1] In all, Wakeford lost fourteen guineas, his silver
plate and two silver watches. He dared complain only to the Duke of
Richmond.

Another Hampshire landowner, Henry Foxcroft, wrote to Richmond of
a similar, though more serious problem. In the early summer of 1748,
Foxcroft wrote:

I have had abundance of mischief done me in the night time: my gardens
have been four times cut to pieces; near seven hundred trees, of nine years
growth, of elms, walnuts, apples, and cherries utterly destroyed; ten or twelve
gaps made with a bill hook in quick set hedges, from one yard to three wide;
nine outside fences of nine years growth; the mounds of my fish ponds broke
down, and the penstocks carried away; and where the mischief could not be
done they have poisoned the water; and within this three months, I have had a
summer house burnt down. . .

Foxcroft also wrote that he had discovered the man responsible, 'by
means of a threatening letter'. The man, Henry Aburrow, a blacksmith,
was tried the following year at the Winchester Assizes. What exactly it
was that led Aburrow (if he was in fact guilty) to take this toll on Foxcroft's property is not known. Foxcroft said that it was 'for turning him
out of work as a blacksmith', which seems possible, but he also said, 'As
firing of houses and doing such sorts of mischief . . . are very much in
fashion in this neighbourhood, and we are unfortunately placed in a nest
of smugglers, I hope your Lordship will think this man a proper person
to make an example of. . .'

Smuggling may not have been directly involved in this affair. Nevertheless it was clearly an aspect of what Foxcroft called the 'fashion of the
neighbourhood', and certainly must have contributed to the fact that 'no
body within five miles of him [Aburrow] dared meddle with him. . .' In

1. West Sussex RO, Goodwood MSS, 155/H 24: Richmond to Pelham, n.d. (November
1748?); affidavit of John Diamond, dated 22 July 1749, but referring to an incident
many months before, probably October or November 1748.

fact, this neighbourhood may well have been one of those in which the 'nest of smugglers' held at least the immediate balance of power.[1]

The system of law enforcement in the English countryside in the eighteenth century was weak and inadequate. The existence of well-organized gangs of smugglers made the delicate balance of force and deference upon which order in the countryside depended even less reliable. Indeed the evidence from Sussex in these years shows, if anything, a serious and widespread breakdown in the system of deference. At any rate, the fears of the gentry were far from unfounded.

Examples of the smugglers openly challenging the authorities are not difficult to find. In May 1744 Christopher Gunman wrote to Collier from the Custom House in Dover of

the two late audacious attempts of nearly 200 men and horses who came down in the daytime to this place with the design to rescue the Dove smuggling cutter, Adam Peak, master, laden with tea, which was taken by Captain Hardy in His Majesty's sloop Drake, brought into this port and delivered into my care. They rode through the town about 5 o'clock in the afternoon with pistols cocked in their hands, each having two carbines and cutlasses, swearing and threatening destruction to the Officers of the Customs and to blow out their brains and burn their houses, and [they] put the whole town into the utmost consternation.[2]

In March 1742 Thomas Clare sent the following report to Collier, describing the efforts of two of his officers, John Darby and Freebody Dray, to secure contraband brandy. The Customs officers were themselves taken by smugglers who

took the said half anchors of brandy from these deponents and ordered them to take off their great coats from their backs which they accordingly did and then took these deponents about two miles and a half towards Dungeness Point where there lay in oil skin bags a considerable quantity of tea to the amount these deponents believe of about four thousand pounds weight and that the gang of smugglers joined together were about fifteen or sixteen men and twenty-five horses on which the gang loaded the said tea ... and carried the same into the country and also took these deponents horses with them ... [deponents then say] ... that the smugglers declared these deponents should get a voyage to France but these deponents desired they would not send them on board but the gang swore they would compel them to go into the boat which lay hovering on the coast ... [they also said] ... that there was on board the said smuggling vessel 15 men, eight swivel guns, and two carriage guns, and two chests of small

1. Brit. Mus. Add. MSS, 32,718, fo. 312 (12 July 1749). And see also Richmond to Newcastle (fos. 309–10), ''tis certain that the fellow is a most notorious villain, a poacher and a smuggler, and so are his whole family, one of his brothers was evidence against him to save himself [at the Winchester Assizes] ...'

2. Custom House Library, Collier MSS, 621.

arms and all or the greatest part of the men were English . . . [they were] . . . carried to Boulogne and landed about two o'clock the next afternoon, and they treated them civilly and Mr. Curlois, a merchant of the said place, who as these deponents believe [sent] . . . the cargo of tea, hired a boat and sent these deponents over to England . . . [then on March 4] that their horses were the same day sent to the George Inn at Rye by the post boy that rides the stage from Stourmouth through Hawkhurst to the said port [Rye] and these deponents having notice thereof went thither and fetched them home the next day.[1]

The best-known case was that of the Hawkhurst gang at Goudhurst in Kent, where the smugglers threatened to burn down the town, and kill its inhabitants. This they apparently attempted to do. The town, however, was defended by a militia, organized by the local gentry. In the considerable fighting which took place (in April 1747), two of the smugglers were killed, and the town saved.[2] In August of the same year, the *Gentleman's Magazine* reported: 'About 24 smugglers well-armed and laden with prohibited goods rode through Rye, Sussex, and stopping at the Red Lion to refresh, fired several times to intimidate the inhabitants, and observing one, James Marshall, a young man too curious of their behaviour, carried him off, and he has not been heard of since.'[3] The same issue claimed that the smugglers threatened the printers for publishing advertisements against them.

A Mr Jordan, Customs officer in Folkestone, wrote to the Treasury in March 1744, to inform them that several large gangs of smugglers were active in his area and that the soldiers quartered near by were refusing to assist him. Only the night before, he wrote, one of the gangs 'came armed to the town, riding about the streets in a riotous manner, demanding drink at private as well as public houses, shooting through several signs, and enquiring after the behaviour of the officers, swearing that if they were bad officers, that they would cure them. . .' Jordan wrote again the next day. There was a smuggler imprisoned in the town gaol, he wrote, and he feared either an escape or a rescue, 'the gaol being a weak one'. And once again he begged 'for some relief from the soldiery as soon as possible'. The entire situation, he concluded in apparent desperation, could 'be compared to nothing more like than a frontier town in a state of war'.[4]

The Government responded to all this in a number of ways. The

1. ibid., 471. Darby and Freebody said they did not 'know "any person of the gang" . . . but believe the gang of smugglers were belonging to Hawkhurst and the adjacent parts commonly called the Curtis gang and that Curtis' right name as these deponents believe is Pollard and believe the smugglin vessel were [sic] the company commonly called the Transports formerly belonging to the Port of Hastings. . .'
2. *Gentleman's Magazine*, vol. XVII (1747), p. 198.
3. ibid., p. 397.
4. PRO, T 1/316.

strength of the fleet off the south coast was increased, as were the land forces. One witness to the parliamentary hearing (itself part of the Government's response), Richard Sclater, another tea dealer and ex-smuggler, testified that the strengthening of the fleet alone had 'totally prevented' the running of goods in Kent and Sussex, while the smuggling trade in general faced 'great interruption'.[1] The fleet, in fact, was a minor factor, especially in comparision to Henry Pelham's tax reforms of 1745. These were designed to end the great decline in the legal trade, which had been particularly sharp in the preceding three years. This decline was universally accredited to the growth of smuggling. Consequently, the duty on tea was reduced – from four shillings per pound to one shilling per pound and a 25 per cent *ad valorum*.[2] Most contemporaries believed that these measures were effective. In 1749, for example, the *Gentleman's Magazine* reported that 'the great mischiefs done of late by the smugglers is in part to be accounted for by the decline of their business. The profits of smuggling, a few years ago, were so considerable, occasioned by the high duties, that the very hirelings had such extravagant gain, as was sufficient to corrupt the most industrious labourer from his honest employment, each man being allowed half a guinea each a journey, and a dollop of tea.'[3]

At the same time, numerous anti-smuggling acts were passed, statutes which equal in savagery any eighteenth-century legislation. The Committee on Smuggling itself called for stricter laws. One of the witnesses had proposed that 'future smugglers should be deemed to be within the description of the Act of the 9th of the late King, commonly called the Black Act, it would greatly discourage them'.[4] In fact, the law passed the following year (19 Geo. II) was in many ways similar to the notorious Black Act. Under the provisions of the new act, numerous activities, such as being assembled 'in the running, landing, or carrying away of prohibited or uncustomed goods', having a blackened face or wearing 'any Wizard Mask or other disguise', or wounding an officer of the Revenue were made felonies, with the convicted to 'suffer death . . . without benefit of clergy'. In addition, entire communities would be held collectively responsible for such things as goods being rescued, or officers being wounded or killed. The beating of an officer could cost a Sussex Rape £40. By the same act, a reward of £500 was offered to persons 'who shall apprehend and take or discover, so that he may be taken, all and every persons, who shall have not surrendered himself within forty

1. *CJ*, vol. xxv (1745–50), p. 103.
2. 18 Geo. II c. 26.
3. *Gentleman's Magazine*, vol. xix (1749), p. 138.
4. *CJ*, vol. xxv (1745–50), p. 109.

days. . .' This referred to the fact that 'notorious' smugglers were to be advertised in the *London Gazette*, their names posted in market towns, and given forty days to surrender themselves.[1]

The large rewards led to the formation of a number of groups, such as the 'Cranbrook Associators', which roamed the countryside in search of 'bounties', and on a number of occasions these groups fought pitched battles with smuggling gangs.[2] The main purpose of the rewards, however, was to gain information, so that the authorities themselves could capture the outlawed smugglers. But this presented problems as well. One pamphleteer complained that the rewards were 'so large' as to 'open a wide door for perjuries, false and malicious informations, and a great variety of oppression'. In addition, he wrote that the rewards gave the informer the 'power' to 'swear away any persons life, unless such person charged has the foresight, or can afford to keep a journal of all his hours and days, and have half a dozen persons continually with him, to prove such a journal, and make entries of it.'[3] The smugglers, then, found themselves attacked not only by the government directly, but also by all those in the country whom the government or the local gentry could buy.

The exact extent to which these measures and the many others taken affected the smuggling trade is difficult to say. Mr Sclater's view that smuggling had been stopped was certainly not true. On the other hand the volume of smuggled tea had been considerably reduced. But the conflict between the smugglers and the authorities was heightened. In September 1746, for example, John Collier wrote again to Henry Pelham, complaining that the Act of Indemnity, passed that year, 'was but of little service to any persons in this County, but on the contrary has made the great lawless gangs more desperate, swearing that [if] they are liable to be gaoled and transported for past offences, they must and will keep on. It has pardoned those that are in the country thought to deserve as great punishment, at least the merchants and tradesmen in London that employed them and received their smuggled goods. . .'[4] In May 1747 George Oxenden of Dean, the M P for Sandwich, wrote to the Duke of Newcastle on behalf of two brothers from his neighbourhood, the Tuckers. These men, he wrote, were 'of the civiler sort . . . who never used any fire-arms nor was ever in any fray, but traded indeed for their quota of brandy as their neighbours did'. They were about to sail for Holland, preferring

1. 19 Geo. II c. 34. A Rape is an ancient administrative division.

2. East Sussex R O, Sayer M S S, 299, a letter from Collier to the Customs Commissioners, 4 August 1747. Also see Sayer M S S, 300, notes, n.d.

3. Anon., *A Free Apology in Behalf of the Smugglers, So Far as their Case Affects the Constitution, by an Enemy to all Oppression, Whether by Tyranny or Law*, 1749, pp. 12–14.

4. East Sussex R O, Sayer M S S, 420.

living there to surrendering in England; surrendering themselves was 'to be hanged, they say'. Other smugglers, however, would stay. Before sailing, they informed Oxenden 'that the Western smugglers (which are those of the Wild of Kent and Sussex) designed resisting to a man. . .'[1]

III

The event which finally fixed the attention of the entire nation on Sussex was the killing, in February 1748, of William Galley, a riding officer for the revenue, and Daniel Chater, an informer. A gang of West Sussex smugglers captured, tortured and murdered Galley and Chater, and this crime, which was also connected with the audacious attack on the Custom House at Poole, became one of the best-known smuggling events of the period. Though these events are well established in the history of smuggling, a few details will help to explain their notoriety. In any event, these murders led directly to the Duke of Richmond's extraordinary campaign against smuggling in Sussex.[2]

Indirectly, the murders were the result of the capture of a load of tea. A West Sussex gang had arranged for William Hollace of Rye, the master of a 'small vessel', to pick up a load of tea at Guernsey and land it near the Hampshire border, at a place between Lymington and Ringwood. Both Hollace and the tea ('30 hundred weight' valued at '£500 and upwards'), however, were captured on their return, by a privateer, a Captain William Johnson, who deposited the tea at the Custom House at Poole. Outraged by the loss of their tea, the smugglers decided to recapture it immediately. Joined by a number of 'East country people', men from the Hawkhurst gang, they met during the night of 6 October 1747, on the edge of Charlton Forest – the Duke of Richmond's hunting ground – and travelled together from there to Poole. In all, they numbered between thirty and sixty.

At the Custom House, the West Sussex gang lost its nerve. One of them, Thomas Willis, told the others that 'there was a large sloop lay up against the key; she'll plant her guns to the Custom House door, and tear us to pieces. . .' But the Hawkhurst smugglers were determined to carry out the attack. Eventually they convinced the others, and in the end they were successful. They broke open the Custom House, apparently with

1. Brit. Mus. Add. MSS, 32,711, fo. 90.
2. The official records of the Special Commission are in the Public Record Office, PRO, KB 8/72. The story is also told in *The Complete Newgate Calendar*, G. T. Crook, ed., 1926, vol. III, pp. 155–8, 170–76, and in *The Proceedings on the King's Commission of the Peace* (*Old Bailey*), no. IV, 1749. The most complete account is that written by the 'Gentleman of Chichester' (see n. 1, p. 128 above).

little or no opposition, and recovered their tea. As for the sloop, 'the tide was low, and that vessel could not bring her guns to bear to fire. . .'

The following day, the smugglers returned triumphantly with their tea to Sussex. They 'breakfasted' in Fordingbridge, a village in Hampshire 'where some hundreds of people were assembled to view the cavalcade'. Among the spectators was Daniel Chater, a shoemaker, who in the past had worked the harvest with John Diamond, one of the smugglers. As he passed, Diamond threw Chater a bag of tea and shook his hand. Unfortunately for Chater, this made him a celebrity. It was not long before he was taken by the Customs officers.

Several months later, in February 1748, Chater, with William Galley, the riding officer from Southampton, set out for Stanstead near Chichester, where Major Battine, the Surveyor of Customs for Sussex and a Justice of the Peace, was to have examined him. Instead the two men were met by smugglers At midday on the journey to Stanstead, Chater and Galley stopped to refresh themselves at the 'White Hart at Rowland's Castle, a public house kept by one Elizabeth Payne, widow, who had two sons, both grown men, and blacksmiths, and reputed smugglers. . .' Mrs Payne's suspicions were aroused by the travellers. She informed the smugglers, who immediately joined Chater and Galley at the White Hart, where they all 'drank plentifully, and made Galley and Chater . . . fuddled. . .'

The smugglers, having captured the two, were then confronted with the problem of what to do with them. Mary Carter, the wife of William Carter, one of the West Sussex gang, advised the others that it was 'no matter what you do with them, whether you kill them or hang them, for they are come to ruin us. . .' The others must have shared this view, for the gang soon set off to kill the two men. Galley and Chater were both tied to their horses. Galley 'rode with his head under the belly [of the horse] . . . wounded, bruised, and hurt', with Jackson another member of the gang, 'all the time squeezing his private parts'. Then, after having 'cut off his nose and privities, [and] broke every joint in him . . .', the smugglers decided he was dead. They threw Galley into a hole and buried him near Rake, in Sussex. Chater suffered much the same. He ended up in Harris's Well, near Harting, in Sussex, into which the gang hurled him. The bodies of the two men were discovered the following autumn.[1]

The Duke of Richmond made the capture and conviction of the murderers his personal responsibility. Moreover, from the autumn of 1748, he undertook to stop smuggling in Sussex altogether, and this campaign

---

1. The above account is based upon 'Gentleman of Chichester', op. cit., esp. p. 7; *The Proceedings*, 1749, IV (April 1749), p. 77; Taylor, op. cit., p. 34; *Gentleman's Magazine*, vol. XVIII (1748), p. 475, vol. XIX (1749), p. 359; PRO, KB 8/72.

lasted until his death, nearly three years later. His first undertaking was to have a Special Commission held in Sussex. In December 1748 he wrote to his friend the Duke of Newcastle, urging him:

> to press the Chancellor upon this point of getting these murderers tried at Horsham directly by a Special Commission, and I hope you will do it as the thing in the world that will do most good in this country, and I am sure nothing but treason can be a stronger claim for such a commission, for this is not only murders of the deepest die attended with the most shocking circumstances of cruelty but also committed by whole gangs of these villains in open defiance of the laws and all government whatever. So though it may not be treason in law, I am sure it is so in common sense...[1]

The Duke of Richmond pressed his proposal for the special assizes on everyone he could. He reminded Henry Pelham, the Prime Minister, of the attacks on Wakeford and Foxcroft. Pelham supported the Duke's requests, and said of his accounts of smuggling in Sussex that 'such a scene of villainy and barbarity I have never before heard of or read of'. 'What,' he asked in apparent despair, 'is to become of the women?'[2] The Duke of Newcastle, the Secretary of State, joined in supporting the Duke of Richmond's plans, but by mid-December these had been changed. By then the Duke of Richmond was petitioning the Chancellor, suggesting that the Commission should be held in Chichester, rather than Horsham. The former, only a few miles from the Duke's estate at Goodwood, would be 'more convenient for us all in this part of the country, where the murders were all committed and all the evidences live, most of the Grand Jury live, and where a sheriff can get a Petty Jury whose probity can be depended upon.'[3]

On 20 December the Duke received word from Henry Simon, of the Custom House in London, that a Special Commission of Oyer and Terminer for the County of Sussex had passed the Great Seal.[4] The judges had been chosen – Sir Michael Foster from the King's Bench, Edward Clive, a Baron from the Court of Exchequer, and Sir Thomas Birch, of the Court of Common Pleas – and they had agreed to meet Richmond at his 'half-way' house in Godalming, to travel from there together to Goodwood.

The Duke, with his agents and servants, made nearly all the arrangements for the Special Commission. From the beginning, he treated it as his personal project, going to great lengths to see that it was neither delayed nor interfered with. He personally gathered evidence, paid informers and interrogated witnesses. His agents travelled throughout London and the south-east. (Later, he even sent them as far as Holland in pursuit of

1. Brit. Mus. Add. MSS, 32,717, fo. 407.
2. West Sussex RO, Goodwood MSS, 155/H 24.   3. ibid., H 42.   4. ibid., H 47.

smugglers.)[1] In one sense, he also acted as judge and jury, for by the time the Commission began his efforts had all but guaranteed hangings. The Duke of Richmond did all this, he explained to Pelham, because 'nothing but an active zeal, manifested by public acts, can give a cheque to these dangerous outrages and barbarous and inhuman murders, with which our part of the country is so justly terrified'.[2]

Seven smugglers were indicted at Chichester. Though many others had been involved in the events, the Duke of Richmond chose to prosecute the seven first and as quickly as possible, partly because he felt that the Special Commission itself would have an effect on the county, and also because he thought that only the immediate setting of examples would intimidate the smugglers. Many others, however, were tried in the following months. All seven of those indicted at Chichester were labourers or rural artisans. The first taken was Richard Mills, junior, who was apprehended in Sussex on 16 August. He was a colt-breaker, though he was commonly known as a smuggler. John Hammond, a labourer from Bersted, Sussex, was taken at the beginning of October 1748, and committed to Horsham Gaol. John Cobby was taken on the 18th of the same month and was also committed to Horsham. He was a labourer as well, thirty years old, from Sidlesham, in Sussex. William Jackson, a labourer from Wellser, in Hampshire, was captured also near Rowland's Castle. These two men were taken near Godalming, and from there carried to London under strong guard and committed to Newgate. Benjamin Tapner of West Stoke, Sussex, a labourer aged twenty-seven, was committed on 16 November. Richard Mills senior was not taken until 16 December 1748. Though he knew all the others had been imprisoned, he remained at home 'never absconding' 'as he knew nothing of the murder of Galley, and as to that of Chater, he was seemingly very easy, as he was not murdered in his house, nor was he present when the evil deed was done'. Old Mills, like his son, was a colt-breaker. He was sixty-eight years old and lived with his sons at Trotton, in Sussex.[3]

The Duke of Richmond's motives in all this are far from clear. His chief interests in Sussex were hunting, cricket and his gardens at Goodwood. As a member of the Whig aristocracy, he was a powerful man, clearly the most powerful magnate in West Sussex. He had also served as Mayor of Chichester. Politically, he was a strong supporter of the Pelhams. Horace Walpole claimed he 'loved the Duke of Newcastle, the only man who ever did'.[4] As to why he undertook the suppression of smuggling,

1. See, for example, in West Sussex RO, Goodwood MSS, 156/G 72, an account of the capture of the smuggler 'Little Blew' and of his return to England.

2. ibid., 155/H 24.   3. 'Gentleman of Chichester', op. cit., pp. 22-3.

4. Horace Walpole, *Memoirs of the Reign of King George the Second*, 1847, vol. I, p. 3.

one can only surmise. His official biographer says simply that 'he was an advocate of stern legislation both as a magistrate and local magnate where poachers and smugglers were concerned'.[1] Henry Fielding, who tried a number of cases involving Sussex smugglers, held up the Duke of Richmond as an example, calling him 'the noble duke' and 'one of the worthiest of magistrates, as well as the best of men'. In his tract on robbery, Fielding singled him out for praise as an opponent of law-breakers, and lamented his death, wishing that 'his life, for the good of mankind [had] been prolonged'. Queen Caroline, on the other hand, found him 'half-witted' and 'muleish'.[2]

On several occasions, the Duke had some contact with smugglers. In 1735, as Mayor of Chichester, he received a threatening letter demanding money. The anonymous authors identified themselves as smugglers. In 1746 he wrote to the Duke of Newcastle, informing him that 'the smugglers have been hereabouts lately, and wherever they go they declare themselves rebels. I think it a much more serious thing than people seem to appreciate it in London.'[3] The Duke of Richmond was a staunch patriot and fanatical anti-Jacobite; he called the Jacobites 'the scum of Scotland'.[4] On another occasion, two of his servants were found with parcels of smuggled tea in their possession. When he first learned of the affair at Poole, it was because two or three of his servants were held to have been involved, though apparently this was not the case.[5]

Most likely, as all his letters indicate, he genuinely abhorred smuggling, particularly when it was conducted in his domain. The crime, after all, had been planned on his own estate, and one of the bodies was discovered just a few miles from Goodwood. All this must have constituted a threat to his power and prestige in the area. More important, with rank and deference seriously challenged in the county, and with the lesser gentry often openly intimidated by the smugglers, the Duke of Richmond may well have been reminded of his customary duties and responsibilities as the principal landowner. At any rate, he pursued the smugglers with a vengeance.

A campaign against smuggling was not a simple undertaking, even for a powerful peer. In the eighteenth century the opponents of smuggling faced almost insuperable obstacles. To begin with, the officers of both the Excise and the Customs were notoriously corrupt and inefficient. Often

1. C. G. H. Lennox, *A Duke and His Friends*, 1911, vol. I, pp. xvi–xvii.
2. Henry Fielding, *An Enquiry into the Causes of the Late Increase of Robbers*, 1751, p. 69; *DNB*.
3. Brit. Mus. Add. MSS, 32,706, fo. 63.
4. ibid., fo. 114.
5. West Sussex RO, Goodwood MSS, 155/H 8, William Sherer to Richmond, 26 February 1747, and H 11, Wood to Richmond, 8 March 1747.

they were smugglers themselves, or at least in league with the smugglers. This is not the place for a history of the provincial Customs officer, but certain of the problems faced by these authorities are particularly interesting. In an area like Sussex, where smuggling was so common and involved so many people, the Customs officers often had to come to terms with their neighbours or move out. The honest revenue man could scarcely find a place to live along the Sussex coast. And this problem faced not only the lowest riding officer or waterman. John Collier, the chief Customs official in Kent and East Sussex, personally wrote to Colonel Pelham on behalf of several Hastings smugglers:

> I am sorry to find it's not proper to countenance our petition as the six persons are natives of this place and we are incessantly teased with solicitations. As John Grayling, now in Newgate . . . will be hanged unless by my Lord Duke of New-castle's favour in obtaining the King's pardon, your good offices therein must be humbly entreated. As to the other five, they must be given up and shift for themselves, but it's hoped His Grace will be pleased to interfere for Grayling's life. . . I really abominate the smuggling practices, but in this case, as circum-stanced, it's absolutely necessary to be made a point of. I hope you would pardon my presumption in writing so much, or so free about so worthless a creature. As he was convicted in Sussex and that is the county where he has been seen at large, I find his trial must be at our assizes and hope it may be prevented because I must have a considerable hand in it which (as a native here) I would willingly avoid.[1]

More often, however, the probem was corruption on a lower level. In 1746 one army officer, sent to Sussex in an effort to control smuggling, wrote to the Treasury that:

> the Custom House officers should be employed as advanced spies to give the

1. Brit. Mus. Add. MSS, 32,703, fo. 170, 30 June 1747. Collier also seems to have used the excuse of ill-health in avoiding involvement in smuggling cases. In December 1744 Simon wrote to him, ' . . . I am very sorry to hear you complain. Whenever you decline these prosecutions, the crown loses a very good solicitor, and the solicitors office here a very kind and able assistant. . .' Customs House Library, Collier MS, 682. Collier's precise relationship with the smugglers is as yet unclear. But he certainly acted in favour of many smugglers, including Thomas Holman, who was his cousin and one of the Hastings Outlaws. In this particular case, Richmond and Collier worked at cross-purposes. William Cranston, Collier's brother-in-law, who was a London solicitor, worked tirelessly to obtain Holman's release, but Richmond believed that Holman 'was the person that carried over to France one Stringer, and other persons that were concerned in the barbarous murder of Daniel Chater and Galley. . .' and he blocked all attempts to free Holman: East Sussex RO, Sayer MSS, 2247. In August 1750 Cranston wrote to Collier, 'The Duke of Richmond is dead and gone. He might be possessed of many good qualities, but he certainly bore too cruelly hard against Tom Holman. He lived just long enough to clinch him. . .' Sayer MS, 1092. Shortly thereafter, however, Collier, with the Duke of Newcastle's help, gained Holman's release.

[army] officers intelligence when any party of smugglers try to come that way, but on the contrary they declare they won't give any [information] under the pretense they are afraid, but it is doubted that is the true reason, for it is very well known when our detachments have been there formerly, the men when they come back have declared how often the Custom House officers have kept them drinking while run goods have passed, this shows something of the bribery. . .[1]

Sometimes the cooperation between officers and smugglers went far beyond pay-offs and profit-sharing, as in the case of a Mr Polhill, a Customs officer at Lydd. In January 1747 Thomas Claire, the Collector of the Customs at Hythe, wrote to Collier to tell him that an informer, William Wyman, had been mistreated by Polhill. According to Claire, the latter had 'not only . . . [made] him [Wyman] bear his own charges from Maidstone home, but when Mr. Polhill came to Ashford, he went into the company with Brooks and other proclaimed smugglers from Hawkhurst, and told them what he had been about himself and that Wyman was an evidence for the King. . .'[2] The most common complaint against the Customs men, however, was that made by General Hawley, the Commander of the troops in Sussex, who wrote the following to the Lords of the Treasury: '. . . it was the general opinion and discourse of the country that the Customs officers were afraid to do their duty on account of the insolence of the smugglers and apprehension of being abused by them. . .' The use of troops was the most obvious means of suppressing smuggling, but even the army faced numerous and unusual problems. Hawley also complained that 'the officers of the Customs often make the soldiers drunk and then buy their share of seizures at an under rate'.[3]

Normally, however, the Government seemed quite willing to deploy soldiers. Several reports to the Treasury, for example, contain requests from Collier and Battine, the Surveyors for Kent and Sussex, asking for more troops for their respective areas. In 1743 Battine was sent 'two troops of Dragoons and a company of foot soldiers to march into Sussex and prevent smuggling'.[4] The next year, the Lords of the Treasury wrote to the Secretary of War requesting him to 'move the King to order a regiment of dragoons into the counties of Kent, Sussex, and Surrey to assist the civil magistrates and Custom House officers against smugglers of Hawkhurst and other places. . .'[5] In November 1747 General Hawley had in West Sussex alone at least one troop of soldiers in Arundel, Petworth, Maidhurst, Chichester and Petersfield.[6]

1. PRO, PC 1/5/111.   2. East Sussex RO, Sayer MSS, 313.

3. Report of the Commissioners of the Customs to the Treasury, 5 December 1746, PRO, PC 1/5/111.   4. PRO, T 1/319.   5. ibid.

6. East Sussex RO, Sayer MSS, 343, Collier to Customs Commissioners, 20 November 1746.

Just how successful the troops were cannot be fully estimated. Of course, there are numerous instances of soldiers seizing contraband goods and capturing smugglers. But there is also a significant number of cases where the soldiers did the opposite. The most common tendency of the troops was, like the revenue officers, simply to avoid combat. When Henry Blaxton, Supervisor of the Customs in West Sussex, heard that a large gang of smugglers was at the coast, he applied to the Commander of the troops quartered at Arundel and got the assistance of nine soldiers. Together they quickly found the smugglers, but the soldiers, after the first shots were fired, fled and 'left ... Blaxton to the mercy of the smugglers who cut and beat his head. . .'[1]

In some cases, the soldiers seem to have actively collaborated with the smugglers, as in Romney and Lydd where they were 'frequently making seizures of brandy and horses and delivering them again to the smugglers for one guinea each horse and the brandy to an officer of the excise from whom they received two shillings for each half-anchor. . .'[2]

On another occasion, in September 1748, a number of men from the Custom House in Southampton travelled to the home of a Captain Gwyn near Bishop's Waltham, in search of contraband goods. *En route* they sought the assistance of soldiers quartered near by. When they arrived at Gwyn's house, they found it defended by a posse of his neighbours, but, seeing the soldiers, 'there appeared such a damp in Captain Gwyn and his posse that the officers went right to work to get the goods out of his house'. While the men gathered the smuggled goods, however, 'the posse still continued there and to advance their spirits to make them more desperate and fit for any mischief, they were well supplied with spirits by the servants of Captain Gwyn's house'. At that point, a lieutenant of the marines appeared, who, after conferring with Gwyn, forbade the soldiers to help the revenue men, and ordered them to move off the highway.

The Customs officers, dangerously outnumbered already, were then confronted by the local constable who told them

that it was a damned scandalous villainous thing, and the most dangerous that was ever known, for them to offer to come to search a Gentleman's house, for to take away such a small sample of liquor; that should they attempt to carry it away, he would not be in their clothes for ever so much; that it would not be possible for them to carry it two miles; that he wondered that anybody dared to come to Waltham on such an account.

Faced with an increasingly hostile crowd, the Customs officers retreated and returned to Southampton, though not before Captain Gwyn's fore-man had told them that 'the captain did not expect they should have come

1. PRO, T 11/22, 11 February 1747. Blaxton apparently died.
2. East Sussex RO, Sayer MSS, 275, Commissioners to Collier, 8 July 1735.

for nothing, they should give them some money for their time and charge if they would go home and be quiet'.[1]

The mere presence of large numbers of soldiers, then, was far from an effective means of suppressing smuggling. But, in addition to the problem of the reliability of the troops, there was also the increasing tendency of the smugglers to defy the Army, as the numerous examples of armed clashes indicate. In one case, the smugglers even went on the offensive against soldiers. Collier described this affair in a letter to his colleague, Mr Freemantle:

> The 8th [of December, 1744] a numerous gang on horseback upwards of 50 of them armed as appears by oath entered a village 6 miles distant from this town in the daytime, colours flying, where about 14 of the detachment of General Harrison's Regiment of foot are quartered into these parts to assist the civil magistrates and officers of the Customs in the execution of their duty. They searched the quarters and took away their arms and abused several of them...[2]

Finally, beyond all this, there was the traditional hostility of rural England to the presence of the Army. For instance, at the very time that the Duke of Richmond was preparing the Special Commission at Chichester, the innkeepers of Lewes were protesting at 'the great number of soldiers marching to and from different parts of the kingdom [and] billeted and quartered in their ... houses'.[3]

The greatest threat to the individual smuggler, then, apart from reduced tariffs, appears to have been neither the revenue officers nor the Army and Fleet, but rather the informer. Nearly all the best-known smugglers of this period lost their freedom because of the confession of one or more of their compatriots. In the Duke of Richmond's campaign, his greatest successes were achieved by his careful cultivation of informants, as well as by his willingness to pay almost any price. In normal circumstances, however, the solidarity of the smuggling communities was remarkable, and this solidarity, while often buttressed by systematic intimidation, also says a great deal about the extent of smuggling in Sussex.

Generally informers were few and the pressure against informing was great. In 1746 John Darby, a revenue officer, wrote to Collier that 'I have

1. PRO, T 1/331. Report of William Cooley and Robert Turvin, Custom House Officers in Southampton, to the Treasury, 6 September 1748. Richard Gwyn's response from the Admiralty Office, 22 September 1748, is attached to this report. He contested the charges.

2. Custom House Library, Collier MS, 673.

3. Brit. Mus. Add. MSS, 35,058, fo. 457 (petition dated 23 January 1749).

done everything that is in my power to induce the man that informed me, but he is a farmer and lives at Reculver and says that he is afraid the gang [of smugglers] will burn down his house and barn if he should discover any of them and so says everyone. . . They all say that there is no force in the country, the smugglers will do as they please with them . . .'[1] Another farmer, Alexander Carr of Beddington, in Sussex, who was rightly suspected of informing, complained to Richmond that his neighbours 'have used me very barbarous in breaking of my windows and sending of a threatening letter to me and opening my barns in the night to spoil my corn and destroy my cattle'.[2]

Sometimes, however, the informer faced not only direct retaliation by the smugglers but also the open wrath of the entire community, especially, of course, where smuggling was most common. In May 1748, for example, John Collier's clerk wrote from the Custom House in Hastings that 'the inhabitants of Hastings were very much incensed at one Harrison for informing against several persons in Hastings and elsewhere for being concerned in smuggling practices, and that one Evers had been arrested on Harrison's information'. Harrison escaped, though only narrowly. An angry crowd pursued him into the countryside. The clerk, Richard Patrick, reporting to Collier who was ill in Bath, went on to say he was 'really surprised to see what a spirit of smuggling is grafted in this town; for the apprehension of Evers has put the inhabitants in the greatest flame imaginable; for I am really of the opinion that nine parts in ten thereof would as freely murder Harrison as they would eat or drink when hungry or dry'.[3] In Chatham, in Kent, a crowd attacked John Lidgater, an officer of the Excise, and John Brewer, a cordwainer, as they walked down the street. Alexander Garner, a victualler, who witnessed the event, swore that he, 'being in his house in Chatham . . . [heard] a great noise of people in the street, there went out of his store door to know the cause of it and there saw . . . [Lidgate and Brewer] followed by a mob of a great number of persons crying out "Informers, they ought to be hanged. It is no sin to kill them" and throwing stones and dirt at them. . .' The crowd 'damned' Garner for 'harbouring informers', attacked his house, and broke several of his windows.[4]

1. East Sussex RO, Sayer MSS, 347.
2. West Sussex RO, Goodwood MSS, 156/G 42 (21 June 1749).
3. East Sussex RO, Sayer MSS, 1391.
4. PRO, KB 32/1 pt 1. The deposition of Alexander Garner and his wife Ruth, and John Brewer, sworn at Chatham, Kent, 29 March 1751. The incident occurred in January 1751. Revenue officers appear to have been very unpopular in Chatham. On 1 January 1744, '. . . John Tomlin, Riding Officer at the Port, seized in the street in Chatham upon a mare from a person unknown two bags containing twelve pounds of tea and also the said mare, and in a few minutes after making the seizure Charles Fresh and Richard

Nevertheless, informants were found. The Duke of Richmond personally paid one man £100 for information concerning a West Sussex gang.[1] The Government, of course, was offering as much as £500 for information against outlawed smugglers, a large sum for anyone to turn down. In addition, captured smugglers often received indemnity in return for informing against those at large. But even such large amounts of money and the promise of indemnity were not always enough to break down the fear of reprisals and the solidarity of the smuggling communities. William Wood, secretary to the Customs Commissioners in London, testifying before the Parliamentary Committee, said that he 'had known of large rewards offered by advertisements published in the country; but they were to no purpose, the people being afraid to inform'.

In preparing for the Commission, the Duke used a large number of informants, whose co-operation he gained primarily through the promise of pardon and financial reward. The fact that he was less interested in seeing the guilty punished than in setting an example for the county was also a great help. Not everyone agreed with his generous use of indemnity, however, and on one occasion he wrote to Simon, saying he 'was sorry to find the Attorney-General has scruples upon permitting pardon to the outlaws, for which there are many good reasons. . . I am very certain that it is the only way to bring these wicked villains [the murderers] to justice and at the same time it will be the greatest means to destroy the gangs of smugglers by breaking into all the confidence they may have with one another. . .'[2] The Duke of Richmond eventually convinced Ryder, the Attorney-General. On this point the Duke was undoubtedly right, for it was the promise of the pardon, even to accused felons, that enabled him to convict as many smugglers as he did.

Read, two coachmen, with a mob of people that lived in Chatham (unknown to Mr. Tomlin) assaulted Mr. Tomlin in such a manner that the mare got out of his hands and he could not recover her again. . .' Custom House Library, Collier MSS, 569.

1. William Fletcher, one of Richmond's agents, did most of the leg work in tracking down smugglers and finding informers. His letters provide an interesting picture of 'detective' work in the eighteenth century. About the Carswell killing he wrote that he had searched for witnesses, 'but I don't find anyone about Hurst Green, or Hawkhurst that way disposed. I was told that the smugglers just before they killed Carswell, went to the Bull (at Hurst Green), there charged their firelocks and stripped themselves into their shirts and put on white caps. I went to that house, the landlord is since dead. I talked with the widow, used fair words but could get nothing of her, then talked to her in other terms, and told her she should certainly be carried to the assizes and at her own expense, unless she would fairly tell me what she knew of the matter, but she would tell me nothing. . .' West Sussex RO, Goodwood MS, 156/G 24.

2. ibid., 155/H 33.

IV

Smuggling was widespread, however, not only because the forces of repression were weak and the officers of the revenue corrupt. The real cause of the inability of the authorities to suppress the illicit trade was that, with duties high, smuggling was extremely profitable for large numbers of people. At the same time, it meant that such things as inexpensive tea and imported spirits were available to an even larger section of the population. Consequently, as Samuel Wilson told the Parliamentary Committee, 'the generality of the people on the coasts are better friends to the smugglers than they are to the Custom House Officers'.[1]

No section of eighteenth-century society was untouched by smuggling. For example, when Henry Jacques of Cranbrook in Kent sent the Duke of Newcastle details of a possible French invasion, he had to beg that his informant 'may not suffer on account of the illicit trade he is concerned in, through my means, and that at the same time my name remain a secret, being by trade an apothecary and having some very good customers among those people with which your Grace can't be ignorant this country abounds'.[2] Apothecaries, like all provincial shopkeepers and tradesmen, played an obvious part in the economy of smuggling, and there are numerous examples of their direct and indirect activities in the trade. In the case of an assault on a Captain Asher and his marines near Hastings, among those standing bail for the smugglers indicted were William Gurr, an innholder from Hastings, and James Hutchinson, a wholesale victualler from the parish of St Margarets.[3] They were joined by two Hastings mariners, Zebulon Morphet and James Hutchins.

Few of these men were ever themselves victims of the law, however, and it is difficult to discover much about those whom Collier described as 'the merchants and tradesmen of London that employed . . . [the

---

1. *CJ*, vol. XXV (1745–50), p. 104.
2. Brit. Mus. Add. MSS, 32,702 fo. 149, 4 March 1744. Jacques also reported that he began his inquiries on hearing a rumour that the masters of two smuggling cutters had been seized and hanged by the French. His informant 'told me on Friday night two persons arrived being the first boat suffered to come from Boulogne this three weeks, and they acquainted him that two (viz. Thomas Harvey and Robert Fuller) masters of two cutters were seized at that place . . . and carried from thence, the reason of which usage they were entirely ignorant of, but since it appears they were detained to serve as pilots in the fleet destined for the invasion of this kingdom. They remain still in custody and are treated a very handsome manner as they express it, but are not suffered to go without a guard. I did not think it proper to be solicitous in the affair by reason people in that business are a little cautious of letting persons into their business. . .' ibid.
3. Custom House Library, Collier MSS, 547: Simon to Collier, 24 March 1744.

smugglers] and received their smuggled goods. . .'[1] Nevertheless, as the
fines levied by the Court of the Exchequer indicate, there were many men
of substance among the dealers in contraband goods. Samuel Hulme,
a Southwark grocer, petitioned the Customs against the fine of treble the
value of 6,000 pounds of tea 'supposed to have come into his hands, he
not knowing the duties thereof not to have been paid'.[2] There were men
in the Fleet Prison with fines as large as £25,000.[3] The fines were fixed at
treble the value of the goods seized. The Duke of Richmond, in the course
of his campaign for the Special Commission, wrote to Henry Simon that
'as soon as Diamond was taken, two very substantial men, one of
Chichester and the other living just out of the town, immediately came
and offered whatever the justices should think fit to ask, which to me is
very strong proof that they must have had great dealings with him. . .'[4]

And, as the opponents of smuggling never tired of pointing out, the
illegal trade corrupted the entire nation. Parson Woodforde, who accepted
gin from Richard Andrews, 'the honest smuggler', was not an exception.[5]
Robert Walpole himself, despite the savagery of the measures he proposed
to suppress smuggling, personally carried his fine French wines past the
Custom House. The 'exceedingly good French white wine' which Celia
Fiennes drank on her Sussex tour was undoubtedly smuggled.[6] The fact
that Richmond left no records of his taste in wine is a great pity. Finally,
the case of Captain Gwyn and his posse, which involved not only his
neighbours but also the local constable and a lieutenant of the marines,
all gathered in opposition to the revenue officers, indicates the extent to
which smuggling involved all classes of people on the coasts of England.

Nevertheless, it was neither the importation of fine wines, nor the
profits of the provincial shopkeeper which most alarmed the authorities
in the 1740s. Rather, in the words of John Taylor, the Ordinary of Newgate, it was the fact that 'the common people of England in general fancy
there is nothing in the crime of smuggling. . .'[7] There is abundant
evidence that this was the case, and the Duke of Richmond made the

1. East Sussex RO, Sayer MSS, 420.   2. PRO, Customs 48, 13/475.
3. C(H) MSS 40/14. David Boys, a merchant, was fined £25,515 by the Court of
Exchequer, '. . . treble the value of a parcel of wine and brandy charged to have come
into his hands.' Boys was said to be a 'very notorious offender. The warden of the
Fleet is under prosecution for an escape by this deponent.' The fact that fines such as
this one were usually paid (or at least compounded) indicates something of the wealth
of some of the people involved in smuggling.
4. West Sussex RO, Goodwood MSS, 155/H 33.
5. Rev. James Woodforde, *The Diary of a Country Parson*, ed. John Beresford, Oxford,
1926, vol. I, p. 282.
6. Celia Fiennes, *The Journeys of Celia Fiennes*, ed. Christopher Morris, 1949. Her
Sussex tour was in the 1690s.
7. Taylor, op. cit., p. 23.

point himself in an angry exchange with Sir Cecil Bishop, another Sussex landowner. Bishop began the argument by writing to the Duke of Richmond on behalf of Thomas Lillywhite, a young labourer, indicted as an accomplice at Poole:

... this poor lad neither saw the Custom House nor was in the town, but attended the horses about a mile's distance. I am sensible this in the eye of the law may make him an accomplice, but in a case where there is no bloodshed, in the poor opinion of a country gentleman, ignorant in the laws, he may deserve some favour. He, at the time of the gallant expedition [to Poole], for such it was esteemed by most of this neighbourhood, was but seventeen years old...

Richmond was outraged by this petition, and sent the following response:

I ... really cannot help wondering at your application in favour of a smuggler, especially for Thomas Lillywhite, who has been guilty of such a heinous offense as that of being assistant to breaking open the Custom House at Poole: and what astonishes me the more ... is your having been lately upon the bench where you heard such a scene of barbarity and murders so evidently proved... I have often heard you say and with great truth, that the common people of this country have no notion that smuggling is a crime. What then can a government do to show them their error but punish the guilty? ... I say it is strongly against him [Bishop's argument in Lillywhite's favour] for it has become necessary to show the common people by example that accessories are to be punished as well as principals ... for you know very well that the common notion in the country is that a man may stand by and see crimes committed and even advise and assist in them with impunity, if he does not commit the fact with his own hands; this shows the necessity for examples, without which, indeed Sir Cecil, neither you nor I, nor any good subject can live in tolerable security in this country.[1]

For the common people, then, smuggling was much more than the chance to earn an extra shilling or consume exotic commodities. The fact that smuggling was considered 'no crime', or, more importantly, that the attack on the Custom House at Poole could be seen as a 'gallant expedition', goes a long way in explaining the determination with which the Government's efforts to suppress smuggling were met. Smuggling, far from being seen as an illegal activity by the Sussex poor, was considered a legitimate part of the local economy. It was one of the many methods used by the eighteenth-century rural poor to maintain themselves, regardless of legal prohibitions. John Taylor was not alone in noting that the poor felt they had 'a right to shun ... paying any duty on their goods...'[2] Like poachers and wreckers, they claimed this 'right' in accordance with custom and tradition.

1. West Sussex RO, Goodwood MSS, 155/H 83 (6 February 1749) and H 96 (17 February 1749).
2. Taylor, op. cit.

Sussex in the 1740s languished in the memory of better days, when the
fine harbours of Rye and Winchelsea were free of silt, and the clothing
trade still flourished in the villages of the Weald.[1] Fishing, another traditional occupation, was also in decline, and the papers of John Collier
contain numerous petitions from the herring fishermen demanding relief.
Even the famous Sussex iron, produced with the charcoal from the great
forests, was in its last phase. By 1720, there were only ten blast furnaces
in all of Sussex.[2] Smuggling, therefore, filled an important gap, and it
should not be surprising that the development of national monopolies
was met with hostility, by both the provincial traditionalist and the rural
poor alike. Duties, after all, protected the monopolies of the mercantile
bourgeoisie, in addition to raising revenue for the national government.
The protection of smuggling was in part a defence of the local economy,
as against the development of commercial capitalism. For the poor it was
even more. Often smuggling meant the difference between a bare subsis-
tence and worse. For a few, it was an escape from everything which
defined the life of the rural labourer or village artisan. The resistance of
the plebeian smugglers to attempts to suppress their trade, therefore, was
also an aspect of the class struggle of the eighteenth century.

While no two persons became smugglers for precisely the same reasons,
there were certain patterns. John Diamond, for example, was a member
of the West Sussex gang involved in the affair at Poole. While testifying
against his former comrades, he gave the Duke of Richmond an account
of his own life. Diamond was thirty-one years old in 1748. Born in Dorset,
he was apprenticed to a farmer at the age of nine. Upon reaching the age
of twenty-one, he left Dorset, working with a succession of farmers until
1744, when he came to work for a Mr Wooden, a farmer at East Whitten
in Sussex. There 'he used to take care of his master's sheep in certain

1. According to Celia Fiennes, Rye 'was a flourishing place before the sea left it'.
Observing the landscape from Beggar's Hill, where she attended 'the saddest fair [she]
. . . ever saw', Fiennes described a 'great tract of land on each side that is choked up with
sand, which formerly was a good haven for ships'. As for the town opposite Rye, she
wrote, 'grass now grows where Winchelsea was. . .' Fiennes, op. cit., pp. 138–9.
Another visitor to Sussex, Dr John Burton, a Fellow of Eton College, gave this picture of
Brighton in 1751: 'It is not indeed contemptible as to size, for it is thronged with
people, though the inhabitants are mostly very needy and wretched in their mode of
living, occupied in the employment of fishing, robust in their bodies, laborious, skilled
in all nautical crafts, and, as it is said, terrible cheats of the Custom House officers. The
village near the shore seemed to me very miserable, many houses here and there deserted
and traces of overthrown walls.' Burton described Shoreham as 'a village despicable in
appearance, but nevertheless with a market and shipyards and officers of the Customs
. . .' Quoted in W. H. Blaauw, 'Extracts from the Iter Sussexiense of Dr. John Burton',
Suss. Arch. Coll., vol. VIII (1856), p. 263.
2. Basil Williams, *The Whig Supremacy*, 1962, p. 113.

marshes known by the name of the ordinary marshes in the parish of East Whitten, and whilst he was close to the sea side . . . he had divers times seen a number of smugglers come down those marshes to and from the sea side . . . they frequently used to call him to come and help them and then gave him for his trouble sometimes money sometimes tea. . .' After helping the gang on several occasions over a period of about three months, Diamond was persuaded 'to enter with them into their society and that he should be concerned and have part of their profit which he did accordingly, and finding he got more by that than he did by service, left his master Wooden and bought himself a horse and joined the gang, which amounted to the number of about twenty. . .'[1]

Richard Perrin was a leader of the Hawkhurst gang. In 1748 he was thirty-six years old. Perrin was born near Chichester and 'being bred a carpenter was looked upon as a good workman'. In addition, he 'had a pretty business, til the use of his right hand, being in a great measure taken away by being subject to the palsey, he thought proper to leave that trade, and to take up smuggling. He was esteemed a very honest man as to every other affair in life, and was therefore often entrusted by others to go over the water to buy goods for them, and for himself too he traded in that way for brandy and tea.' Perrin was the man who purchased the tea, which was subsequently taken by Captain Johnson, lodged at Poole, and then retaken by the smugglers.

Another Sussex smuggler, John Cook, of Hawkhurst, was 'born at Hastings in Sussex of poor but honest parents'. He was first employed for several years as a labourer 'in helping lade and unlade vessels at that port'. This he continued until 'getting acquainted with the smugglers'. Francis Andrews, aged thirty-three, testified that he had 'been a smuggler in his time'. But since May 1745 'he had not done anything . . .' for 'he had got some money by that way of trade which enabled him to rent a small farm of Mr. Justice Day, which he cultivated, and maintained his family by. . .'[2] Andrews was indicted in Suffolk for not surrendering himself.

There were countless men like these, for smuggling was easily more profitable than 'honest work'. At the beginning of the nineteenth century, Arthur Young, in his study of Sussex agriculture, contrasted the wages of labourers with the returns from smuggling. At that time, according to Young, a task-worker could earn between 1s. 6d. and 2s. a day, while a labourer earned from 16d. to 18d. Compared to this, a smuggler could earn 10s. 6d. a night. The men who helped the smugglers, as Diamond

1. West Sussex RO, Goodwood MSS, 155/H 27.
2. Taylor, op. cit., pp. 30–31, 41, 83.

did, might make a guinea a week. For merely conveying goods from the smuggling vessel to the shore, a man could earn 2s. 7d. a night.[1]

While these figures represent the wages of a later period, they are still useful, for in the absence of better evidence they serve as an indication of the disparities that existed. For the 1740s, we know that a man might receive 'half a guinea a journey', but this says nothing of the job or the journey.[2] Probably the best evidence for this period is the account of the author of *The Trials of the Smugglers*, who thought

it very necessary to give the public some account of what encouragement is given to poor men to serve the smugglers as servants, to fetch their goods up from the sea-side, by which time they become smugglers themselves. Each man is allowed half a guinea a time, and his expenses for eating and drinking, a horse found for him, and the profits of a dollop of tea, which is about 13 pounds weight, being half a bag; which profit, even from the most ordinary of teas, comes to 24 or 25 shillings; and they always make one journey, sometimes two, in a week; for they have always certain intelligence of the exact time and place that the cutter, which brings the tea, is come to land.[3]

And we also know that the residents of the neighbourhood of Hawkhurst were promised twenty guineas each to protect the smugglers' goods from the revenue officers.[4] While this was probably an exaggeration, we can still be certain that in the mind of the informer the amount promised was a lot. In some ways the impressions of contemporaries can be just as useful as the actual wage figures. For example, when George Spencer, a landowner from Field Place in Sussex, wrote to the Duke of Richmond on behalf of a condemned smuggler, he contrasted the smugglers with 'fine horses, gay clothes, watches in their pockets, and a seeming plenty of money . . .' to the 'poor fellow who has to earn his bread by the sweat of his brow'.[5] Even if Spencer overstated his case, his comparison tells us a good deal about how his contemporaries looked at smuggling.

The exact social composition of the smuggling gangs is not always easy to determine, yet the evidence suggests that nearly all of those involved in the gangs of the 1740s were plebeian. If those innkeepers, dealers in tea and farmers who smuggled were ever involved in the gangs, they were rarely either caught or prosecuted. In the years of the Duke of Richmond's campaign, there were at least five major trials concerning Sussex smug-

1. Arthur Young, *General View of the Agriculture of the County of Sussex*, 1813, pp. 404–5.

2. *Gentleman's Magazine*, vol. XIX (1749), p. 138.

3. Anon., *The Trials of the Smugglers, and the other Prisoners, at the Assizes held at East Grinstead . . .*, 1749, p. 19.

4. See above, p. 129.

5. West Sussex RO, Goodwood MSS, 156/G 83, n.d., probably March 1750.

glers. Of all the men convicted in these cases, none, so far as the evidence shows, ranked higher on the social scale than labourer or artisan. Twelve of the twenty-eight convicted were labourers. Three were artisans, two were colt-breakers, and the rest were either 'bred to no business' or identified simply as smugglers.[1]

In November 1748 William Wood issued a proclamation from the Custom House, which, in accordance with the Act of 19 Geo. II c. 10, listed 103 persons, all charged with smuggling, commanding them to surrender themselves within forty days. Nearly all of these men came from Norfolk, Suffolk, Kent and Sussex, with one or two each coming from Cambridgeshire, Essex and Hampshire. Of the 103, 69 were listed as labourers. The next most numerous group was that of yeoman, with seven. There were six butchers, four farmers, four carpenters and four victuallers. And there were one each of the following: basketmaker, bargeman, mariner, innkeeper, shoemaker, cordwainer, locksmith, pattern-maker, thatcher and husbandman.[2] Of course evidence like this must be treated with care. The category 'labourer', for example, was often given to any person with no other obvious occupation, including many who were professional smugglers. On the other hand, most of these people appear more than once in the legal records of the period, and there is a surprising consistency. Similarly, care must be used with those identified as yeoman. At least three of the seven were well-known professional smugglers: Jeremiah Curtis, Uriah Creed and Robert Mapesden, all of Hawkhurst. The distinction 'yeoman' may have been applied to them in recognition of their financial success in smuggling, for other evidence shows that they were all born into poverty.[3]

1. See the following: 'Gentleman of Chichester', op. cit.; GLRO, MJ/GDR 2919, Indictment 33; PRO Assi 31/2; PRO, KB 8/72; and *The Trials of the Smugglers*.
2. West Sussex RO, Goodwood MSS, 155/H 17.
3. Some smugglers did very well by their trade, even socially it appears. Three leaders of the Hawkhurst gang are interesting examples. Arthur Gray was born at Hawkhurst, and later 'put apprentice to a butcher at Malden near Maidstone, to whom he served seven years, after which he returned to Hawkhurst and there carried on his trade for about three years...' at which time he became a smuggler. Gray figured prominently in Sussex smuggling until he was captured and sent to Newgate. He escaped from Newgate in 1748, with his brother William and Thomas Kemp, was recaptured, and finally was executed at Tyburn in May 1748. When he died he was thirty-four years old and said to be worth £10,000: Taylor, op. cit., pp. 49–52; and East Sussex RO, Sayer MSS 3871. William Gray was first taken by the Cranbrook Associators. At that time, according to Collier in a letter to Simon, he had 'lately built a house at Hawkhurst which is thought cost at least £1,200 to £1,500'. After he escaped, he, with Thomas Kemp, 'was seen in this neighbourhood ... drinking at a public house door at Battle at the very time when some of the townspeople were inside reading the advertisement for their apprehension'. William Gray was 'universally looked on [as] ... one of the most desperate of the gang'

Regardless of the number of others involved in smuggling, it is evident that those from the 'common people' took the risks, fought the battles and received the vengeance of the authorities. Undoubtedly these men were themselves exploited by others, the 'men of substance' who made the greatest profits, for smuggling was also an increasingly important business. Hoh Cheung and Lorna Mui are certainly correct in stressing the importance of smuggling in pioneering and 'developing trade facilities in areas not easily reached from established centres of distribution', and, more importantly, 'promoting the international and domestic trade of the kingdom, which, in turn, contributed to the growth of the British economy in the latter part of the eighteenth century'.[1] What they omit is any mention of the bloody conflict which was at the bottom of this aspect of British commercial development. The smugglers both resisted and enhanced the development of capitalism; in each case they paid dearly for their efforts.

Whatever part of their earnings may have gone to others, the smuggling gangs of the 1740s grew steadily more defiant in the face of Government repression. When smugglers became involved in other forms of crime, particularly house-breaking and highway robbery, contemporaries usually attributed this to the decline in smuggling caused by the Pelham reforms. In October 1747, for example, the *Gentleman's Magazine* reported, 'A great number of robberies have been committed, since the beginning of this month, within ten miles of London, mostly as it's thought by smugglers; for two of these people having robbed a gentleman who knew them, declared that they had lost their trade, could not follow any honest employ, their lives being forfeited, and while they did live, they would not starve.'[2] It would be wrong, however, to view the increase in robbery in solely

---

according to Collier. When he was tried in London, Simon wrote that 'Mr. Lance a brewer at Rye (I think that is his name) interests himself much in favor of both these men [the Grays], as to William, I find many are to appear for him, and (what I am sure even you will think very strange) many are Custom House Officers.' Sayer MSS 319 and 311. Jeremiah Curtis, who was also called William Pollard, was listed as a labourer, when he was first indicted at the summer Assizes in Lewes, 1737, but as a yeoman when he was outlawed in 1748. He too escaped from Newgate, though at a different time, and he also escaped the country, going to France, though he apparently crossed the Channel frequently. In 1749, Richmond heard from a correspondent in Boulogne, 'I have heard that villain Curtis at Dunkirk is listed in the Brigade [Irish], if so it will be difficult to touch him. . .' and the same year a Mr Dobson, a Customs officer at Rye, wrote to Richmond that he had to be very cautious in watching for Curtis [who was said to be returning to visit his wife] as 'Curtis is here looked upon as the natural son of Mr. Lamb, one of our great men. . .' West Sussex RO, Goodwood MSS, 155/H 83 and 156/G 62.

1. H. and L. Mui, op. cit., p. 73.
2. *Gentleman's Magazine*, vol. XVII (1747), p. 496.

economic terms, just as it is wrong to see smuggling as nothing more than an economic response by the poor to their poverty. In this period house-breaking and other crime went along with intimidation, reprisals and a general defiance of authority. Smugglers 'took to the highway' not only because they lost their trade, but because they were determined, in the Tucker brothers' words, 'to resist to a man'.[1]

In addition to these explanations, there is another possible reason for the increase in robberies in Sussex during these years. For example, when four men armed with pistols and a blunderbuss broke into the house of Richard Haffenden in Sussex and took 'thirty five pounds in money, five pieces of old gold, two silver spoons marked I.H., a silver watch, a two-handled tumbler, and three gold rings . . .'[2] they may have been collecting capital for a future smuggling endeavour. They were said to have been 'part of a gang of smugglers', and smugglers had to find capital somehow. Men who were either poor or strong enough to be independent of the merchants and tradesmen may have used stolen money and tribute as one means of financing their trade.

The threatening letter which Richmond received some years earlier suggests such a possibility:

This is for his Grace to know that we desire him to put 2 hundred and 50 ginnes in a bag and put them on the outside of the park pales under the lader stile of the Southeast Corner of the park against the pond this night and in four months you shall have all your money and fifty ginnes for the use of it, if not we will beat down all your buildings and destroy all that you have, for hear are 2 hundred and 50 of us, and in too days time we can raise our company to 6 hundred so if you do not deliver your mony quitly we will destroy all that you have and we will shoot his Grace whearever we sees him for we are all smugglers and we have lost a great deal of goods.[3]

One account of the conflict at Goudhurst is also suggestive; it describes the smugglers as having 'arrived at that pitch of wantonness and cruelty that they would frequently ride into a town in a large body, and plunder the houses where they thought there was the most to be acquired. . .'[4] This implies something of a *system* of robbery, and as Goudhurst was situated near Hawkhurst and in the midst of other smuggling villages, the system may well have involved the collection of a form of tribute in conjunction with the smuggling trade. At any rate, the situation was serious. The local gentry raised the Goudhurst militia.

1. See above, p. 136.   2. *LG* 8797, November 1748.
3. Lennox, op. cit., vol. II, pp. 573–4.
4. Kent RO, East Barming Parish Register, 1868 (a copy of what is claimed to be an eye-witness account).

Two anonymous letters to Henry Pelham suggest the same thing. The first (both were signed 'Legion') complained that 'the number of these southern rebels [the smugglers] is far greater than those of the north [the Jacobites], and if not timely suppressed will be equally dangerous to the best of governments.'[1] The second letter concluded that 'we [presumably the inhabitants of Sussex] are in as bad a condition as they were in Scotland, when plundered by the rebels ... when they [the smugglers] plunder so or as they call it 'visiting of 'em', or say 'tis only 'neighbours fare and hope they'll not take it a miss. . .'[2] 'Neighbour's fare' could well have been tribute, and extortion might possibly be added to the history of smuggling and social crime. At the very least this evidence continues to create a picture of exceptionally audacious smugglers, as well as of a serious breakdown of authority in the countryside.

On some occasions, the defiance of the smugglers appears to have included at least verbal support for the Pretender. While it would be a mistake to make too much of this, it is worth recalling that in later periods, smugglers were prominent in both the Swing riots of south-east England and the crowds of revolutionary Paris.[3] In Scotland, smuggling and Jacobitism seem to have gone hand in hand. In Sussex in the 1740s, the smugglers appear to have gone no further than oaths and boasting in country inns, though the Duke of Richmond thought such declarations

1. Brit. Mus. Add. MSS, 32,709 fos. 273-4, 27 November 1746.
2. ibid., 32,711, fo. 211, 4 June 1747. In another letter signed 'Legion', the anonymous writer wrote the following: 'We who are his Grace's (real) friends think it our duty to acquaint your honour with the clamours that have been raised by his Grace's enemies since one of the chiefs of the plunderers of this country has been apprehended by the soldiers at the seaside. His Grace's enemies have declared that he'd be released by his Grace's interest. Some of his Grace's pretended friends having offered £500 for that purpose. If the heads are crushed, the lesser ones will fall, of course, and we shall see the [Pelham] interest likewise raised to its former luster, which every step taken towards subduing these destroyers of the country contributes to. Without such, a revolution like that in Holland must inevitably ... follow': ibid., 27 May 1747. 'Legion' said more than once that the Pelhams' 'enemies' were charging that the Pelhams were protecting the smugglers. Apart from Collier, I have found no direct evidence of this, aside from the normal sort of corruption involved in Sussex electioneering. Many petitioners promised the Duke of Newcastle votes if the neighbourhood smuggler might be let off. At the same time, however, others asked for protection against the smugglers. I have not come across any well-known smugglers released in the spring of 1747, though Curtis escaped from Newgate on 4 July 1747. PRO, T 1/327.
3. See Rudé and Hobsbawm, *Captain Swing*, 1968, p. 63, and Rudé, *Paris and London in the Eighteenth Century*, 1970, p. 174. In the first, Hobsbawm writes, 'Poachers and smugglers – in the nature of things mostly young and strong men with no prejudice against violence – and those who organized their work, were notoriously involved in the risings of 1816 and 1830. On the other hand, such "natural rebels" among the agricultural workers were likely to be the least educated and "ideological" of their kind.'

were 'a much more serious thing than people seem to appreciate it in London'.[1] One such case was reported to Collier by his clerk, Richard Patrick, in May 1744:

> On my journey to Folkestone, I called upon Mr. Darby at Lydd who informs me that the large gangs of armed smugglers frequent that place as much as ever, that the Transports and one Betts of Rye have leave from the French King to go out and in any of the harbours and ports in war with France, and that there has since the commencement of the war with France been great quantities of run goods landed in Romney Marsh and places adjoining from those cutters, and that the land smugglers have been so impudent as to publically drink to the Pretender and his sons' health, wish success to their arms and confusion to his Majesty's King George...

During the same week, Thomas Clare, the officer at Hythe, wrote Collier that:

> On Monday, the 7th [of May] Messrs. Rogers and Bayly, Officers at Hythe, came to acquaint me that the Hasting's Outlaws had their goods between Brockman's Barn and Hythe which goods were immediately carried off by Hawkhurst Gang, who were a great number and armed. I am credibly informed that the Hasting's Outlaws have taken an oath of allegiance to the King of France, and carry people from England thither, which at this time of day is a thing of bad consequence...[2]

Too little is known about popular Jacobite sympathy to say whether the Duke of Richmond was right in taking these kinds of reports seriously. The most that can be said now is that they are at least an indication of the unpopularity of George II and of the Hanovers. In the absence of any real popular opposition of a radical kind, however, such threats were one way of expressing opposition, if only for the sake of frightening the Whigs.

If there were in fact no smugglers as politically rebellious as these oaths would suggest, there were certainly rebels of another sort. For smuggling offered more than money. There were smugglers in Sussex who remind one of Hobsbawm's social bandits; 'men who are unwilling to accept the meek and passive social role of the subject peasant; the stiff-necked and recalcitrant, the individual rebels'.[3] Smuggling was for the poor a way out, an escape for those who refused to submit. Thomas Kingsmill, another of the smugglers at Poole, 'wanted not business'. Born of a poor family at Goudhurst, he was 'a bold resolute man, undaunted, and fit for the wicked purposes of smuggling'. Kingsmill was twenty-eight when he was executed. William Fairall had also been at Poole. He was executed at the age of twenty-five. Born at Horsendown Green in Kent, Fairall was 'bred to

1. See above, p. 140. 2. Custom House Library, Collier MSS, 613, 629.
3. E. J. Hobsbawm, *Bandits*, 1969, p. 28.

no business . . . [and] inured to smuggling from his infance'. He too was contemptuous of the authorities, and at his trial he 'seemed to show the utmost daringness and unconcern, even showing tokens of threats to a witness, as he was giving his evidence to the court, and standing all the while in the bar with a smile or rather a sneer upon his countenance. . .'[1]

Many examples of the smugglers openly challenging the authorities have already been given. There existed in this period a serious threat to the system of deference and authority in the countryside, and the defenders of property were clearly alarmed. Justices of the Peace were often afraid to prosecute smugglers. Those who opposed the gangs were intimidated and even attacked – barns were burned and informers were murdered. Officers of the revenue could never be certain how a night's work might end (unless they made their own peace with the smugglers). In 1742 the Excise officer at Sevenoaks, according to another officer, Daniel Barker,

was taken prisoner by upwards of 20 smugglers who beat him and carried him to the Bull Head at Sprats Bottom . . . where they unloaded their goods, kept him all night til they loaded again and went clear off. And last night Mr. Griffin, Supervisor of Excise [the report continued] was doing his survey with the Excise Officer of Tunbridge and was beat and cut in so violent a manner that his life was despaired of, by a large parcel of smugglers within a mile of Tunbridge. They likewise beat and misused several private people in the road and made them kneel down in the mud and beg their pardons.[2]

Other people were similarly humiliated, and the smugglers often 'dared' the authorities to oppose them. They rode 'triumphantly' through the villages of Sussex, often in daylight, defying the Army and local authorities alike. More than one person compared this conflict on the south coast to that of war.

Eighteenth-century smuggling involved a mixture of social forms of resistance. Because most of the actual fighting was between the plebeian gangs and the forces of the Government, and because the smugglers believed they were protecting their 'rights', the conflict contained elements of class war. This is also the case in the plunder of the gentry, to the degree that it actually happened. Moreover, while many people benefited from smuggling, only the poor went to the gallows, a fact that was not missed by the common people of Sussex. On the other hand, in some cases, as in Hastings and Hawkhurst (and perhaps even in the confrontation at Captain Gwyn's), entire communities supported the smugglers and would rise in their defence '500 in less than an hour', it was said at Hawkhurst.[3] The conflict was also, therefore, partially a

1. Taylor, op. cit., pp. 40–41.
2. Custom House Library, Collier MSS, 497. Letter to Collier, 24 October 1742.
3. See above, p. 124.

regional and traditional response – in this case to the centralization and monopoly of commercial wealth and power. Before these elements can be thoroughly untangled, a great deal more research must be done, particularly into the smuggling communities themselves. As yet, very little is known about the population of the towns and villages of the Weald and the coast, where smuggling, apparently, was the primary activity.[1]

Still, there are some things which we can say about the smugglers. For one thing, certain of their activities, including the collective struggles of entire communities, as well as frequent direct action against informers, revenue officers and soldiers, can be seen as a variation upon what is known of eighteenth-century crowd activity, although with important differences. The absence of any vestige of deference is the most striking of these, as is the willingness to go quickly beyond violence to property, the point at which price-fixing crowds, for instance, usually stopped. Those individual smugglers, such as the men who made the attack on the Custom House at Poole, who went beyond mere smuggling and who also supported themselves and their trade by highway robbery and housebreaking, were often the rebels of the countryside. And, again like Hobsbawm's 'social bandits', they were 'robbers . . . who are *not* regarded as simple criminals by public opinion'.[2] In other ways, smugglers do not fall into Hobsbawm's categories. Nevertheless, to the common people they were certainly not seen as criminals. Cecil Bishop's neighbourhood actually applauded the march to Poole, as did many others, and on their return to Sussex the smugglers were admired by 'hundreds of people' who gathered to watch them pass at Fordingbridge. The smuggler was often a symbol of resistance, to the authorities in general, and in particular to the hated Excise. Whether or not the smuggler was anything more than this remains to be seen, but it would be premature to agree with Hobsbawm that in England 'the miserable village labourers have risen to little

1. It is interesting to note that whatever regional solidarity there was concerning smuggling may have broken down in 1747 and 1748. Cranston, for example, who was certainly sympathetic to the smugglers, wrote to Collier in November 1747: 'I read yours today, am sorry the Hawkhurst people have brought themselves into such a scrape, the very devil must be fully in them, or they could never act in so unaccountable and shocking a manner. How they will get out of it, I know not. . .' East Sussex RO, Sayer MSS 909. Richmond's successes may have been in part due to the fact that, in such acts as the killing of Galley and Chater, the smugglers alienated people who were ordinarily sympathetic. It would also be interesting to know more about the social composition of groups like the Goudhurst Militia and the Cranbrook Associators. It seems clear that they were at least initiated and financed by the gentry, but beyond that we know very little. Collier wrote to the Commissioners of the Customs that he felt 'that their taking up arms was very laudable and of very great service towards dispersing the infamous gangs of smugglers at and about Hawkhurst. . .' Sayer MSS 300.

2. Hobsbawm, op. cit., p. 13.

more than the modest admiration for exceptionally daring poachers.'[1]
The truth is probably that very little is known about the heroes of the
eighteenth-century poor.

V

The Duke of Richmond believed that only a great amount of publicity
and a large number of capital convictions could stop smuggling. He also
insisted that pardons should be available to any who would act as
informers, even if that person had broken the revenue laws or been outlawed, so long as the informer had 'not been concerned in any murders
or in breaking open the Custom House at Poole'. Such pardons were
essential, he told the Prime Minister, because 'the taking of Carter,
Jackson, Mills, Curtis and the others chiefly concerned in the murders in
Sussex is attended with so much difficulty, the whole country is being
intimidated'.

For the Special Commission itself, the Duke insisted on bringing down
judges from London. The justices of West Sussex, he told Pelham, could
not be trusted to convict smugglers. He had heard that 'Mr. Wicker of
Horsham, Mr. Mitford and Mr. Goodwin of Petworth, have declared
they would act in nothing relating to smuggling.'

After the smugglers were captured, the problem remained of ensuring
that the prisoners, the witnesses, and even the judges lived until the
commencement of the Special Commission. From the beginning, there
was the fear that others might share the fate of Chater and Galley. And
such fears were not entirely unjustified. In addition, the threat of an
escape or attempted rescue was a problem in every case involving
smugglers. Only eight months earlier, members of the Hawkhurst gang
had been rescued from Newgate in London. Accordingly, the Duke of
Richmond ordered additional soldiers into the county, to be stationed in
all places related to the Commission. He also asked Pelham to order the
gaoler at Horsham 'to be very careful that the prisoners make no escape
and threaten him with the severest punishment that the law can inflict
in case anything of that kind should happen...'[2] The possibility of an
actual attack on, or interruption of, the proceedings of the Commission
must have been small, but it was not imaginary.

A most extraordinary threat, if it is to be believed, was reported to the
Duke of Richmond by a number of West Sussex magistrates who wrote
that they were 'alarmed by intelligence from Portsmouth, brought by

1. Hobsbawm, *Primitive Rebels*, New York, 1965, p. 23.
2. West Sussex RO, Goodwood MSS, 155/H 24 (n.d. but probably November 1748).

farmer Lambert of Rumbaldsweek, who there heard Mr. Carter, a merchant of great credit in Portsmouth, say that a suspicious person bought last Thursday of Mr. Ballard, a noted sail-maker in Portsmouth Point, four hundred French muskets; he seemed in a great hurry when he bought them, put them into a wagon immediately, and said he must be at Rowland's Castle that night. . .' A troop of dragoons from Chichester was sent to Guildford, to 'strengthen the escort of the persons on the road . . . in case this should be true and ill use made of them either against the witnesses or the prisoners'.[1]

Mr Ballard, the man who sold the rifles, contacted the Duke of Richmond the next day, however, and it turned out that only twenty-five muskets had been sold, though the buyer had asked for 'four or five hundred'. He had also given Ballard earnest money for one hundred guns. Ballard said he sold the man only twenty-five because he 'made me imagine they were for some desperate case, especially when I found (by their discourse) that they lived somewhere in Sussex. . .'[2]

As it happens, no more was heard of the rifles. If there was any threat to the Commission, it was only the threat of John Mills, the other son of the defendant, Richard Mills, senior, to stop the judges as they travelled to Chichester and rob them. After the conclusion of the Special Commission, William Mitchell, an Under-Sheriff from Lewes, reported that he had been harassed by smugglers as he returned home from Chichester. In the first case, Mills's companions apparently thought the risks involved in such a robbery were too great.[3] In the second, Mitchell was followed and repeatedly passed by a man whom he 'guessed . . . was a smuggler', but the worst appears to have been when the man 'passed' Mitchell and 'snapped his whip very loud'.[4]

The accused smugglers were brought to Chichester under heavy guard. On Monday, 9 January 1749, Jackson and Carter were removed from Newgate. Richard Mills, junior, was taken from 'the New Gaol' (Guildford?), Surrey, the same day. These three were then carried to Horsham where the other prisoners were kept. The smugglers there, Richard Mills, senior, Benjamin Tapner, John Hammond and John Cobby, were placed in a wagon with the other three and taken, under even heavier guard, to Chichester, where they arrived on Friday, 13 January. In Chichester, they were all bound in heavy irons and confined in a single cell, except for Jackson, who 'being extremely ill was put into a room by himself, and

1. ibid., H 65.
2. ibid., H 66 (7 January 1749).
3. *The Complete Newgate Calendar*, vol. III, p. 173.
4. Brit. Mus. Add. MSS, 32,718, fo. 57 (deposition of William Mitchell, 31 January 1749).

all imaginable care was taken of him, in order to keep him alive (for he was in a very dangerous condition) til he had taken his trial'.

The judges travelled down from London over the weekend, spending one night at the Duke of Richmond's 'half-way house' at Godalming. The next day they dined with the Duke in his hunting lodge at Charlton. On Monday morning, the 16th, the judges rose and went in procession from the Bishop's Palace to the Guildhall, led by the High Sheriff of Sussex. There they were met by the Commissioners, among whom were the Duke of Richmond and Sir Cecil Bishop. When all this was done, Justice Foster, the Chief Justice at the Commission, announced the purpose of the trial; 'that the several murders, and other crimes committed by armed persons gathered together contrary to all law, in this and the neighbouring counties, loudly demanded the justice of the nation. . .' Foster concluded that he 'likewise took notice of the dangerous confederacies that had been formed for many years past in Sussex, and its neighbouring counties, for very unwarrantable and wicked purposes; even for robbing the public of that revenue which is absolutely necessary to its support, and for defeating the fair trader of his just expectation of profit. . .' Then Foster made a number of legal points which recall Richmond's admonitions to Sir Cecil Bishop. He contended that all persons concerned in smuggling, even accomplices, had to be made examples of, if crime in general and smuggling in particular was to be stopped.

For instance: numbers of people assemble for the purpose of running uncustomed goods . . . with a resolution to resist all opposers (and the riding with fire-arms and other offensive weapons is certainly an evidence of that resolution) . . . they are met by the officers of the revenue; one of the party, *in the prosecution of this unlawful design*, fires on the King's officer, and kills him or any of his assistants: the whole party is, in the eye of the law guilty of murder, though their original intention went no further than smuggling. . .[1]

This was the ruling which the Duke of Richmond had demanded, and it was this ruling which led to the conviction of Richard Mills and his son. In the Duke's opinion, the execution of these two was the single greatest accomplishment of the Special Commission. It was the 'example' he wanted, and he believed it did 'more service than the executions even of the principals'.[2]

The Special Commission lasted three days. On Wednesday, 18 January 1749, the final day, Justice Foster concluded the proceedings and gave instructions to the jury. After consideration, the jury as expected found Jackson, Carter, Tapner, Cobby and Hammond guilty as principals in the

1. 'Gentleman of Chichester', op. cit., pp. 26–9.
2. West Sussex RO, Goodwood MSS, 155/H 96 (17 February 1749).

murders, and the two Mills guilty as accessories.[1] That afternoon, the prisoners were fitted for the chains in which they were to be hung. The fitting seems to have upset them as much as anything, and the Mills were reported to have been greatly relieved on hearing they would be spared the chains and 'hung only as common malefactors'. According to the 'Gentleman of Chichester', it was the opinion of all those present that the fitting was the immediate cause of Jackson's death, for he 'was seized with such horror and confusion that he died in two hours afterwards. . .'[2]

The Duke of Richmond considered these convictions to be a great success, though even after the Commission he continued his campaign against the smugglers. Henry Simon congratulated the Duke and contrasted the Carswell case with that of Chater and Galley. The difference, he explained, was that 'the best endeavours of the Board of Revenue on prosecutions of this sort must fall short unless they are seconded and supported by the spirit and exertion of the country'.[3] To the extent that a number of the strongest gangs, including the Hawkhurst gang, were broken, and their leaders executed, the Duke of Richmond was certainly successful. But just how far his personal 'spirit and exertion' was shared or even approved of in the countryside is far from clear. The Duke, as far as possible, would allow no accommodation with smuggling, but he faced neither the problems nor the temptations of the majority of those living in Sussex. Two Sussex Under-Sheriffs apparently felt differently about the Commission, for William Mitchell wrote to Richard Rideout that he 'feared . . . the ensuing year will be much more hazardous than the former one on account of the vigorous prosecution of the smugglers, in which we must run great hazard and have great trouble. . .'[4] John Page, a Justice of the Peace from Stockbridge, wrote to the Duke of Richmond in a similar vein: 'I can't help observing to your Grace that whilst we are acting with so much vigour in one part of the country, there seems to be a sort of counter-acting in another. . .'[5] This 'counter-acting', apparently, was the unwillingness of some East Sussex justices to prosecute smugglers. Another observer of all these events, however, went far beyond these complaints and described the results of the Special Commission as 'the most savage and inhuman butcheries at Chichester . . . a melancholy instance of what cruel ravages the laws may sometimes give sanction to'.[6]

As far as the smuggling trade was concerned, however, the Duke's efforts were in vain. Nor was he successful in convincing the common

1. PRO, KB 8/72.   2. 'Gentleman of Chichester', op. cit., p. 74.
3. West Sussex RO, Goodwood MSS, 155/H III (30 May 1749).
4. Brit. Mus. Add. MSS, 32,718, fo. 59 (30 January 1749).
5. West Sussex RO, Goodwood MSS, 156/G 59.
6. *A Free Apology*, p. 18.

people that smuggling was a crime. He did, nevertheless, inflict a severe punishment on the smuggling community.

The trials of the smugglers continued through the spring and summer of 1749. In March, at the East Grinstead Assizes, John Mills, another of the gang at Poole, was indicted for the murder of Richard Hawkins, a labourer from Yapton in Sussex. Jeremiah Curtis was also charged but he had not been taken. Curtis was said to be living in France, where he was involved with the Irish brigades.[1] Witnesses said the murder stemmed from 'stolen tea'. Henry Murril said he had come upon Curtis in a public house in Yapton, drinking and angry because 'some rogues had stolen two bags of tea from him'. Hawkins, a labourer, apparently was found with the tea, and the jury found Mills guilty of killing him and, along with Curtis, throwing him into a pond which belonged to Sir Cecil Bishop. Another witness, Mr Serjeant Wynn, testified that this crime and 'the most daring robberies and insults . . .' were 'committed by these sort of men [Mills, etc.] who thought themselves above all law. . .'[2]

At the same time, five other well-known smugglers were charged with various crimes. Henry Sheerman was indicted for the murder of Galley. John Brown was charged with 'assaulting and putting in fear' John Walter near Burstead and of robbing him of twelve guineas in gold and £12 in silver. Thomas and Lawrence Kemp were indicted for having robbed Richard Havendon of Heathfield 'with crepes over their faces'. And Richard Savage was charged with 'stealing scarlet cloth out of the Lewes wagon'. All were found guilty, though Savage was not sentenced to death. He received seven years' transportation. Thomas Potter, William Priggs, James Bartlett and Stephen Dispose, 'all notorious smugglers' from Hawkhurst, were tried at Rochester, the first for horse-stealing, and the others for robbing John Rich of Linton of £170, plus plate. They were executed on Pickindon Heath near Maidstone in April.[3]

At the Old Bailey in London, Thomas Kingsmill, William Fairall and Richard Perrin were convicted of taking part in the attack on the Poole Custom House. They were hanged at Tyburn on 26 April 1747. The bodies of Kingsmill and Fairall were delivered to the Sheriff of Kent, to be hung in chains, the former at Goudhurst and the latter at Horsendown Green, 'where he once lived'.[4]

At the summer Assizes in Lewes, 1749, Edmund Richards, George Chapman and Richard Double were found guilty of the murder of Thomas Carswell. William Trower, John Geering, Thomas Holman and John Blue were also found guilty, having been charged in the murder of Michael

---

1. See above p. 153, n. 3.   2. *The Trials of the Smugglers*, pp. 4, 12–13.
3. ibid., pp. 12–13, 19.   4. Taylor, op. cit., p. 43.

Bath, an army officer, during an affray involving smuggling. The following year at the East Grinstead Assizes, another smuggler, Thomas Carey, was convicted of also having been involved in the murder of Carswell. In a contemporary account of two of these trials, the writer concluded with thanks to the Duke of Richmond: 'It must be allowed, that the country in general is greatly obliged to a certain noble duke. . .'[1] The Duke died in 1750.

In Chichester, the Special Commission was concluded with the march to the gallows. On Thursday, 19 January 1749, the prisoners were removed from the gaol and, escorted by a company of Foot Guards and a party of dragoons, taken to the place of execution, a place called the Broyle, about a mile outside the town. The procession was slow and solemn. When the six smugglers reached the tree, they found a great number of spectators had assembled to watch. Of the six, four – Carter, Hammond, Cobby and Tapner – were said to have confessed their guilt and agreed that their sentences were just. Richard Mills, junior, on the other hand, was said to have 'talked very merrily, and said "We shall have a jolly hang of it" '. At the tree, he complained that it was 'very bad to be refused a pint of beer', which he had asked for. Just before his execution, he was also reported to have told a gentleman in attendance 'that he did not value death, but was not guilty of the murder of which he was accused, since he was not present when it was done; though if he had he should not have thought it any crime to destroy such informing rogues'. His father, aged sixty-eight, 'would have smoked from the gaol to the gallows, but was prevented'. He also refused to plead guilty, saying that 'he was only sorry for his sons, for as to himself, he was under no trouble, for he was sure he could not, according to the common course of nature, live above a year or two longer. . .' As for the murder, he told the clergyman that 'it gave him but little trouble, since he was not guilty of it, but as to the charge of smuggling, he owned he had been concerned in that trade for a great many years, and did not think there was any harm in it'. The other Mills, John, convicted at East Grinstead, was hanged in chains on Slendon Common.

John Hammond broke down at the last minute, pleading for his 'poor wife and children'. He had been known as an exceptionally hard man, with

1. PRO, Assi 31/2; 'Gentleman of Chichester', op. cit., p. 72. Richmond had a hand in all these trials. For example, William Mitchell, the Under-Sheriff at Lewes, wrote to Richmond on 22 July 1749, concerning the coming assizes. 'I am favoured with your Grace's letter and have sent enclosed a copy of the jury, which I have made out as well as I can, and have returned a great part of them out of the West Sussex, that your Grace may be the easier informed about them, and if they should not be the proper persons, they may be challenged by the Crown at the assizes. . .'; Goodwood MSS, 156/G 50.

a particular antipathy for revenue officers. And he had often said that he did not think it a crime to kill an informer.[1]

The body of William Carter was taken down and hung in chains on the Portsmouth Road near Rake in Sussex. Benjamin Tapner's body was hung on Rook's Hill near Chichester. The bodies of John Cobby and John Hammond were taken to Selsey Bill and hung there, where they could be seen from a great distance in all directions. The two Mills's were thrown with Jackson into a hole just near the gallows.

The Duke of Richmond kept lists of the smugglers he pursued. On one of these, he wrote the names of those executed during the two years of his campaign. In all there were thirty-five; another ten were spared the gallows by dying in gaol.[2]

1. 'Gentleman of Chichester', op. cit., pp. 72–3; M. A. Lower, 'Newspaper Cuttings relating to Sussex: 1678–1771', *Suss. Arch. Coll.*, vol. xxiv (1872).
2. West Sussex R O, Goodwood MSS, 154/J7.

Wrecking and Coastal Plunder

'Wreckers', explained the author of a nineteenth-century tract to his inland readers, were people, 'often smugglers and their connexions, who inhabit those parts of the coast where vessels are most frequently wrecked. These hard-hearted persons, not only men, but women also, consider the stranded vessel as their property as soon as the waves have thrown it on their coast. – Under this unhallowed impression they plunder all they can, although the owner should survive and protest against their proceedings'.[1] He was describing a form of coastal plunder which occurred not infrequently around the British coastline in the eighteenth and nineteenth centuries. Wrecking had been the subject of a specific prohibitive statute as early as the reign of Edward I, but it was in the eighteenth century that increasing attention began to be paid to the depredations of coastal dwellers on the cargoes and materials of wrecked or stranded vessels. An act of 1713, finding 'that many ships of trade after all their dangers at sea escaped have unfortunately near home, run on shore ... and ... have been barbarously plundered by Her Majesty's subjects', was designed to reinforce existing legislation. It stressed that part of 3 Edward I. cap. 4. which stated that where any living creature escaped alive out of a ship, that ship could not be regarded as a wreck, even by those who claimed the right of wreck in a particular vicinity. This act was ordered to be read four times a year in all the churches and chapels on the sea coast.[2]

Wrecking persisted, and in 1735 the Commons received a petition from London merchants complaining that their ships were still being plundered, and their crews cruelly treated if they made any attempt to check the plundering. A statute was passed in 1753 which was more comprehensive than any existing prohibition. Its preamble referred to the persistence of

1. Anon., *The Wreckers, or a View of what sometimes passes on our Sea Coast*, n.d., p. 2.
2. 12 Anne c. 18 (1713).

the practice despite 'the good and salutary laws now in being', and claimed that many 'wicked enormities' had been committed. This act made it a capital offence to 'plunder, steal or take away, cargo, tackle, provision or part of such ship', whether any living thing remained on board or not. It also made it a capital offence to beat, wound or hinder the escape of any person trying to save his life from the wreck, or to put out 'any false light or lights with intention to bring any ship or vessel into danger'. The stealing of goods cast on shore, if not attended by any outrage or violence, was to be treated as petty larceny, and six months' imprisonment was prescribed for receiving and concealing wrecked goods. Anyone assaulting an officer or justice who was attempting to protect a wreck could be sentenced to seven years' transportation.

Merchants continued to complain of the activities of wreckers. In 1775, following petitions from the merchants of Poole and Bristol, Burke introduced a bill for a further act against wrecking. He spoke of the 'shameful and horrid practices' which were frequently committed on the British coastline. He proposed strengthening existing legislation by adding the imposition of a fine on the hundred in which any wrecking incident took place. His bill was lost, the opinion of the House being that what was needed was the better enforcement of existing legislation rather than the introduction of fresh. During the course of the bill, a petition against it was received from the coastal districts of Carmarthen a district where a high proportion of such fines would have been levied.[1]

The peak of wrecking activity was reached in the eighteenth and early nineteenth centuries, and there is some evidence to suggest that it became more frequent about the middle of the eighteenth. This increase most probably reflects the greatly increased opportunities for plunder provided by the tremendous increase in merchant shipping over the period. One authority suggests that English activity on the sea increased roughly fourfold during the eighteenth century. The associated growth of marine insurance added another pressure group to the merchants in support of the case for a more effective prevention of the practice.[2]

Wrecking continued into the nineteenth century, and its eventual decline from the middle of that century was probably due to a combination

1. *CJ*, vol. XII (1735), p. 603; 26 Geo. II c. 19 (1753); *CJ*, vol. XXV (1775), pp. 204, 705, 738, 745; *Cobbett's Parliamentary History* (1774–6), vol. XVIII, clm 1298.
2. W. Coxe, *Memoirs of Henry Pelham* (1879), vol. II, p. 272; T. S. Ashton, *An Economic History of England: The Eighteenth Century*, 1955, p. 144. The petition of 1753 in support of the act of that year came from the 'Merchants, Traders and Insurers' of London (*CJ*, vol. XXVI, (1753) p. 589). Although most of the surviving letters in the State Papers come from magistrates or Customs officers, a few do come from insurers' agents. For an account of the growth and development of marine insurance in the eighteenth century see L. S. Sutherland, *A London Merchant 1695–1744*, 1933, pp. 42–80.

of several factors: more effective policing, improved navigational methods, increasing use of coastal warning devices, the gradual replacement of sail by steam, and changing ideas of permitted behaviour on the part of the coastal populace. Wrecking was still prevalent enough in 1839, for the Constabulary Commissioners to use its existence as a major argument for the establishment of a rural police force. A clause in the Merchant Shipping Act of 1854 empowered the Receiver of the Board of Trade to use force in suppressing plunder at wrecks. A writer, commenting on this act in 1874, described it as 'not too stringent to suppress the lawlessness even now prevailing when wrecks take place on remote parts of our coasts'.[1]

The term 'wrecking' has no single and precise meaning. It refers to a range of activities varying from the casual pocketing of articles cast up by the sea to the deliberate luring of vessels ashore; from petty larceny to armed defiance of the law; from near beachcombing to open looting. If the term is used in a comprehensive way to imply simply the illegal appropriation of the cargo and materials of shipwrecked vessels, then it is clear that wrecking was prevalent at many places on the British coastline. Especially notorious were the long shores of Cornwall and the Isles of Scilly. 'Cornish' became an adjective which almost invariably preceeded any literary use of the word 'wrecking'. Lecky explicitly associates wrecking with Cornwall, and David Macpherson in 1805, singled out the 'farther south-western shores of England' for special mention in this context. Defoe was especially severe on the islanders of Scilly, and in 1732 Alexander Pope employed the couplet:

> Then full against his Cornish lands they [winds] roar,
> And two rich shipwrecks bless the lucky shore.

In a footnote he explained that he had located this scene in Cornwall, not only because of the frequency of wrecks there but also because of 'the inhumanity of the inhabitants to those to whom that misfortune arrives. When a ship happens to be stranded there, they have been known to bore holes in it to prevent its getting off; to plunder and sometimes even to massacre the people.'[2]

There was some justification for this regional association, but Cornishmen were, without denying the existence of wrecking along their own

1. *First Report of the Constabulary Force Commissioners, PP*, 1839, vol. xix; W. S. Lindsay, *History of Merchant Shipping and Commerce*, 1876, pp. 316–17.

2. W. E. H. Lecky, *History of England in the Eighteenth Century* (1892 edn), vol. ii, p. 114; D. Macpherson, *Annals of Commerce*, 1805, vol. iii, p. 40; A. Pope, 'Moral Epistle No. 3', in *Works*, ed. W. Elwin and W. J. Courthope, *Poetry III*, 1881, p. 156.

shores, indignant enough to. point out that there was nothing uniquely Cornish about it. A local magistrate wrote in 1792: 'Cornwall hath long been infamous to a proverb, for the inhospitality of the inhabitants on occasions of shipwrecks . . . Instances of shipwrecks in other parts of England and in Wales, have happened when the inhabitants have behaved altogether as bad, if not worse, than Cornishmen.' The *Western Luminary* in 1819 gave prominence to an incident at Deal under the heading: 'Wreckers out of Cornwall'.[1]

Eighteenth-century records document wrecking incidents on the eastern coast of Ireland, on the north and south coasts of Wales, on the coasts of Devon and Dorset, and at Deal in Kent, as well as from Cornwall and Scilly. The Report of the Constabulary Commissioners of 1839 which provides a comprehensive survey of wrecking activities based on returned questionnaires from the coastguards extends the list. In addition to places already mentioned incidents were reported from the coast of Lancashire and Cheshire, Folkestone and Whitstable in Kent, Raynham in Sussex, several places in the Isle of Wight, Sunderland, Bridlington, Lincolnshire, Mundesley in Norfolk, and Yarmouth and Aldeburgh in Suffolk.[2]

Wrecking was not equally prevalent in all these places. Cornwall and Scilly, the north and south coasts of Wales, the Wirral peninsula and the Kent coastal villages were to be especially noted. At Deal it was said of the inhabitants that they assembled for plunder in 'every instance' of a wreck, and the same was said of places on the Norfolk coast. Other places witnessed less frequent, but not necessarily less determined, instances of plunder.[3]

To coastal dwellers materials obtained from wrecks contributed importantly to meeting their needs for certain kinds of commodities, supplying materials much in want in poor households, or even a surplus for sale.

> The *Good Samaritan* came ashore
> To feed the hungry and cloathe the poor,
> Barrels of beef and bales of linen,
> No poor man shall want a shillin'.

runs a verse about a ship wrecked on the Cornish coast in 1846. But it was not just the cargoes which were important. The timber from which a ship

1. J. Pearce, *The Wesleys in Cornwall*, Truro, 1964, pp. 158–9 n; *West Briton*, 19 February 1819.
2. The returned questionnaires are in the Home Office Papers. In subsequent references they will be cited as P R O, HO 73/3, followed by the name of the coastguard station making the return. In the printed report the places mentioned are listed in *PP*, 1839, vol. XIX, pp. 61–2.
3. P R O, HO 73/3 Deal; ibid. Wells.

was constructed, the ropes which formed her rigging and the copper which sheathed her hull were all valuable commodities to the poor. Defoe provides a description of how important such materials could be for local constructional activities:

> As I went from Yarmouth northward, along the shoar towards Cromer . . . I was surprized to see in all the way from Winterton, that the farmers and country people had scarce a barn, or a shed, or a stable; nay not the pales of their yards, and gardens, not a hogstye, not a necessary-house, but what was built of old planks, beams, wales, and timbers etc. the wrecks of ships and ruins of mariners' and merchants' fortunes; and in some places were whole yards fill'd and piled up very high with the same stuff laid up, as I suppos'd to sell for the like building purposes.[1]

Nowhere was wreck timber of more importance than on the Isles of Scilly. Robert Heath, in his description of the islands published in 1750, said that no timber then grew on the islands, and the inhabitants depended upon imported supplies or else wreck timber. He refers to 'wreck furniture' which was sent to the islanders by 'the Hand of Providence', and informs that the inhabitants of the island of St Agnes even had a patron saint, St Warna, who was believed to be instrumental in sending them wrecks. Defoe had painted a black picture of the islanders, claiming that those wrecked on the islands would 'find the rocks themselves not more merciless than the people who range about them for their prey'. Heath, who had been for a time commander of the garrison stationed on St Mary's, hotly rejected Defoe's accusations, describing them as the product of his imagination, and suggesting that it was impossible for such barbarities to occur on a small island group on which a permanent garrison was stationed. It was optimistic of Heath to believe that as garrison commander on St Mary's he was always aware of what was going on on some of the smaller outlying islands. When the *St Joseph* was wrecked on Sampson in 1739, the Scillonians carried off its cargo of brandy and refused to give it up. When the Penzance Customs went across to investigate, the loot was removed to another island, Tresco, and although the officers did succeed in seizing it, it was later recovered from a locked warehouse by the islanders. During the winter of 1740 several other vessels were wrecked on the islands, and about 9,000 gallons of brandy were brought ashore. The islanders cellared about 3,000 gallons, claiming it as their salvage – 'one third being the custom of the island'. This claim was supported by the deputy steward to the Lord Proprietor, an official who was said to govern the islands very much as he pleased. Heath was also

1. A. K. Hamilton Jenkin, *Cornish Seafarers*, 1932, p. 116; D. Defoe, *A Tour through the Whole Island of Great Britain*, 1962, vol. I, p. 71.

a supporter of the islanders' claim to high rates of salvage. He thought that they did not gain as much from wrecks as was sometimes supposed since 'of what they get out of the sea they only enjoy a proportionable part for salvage; the rest belonging to the Proprietor, or perhaps to the merchants... What is saved at the hazard of lives from the devouring of the sea, the salvors are, by right of nature as well as of reason entitled to a share of...' He thought them sometimes 'ungratefully rewarded' by merchants whose property they salvaged.'[1]

Customary notions about entitlement to salvage sometimes blur the edges of a definition of wrecking. Clearly wreckage could contribute to a local economy. There were, for example, groups of men from Liverpool who ran what were known as 'speculative boats'. They went out to save as much as possible from wrecked or stranded vessels, and received salvage to the extent that they were successful. The basic distinction between salvors and wreckers is, however, a clear-cut one. When the Penzance Customs officer told the Commissioners in 1839 that in his district the lower classes assembled 'for the purposes of plunder, very few to act as salvors', he had a distinction clearly in mind. Motivation was quite distinct: salvors rescued wrecked or stranded property in order to receive a share from the legitimate owners or insurers: wreckers appropriated such property for their own use. The distinction between salvage as the legitimate and wrecking as the illegitimate activity is complicated because popular and customary notions as to what constituted salvage, and who had the right to it, were not always in accordance with the ruling of the law on the matter. Especially vehement in following their own customary notions of salvage rights were the beachmen of Lowestoft. In an incident in 1821, they were the first to reach a stranded vessel, but subsequently she was also reached by the life-boat from the harbour. The beachmen forced the life-boat to go away, but in the confusion they failed to take off four of the crew whose lives were consequently lost. In the resulting hearing, the presiding judge was told that the beachmen held to the salvage doctrine of 'first come, first served'. He interjected that if such an impression existed, nothing could be more erroneous. It was without the slightest foundation in fact: 'It is most absurd to suppose that, because a boat gets alongside a vessel in distress, the crew have a right to take possession of her, supersede the authority of the captain and say who shall or shall not afterwards come on board. Such a doctrine is wholly devoid of foundation; and I cannot but say that if salvage was claimed under such circumstances the owners were extremely ill-advised in paying one sixpence.' In 1850 the beachmen were accused

1. R. Heath, *The Isles of Scilly* (1750), reprinted Newcastle, 1967, pp. 30, 37, 53, 56; Defoe, op. cit., vol. 1, p. 244; J. Vivian, *Tales of the Cornish Wreckers*, Truro, 1969, p. 10.

172

in the national press of being wreckers, following an incident in which they fought a fierce battle with the crew of a steam tug attempting to assist a stranded vessel. But once again they were not claiming right of wreck, but right of salvage. They were very hostile towards the tug, which they said was taking the bread out of their mouths. At the inquiry into the riot, the chairman remarked: 'They seemed to have the idea that custom had given them the right exclusively to go to those vessels. It might be the custom, but it was not the law, and therefore they must be on their guard in future.'[1]

In few places can wrecking have contributed more to the local economy than it appeared to have done in the Wirral peninsula of Cheshire, where Liverpool shipping came often to grief. The evidence collected from this district in 1839 suggests that wrecking was practically a full-time occupation for many of the inhabitants of this stretch of the coast. 'They are all wreckers,' said a witness, 'almost all the inhabitants along the coast are decidedly wreckers.' The villagers of Hoylake were especially noted for their wrecking proclivities: 'The greatest portion are men calling themselves fishermen, but who, in fact, live by plundering wrecks. They intermarry and are nearly all related to each other.' Another witness claimed that although he had lived there for some time he had neither seen nor tasted fish. Wreckage and plundered cargo were not appropriated just for village use. They were a saleable commodity. The villagers of Hoylake were said to dispose of some of their spoils in the neighbouring villages, but to send most of it to Liverpool, where it was bought by marine-store dealers. Strangers from all parts came to deal with the wreckers, so that there was no need for them to carry the goods inland themselves and risk being apprehended *en route*.[2]

A similar traffic in wrecked goods existed elsewhere in England and Wales. In Cornwall in 1796 it was reported that staves from a wreck were being openly sold in the streets of Helston in great quantities. A Norfolk witness in 1839 doubted that paid constables could be effective in dealing with wreckers unless they were independent of the local inhabitants, who were generally ready purchasers of wrecked goods. When a Liverpool ship was wrecked in Carmarthen Bay in 1833, a local tradesman hired out carts to wreckers to assist them in carrying off a valuable cargo of cotton bales.[3]

Some cargoes were destined for immediate consumption on the shore.

1. *PP*, 1839, vol. XIX, p. 57; PRO, HO 73/3 Penzance; R. W Maltster, 'Suffolk Lifeboats – The First Quarter Century', *Mariner's Mirror* 55 (1969), pp. 268–75; *Standard* (London), 5 November 1850.
2. *PP*, 1839, vol. XIX, pp. 56, 59.
3. 'Journal of Christopher Wallis' (MSS County Museum, Truro), 2 January 1796; PRO, HO 73/3 North Walsham; HO 52/23, from J. H. Rees, Llanelli, 26 December 1833.

When a ship went ashore in the road of Liverpool in 1758, part of its cargo of wine and spirits came ashore on the Welsh side. Despite attempts to prevent them, the local populace 'broached the wine and spirits, got immoderately drunk, and committed the most violent outrages'. Two men in the vanguard of wreckers at Dartmouth in 1738 broke open a hogshead of wine and encouraged the crowd to come and drink it. It was said of the Mount's Bay wreckers of Cornwall that if a vessel containing wine or spirits was wrecked, it was not uncommon for five or six persons to drink so much that they perished on the beach. In fact it was uncommon for fatalities to occur at such chance orgies, but a report in the local paper makes it clear that it was not unknown. The whole of a large cargo of alcohol could prove beyond the immediate capacity of even a large crowd. When such abundance came ashore the Wirral wreckers knocked the heads of the casks out, and men, women and children would bail the contents out with kettles, pails, or whatever household utensils came to hand, and carry their plunder home.[1]

So far wrecking has been considered from a comprehensive viewpoint as the plundering of wrecked vessels and goods. A more detailed analysis of its forms is needed. In some respects wrecking can be considered as a form of crowd activity. By weight of numbers, with sufficient determination rooted in a belief in the legitimacy of their action, the inhabitants of certain coastal districts would plunder stranded vessels in open defiance of the forces of law and order. Numbers were usually on the side of the wreckers. An agitated report from Cornwall in 1700 concludes: 'The number of the rioters was so great and their threatenings so high, and their proceedings so outrageous that the ordinary ministers of justice durst not attempt to suppress them.' The people on the eastern coast of Ireland were particularly emphatic in their determination to profit from shipwrecks. When an American vessel came ashore in Clonderlaw Bay in 1811, the local people made a determined attempt to take possession of her: 'They assembled about ten in the evening to the number of about 2–300, and commenced the firing of musketry, which they kept up at intervals for three hours; when finding a steady resistance from the crew and a guard of yeomanry, which had been put on the vessel on her first going on shore, they retired.' In the same year some wreckers arrested at a wreck near Broadhaven were rescued by a large mob of their fellows, and in 1817 the police protecting a stranded vessel in the Shannon found themselves confronted by a mob several thousand strong, who openly

1. *Annual Register*, vol. 1 (1758), p. 113; PRO, SP 36/45 fo. 226, from Customs Officer, Dartmouth, 14 April 1738; C. G. Smith, *The Wreckers: or a Tour of Benevolence from St. Michael's Mount to the Lizard Point*, 1818, p. 5; *West Briton*, 10 January 1817; *PP*, 1839, vol. XIX, p. 57.

declared their defiance of them and their determination to repossess plundered property which the police had recovered. The police were assailed with stones, scythes, sticks and axes and were forced to fire in self-defence before the crowd retreated. Such incidents can be found in other wrecking districts. The Deal coastguard reported in 1829 that they had sometimes to fire over the heads of crowds assembled to plunder before they would desist, and similar assertions came from Weymouth, Dartmouth and Beachy Head. Cornish wreckers in 1722 overpowered thirty-five armed men placed on a vessel to protect her.[1]

Generally wreckers did not carry fire-arms. Some pistols were carried by Wirral wreckers in 1839, but this was said to have been the first time they did so. More usually they carried bludgeons or pitchforks. The Cornish wreckers who threatened in 1838 to destroy the coastguard if they attempted to prevent their plunder were armed with pieces of wood and staves – *ad hoc* weapons obtained from the wreck itself. The tools of the wrecker's trade, axes, crowbars, and so on, were in themselves formidable weapons. A Dartmouth Customs officer's horse was struck with the pole of an axe, and he himself threatened with murder if he persisted in his attempts to prevent the plundering of a cargo. Such confrontations from time to time produced fatalities. At Dartmouth in 1721 several wreckers were shot by soldiers protecting a stranded East Indiaman from a determined crowd. Three persons were killed and several wounded in a confrontation near Bridgend in 1782, and in the same year two wreckers were shot and more than a dozen wounded at a wreck in Galway Bay. The Volunteers shot a Cornish wrecker at a wreck in 1795.[2]

Sometimes in its haste for plunder the crowd behaved with a direct callousness towards the survivors of shipwrecks, as when they robbed and assaulted sailors, or with an indirect callousness as on the occasions when they concentrated on securing plunder instead of rendering assistance in the saving of lives. This was evident at Dartmouth in 1838 on the wreck of the *Barbara*: 'During the time they [the coastguard] were employed in endeavouring to save the lives of the crews, the country people, who had assembled in great numbers, were plundering in all directions.' Not only were the bodies of drowned men stripped of anything of value, but survivors sometimes lost their clothes and any pieces of personal property

1. PRO, PC 1/1/50, 18 March 1700; *Annual Register*, vol. LIII (1811), pp. 4, 114; ibid., vol. LIX (1817), pp. 13-14; HO 73/3 Deal; *PP*, 1839, vol. XIX, p. 62; SP 44/123, p. 85, from Helston, 7 April 1722.

2. PRO, HO 73/3, letter from Liverpool 12 February 1839; *PP*, 1839, vol. XIX, p. 64; Vivian, op. cit., p. 11; SP 36/45, fo. 216, deposition of Peter Eliot, 27 April 1738; SP 35/29, fo. 50, from Plymouth, 20 December 1721; *Gentleman's Magazine*, vol. LII (1782), p. 44; Wendron Parish Burial Register 1795 (transcript in County Record Office, Truro).

which they had succeeded in saving. The captain of the *Charming Jenny* and his wife were the only survivors when she was wrecked on the coast of Anglesey in 1774:

> Nearly exhausted they lay for some time, till the savages of the adjacent places rushed down upon the devoted victims. The lady was just able to lift a handkerchief up to her head, when her husband was torn from her side. They cut his buckles from his shoes, and deprived him of every covering. Happy to escape with his life, he hastened to the beach in search of his wife, when horrible to tell! her half-naked, and plundered corpse presented itself to his view.

The woman had been carrying two large bills and about 170 guineas in cash. A Cornish magistrate, writing in 1753, referred to the 'monstrous barbarity' practised by the miners upon the survivors of wrecks. He claimed to have seen many a survivor, 'half-dead, cast ashore and crawling out of the reach of the waves, fallen upon and in a manner stripped naked by these villains, and if afterwards he saved his chest or any more cloaths they have been taken from him.' This assertion is supported by the experience of the crew of the French ship *Marianne* who were stripped of their clothes by the miners of Perranzabuloe when they were wrecked there in 1764. When an Italian ship was wrecked on the Welsh coast in 1839, wreckers robbed the survivors and took the clothes from their chests before their faces.[1]

Such behaviour may have been exceptional. There are few specific recorded cases of such direct inhumanity. Rescue of seamen at considerable hazard to life would often precede plunder of cargoes and materials. As a letter from Cornwall in 1792 emphasized (see appendix, page 187), the crowd would not always see anything incompatible in combining rescue and plunder.

Much evidence suggests that wreckers believed themselves to have a perfect right to the property which they appropriated. The Cornish were said to have inherited from their ancestors an opinion that 'They have a right to such spoils as the ocean may place within their reach, many of the more enlightened inhabitants secure whatever they can seize, without any remorse; and conclude without any hesitation, that nothing but injustice, supported by power and sanctioned by law, can wrench it from their hands.' The magistrates of Glamorganshire wrote in 1837 that wrecking had been carried out on their coast 'almost uninterruptedly from time immemorial', and was regarded by the country people as a right which 'in

---

1. PRO, HO 73/3, from Capt. Pulling, Dartmouth, 29 November 1838; *Annual Register*, vol. XVII (1774), pp. 113–14; Hamilton Jenkin, op. cit., p. 90; *Calendar of Home Office Papers of the Reign of George III, 1760–65*, document no. 1460, 24 September 1764; *PP*, 1839, vol. XIX, p. 57.

some instances has been most barbarously exercised'. In Denbighshire in 1824 the feeling that stealing from wrecks was no great moral offence was said to be very prevalent, and almost a century earlier, a Customs officer in Anglesey had been told by some wreckers that they had as good a right to be there as he had. In 1839 a witness, asked if the Wirral wreckers thought anything of plundering the effects of passengers and sailors, replied, 'They think nothing of it; they think they are entitled to it, it is a common occurrence.' This belief they passed on to their children: 'They all bring up their children in the same line of crime as themselves, and there are generations of wreckers.' Cyrus Redding said of the Cornish in 1842 that they believed that property saved from shipwreck belonged to any survivors, and that if no one survived to anyone who might pick it up from the beach. He was being ingenuously optimistic if he really believed that respect for the property rights of survivors was part of the wrecking ethic.[1]

A Lloyds agent at Liverpool who tried to prevent the plundering activities of a group of Wirral wreckers in 1838 told them that they should desist from plundering. The wreckers replied, 'We are not taking anything. I suppose every man has a right to take what is here, one as much as another.' There is evidence that wreckers did not recognize the authority of the coastguard to secure wrecked property, in spite of their lawful duty to do so. The opinion that the coastguard acted without authority in this context, and did so from interested motives, was generally held in Norfolk in 1839, and in the same year the people of the district around Dartmouth were said to be under the general impression that the authority of the coastguard was confined to the protection of the revenue. A further support for notions of legitimacy was evident in Anglesey in 1745, when one man, encouraging others to follow his lead in plundering, shouted that it was a wreck and insured and they might take what they would.[2]

Beliefs in the legitimacy of appropriating wreck goods had no basis in fact. The legal position was clear. Under an act of Henry II, if anyone escaped alive from a ship, or if ownership of any of the property which came ashore could be established, then such property could not be forfeited as wreck. If neither of these two conditions applied, then such goods or materials were considered wreck, and as such formed part of the

1. Smith, op. cit., p. 13; PRO, HO 52/35, from magistrates of Glamorganshire, 4 February 1837; HO 52/4, from James Aiken, Denbigh, 6 April 1824; KB 33.5/4, affidavit of W. Prytheric of Anglesey, November 1745; *PP*, 1839, vol. XIX, p. 59; C. Redding, *An Illustrated Itinerary of the County of Cornwall*, 1842, pp. 187–8.

2. *PP*, 1839, vol. XIX, p. 59; PRO, HO 73/3, North Walsham and Dartmouth; KB 33.5/4, affidavit of William Prytheric, November 1745.

maritime revenues of the Crown. In the past the Crown had granted revenue from wreck as a royal franchise to lords of the manor. The act of Henry II also ordained that the sheriff of the county should retain any wrecked goods for a year and a day, during which time representation of ownership could be made. If the goods were of a perishable nature then they were sold and the money value held instead. By an act of Edward III it was allowed that any goods recovered from wrecks should be returned to the owners, who were expected only to pay a reasonable reward as salvage to those who had recovered them. Under a statute of 1713, confirmed by an act of 1718 and better enforced by an act of 1753, the officials of towns near the sea should, upon application being made to them, summon as many hands as necessary and send them to the relief of any ship in distress. In the case of assistance being given salvage was to be paid by the owners, the amount being assessed by three neighbouring justices. The Merchant Shipping Act of 1854 did nothing to alter these very specific rights to wreck. The position throughout the period under study was straightforward. Original right to wreck was a Crown prerogative. Some lords of the manor had been granted this right, but even where the right existed, the definition of what could be regarded as wreck was a specific one. No property could be regarded as wreck where rights of ownership could be established. All stranded and wrecked goods were to be kept for a year and a day to enable ownership claims to come forward. There was no right to wreck on the part of the general populace, and no right immediately to appropriate wrecked goods on the part of anyone.[1]

Wreckers were certainly adept at securing the goods to which they believed themselves entitled. Cornish miners were said to be able to cut a large trading vessel to pieces on one tide, and when the *Lord Rockingham* was wrecked on the Irish coast in 1755 so effective was the work of the local people that not two planks remained together. A description of the Mount's Bay wreckers indicates how quickly they took advantage of a wreck:

1. This summary of the legal position is based upon Sir William Blackstone, *Commentaries on the Laws of England*, 9th edn, ed. R. Burn, 1783, vol. I, pp. 291–3; R. Burn, *The Justice of the Peace*, 23rd edn, 1820, vol. V, pp. 613–21 and T. Williams, *Everyman his own Lawyer*, 2nd edn, 1818, pp. 24–5. Among the relevant statutes are: 27 Edw. III c. 13, 12 Anne st. 2, c. 18, 4 Geo. I c. 12, 26 Geo. II c. 19, and 17 & 18 Vict. c. 120. The archivist of the Customs and Excise Mr Edward Carson has commented on the occurrence of disputes as to right to wreck between the Customs and lords of the manor in the eighteenth century in his recent book, *The Ancient and Rightful Customs*, 1972, p. 110. In a letter to me Mr Carson has suggested that such conflicts may have contributed to the unwillingness of landowners to sell or rent land for coastguard cottages. On the claims made by lords of the manor see also Hamilton Jenkin, op. cit., pp. 79–84.

When news of a wreck flies round the coast, thousands of people are instantly collected near the fatal spot; pickaxes, hatchets, crow bars and ropes are their usual implements for breaking up and carrying off whatever they can. The moment the vessel touches the shore she is considered fair plunder, and men, women and children are working on her to break her up, night and day. The precipices they descend, the rocks they climb, and the billows they buffet, to seize the floating fragments are the most frightful and alarming I ever beheld.[1]

On some shores, even if a sound vessel came ashore, she could, if not immediately protected by a sufficient force, be as quickly rendered as unseaworthy by the local inhabitants as she would have been by the storm which she had escaped. The *Inverness*, stranded in the Shannon in 1817, was so little damaged that she could have been refloated at the next spring tide, but the local inhabitants rendered her a wreck by scuttling her and tearing away all her rigging. When the authorities regained control of her she was a complete wreck. An unidentified ship of 250 tons driven on shore near Mawgan in Cornwall in 1754 remained in good condition, but only until a party of miners from the neighbouring villages came and demanded the whole as wreck. The captain of the *Squirrel*, obliged to run ashore near Marazion in the same county, claimed that he could have easily got off had not a crowd arrived armed with poleaxes and clubs and made themselves masters of the vessel and cut down her masts, cables and rigging. A ship was plundered in Carmarthen Bay in 1840 even though she was undamaged. When a ship grounded on the Goodwin Sands in 1784 she had almost been refloated when about two hundred men arrived from Deal, prevented her refloating and plundered her.[2]

An assembly of Dee estuary wreckers at the scene of a wreck was described in 1839 as 'the most instantaneous thing you can imagine'. They saw from their residences what was likely to happen to a ship off-shore, and hit the beach simultaneously with the vessel. The country people of Carmarthen Bay were said to always arrive at the scene of a wreck fully prepared with their hatchets and hammers in hand, and the Cornish miners, as soon as they saw a ship in trouble off-shore, were said to arm themselves with similar tools, leave their mines and follow the ship.[3]

There is little doubt that the determined plunder of wrecked vessels was a feature of many British coastal districts in the eighteenth and early

1. Hamilton Jenkin, op. cit., p. 90; *Calendar of Home Office Papers of the Reign of George III, 1773-5*, pp. 511-12; Smith, op. cit., p. 8.

2. *Annual Register*, vol. LIX (1817), p. 14; Vivian, op. cit., p. 12; PRO, SP 44/85, Bedford to Mt Edgcumbe, 26 May 1750; HO 52/47, from J. H. Rees, Llanelli, 11 December 1840; *LG*, 12 November 1784.

3. *PP*, 1839, vol. XIX, p. 57; Hamilton Jenkin, op. cit., p. 89; PRO, HO 52/23, from J. H. Rees, Llanelli, 26 December 1833.

nineteenth centuries, but there is a further aspect of alleged wrecking practice which demands investigation. The act of 1753 referred to the putting out of false lights to lure vessels onto dangerous shores. Such practices are part of the folklore of wrecking and, like that other piece of wrecking lore, the biting off of dead men's fingers to secure rings, are to be found in the wrecking traditions of several districts. The evidence on this point is rarely specific. Vague references are made to the practice in this or that district, but the accusations are invariably couched in general terms. A witness said of the Wirral wreckers that they would 'use every endeavour to bring a vessel into danger rather than help her, in order that she should become a wreck'. But the Constabulary Commissioners were given no specific evidence in support of this assertion.[1]

A visitor to the Isle of Wight in 1796 was told by sailors that the villagers of Chale 'allured the unwary mariner to his destruction by fixing a lanthorn to the head of an old horse, one of whose forelegs had been previously tied up'. The up-and-down movement of the light as the horse hobbled along gave the impression that it was a masthead light and beguiled unfortunate masters into coming further inshore than was safe. The gentleman to whom this story was related did not believe it. Popular writers on the subject of wreckers tended to emphasize this unsubstantiated aspect of wrecking. In a novel published in 1857, one of the characters in delirium cries out when he imagines he sees a ship close inshore: 'Hold up the light! – so – now plunge it in the hollow. That is the floating beacon. Hurrah! Lift it – now lower again. All's right!' Cornish wreckers were also accused of employing false lights to lure ships ashore, but again the accusation is general, referring neither to specific individuals nor instances.[2]

A specific recorded case is that of the *Charming Jenny* wrecked on the coast of Anglesey in 1774, for which disaster the following reason was given: 'In consequence of false lights being discovered, the captain bore for those, when his vessel . . . went to pieces; and all the crew except the captain and his wife perished.' It is this same case which provides us with one of the most disturbing accounts of inhumanity towards survivors (above, p. 176).[3]

Robert Heath, staunch defender of the islanders of Scilly against Defoe, was a little less certain when describing the conduct of the keepers of the St Agnes light: 'Before the coming of this present Light-keeper, I've

1. *PP*, 1839 vol. XIX, p. 59

2. E. Boucher James, *Letters Archaeological and Historical Relating to the Isle of Wight*, 1896, vol. I, pp. 159–60; Anon., *The Wreckers*, 1857, pp. 14–15; Hamilton Jenkin, op. cit., p. 87.

3. *Annual Register*, vol. XVII (1774), pp. 113–14.

known it scarcely perceivable in the night, at the island of St Marys, where it now looks like a comet. And some are of opinion (not without reason), that in the time of the former Light-Keeper, it has been suffered to go out, or sometimes not lighted.' A comparable attitude towards lighthouses seems to have existed in west Cornwall. When Sir John Killigrew erected the first lighthouse at the Lizard in 1619, the locals were enraged by his action, complaining that he took away 'God's grace from them': 'meaning that they shall receive no more benefit from shipwrecks. They have so long been used to reap profit by the calamity of the ruin of shipping that they claim it as hereditary.'[1]

Not only were lights used, or not used as the case may be, but there were other methods. When the East Indiaman *Albemarle* was driven in to shore near Polperro in 1708, a request was sent to London that the company should send down pilots to assist in refloating her, for fear 'these Cornish pylots may run her aground or do some other mischief to make a wreck of her'. If legend is to be believed, the islanders of Scilly were not above invoking divine intervention in the matter. Parson Troutbeck was said to offer the prayer: 'We pray thee, O Lord, not that wrecks should happen, but that if wrecks do happen, Thou wilt guide them into the Scilly Isles, for the benefit of the poor inhabitants.' It is difficult to dismiss entirely the suggestion that ships were sometimes deliberately wrecked, but there is a marked lack of specific, conclusive evidence on this practice.[2]

Who were the wreckers? The clearest group identity which can be discerned is that of the Cornish miners. In that county large groups of industrial workers, with a reputation for collective action and for adherence to customary and traditional forms of behaviour, lived near a long and dangerous coastline. But the fact that Cornish wreckers were industrial workers is in itself sufficient to make them exceptional in the context of wrecking. It is this difference which accounts for the observation, made in 1839, that whereas on other parts of the coast persons assembled in hundreds to plunder wrecks, in Cornwall they did so in thousands.[3]

Not surprisingly, since the coastlines on which wrecks were most likely

1. Heath, op. cit., p. 37; Hamilton Jenkin, op. cit., p. 85.
2. Sir E. Cotton and Sir C. Fawcett, *East Indiamen*, 1949, p. 129; Hamilton Jenkin, op. cit., p. 87.
3. *PP*, 1839, vol. XIX, p. 64. Especially notorious were the miners of the neighbouring villages of Breage and Germoe. An early description of their activities is contained in a letter of 1721. That a familiar activity was being described is suggested by the use of the term 'notorious wrecker' as a description of one miner: PRO, SP 35/29, from Budock, Helston, 17 November 1721.

to occur were backed by rural hinterlands, wrecking was essentially a rural crime. The nomenclature commonly used in the documents, 'the country people', is a substantially accurate description of the wreckers of most parts of the coast. Some court records provide a more precise analysis. After an incident at Dartmouth in 1738 eighteen persons were identified by eyewitnesses. Of these two were shopkeepers, two sailors, two artisans, six labourers, two yeoman and four husbandmen. Seven men were charged with wrecking offences at the Devonshire summer Assizes of 1762. They were five husbandmen, a yeoman and a carpenter. In 1745, thirty-six persons were indicted for riot at the scene of a wreck in Anglesey. These indictments fully reflect the rural nature of the area: twenty were described as yeomen, six as labourers, eight as artisans, one as a mariner and one as a housewife.[1]

Although the lower orders of rural society, either labourers or small farmers according to the local form of rural economy, formed the bulk of the wrecking crowds, from time to time more substantial citizens were implicated. Wrecking was as much a matter of regional community traditions and attitudes as of social class. Three opulent inhabitants of Anglesey, one of whom was able to offer £5,000 bail, were found guilty of wrecking at Shrewsbury Assizes in 1774. At Hereford Assizes in the following year the death sentence was passed on a wrecker from Glamorganshire, said to be a farmer of considerable property. In the nineteenth century prosperous Welsh farmers continued to be involved. A Llanelli magistrate confessed to the Home Secretary in 1833 that he did not know how to proceed following the plunder of a wreck, because so many involved had been persons of great respectability. Some farmers, he claimed, had employed men to saw off the bowsprit of the wreck. Following a wreck near Dunraven in 1836, some of the plundered materials were traced to three farmers who were believed to have been leaders in the incident. Well-to-do farmers were also involved in the plunder of a wreck near Dartmouth in 1738, following which a local justice thought that a reward might encourage information against 'some of the more substantial ones'. Such persons he thought quite able to make recompense to the owners of the plundered property. On the occasion of a wreck near Looe in Cornwall in 1751, horses and carts were loaded with plunder by 'the whole country . . . as well reputable farmers and tradesmen as the poor'.[2]

1. PRO, SP 36/45, affidavits of William Saunders, Peter Eliot and Thomas Grove, 17 April 1738; Assize Process Book, Devon Summer Circuit 1762 (Assi 24/40); KB, 33.5/4.

2. *Annual Register*, vol. xvii (1774), p. 148; ibid., vol. xviii (1775), pp. 113, 154; PRO, HO 52/23, from J. H. Rees, Llanelli, 26 December 1833; HO 52/35, from magistrates of Glamorganshire, Bridgend, 4 February 1837; SP 36/45, from W. Rogers, Kingsbridge, 16 April 1738; *Gentleman's Magazine*, vol. xxi (1751), p. 41.

The fact that a whole community might involve itself to a greater or lesser extent in wrecking activities presented severe problems to the authorities seeking to press prosecutions. The Secretary of State was reminded from Dartmouth that it would be a long time before information against wreckers could be gathered, 'the people being unwilling to inform against their neighbours, almost the whole county for 15 to 20 miles around being concerned therein either in person or by their servants'. A Lloyds agent complained from Denbighshire in 1824 that it was little use offering rewards, 'all being equally guilty'. Some of the Cornishmen who plundered the *Albemarle* in 1708 were convicted although evidence against them had proved hard to obtain, and false information had led to the prosecution of an innocent man who had exhibited the locally deviant behaviour of assisting the crew to save what they could from the wreck.[1]

There are accounts of wreckers quarrelling on the beaches over the division of spoils, but there is some evidence that rudimentary conventions helped to avoid this. Thus it was said of the wreckers of the Dee estuary that 'if a man saw a bale of goods or a barrel floating in the water, he would run almost any risk of his life to touch that article as a sort of warranty for calling it his own. It is considered such fair game, that if he could touch it he called out to those about him, "That is mine". That is marked as his, and the others would consider that he had a claim to it and would render him assistance.' Combined operations seem to have been the order of the day at Atherfield on the Isle of Wight in 1839, when two vessels broke up in a storm. The women concealed the plunder under their cloaks, and the men passed goods from one to another and hurled them up the cliffs.[2]

In some districts the wreckers would certainly have been fishermen. This would have been the case on the Kent coast, in some of the districts of Sussex and Norfolk and, as we have seen, it was the claimed occupation of the villagers of Hoylake. It is interesting to speculate whether attitudes on the part of men who were themselves seamen towards shipwrecked sailors, if not towards shipwrecked property, would differ from that of miners or countrymen. Three pieces of evidence from Cornwall, where fishing and mining communities existed in close proximity, are interesting in the context. All three incidents took place in St Ives Bay. When Commodore Walker was wrecked there in 1745, the inhabitants of St Ives treated him so well that he, knowing of the reputation of Cornishmen, reflected: 'How weak a creature is general belief, the dupe of idle fame!' It was not a lasting impression. In the night a party of miners arrived at his

1. PRO, SP 36/45, from Dartmouth, 14 April 1738; HO 52/4, from J. Aiken, 6 February 1824; Cotton and Fawcett, op. cit., p. 129.
2. *PP*, 1839, vol. XIX, p. 57; HO 73/3, Yarmouth (Isle of Wight).

ship, and set about sharing the wreck among themselves. They were beaten off by the crew assisted by some armed townspeople. The second incident took place in 1817, when the villagers of Gwithian assisted the crew of a wreck, while a party of miners plundered it, and even stole the seamen's clothes which the villagers had hung up to dry. Nine years later, when the people of St Ives at considerable risk to themselves rescued the crew of a French vessel driven onto Hayle Bar, the inhabitants of the neighbouring mining villages arrived to plunder its stores.[1]

The most striking feature of wrecking is its persistence in the face of centuries of prohibitive legislation. It persisted in the face of moral as well as legal pressure. There is little evidence that wrecking as a moral problem received much attention from the Established Church. The act of 1713 was required to be read from the pulpit four times a year, and there were individual initiatives, such as that of the Bishop of St Davids, who, in the early nineteenth century, ordered the clergy of his diocese to preach an annual sermon against wrecking. A commentator thought it would have little effect: 'Seldom or never have I known evil habits and old practices broken by violent threatenings from the pulpit.'[2]

On occasion members of the rural clergy were not above identifying themselves with the local community sufficiently to indulge in some old practices themselves. The story of the clergyman who, on hearing of a wreck, admonished his congregation who were rushing out of church to slow down and given him an equal chance is part of the folklore of wrecking:

> Stop! Stop! cried he, at least one prayer,
> Let me get down, and all start fair.

One congregation at least is claimed to have left divine service precipitately on the news of a wreck. In 1720 Cornishmen rushed out of church with their hatchets in their hands. Presumably they had taken these implements with them, being always optimists in bad weather.[3]

Cornish parsons are known to have received wrecked goods. The Reverend Thomas Whitford of Cury was discovered to be in possession of wine from the *Lady Lucy* of Bordeaux, wrecked at Gunwalloe in December 1739, and when Richard Polwhele moved into the vicarage of Mannacan he found that the wine left in the cellars by the previous incumbent tasted of salt water, it having been 'picked up at wrecks'. Such

1. H. S. Vaughan, ed., *The Voyages and Cruises of Commodore Walker*, 1928, pp. 90–91; *West Briton*, 28 March 1817 and 14 April 1826.

2. Smith, op. cit., pp. 11–12.

3. H. Shore, *Old Foye Days* (1907), reprinted Newcastle 1966 with new title: *Smugglers of Fowey*, p. 57; Vivian, op. cit., p. 7; J. S. Buckingham, *Autobiography*, 1855, vol. I, p. 176.

clergymen were surely not typical, but there is little evidence of positive action against wrecking on the part of the Church to set against them.[1]

In Cornwall religious opposition from the direction of Methodism might have been expected to have some effect. In that county wrecking practices were in conflict not only with the law, but also with the important value system provided by Wesleyanism. In few places was John Wesley's influence stronger than in Cornwall, and he was a firm opponent of wrecking. At Cubert in 1776 he inquired if 'that scandal of Cornwall, the plundering of wrecked vessels', still persisted. He was told that it did, as much as ever, but that the Methodists would have nothing to do with it.[2]

Yet it is difficult not to believe that many Methodists were able to reconcile religious fervour with wrecking (as Wesley had discovered to his discomfort, many were able to reconcile it with smuggling). To those who know the Cornish Methodism of the time, the following account does not sound especially improbable: 'In this neighbourhood, it seems, some having a little more light than others, scrupled to visit a wreck that came on shore last winter, on a Lord's Day, lest it should be breaking the sabbath; but they gathered all their implements into a public house, and waited until the clock struck twelve – at midnight, therefore, they rushed forth, all checks of conscience being removed.' The *Cornwall Gazette* clearly had local preachers in mind when, in 1846, it reported that among those who plundered a wreck were those who 'stand up in the pulpit to preach the word of God'.[3]

The fact which really suggests that the influence of Methodism in inhibiting wrecking must have been minimal is the sheer size of the crowds which assembled to plunder. The Commissioners of 1839 claimed that the Cornish assembled in thousands. Given the strength of Methodist membership among the miners, and the justified claims made for the extent of its influence, the conclusion is inescapable that many miners must have been able to reconcile religion and wrecking. The old story of the man told by his wife that John Wesley had condemned wrecking has the ring of truth: he is said to have replied, 'Wesley? What do 'ee knaw 'bout wreckin'?'.

The sanction of custom can be resilient enough to permit the survival of forms of action which are in direct conflict with existing law, and perhaps also at variance with the teachings of powerful cultural and religious agencies, which in other directions may exert strong control on behaviour. The conflict of custom with legal prohibition is a recurring theme of the

1. Vivian, op. cit., p. 8; R. Polwhele, *Traditions and Recollections*, 1826, vol. II, p. 377n.
2. J. Wesley, *Journal*, Saturday, 17 August 1776.
3. Smith, op. cit., pp. 8–9; C. Carter, *Cornish Shipwrecks. Vol. 2. The North Coast*, Newton Abbot, 1970, p. 126.

social history of the eighteenth and early nineteenth centuries. It is clearly seen in such activities as smuggling and poaching, but it is present also in the enclosure debate, and inherent in the food riot. This study has been concerned with a further, perhaps less well-known, example of such a conflict. The study of wrecking practices illuminates an area of conflict between law and custom. It shows how strong was the local strength of tradition, if such a form of criminal action could be persistently employed by whole communities, when its only legitimacy lay in the realm of custom. It emphasizes the enormous problem facing the authorities in enforcing law and order in the rural districts. It was fitting, from this point of view, that the Constabulary Force Commissioners should have so emphasized wrecking in arguing their case for the establishment of a rural constabulary, for here was a clear case of an authority, the coastguard, set up for one purpose, being entrusted with the maintenance of law and order in a further direction for which its manpower was woefully inadequate.

Like poaching, despite the occasional involvement of the better-off, wrecking obviously bears some relationship to poverty. In the context of the economy of the coastal poor, it reminds us how various were the sources from which the poor supplemented their meagre living. Forgetting the silks and wines of exceptional wrecks, the timber, ropes, nails, sails and so on were needed in the homes of the poor. Timber would have been all the more welcome at a time which saw the closing to the poor of much wood and common land. Wrecking needs to be placed alongside scavenging, totting, poaching, mud-larking, taking of cast-off clothes and 'translating' boots in any real study of the living of the poor.

Wrecking attracted less persistent attention from the authorities than poaching or smuggling. It was an offence against property, but not, like poaching, a violation of the sacred property of the landed magistracy. Nor, like smuggling, did it offer the insult of an offence against the royal revenues. Unlike smuggling it was of its nature something of an *ad hoc* activity and did not call into being permanent gangs providing a continuous threat to order. Nevertheless from time to time the authorities did react with a determined example-making rigour. In particular, assize judges in the second half of the eighteenth century began to emphasize the necessity of making local examples. In 1775 the execution of a wrecker was carried out at Shrewsbury, and in the same year the death sentence was passed on another wrecker at Hereford Assizes. In 1782 a wrecker was executed at Hereford, and the opinion expressed that this example might be hoped to put a final stop to the practice of plundering wrecked vessels. In 1767 a Cornishman was sentenced to death for his part in the plunder of a wreck. The judge was clearly concerned to make an example. He admitted that in some respects the condemned man was not so criminal as others who had escaped arrest, but as there were many common people in court he took the opportunity of 'inveighing very warmly against so savage a crime, and of declaring publicly that no importunities whatsoever should induce him to reprieve the criminal'. The condemned man was eighty years old. He had taken an 'inconsiderable quantity of cotton', and a piece of rope.[1]

APPENDIX

Extract from a letter from Joseph Banfield to Mr Knill, 28 February 1792. Falmouth (PRO, HO 43/4 Entry Book).

Respecting the Brielle Dutch Frigate (being Dutch Vice Commissary) I was sent for soon after she struck & being one of the first that came upon the spot which was the morning after she touched the ground, I can give you a pretty just account of the behaviour of my Countrymen. This ship ran plump on shore on the rocks near Coverack the 22nd Decr. at 8 a night & with the force she struck had very soon 10 feet of water in her hold; when she struck it was near low water & she filled as the tide rose. She lay about half a cable's length from the land about a mile to the westward of Coverack. Signal guns of Sixteens being fired a small boat from Coverack went off to go to the ship, it was very dark they came near the ship and by the light of the guns firing they discovered a ship on shore. They took in one of the Lieutenants and brought him onshore to Coverack, he acquainted the people it was a Dutch frigate and requested they would send out boats to save the people as the ship would fill as the tide made. The Coverack men then launched some sean boats (which were hauled up on the bank & laid up for the winter) & with great alacrity and activity tho' there was a great sea & they ran some risk of the boats and their lives very humanely brought all the ships company together with the Soldiers safe to land excepting only some few who were unfortunately drowned. The first part of this business did the Coverack men great credit, as to the accounts given in the papers of their plundering the people of their cloaths as they came on shore I believe its totally destitute of truth. This is a justice I owe to the people of Coverack, and this is all

1. *Gentleman's Magazine*, vol. XLV (1775), p. 202; *Annual Register*, vol. XXV (1782), p. 219; *Calendar of Home Office Papers of the Reign of George III, 1776–9*, pp. 184, 251.

I can say in their favour; for as to other matters no persons could behave more rascally. We agreed ... the next day to give them 1/3 of the value for salvage & bringing on shore to Coverack the stores and materials, but they took every opportunity they could to throw overboard near the shore as they rowed from the wreck towards Coverack such of the goods as they knew when to creep for and pick up at a future opportunity: they plundered the wreck by night and brought nothing they took in then to the proprietors ... not only the Coverack people but boats from different parts of the coast plundered and carried off from the ship while she lay at a distance from land ... after lying there 5 days the upper part separated from the bottom below her lower deck and floated on shore. What was then the behaviour of the country? Hundreds of people men and women came down with avidity entered the vessel provided with axes and cut up and destroyed everything ... It is shocking to reflect on the behaviour of the people of this county. No person could suppose it was the practice of people professing Christianity, for strangers driven on shore would naturally suppose the multitude of people they should see collecting on the shore were persons attending to save their lives, & the property that might escape from the waves. No such thing: tis true they have humanity enough to save men's lives at the hazard of their own: when that is done, they look upon all the rest as their own property. They imbibe this idea from their infancy, & nothing but some of them being brought to condign punishment will remove their delusion. It is an indelible stain & disgrace to this nation that this practice this infamous annual practice has not been put a stop to before...

Poaching and the Game Laws
on Cannock Chase

> Honest alike, you own, but wiser far,
> The Knave upon the Bench than at the Bar:
> Where lies the Diff'rence? only in Degree,
> And higher Rank is greater Infamy.
> Poor Rogues in Chains but dangle to the Wind,
> Whilst rich ones live the Terror of Mankind.

THOMAS CATESBY PAGET[1]

I

True equality before the law in a society of greatly unequal men is impossible: a truth which is kept decently buried beneath a monument of legislation, judicial ingenuity and cant. But when they wrote the laws protecting wild game, the rulers of eighteenth-century England dispensed with such hypocrisies. By an act of 1670 a man had to be lord of a manor, or have a substantial income from landed property, even to kill a hare on his own land. The basic game qualification was an income of £100 yearly from a freehold estate, which in 1750 was between five and ten times the annual income of a labourer, and fifty times the property qualification to vote for a knight of the shire.[2] From the beginning of the century a mass of other statutes re-enacted and stiffened the penalties for unqualified hunting: a £5 fine or three months in gaol for keeping dogs or snares, the same for killing rabbits in warrens, £30 or a year's imprisonment for killing deer. These were the most common sanctions, but there were other,

---

1. *A Essay on Human Life*, 1734, 'composed in the intervals of bad weather in hunting seasons'; G. E. C[ockayne], ed., *The Complete Peerage*, 1910–59, title 'Paget'. Uxbridge was his son.

2. Other qualifications were leases of ninety-nine years worth £150, being the son and heir of an esquire, or owning parks, warrens, chases or free fisheries (22 & 23 Chas. II c. 25, the basic qualification act until that of 1831, 1 & 2 Wm. IV c. 32).

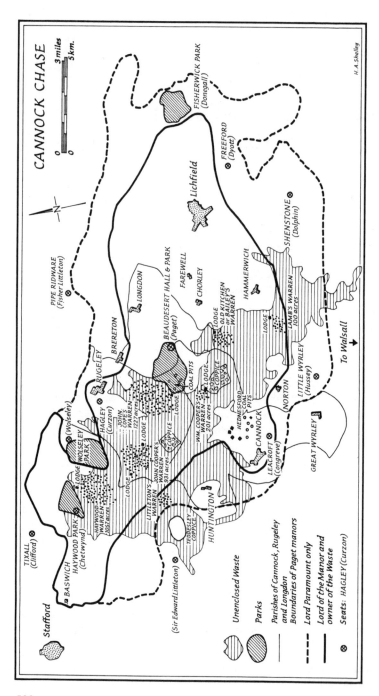

CANNOCK CHASE

3 miles
5 km.

H. A. Shelley

Stafford

TIXALL (Clifford)

BASWICH

HAYWOOD PARK (Chetwynd)

(Wolseley)

WOLSELEY PARK

LODGE

HAYWOOD WARREN 1057 acres

HAGLEY (Curzon)

RUGELEY

BRERETON

PIPE RIDWARE (Fisher Littleton)

(Sir Edward Littleton)

LODGE

JOHN COOPER'S WARREN 1227 acres

LODGE

LITTLETON'S WARREN

JOHN COOPER'S WARREN 931 acres

COPPICE

LODGE

TEDDESLEY COPPICE

HUNTINGTON

LONGDON

BEAUDESERT HALL & PARK (Paget)

FAREWELL

CHORLEY

LODGE

COAL PITS

WM. COOPER'S WARREN 201 acres

LODGE

COPPICE

HEDNESFORD COAL PITS

LEACROFT (Congreve)

CANNOCK

NORTON

GREAT WYRLEY

Lichfield

FISHERWICK PARK (Donegall)

FREEFORD (Dyott)

SHENSTONE (Dolphin)

HAMMERWICH

OLD KITCHEN or BAILEY'S WARREN

LODGE

LAMB'S WARREN 100 acres

LITTLE WYRLEY (Hussey)

To Walsall

Unenclosed Waste

Parks

Parishes of Cannock, Rugeley and Longdon

Boundaries of Paget manors

Lord Paramount only

Lord of the Manor and owner of the Waste

Seats: HAGLEY (Curzon)

extraordinary ones. Deer were very heavily protected, and transportation, or death under the Black Act, could be invoked at the pleasure of the prosecutor if they had been killed within his park. Beyond these powers many great landlords held rights of free chase and free warren, which gave them sole privileges of game over large areas of land. And the statute laws became more severe throughout the century.

The lawyers argued about the legal status of game, but usually agreed on the practical reasons for the code: the laws were 'to prevent persons of inferior rank, from squandering that time, which their station in life requireth to be more profitably employed'.[1] The gentlemen of England chorused in agreement, usually concluding that a law to protect the poor from their own idleness was 'a salutary restraint' – indeed, the essence of good government.[2] But the unanimity of the propertied on the subject of poachers broke down when other effects of the game laws were considered. Pamphleteers for 'the monied interest' ridiculed a situation in which little country squires could shoot at will but men with £10,000 in the funds were barred. Farmers protested against the despotism which allowed gentlemen to flatten their crops in pursuit of hares, but forbade yeomen even to buy them. 'The subject of the Game Laws', wrote Chitty in 1816,

in whatever light it is considered, is one of no common importance. The property which they protect is viewed with peculiar jealousy, both by those who are precluded from taking it, and those to whom its enjoyment is secured. The former consider it as a common right of which they are unjustly deprived; the latter as more sacred than any other class of property, on account, not only of its intrinsic value, but of the amusement which it affords them. These opposite feelings are continually called into exercise, not only by their immediate object, but by all the local disputes and antipathies with which they mingle.[3]

Meanwhile the poor ignored the war of words, reminded themselves that Genesis said the animals were made for man, and poached with passionate determination and courage. Gentlemen combined in local associations all over the kingdom to prosecute them with equal ardour; a critic observed

1. Bacon quoted in Richard Burn, *The Justice of the Peace and Parish Officer*, Title 'Game', 12th edn, 1772, vol. II, p. 218; but see also below, p. 219 n. 1.
2. Edward Christian, *A Treatise on the Game Laws*, 1821, p. 326.
3. J. Chitty, 'Observations on the Game Laws' (1816) in *The Pamphleteer*, vol. IX, no. 17 (January 1817), pp. 172-3.

(*Opposite*) Cannock Chase in 1750

Sources: William Yates, *A Map of the County of Stafford*, 1775; three sketch maps, Staffs R.O. D(W)1511/34/58/1, D603/S163; Littleton, 'Records', pp. 188-200; Staffs R.O. D603 *passim*.

in 1771, 'One would almost be tempted to think . . . that there was some sovereign medicinal quality in the blood and juices of these animals. . .'[1]

In short, the game laws cast a flood of light on class conflict in many parts of rural England. Enacted to determine contentious questions of property and status, their administration tells us much about that world. Yet when we turn from statutes and pamphlets to poaching and prosecutions, there are immediate difficulties.[2] Most of the game laws were part of that large and growing body of legislation that was executed by individual Justices of the Peace, acting in their own neighbourhoods, hearing cases more often than not in their own houses, and neglecting almost always to record the conviction. Hence game offences figure hardly at all in most legal records before the nineteenth century, although they obsessed Parliament and occupied most of the time of many country magistrates.[3] To see the laws in action, to rediscover the world of the poacher, we must forget the courts and look at that characteristic institution of the eighteenth-century ruling class, the great landed estate.

Between the industrial centres of Stoke and Birmingham lies Cannock Chase, a rolling stretch of heath and woodland preserved for walkers and picnickers, and for the herd of wild deer which has roamed it for centuries. Near the highest point of land are the few ruins of Beaudesert Hall, the ancient Staffordshire home of the Pagets. The topographer Shaw, inspired by its beauty and the patronage of its owner, described it in the eighteenth century as a 'princely seat . . . boldly situated on the side of a lofty sloping eminence . . . embosomed with rich foliage, commanding in front, over the tops of far subjacent woods, a most extensive and delightful prospect . . . The park, replete with deer, exhibits a continued series of hills and dales alternately tossed about in wild and beautiful disorder.'[4]

After inheriting the estate in 1743 the new Earl of Uxbridge heard a great deal about disorder: mostly poaching, riot and arson.[5] Within a

1. [Samuel Purlewent], *A Dialogue between a Lawyer and a Country Gentleman, Upon the Subject of the Game Laws*, 4th edn, 1775, p. xi.

2. For an outline history of the game laws, based on printed sources, see Chester and Ethyn Kirby, 'The Stuart Game Prerogative', *English Historical Review*, 1931, vol. LXVI, pp. 239–54; C. Kirby, 'The English Game Law System', *American Historical Review*, vol. XXXVIII (January 1933), pp. 240–62; C. Kirby, 'English Game Law Reform', in *Essays in Modern English History in Honour of Wilbur Cortez Abbott*, Cambridge, Mass., 1941, pp. 345–80; and C. Kirby, 'The Attack on the English Game Laws in the Forties', *Journal of Modern History*, vol. VI (March 1932), pp. 18–37.

3. See below, p. 251 n. 2.

4. Stebbing Shaw, *The History and Antiquities of Staffordshire*, 1798–1801, vol. I, p. 221.

5. Henry Paget, the ninth baron and the second Earl of Uxbridge, died a bachelor in 1769, when the estates went to Henry Bayly, son of the great-granddaughter of the fifth

year his keepers caught two labourers from Longdon who had broken into the deer barn in the Park and butchered two bucks and a doe. On his orders the men were prosecuted at Stafford Assizes under the Black Act, convicted, and sentenced to death.[1] He intended to make an example *in terrorem*, but it had little success. During his lifetime and that of his successor, Lord Paget, poachers from the villages near the Park and the Chase waged a small war on the keepers and the game. There were hundreds, perhaps thousands of encounters – in the half-century after 1750 the estate stewards mentioned some two hundred poachers by name in their letters to the Pagets, and dealt with at least four times that number.[2] About a third were men coursing and killing deer; another third were caught poaching in the warrens or snaring hares. The rest were a mixed bag of anglers, labourers keeping illegal guns or dogs, and men taking birds or burning the heath – an offence against the game because it destroyed their cover. While the stewards gathered evidence, prepared informations and informed local magistrates of the wishes of the Pagets, seven warreners and keepers patrolled the chase and deer walks, assisted by their sons and servants.[3] They had an immense property to protect. There were 400 deer in the Park and on the Chase, thousands of hares, scores of pheasants, well-stocked streams and pools. The Chase, some thirty square miles in extent, abounded in grouse and partridge, and the

---

baron. Bayly became the tenth Baron Paget and, in 1784, first Earl of Uxbridge (second creation). For clarity I have referred to him as Lord Paget throughout, and to both men together as the Pagets. The Earl of Uxbridge inherited eleven manors and over 10,000 acres of land in Staffordshire and Derbyshire, in addition to Beaudesert Park, Sainai Park near Burton and Cannock Chase. During the eighteenth century estates were acquired in Dorset and Berkshire. The Earl held others in Middlesex, and Bayly also inherited his father's Irish estates; he enjoyed the income from the copper-mines and 100,000 acres of land he held in Anglesey. The income from land alone was £28,000 in 1802. (Marquess of Anglesey, *One Leg, The Life and Letters of Henry William Paget, First Marquess of Anglesey*, 1961, p. 356; *Complete Peerage* (account of tenth baron); Staffs. R O, D603, Adey to Earl of Uxbridge, 14.11.43). References to D603 are by date, writer and recipient because the collection is unsorted; where necessary the temporary classification is also given. Other references are to collections in the Staffordshire Record Office, or as noted. 'Plas Newydd' denotes material still held there by the Marquess of Anglesey.

1. See below, p. 238 n. 3.

2. In the decade after 1752, when the correspondence is most complete, over eighty common poachers are mentioned, and about sixteen are named in a summary of incidents between 16 January 1777 and 5 December 1778 (in the financial accounts). Assuming the same rate for the period 1743 to the end of the century, the stewards caught and dealt with at least 500 cases in this period, and the addition of qualified trespassers to the total would probably double it, according to the financial summary cited. These estimates are of poachers *known* to the stewards; most went undetected.

3. D260/M/E/429/31, large vol., p. 189.

Pagets kept six warrens with some 15,000 rabbits.[1] For the men of Rugeley, Longdon and Cannock, poaching was a 'custom of the manors' that they and their fathers had followed long before the Pagets acquired the Chase in the sixteenth century. It meant sport, money, a bit of meat. It was also a skilled craft that demanded patience and courage as well as guile.

The tools of the trade were an arsenal of what the game laws called 'engines of destruction'. In the hands of anyone but keepers and landlords they were all illegal. Guns were effective with deer and birds, but dangerously loud, and many more men used nets. They set staff nets, ten yards long and more, for hares; and purse nets put over the entrances to burrows entangled bolting rabbits frightened out by the ferrets. Stronger nets, set across roads and along banks near the Chase, trapped many of the deer.[2] But nets were expensive, tedious to make and repair, and often lost to keepers. The screams of hares caught in them often attracted attention. Much cheaper was the simple wire snare, pegged in the ground one night, and easily checked for hares and rabbits on later evenings. One warrener collected over 200 snares in a few years from his ground alone.[3] Rabbits could also be caught without any snares at all, by covering the burrows during the day with pieces of heavy cloth, then returning at night to dig the conies out.[4] Above all else the poacher relied on his dog, a crossbred lurcher or a greyhound with docked ears. Carefully selected and patiently trained, they were inseparable companions that warned of keepers, drove hares into the nets, and could pull down injured deer.

Stealth was essential. Night was the time for most of the work. If by luck a deer was taken during the day, it was usually covered with boughs or concealed in a ditch until it was safe to carry off or butcher it. After dark it could be cut up in a cottage near the Chase – one poaching butcher used his slaughterhouse – and most men buried the skins rather than risk discovery by keeping them for sale.[5] On the Chase, Dickin, the head keeper, sent his men on constant patrols in the deer walks and warrens. Often on horseback, they listened for shots or the screams of netted hares, and watched the hills for villagers with spades and sacks. If they found a wounded deer they might call out a posse of servants to search the woods

1. Nichols to Earl of Uxbridge, 20.10.44; Harrison to Page, 3.11.77; game surveys of 8.8.68 (D603/CE569–606), 1.7.65 and 5.9.69 (D603/E31–70). There were another seventy-eight deer at Sainai Park near Burton; Wyatt to Earl of Uxbridge, 24.5.55.

2. Ridgway to Earl of Uxbridge, 1.1.57, 24.2.59; deposition and record of conviction of Price and Cope, 4.7.89.

3. John Cope to Earl of Uxbridge, 11.9.53.

4. Examination of Robert Harriman, 18.9.61 (D603/C37/10).

5. John Cope to Earl of Uxbridge, 18.9.57; notes by Paget, 9.11.73 (D603/E143–254); p. 238 n. 3 below.

and corn for trespassers.[1] More often, as they hunted the hunters, the keepers used the poachers' own tactics, setting all-night watches on warrens and cottages, lying long hours under wet hedges waiting for the owners of snares to return to them.[2] Even the slight tapping of a peg could attract a keeper on a quiet night. Above all it was important to remain unseen. The keepers often carried search warrants, and if they glimpsed a man near the warrens they could search his cottage before he had a chance to return; when he did his nets or venison would be already discovered. The right to search was the keepers' greatest weapon. In the summer of 1762 the hares were decimated, and acting on a tip Dickin took three of his men and the constable of Longdon to several cottages near the Hall. It was seven o'clock in the morning and all three suspects had the bad luck to be surprised in bed. John Wilkins, a labourer, 'so soon as he discovered them in the utmost hurry got on his Breeches' and dashed through the back door with his eleven nets. Dickin seized them and killed his dog on the spot since it 'appeared to be kept for a driver'. At the house of George Dytch, another labourer, the keepers seized a fishing net and four pike lures. George Lander, a farmer, lost five nets, three wire snares, a gun and a live hare. They took his dog, too, again on the grounds that it had a poaching look about it.[3] The punishment for Lander and Wilkins was a £5 fine – perhaps half the annual wage of the labourer, and a stiff enough penalty for a small farmer.

Faced with gamekeepers who were armed with the law, attracted by rewards, and backed by a great landlord, the poachers sometimes resorted to combination and violence. While some men dug in the warrens, others posted on near-by hills would watch for spies and blow horns in time to allow escape.[4] One man well known to the keepers took a stranger with him to carry the nets and the game, and challenged, his mate fled with the evidence while he fought the keepers. Others always gave false names, and would take a stand to prevent being searched or identified, by threatening the keepers with their guns.[5] At such times there was strength in numbers. The agent at the Burton estate complained in 1763 that the poachers had grown 'so audacious' that gangs of them patrolled the Park pale with dogs, watching for rabbits, hares or deer. 'I had lately two men

1. Scott to Earl of Uxbridge, 21.7.53.

2. Scott to Earl of Uxbridge, 18.8.55; examination of William Cooper, 27.9.60 in D603/C35/57; Ridgway to Earl of Uxbridge, 15.7.56, 23.9.58, 7.9.62; Plas Newydd, Harrison to Paget 3.7.82, Box XXIV; p. 194 n. 4; Price and Cope, p. 194 n. 2.

3. Ridgway to Earl of Uxbridge, 16.10.61, 30.10.61; examination of William Cooper, 14.10.62, D603/CE538–68.

4. Examination of William Cooper, 13.10.61, D603/37/7; 'Case', D603/C35/138.

5. Scott to Earl of Uxbridge, 18.8.55; Cooper to Paget, 6.9.86; case of Price and Cope, 4.7.89, D603/L1–46.

watching who met with five men & dogs on the outside of the pale. My
Men could only hold a parlez and take abuses of the Others who overpowered them with numbers.'[1] This hostility at times was formalized in
a sort of trial by battle. Jeremiah Cope, a warrener's son, found two men
near a dug burrow and chased them on his horse. Cope later testified
that one of them 'refused to stand a Search and after a Short Struggle
prepared himself for a resistance by throwing of his Cloathes and this
Examinant doing the like they fell to Blows. . .' The warrener won, and
found two nets in the poacher's pockets.[2] Three other rabbit diggers did
not feel so sporting the day the head keeper tried to take them to be
identified. They shouted threats and stoned him off; he looked back to see
one of them take a rabbit from his pocket and shake it, while yelling
insults. The same men thrashed him two years later.[3] Such attacks and
affrays were not uncommon, and the keepers gave as good as they got,
breaking men's arms, smashing heads with hickory staffs. Several times
they thrust guns in the faces of trespassers, threatening to blow out their
brains, and on one occasion Cope fired at a man's feet during a violent
quarrel about dogs on the Chase.[4] The destruction of their prized dogs
caused almost as much outrage and pain to the poachers. Usually the
keepers shot lurchers on the spot, but sometimes they took them before
JPs who ordered them hanged in a parody of the rites of Tyburn.[5] One
Staffordshire keeper, struggling to seize a dog from eight women in a pub,
slit its throat before they could rescue it from his hands.[6]

Not surprisingly, keepers and warreners were hated men, and targets
for revenge. In 1750 William Tipper, a labourer on the chase, accused
Cope of stealing fish from a neighbouring gentleman's pools, and the
neighbour prosecuted. Tipper made a second accusation – that Cope had
been shooting deer in the Park. It is impossible to judge the truth of
Tipper's claims. Certainly gamekeepers everywhere were suspected of such
acts, and two men at Beaudesert lost their jobs after similar accusations.[7]

1. Wyatt to Earl of Uxbridge, 7.11.63.
2. Examination of Jeremiah Cope, 8.12.61, D603/CE569–606.
3. Ridgway to Earl of Uxbridge, 26.5.56; information of Francis Dickin, 25.5.56, D603/CE248–359; p. 237 n. 4 below.
4. Informations of Dickin (18.10.55, D603/C32), Cope and Cope (15.4.51, D603/C35/124); Ridgway to Earl of Uxbridge, 12.6.56, 3.3.59, 18.4.61. Cope was found guilty of special assault at assizes, and paid nineteen guineas (PRO, Assi 5/81 Staffs. Summer and Assi 5/82 Staffs. Lent; D260/M/E/429/31, large vol., p. 207).
5. Ridgway to Earl of Uxbridge, 12.6.56.
6. *Ashmall* v. *Cotrill*, D1851/5/2, 23 June 1790. Cotrill was gamekeeper to the manor of Shenstone.
7. Case of Bailey, below p. 206; case of Hill (Hill to Paget, 15.8.74; Paget to Harrison, 18.8.74; Plas Newydd, testimony of Benjamin Hall, in 'Bills etc. 1942–9'). The agent at Sainai wrote in 1753 that 'the game keeper this last year [John Silvester] has not only

In Cope's case, however, the assize jury acquitted after hearing several hours of evidence. But the steward was undoubtedly right when he declared that the prosecution for the fish was begun in 'Malice and Revenge' for Cope's zeal in protecting the game. The warrener had recently taken one William Beeland before a magistrate for having a gun, and Beeland's wife had declared she would be revenged. Tipper was her nephew, and Cope had no doubt that he had faced possible transportation because of a conspiracy between them.[1] Several years later two poachers grimly warned him that they intended to 'destroy him in the night time, or at proper opportunity'.[2] On another occasion a poaching farmer successfully convicted an underkeeper of theft after being fined himself for keeping snares and a dog.[3] Even the steward was not immune from threats, as Nichols reported to Uxbridge in 1751: 'We have had the good fortune at our Sessions Yesterday to Transport for 7 years one of the principal Rogues in the Neighbourhood of Beaudesert for stealing a few geese & notwithstanding I am greatly threatened, I will neglect no opportunity of sending the whole Body of them after their comrade.'[4] Respectable yeomen too did not hesitate to show their hatred and contempt by attacks on the Pagets' servants. About eleven o'clock one night in January 1792 two Rugeley farmers entered the grounds of the keeper, killed his horse by shooting it in the head, then waited with the gun pointed at his bedroom window in case he decided to inquire. They were very merry on the way home, and a witness heard one of them declare he wished it had been the owner rather than the horse.[5]

The keepers led lonely lives as well as dangerous ones. They lived in isolated lodges on the Chase, guarding the rabbits and the deer, and passing their positions on to their sons. Occasionally an underkeeper was tempted to make peace with his neighbours by winking at poaching, but zealous servants such as the Copes and Coopers and Frank Dickin were ostracized by local people. Over a third of the men caught by the keepers came from the villages of Longdon and Rugeley, over two thirds from

---

conniv'd at 'em but been the Greatest Game Killer himself and Destroy'd more than all the people in ye parish besides'; Henry Hayne to Earl of Uxbridge, 17.2.53.

1. John Cope to Earl of Uxbridge, 11.2.50/1; Nichols to Earl of Uxbridge, 27.7.51. Cope expected to be prosecuted for the deer under 5 Geo. I c. 28, but the indictment was only for the fish, for which the possible penalty was three months in gaol by 5 Eliz. c. 21; PRO, Assi 2/16 Staffs. Summer 1751, and gaol calendar for same assizes, WSL.

2. Nichols to Earl of Uxbridge, 14.7.53.

3. The farmer was George Lander (above, p. 195) and the warrener was Bailey (below, p. 206); Staffs. RO, Q/SR, Epiphany 1766, indictment of Theophilus Bailey.

4. Nichols to Earl of Uxbridge, 16.1.50/1.

5. Joseph Perks to Paget, 11.3.92; depositions of Richard Pace, John Pace, William Walbank, PRO, Assi 5/112, Staffs. Lent.

within three miles of Beaudesert Park, and all the evidence suggests that this small community of labourers, colliers and farmers was united solidly in defence of poaching.[1] The keepers met a wall of silence when they tried to make inquiries, but found that word spread like lightning when they obtained a search warrant, and that the suspects had escaped with 'the apparatus' just before they arrived.[2] Witnesses lost their memories, like the dozen colliers who saw three 'most notorious' poachers taking hares an eighth of a mile from the coal pits, but could not identify the offenders.[3] Other witnesses were only too willing to testify, an outraged keeper complained to Uxbridge in 1758: 'there his one John Otty that has been ketch'd killing your Lordship's Deer & as paid the penalty some years agone and appears before the Justices when Francis Dickin and I take any porchers before them Otty appears in the behalf of the porchers. . .'[4] Poachers not only gave alibis for one another; they also took measures against informers, as several discovered when they themselves were before magistrates to answer false charges.[5] Such perjury before a justice did not always succeed, but there were other co-operative ways to evade the law. If a friend laid an information before the keepers could, it prevented their prosecuting, for the informer had rights in the fine. Five pounds sterling went from the poacher to the JP, then to the friend (as informer) and back again to the poacher over a pint in the alehouse.[6] In 1777 two labourers succeeded in an even more audacious attempt to outwit the law. Jeremiah Price informed on Robert Harvey for having a deer in his possession; Harvey confessed, but swore that Price had killed it, which Price in turn admitted. Since Price had informed on Harvey he claimed he was entitled to the pardon extended to informers by the new Deer Act of 1776, and since Harvey had revealed who had given him the

1. There were 6,000 people living in the parishes on and around the Chase in 1801, perhaps twice the number a hundred years previously. The three most populous parishes were Rugeley, 2,030, Cannock, 1,359, and Longdon, 909. Cannock and Rugeley both contained coal-pits and forges; hatting and feltmaking were also carried on in Rugeley, the home of most poachers. It was only 5 per cent agricultural and 95 per cent industrial; Cannock's corresponding figures were 43 per cent and 57 per cent, while 77 per cent of the population of Longdon were in agricultural occupations. (Figures from the 1801 census, assuming that 'Other' occupations for Cannock and Longdon represent dependants of those in other classifications.)

2. Ridgway to Earl of Uxbridge, 27.1.66.

3. Ridgway to Earl of Uxbridge, 23.9.58.

4. Cope to Earl of Uxbridge, 17.5.58.

5. Ridgway to Earl of Uxbridge, 3.2.63; warrant of Dormer Parkhurst, 12.1.53; deposition of Young, Snape, Ward, 15.1.53, D603/CE538–68.

6. Cope to Earl of Uxbridge, 31.8.58; Ridgway to Earl of Uxbridge, 4.10.60. This was a common trick; see *Some Considerations on the Game Laws, and the Present Practice in executing them; with a hint to the non-subscribers*, 1753, p. 26.

venison, he too was immune by another clause of the same statute. Completely at a loss, the steward asked for expert legal advice, and was told the defence was good.[1]

Occasionally the solidarity against the keepers broke down. Fear of a death sentence caused one of the burglars of the deer barn to reveal his accomplices.[2] Someone else seeking a reward ratted on three poachers when the keepers agreed not to reveal any names.[3] An alarmed father forced his sixteen-year-old son to reveal the man who had 'enticed' him to hunt deer.[4] And it must have been tempting at times to use the laws of peers and gentry to settle personal scores. After their guns, snares and fishing tackle were seized in a search, four colliers and labourers living in cottages near the Park knocked about some neighbours whom they suspected of informing. One of the women, outraged, stormed off to the nearest keeper and asked to be taken to a magistrate, promising that she would 'open a nest of them'. Nine months before one of the colliers had brought a deer home on his back, and all four had celebrated Christmas with venison. She had protected them then, but being beaten loosened her tongue and her testimony gaoled two of the men for a year.[5] In two other cases of betrayal there is no evidence for the motive. In another, however, the poacher was informed against because he had betrayed others: he had testified on behalf of Lord Paget against enclosure rioters at the Burton estate.[6] And the striking fact remains that these eight cases are the only impeachments of poachers by mates or neighbours in over 200 incidents spread over half a century. The stewards and keepers constantly tried to find informers, and were delighted when they thought they had one in hand: '[he] may be able to bring a good deal of this kind of mischief to light, and he should be encouraged to do it [wrote the steward about one impeacher] as it may tend to disunite the Gang, and you know the old Proverb says, "when knaves fall out honest men come at their own".'[7]

1. Case, and opinions by Lloyd Kenyon, 2.12.77, 23.12.77, D603/L51–67. The statute was 16 Geo. III c. 30, sections 4 and 17. Richard Burn (*Justice of the Peace*, 14th edn, 1780, vol. II, pp. 266–73) notes several contradictory clauses in the act, but not this one.

2. p. 238 n. 3.   3. p. 195 n. 3.   4. Nichols to Earl of Uxbridge, 9.12.52.

5. Cope to Earl of Uxbridge, 18.9.57; Ridgway to Earl of Uxbridge, 25.9.57, 18.10.57, 13.11.57.

6. Examination of William Dangerfield against Smith, 6.9.67, D603/E143–254; Ridgway to Earl of Uxbridge, 3.2.63, 7.9.67; case of Bailey, p. 206 below; case of Lightwood, 4.9.54, D603/E1–46; case of Oldfield, Harrison to Priest, 9.2.76, Harrison to Paget, 19.2.76, Paget to Harrison, 22.2.76. The William Dangerfield who informed on Smith may be the Samuel Dangerfield who testified against Bailey ('Samuel Dangerfield alias William Edward'; Staffs. R O, Q/S R Epiphany 1766 and Q/S O 15, p. 243).

7. Harrison to Priest, 9.2.76.

In almost every case, including this one, he was disappointed. Pointing out the difficulty of getting evidence, another steward wrote to Paget twenty years later that 'poachers are for the most part in strict friendship with one another, till their Interest dissolves that Tye'.[1] 'Interest' seldom did. The solidarity of the villagers was virtually complete.

Part of that solidarity arose from bonds of blood and marriage, the tangled skein of alliances in small communities where degrees of kinship merged imperceptibly into those of friendship and acquaintance. John Lane, once assaulted by the keepers, was brother-in-law to Sanders, who coursed hares.[2] Bill Tipper, caught repeatedly on the chase by the keepers, was the nephew of the wife of Bill Beeland, another poacher, who in turn was the father-in-law of Tom Benton, a pilferer, and the grandfather of James Moss, caught snaring rabbits.[3] And so on. But it is probably wrong to exaggerate the importance of such ties, particularly later in the century, when villages like Rugeley were growing fairly rapidly as the coal pits expanded. The real basis of the conspiracy of the villagers was their common opposition to the game laws in general, and the Pagets' interpretation of them in particular. Although men of different classes had different kinds of interest in the game of Cannock Chase, the reservation of hunting rights to qualified men – only 800 in all Staffordshire – united the great majority of the rural community against them.[4]

II

Most poachers were poor, if only because most Englishmen were poor. Of the 121 men caught by the keepers for whom there is occupational information, 30 per cent were poor labourers, colliers and weavers, 12 per cent are described as servants and 14 per cent were tradesmen or artisans. Of the last group a few undoubtedly were masters themselves, and therefore properly belong with the other 'middling men' who trespassed – several curates, a clerk, and twenty-one farmers and husbandmen – 20 per cent of the total. The remaining 15 per cent were qualified sportsmen, hoping for the customary indulgence extended to gentlemen sporting on others' property.[5] But it was the poor poacher, the 'common' poacher,

3. Weston to Paget, 17.1.90.
2. Ridgway to Earl of Uxbridge, 14.12.61.
3. p. 194 n. 4; p. 197 n. 7; Ridgway to Earl of Uxbridge, 27.2.62.
4. In 1786 in Staffordshire 739 sportsmen and 124 gamekeepers (some of them gentlemen) took out certificates; *Aris's Birmingham Gazette*, 27 February 1786. The population of Staffordshire at this time was about 205,000.
5. The first group comprised 7 'poor men', 14 labourers or day labourers, 8 agricultural labourers, 10 colliers or ground colliers, 4 poor weavers, 2 nailers and a widowed

who most exercised the keepers. They knew many of these men very well: Lightwood, 'a notorious Pocher'; Turner and Woodward, 'long most notorious pochers'; Veroe, Tipper and Steward, 'three of our most notorious Fellows'. There were many more. Most of them lived in Rugeley; others had cottages on the Chase or near its edge, valued refuges where nets and hares could be concealed quickly. It was one of the steward's tasks to avoid letting such cottages to the worst offenders, and to prevent the building of new ones.[1] There was little he could do about the colliers, however, for many of the pits lay within Beaudesert Park itself, and most of the rest, at Hednesford, were no more than a mile from the warrens and the deer walks.[2] Frequent reports reached Uxbridge that his colliers were not only felling his oaks and heating their cottages with stolen coal, but also feasting on rabbits and venison. Thomas Brown was one of these ungrateful men. In 1757 the steward reported to his employer that

from a Small Boy 'till about Six or Seven years Since, he hath been imployed as a Collyer in your Lordship's Work, And as a Superannuated Collyer, hath the Allowance of Bearing Coals being 5d each Week from the Works; That he hath for a long time, & still doth enjoy a Cottage, & about 5 Acres of Land to it, Value yearly about three pounds, under the rent 11s:8d, which is not in Lease; that notwithstanding these Generosities, he hath all his time been a rude, disorderly man, & a most notorious Pocher, almost continually (whilst able) exercising Some Device by Guns, Wire, or other Engines, for the Destruction of Venison, Hares, & Coneys.[3]

The eighteenth-century poor have not left a literature about the joys of poaching to match the gentry's endless eulogies of the hunt. The excitement of snaring hares, eluding keepers and shooting deer were very real pleasures for Thomas Brown and his friends, although they had no Somerville or Nimrod to record their sport, only magistrates who wrote the stiff prose of convictions. But cottagers took pride in their exploits.

---

cottager and her daughter; there were 13 'servants' and a butler and a keeper; 4 alehouse-keepers and innholders, 3 maltsters, 2 forgemen, 2 butchers, and 1 painter, carpenter, feltmaker, cutler, cordwainer and colliery engineer; 14 farmers, 6 yeomen, 1 husbandman; a clerk, a curate and 4 other clerics, at least two of whom were qualified; and 16 men described as gentlemen, or known to be qualified. The actual proportion of poor poachers was undoubtedly higher than these figures suggest, because they would be less likely to be identified, and hence caught; and wealthy men were far more likely to appear by name in the stewards' correspondence to the Pagets.

1. Cooper to Earl of Uxbridge, 11.2.54; Cope to Earl of Uxbridge, 18.9.57, 30.5.61; Ridgway to Earl of Uxbridge, 13.6.61 and 22.1.72.

2. William Yates, *A Map of the County of Stafford*, 1775; sketch map, D(W) 1511/34/58/1.

3. Ridgway to Earl of Uxbridge, 8.2.58.

Although it was risking a £10 fine (and therefore a year in goal, for few could pay it) some men kept hidden in their cottages the heads and antlers of deer they had felled, trophies of the chase.[1] The convictions of those caught are the only direct evidence the historian has of a rich sporting tradition of thousands of working men on Cannock during a whole century. The rest is silence. The labourers of Cannock could not write, and the few who did, did not risk recording a tradition that was criminal. And the gentry, in their endless pamphlets and parliamentary speeches on the evils of poaching, refused ever to acknowledge that low fellows could have anything but a mean and mercenary interest in game.

Everyone admitted that poachers often had good material reasons: 'For what purpose does every Labourer keep his cross-bred, coney-cut long Dog and take him daily to his work [asked a pamphleteer in 1772]; but that in his going or coming he sometimes starts a Hare, and the very next Day she makes a very decent appearance in a homely Pye, for the use of his family'.[2] As meat became scarce in the diet of labourers in the second half of the century, replaced by bread and cheese which was bought at market, poached game became more important to the cottager's family.[3] In the period of constantly rising food prices after mid-century, and particularly during the years in which poor harvests caused acute distress among the poor, a hare in a 'homely pie' was a boon. A side of venison such as Tom Brown and his butties enjoyed through the Christmas season of 1756 was worth a good many hares, and especially welcome that winter. 'The weather has been very sharp and severe for this last month,' wrote one of the Staffordshire stewards. Prices of all kinds of food were twice their normal level, 'which makes it extremely hard with the poor people. . .'[4] Sometimes we get other glimpses of the want that poaching eased: the wife of an imprisoned labourer who came to the steward with her small children and begged for her husband's release as they were without food, or the labourer who in January 1776 'happened to take a Gun out in that very severe weather when he could not work at home'.[5] The household economy of cottagers conflicted with the game rights of the Pagets even when the animals themselves were not involved. Game required cover, and grouse and deer in particular required the fern on the Chase. It was therefore an offence to burn any of the sparse and scrubby vegetation there; this was punishable by whipping and three months'

1. Staffs. RO, Q/SB 1786, Ep/21: Conviction by James Falconer 20.10.85 of Edward Ealam, late of the parish of Cannock, labourer; also Q/SB 1778, Ea/96. On the infrequency of recording convictions, see below, p. 251.
2. William Taplin, *Observations on the Present State of the Game in England*, 1772, p. 30.
3. J. Drummond and A. Wilbraham, *The Englishman's Food*, 1957, p. 206.
4. Wyatt to Earl of Uxbridge, 26.1.57.
5. Ridgway to Earl of Uxbridge, 27.1.66; Harrison to Paget, 19.2.76

imprisonment. Yet many cottagers risked it – twelve who were caught appear in the estate correspondence – because the ashes could be sold to make lye.[1]

For a number of the villagers the Chase had an even greater economic importance. Rather than being a supplementary benefit to an ill-paid or irregular job, poaching was the trade itself. Sanders, according to the steward,[2] was 'a most notorious loose Young Fellow who chiefly maintains himself by Poching'; and in Rugeley the word was that 'Wilkins & Dytch ... tho' they have families to maintain & are labourers by Profession are Seldom Seen to Work but are patrolling & Poching in the Night time & in Bed in the Day.'[3] Early in the nineteenth century the steward declared that 'as many of the poachers are nail makers & as many do no work *at all* and if disappointed of their Game here I think they would remove to Bilstone or Wednesbury from whence they came and where they could again get employment.'[4]

Labourers and nailers were able to 'maintain themselves' by poaching because of the extensive national market in game, a trade which was strictly proscribed by law but countenanced everywhere.[5] John Lightwood, for example, killed nearly eighty hares during the winter of 1764, and sold them in Lichfield at three shillings each, a return of some £12, which was probably as much as he earned in a year as a labourer.[6] There is little evidence in the stewards' letters about this traffic; they

1. The estate correspondence says nothing about this trade, but its details, if not its scale, perhaps resembled that near Loughborough, Leics., where it still flourished in the 1790s. During the 'fern-harvest' in the autumn the poor of the surrounding villages burnt the fern and made the ashes into balls, which sold for 4s. 6d. to 6s. the hundred. What was still a customary right in Charnwood was a crime on Cannock Chase. A seventeenth-century legal opinion on the terms of the Pagets' 1605 agreement with the commoners declared that it was an offence for them to burn fern for making ashes 'for bucking of cloathes', or for sale. The frequent fires on the Chase were perhaps evidence of a lingering tradition, although several other motives may also have been involved. Some copyholders burnt turf for fertilizer, a practice Paget considered prosecuting in 1775. It was also customary in some regions for shepherds to burn fern in the spring to bring down rain; there is also the possibility that more than one fire was lit from malice. (J. Nichols, *The History and Antiquities of the County of Leicester*, 1795–1815, vol. III, pt 1, p. 132 n. 1; opinions of counsel, Staffs. RO, D(W)1734/2/3/123; Lloyd Kenyon's opinion, 20.3.75 in D1511/20; Joseph Wright, *The English Dialect Dictionary*, Oxford, 1898, vol. I, pp. 78–9, title 'Ash', p. 425, title 'Buck', and vol. II, p. 336, title 'Fern'; see also below, p 253 n. 3).

2. Ridgway to Earl of Uxbridge, 14.12.61.

3. Examination of William Cooper, 14.10.62, D603/CE538–68; Ridgway to Earl of Uxbridge, 16.10.62.

4. Letterbook, D603/CE400–41, 18.1.1813, 24.1.1813.

5. See Kirby, 'The English Game Law System' and 'English Game Law Reform'.

6. Ridgway to Earl of Uxbridge, 27.1.66.

would be the last men in Staffordshire to know many details. But there were probably many like Lightwood who drove a profitable trade with poulterers and inn-keepers. Pamphleteers on the game laws pointed out that any country inn-keeper could supply almost any quantity of game, that it was sometimes sold as openly as 'a joint of meat in the public shambles', and that stage waggoners on the great roads acted as agents for London buyers.[1] Lichfield, only six miles from Beaudesert, was the crossroads of the main routes to the north. The city was noted for its inns, and also for its lively intellectual and social life.[2]

Defoe characterized it as 'a place of good conversation and good company', and it doubtless boasted equally good dinners.[3] All these factors suggest that it was an excellent market for game. At certain times sales were particularly profitable because of unusual demand. During Lichfield races, the chief social occasion of the county, the stewards tried to keep a closer watch than usual.[4] Burton was a similar market for game from the other Paget estate. Sainai Park was less than two miles from the town, and control of the trade was an impossibly difficult task: 'the keeper is continually on the Alert', wrote the Burton steward in 1812, 'but on so extensive a Manor, he does not stand much chance there being so many ways into the Town, we have watched all the coaches Waggons etc. but at present without being able to do much. . .'[5] Even a small village like Rugeley provided customers for poachers. An informer claimed that Mr Brindley, the operator of the collieries, had received a haunch of Paget's venison, and that another Rugeley gentleman had forwarded a side to Birmingham.[6]

This black market in game was regularly denounced by angry pamphleteers, and one of the many arguments they used was that by encouraging poaching the buyers of stolen game led men step by step to the gallows.[7] After 1803 this was sometimes literally so, for Lord Ellenborough's act

1. Taplin, op. cit., p. 19; *Facts, fully established, and submitted to the Consideration of every member of both houses of parliament, to the Lords of Manors, and to the Attention of the People at Large, who consider themselves aggrieved by the abuse of power, displayed in the Cruelty and Oppression of the Game Laws*, Bath, 1784, pp. 30, 33.

2. Harry Thorpe, 'Lichfield: a study of its growth and function', *Staffordshire Historical Collections 1950–51*, 1954, pp. 189–96.

3. Daniel Defoe, *A Tour Through the Whole Island of Great Britain*, [1724–27], 1962, vol. II, p. 80.

4. Weston to Paget, 3.8.76.   5. Letterbook, D603/CE400–441, 30.8.1812.

6. Evidence of Alex Watson, n.d., D603/CE538–68. A few men dealt in only the skins of deer: Nichols to Earl of Uxbridge, 13.12.52.

7. Among other examples: *Considerations on the Game Laws, together with some Strictures on Dr. Blackstone's Commentaries relative to this Subject*, 1777, p. 4; William Elford, *A Few Cursory Remarks on the Obnoxious Parts of the Game Laws*, 2nd edn, Bath, 1817, p. 21.

of that year punished with death poachers who threatened keepers with guns. But even before gentlemen in Parliament had passed legislation to confirm their beliefs, they often claimed that poaching and violent crime, if not identical, were intimately connected. The author of a broadsheet describing the death of Samuel Capewell, hanged in 1793 at Stafford for breaking open the Tamworth turnpike house, attributed his crime to 'the practice of poaching, which with the greatest concern we lament, has been too much encouraged and countenanced by those, who should have instilled the principles of honesty and industry into his mind, and checked the connections he had formed, which has been the means to induce him to commit the act for which he now suffers. . .'[1] Christian, the judge and Cambridge professor, elevated the theory into a form of natural law when he described 'that desperate character, a poacher': 'He who sleeps by day, and prowls for food in the night, soon acquires the disposition of a savage or a wild beast – a disposition which must lead to robbery, and every species of nocturnal depredation. This must have been true at all times. . .' (He quoted Plato to prove it.)[2] The Earl of Uxbridge's agent at Burton had less pretension to science than either of these men, and argued only that the poachers who besieged him were 'of the lowest rank and not unlikely to Break Houses Rob on the Highway or do any other Mischief in their Power'.[3]

Without doubt many of the Staffordshire men who were sentenced for theft in the eighteenth century had tried their hand at poaching. Certain common rural felonies, especially sheep-stealing, called for much the same skills and had similar motives. The black market in mutton was similar to that in game, though not so extensive, and some butchers dealt in stolen meat just as poulterers bought poached pheasant or hare with no questions asked. Both crimes, too, often arose from simple hunger. One man convicted at Stafford in 1757 had gone with friends to Needwood Forest to try for a deer, and was returning home empty-handed when his dog killed a sheep. Food was very scarce that year, and he pleaded in court that 'they were loath to leave it behind, as all of them wanted meat very much', but he was transported for fourteen years none the less.[4] Another poacher, disappointed in his search for crayfish near Beaudesert, also turned to sheep-stealing a few days later. He was hanged.[5] There is no evidence in the Paget correspondence, however, to show that crimes like

1. *The last Dying-Speech and Confession, Birth Parentage and Education, of Samuel Capewell, and James Stubbs, Who was Executed at Sandy-Ford, near Stafford, on Saturday, the 6th April, 1793*; WSL, Broadsheets 2.
2. Christian, op. cit., p. 333.
3. Wyatt to Earl of Uxbridge, 7.11.63.
4. Examination of William Horobin, Staffs. Lent Assizes, 1757, PRO, Assi 5/77.
5. Examination of William Wilson, Staffs. Lent Assizes, 1753, PRO, Assi 5/73.

burglary or robbery, or even sheep-stealing, were alternate occupations of many poachers. Their other crimes were almost invariably stealing wood, turnips or chickens.[1] Fowl-theft was especially common, although it concerned the farmers rather than the Pagets. William Pitt reported to the Board of Agriculture in the 1790s that 'The Profits of poultry are a matter of but little consideration, in or anywhere near the populous parts of Staffordshire; for ... the risk of having their progeny carried off by thieves is so great, and is so often actually the case, that little attention is paid to them as an article of profit.'[2]

One man active near Beaudesert illustrates the way in which poaching and other crimes were most likely to be combined. Theophilus Bailey 'long had the Character of being addicted to Poching' but nevertheless found work under Cooper at Beaudesert.[3] It was common practice to use a few men who moved between the world of the poachers and that of the keepers, in the hope that they would betray their friends.[4] Bailey proved useful in protecting the rabbits from the villagers, for which they hated him fervently, but he continued to poach himself.[5] Eventually he was given an ultimatum, and when a keeper caught him with a ferret a few days later the steward gave him notice.[6] Two years later he had a dispute with one of his mates, who gave a full and detailed account of Bailey's other activities over a period of nine months. In March he had taken posts and rails from Beaudesert Park pale, in May two chickens from a widow's barn, in midsummer carp from the pool of a gentleman in Longdon. Thomas Quinton, another poacher who helped him catch the fish, joined him in October to steal three geese from a farmer's stable. Later that month Bailey took four more geese from another farmer's outbuildings in Longdon, another goose wandering on Brereton Hill, and broke a dozen vermin traps belonging to the Earl's keepers. He took another post from the Park in December. Not that he or his friends had given up poaching: he still kept nets for deer and the steward claimed, 'There is scarcely thro' those fellows now an Hare left about the Hall or Park.'[7]

1. Wyatt to Uxbridge, 30.10.69; letter to Fowler, 6.12.1812, letterbook, D603/CE400–441; Elford, op. cit., p. 1; case of Bailey and Quinton, below.

2. William Pitt, *General View of the Agriculture of Staffordshire*, 1796, pp. 152–3.

3. Ridgway to Earl of Uxbridge, 13.7.52.

4. For another, see Ridgway to Earl of Uxbridge, 27.1.66. Bailey's family may have been keepers: the witnesses against the burglars of the deer barn (p. 193) were Edward Bailey, keeper, James Bailey, and Theophilus Bailey.

5. Below, p. 229; warrant of Dormer Parkhurst, 12.1.53, and deposition of Young, Snape, Ward, 15.1.53, D603/CE538–68; Nichols to Earl of Uxbridge, 2.2.54; information of Francis Dickin, 1.1.57, 'Bills, etc. 1742–9', Plas Newydd.

6. Ridgway to Earl of Uxbridge, 29.1.64.

7. Information of Samuel Dangerfield, 1.1.66, D603/CE248–359; Ridgway to Earl of Uxbridge, 5.1.66, 23.1.66.

Bailey was probably typical of those poachers who stole things other than game. They took geese, turnips and wood, not gold from travellers or plate from the gentry's homes. The larger problem remains, however: the degree to which theft and poaching overlapped. It was a question which contemporaries could not answer, because even if the local history of poaching was an open secret in the villages, that of theft was not. And the gentry, of course, were willing to believe that anyone touching their precious game was capable of any infamy. The most the historian can do is suggest the relative limitations on theft and on poaching that might affect a labourer living near the Chase. Those limitations can be characterized shortly as practical problems and legitimating beliefs.

Practical problems were a matter of profits and risk. The quantity of game on the Chase was so large, the number of servants protecting it relatively so few, that poaching was an immediate attraction. A cottager of Rugeley could easily find plenty of game at almost any time of year, either for the pot or for sale. He had been bred in the craft and knew how to avoid the keepers. If he sold game as a commodity rather than using it himself, he ran few risks in finding buyers, whether passing wagoners or discreet innkeepers. The distribution network for game was undoubtedly much more secure than that for stolen goods, simply because of the massive support of the rural community, and the collusion of even magistrates in the practice. Finally, until the nineteenth century the usual penalties for serious game offences were less than those for thefts of equal value. The one exception was prosecutions under the Black Act for taking deer or fish, and it was relatively rarely used; prosecutors far more often used earlier and later statutes with penalties of a year in prison, and, very rarely, transportation.

At the same time the great majority of men in rural England considered the game laws rank injustice. The conviction of middling men that an arbitrary property qualification was oppression was undoubtedly held also by the mass of labourers and cottagers. 'Every magistrate knows,' wrote Christian, 'that it is the common defence of a poacher, that it is very hard that he should be punished for taking what he had as good a right to as any other man.'[1] But at the same time there were very strong communal sanctions against casual theft. Only the gentry lost by poaching, but loss by theft was a common occurrence at every social level. A large part of the ideological importance of the criminal law in eighteenth-century England came from its recognition of this fact. The judicial definition of theft did not coincide, of course, with the popular one. A wide variety of practices that were punished by law were considered legitimate by the rural poor: miners taking coals as perks, cottagers taking wood

1. Christian, op. cit., p. 293.

from ancient commons, smugglers and tradesmen evading excise. In all such cases, however, the practices were rigidly defined by custom, and the goods involved were sharply distinguished from other property. Legitimating ideas must be clear to the whole community concerned, and the practices they sanction unambiguously defined. Poaching was such an offence; promiscuous pilfering could not be. Casual theft appeared to the villager, as to the landlord, as a conspiracy of the unknown. Because cottagers lost shirts from hedges, tools or bits of bacon from their houses, their suspicions would always turn to those who they knew were thieving from the rich. The clear communal solidarity of the poor with regard to poaching could not, therefore, extend to many other crimes against property. The petty thief could never enjoy the unqualified support of the community, even if he preyed only on gentry and wealthy farmers, because he was never above suspicion among his neighbours.

Some circumstantial evidence is the character of Bailey, the one man who thieved and poached for whom we have much biographical detail. He was not an ordinary villager. He had been an underkeeper, and had forfeited the trust of the poaching community by his violent defence of Uxbridge's rabbits. He married the daughter of a widow, reputed a bawd, who lived away from the village of Rugeley in a cottage on the waste. After his marriage he moved into a similarly isolated cottage, beyond the observation of the community. He worked as a keeper, shared his poached game and stolen goods with a few accomplices, and was probably suspected as a man who might very well betray other poachers if it was worth his while. It is significant that in the end he was betrayed himself.[1] Evidence from court records too suggests that the petty thefts most often associated with poaching were very often the work of men who did not belong to the local community. Fowl-theft was very often committed by labourers from the populous metal-working villages of the Black Country who made periodic sweeps through near-by rural parishes in search of chickens, geese, fish and game. The question must remain open, for the evidence is sparse and difficult to interpret, but it seems likely that the poaching cottagers in the villages about the Chase were seldom active thieves, and that those men who were both were often strangers from outside.[2]

Colliers, labourers and impoverished weavers, 'men of the lowest rank', were not, however, the only poachers. The most articulate opponents of the game laws were middling men and many of them trespassed on the Chase. An alehouse-keeper and a cutler came up from Birmingham for a

1. Mary Ellits to Earl of Uxbridge, 28.3.52; John Cope to Earl of Uxbridge, 11.9.53; entry in Rugeley Parish Marriage Book, 9. 10.59; Ridgway to Earl of Uxbridge, 29.1.64.
2. On relative frequencies of thefts and poaching see below, p. 251.

day's shooting, the son of an ironmaster hunted in the Park, and other offenders included maltsters, law clerks, and the curate of Longdon who kept a pointer, gun and net in his house. There were also twenty-one farmers. They were all men of property who were in the curious position of having no property rights whatsoever where game was concerned. Many had wealth and position in the villages, yet most were 'unqualified'. Because they lacked the £100 per annum from freehold set by the statute of Charles II, small freeholders and large renters alike were excluded from killing a single hare or partridge, even if it came into their own fields:

> Ye Sov'reignes of *Manors*, in Verse
> (Dull Prose will dishonour your Name)
> The Muse shall your Triumphs rehearse
> High sounding the *Laws* of the *Game*.
> The Farmer your *Sport* shall supply,
> Your Beagles his Fences shall break:
> But 'touch not and taste not,' you cry,
> The Law will its Talons awake.
> *One Hundred a Year* gives the Right
> To challenge all Nature your own;
> Tell short of the Sum but a *Mite*,
> And your *Ninety-Nine* Pounds are as none.[1]

Even the wealthiest farmers, men who were qualified, were forbidden by Uxbridge to hunt within the wide bounds where he claimed privileges of free chase and free warren, although some believed they had the right by ancient custom.[2] Meanwhile the deer strayed into their fields and damaged the corn,[3] the rabbits cropped the Chase where they had rights of common for their sheep,[4] and the keepers insulted and threatened them if they took their dogs there.[5] A mass of pamphlets on the game laws denounced such 'unconstitutional oppression'. Taplin, writing in 1772,[6] claimed that 'the Sons have Courage enough to revenge their Fathers' Wrongs', and many of the men of this class, like Thomas Quinton, went at poaching in earnest. 'This young Quinton,' reported Ridgway, 'has a Small Estate that lies near [Hednesford], of about thirty Pounds a year, but Seems to be Spending it as fast as he can; being link't into a Set of bad Company, & giveing his Mind almost totally up to poaching, so that about [Hednes-

1. From the fourth dialogue of 'The Anglers', quoted by W. B. Daniel in *Rural Sports*, 1813, p. 90.
2. Ryder's opinion, 2.6.51, WSL, HM uncatalogued, Box 7, 'Cannock'; see below, p. 219.
3. Ridgway to Earl of Uxbridge, 12.3.57; Samuel Stretton to Earl of Uxbridge, 27.9.44; Ridgway to Earl of Uxbridge, 17.11.65; Ridgway to Earl of Uxbridge, 22.1.72; William Cooper, 12.7.75.
4. See below, p. 221.   5. Below, p. 224.   6. Taplin, op. cit., p. 16.

ford] (I am inform'd), there is not an Hare to be found.'[1] Mr Thomas Birch, a rich farmer in Brereton, was caught coursing hares, and his son Andrew was a constant poacher. When Andrew was taken before a magistrate in 1769 for killing a buck he said he would appeal the conviction to King's Bench, and continue to kill any deer that came into his father's fields. He went as far as to plant turnips at the edge of the Chase to lure the deer there.[2] John Thomas, a farmer of Cannock, set snares in his hedges to take deer leaping into his fields, and set razors too in the hope of maiming them. When the keepers caught him in 1783 he said he would set snares as he liked. He had left a strangled doe in his hedge, slit open so that the guts and unborn fawn hung out.[3]

Such open contempt was not uncommon among men of middle rank, particularly when they could afford to mount a legal defence. Another farmer snatched back the hare taken from him and horsewhipped the keeper, for which he paid the £5 penalty and five guineas damages.[4] A young 'clerk' caught beating with a spaniel and a gun by the gamekeeper of Burton manor resented the man's impertinence; he 'in answer gave me Very Roof langwag', complained the keeper, 'beding me to kiss his Bakside to which I answered in such words as I thought Propper to that Language.' He added that the manor was overrun with such Burton men who 'set up for Quallaty by keeping Grahounds Pinters or Goons or Spanells or Neets or other Ingens ... Tanners Buchers Brewers Parsons and Lawyars and Navagators. Likewise common Bombalifs. ..'[5]

The most troublesome of these 'middling men' was Joseph Harding of Chorley. He was a substantial maltster, a trade known for ambitious men, and for over a decade he coursed and netted hares.[6] The keepers caught or

1. Ridgway to Earl of Uxbridge, 17.12.61.

2. William Scott to Earl of Uxbridge, 27.9.55; opinion of Fletcher Norton, 21.1.69; Ridgway to Earl of Uxbridge, 18.2.69; Ridgway to Earl of Uxbridge, 1.7.69. There were other reasons for the Birches to dislike the Pagets: see below, p. 224. Andrew may also be the 'young Birch' of Longdon (Brererton lay half-way between Rugeley and Longdon) who was prosecuted for poaching in 1776 (Weston to Harrison, 13.3.76 and 10.7.76). He was prosecuted again in 1785; Staffs. RO, Q/SR 1785Tr.

3. Weston to Paget, 17.5.83 and enclosed information of William Cooper against Thomas and Jellico.

4. Weston to Paget, 26.2.80.

5. J. Silvester to Earl of Uxbridge, 14.8.53; warrant of John Turton, 13.11.50, D603/E142–254; Staffs. RO, Q/SO 14, Keeper's deputations for 1749. See also 'A List of Persons Keeping Grey Hounds within the Manor of Burton November 1776' in E422–66; in addition to five gentlemen, probably qualified, there were 5 brewers, 3 butchers, 4 farmers and a watchmaker, smith, chandler, whittawer, mercer and postmaster.

6. He is identified as a 'yeoman' in the indictment at Staffordshire Lent Assizes for 1752; PRO, Assi 5/72.

glimpsed him in 1754, 1758 and 1760; in the last year he was netting carp as well. Repeatedly assuring the keepers he had reformed, he continued poaching without remorse. He killed hares even within the Park, threatened to sue the keepers who shot his dog, and continued with 'abominable assurance', as Ridgway complained to Uxbridge in 1758, to plant his nets up to the Hall itself. Moreover, he was thick with other poachers and pilferers. In 1751 the steward supported a successful prosecution against 'one of the principal Rogues in the Neighbourhood of Beaudesert'.[1] A labourer, he was transported for stealing a few geese, but before the trial Harding had attempted to bribe the chief witness, a servant of Uxbridge, into changing his testimony. Tried at the assizes for subornation of perjury, the maltster was acquitted on insufficient evidence, although 'the Judge said he was sorry a Rogue had escaped'.[2] Harding continued in league with other poachers, for the colliers in the Park refused to give evidence against him a few years later for taking hares there. His career apparently ended in 1760. Caught taking hares, he had a friend file an information against him before the keepers could, but Harding could not resist boasting, and the steward soon had enough evidence to arrest both him and his mate on a King's Bench information.[3]

Harding's friendship with poachers who were labourers and colliers was notorious, but there were other propertied men trespassing who poached with labourers. Eighteenth-century farmers winked when their men destroyed eggs or leverets during harvest or haymaking, and bought game from them.[4] They did more. Farmers and tradesmen made up the panels of common jurors at Quarter Sessions and assizes, and as the steward complained while preparing to prosecute a poacher for assault, 'there is no answering for a Common Jury (who must Try the Indictment) as they have in general a Strong Byass upon their Minds in favor of Poachers, being professed Enemies to all Penal Laws that relate to the Game.'[5] This contempt of jurymen for laws that did not suit them was no great danger, because the legislature had thoughtfully made most game offences punishable by justices sitting without juries. However, in two other cases, the Pagets took a game case into the courts, with unfortunate results. One was the prosecution of Dangerfield and Bailey, the other that

---

1. Thomas Butler (Staffs. R.O. Q/SR, and Q/SO Epiphany 1751; Nichols to Earl of Uxbridge, 16.1.51).
2. Nichols to Earl of Uxbridge, 28.3.52.
3. Nichols to Earl of Uxbridge, 1.4.51, 21.3.52, 28.3.52, 2.2.54; Ridgway to Earl of Uxbridge, 23.9.58, 11.10.58, 27.9.60, 4.10.60, 18.10.60, 20.12.60.
4. Taplin, op. cit., pp. 16–17; *Facts, fully established . . .*, p. 24; Elford, op. cit., p. 4; Anon., *Thoughts on the Present Laws for Preserving the Game*, 1750, p. 25.
5. Weston to Paget, 17.2.90; Blackstone, *Commentaries*, vol. III, p. 362.

of the two farmers who shot the keeper's horse in 1792. All four men were acquitted.[1]

The game statutes thus created a curious anomaly in the administration of the criminal law. They antagonized a great many men who usually were the first to support the defence of property and the conviction of thieves. They also weakened the power farmers and tradesmen had over their labourers and servants, by putting a powerful weapon in the hands of the poor. When farmers hunted illegally, suggested one critic,

> it is most likely that their offences are known to the Poachers, Smugglers, Wood-stealers, and all Sorts of mischievous rascally Night-Walkers, whom the Farmers dare not bring to Justice, for fear of having Reprisals made upon themselves, by Means of Informations. But, if Farmers were set free from those Fears [by being allowed to shoot game] ... they would be constant Scourges to those Miscreants, and for the Sake of their own Hen-roosts and Wood-stacks, would endeavour to keep the Country clear of such Vermin.[2]

The author thought the game laws disturbed the natural order of provincial life. Perhaps, paradoxically, their effect was to increase the stability of eighteenth-century rural society. Although they created friction and sometimes violent hostility between gentry and farmers, they created something of an alliance between farmers and labourers, who poached together and supported one another with alibis and verdicts of not guilty. In all other kinds of criminal prosecutions concerning property, labourers formed the majority of the accused and most of the prosecutors were farmers. The game laws thus not only smoothed relations between two classes of men whose interests were often sharply opposed; they helped to obscure the nature of the law as an instrument of class power. A £20 fine hurt rich farmers like the Birches more in their pride than their pockets, but such incidents blurred the usual divisions between those who used the law in defence of property and those who suffered it. And the power which the threat of an information gave to a poor man over his master helped partially to redress the balance of power between propertied and propertyless. In addition to forestalling prosecutions for theft, it may occasionally have made a farmer more generous with wages, or an overseer of the poor more charitable, than he otherwise would have been.

Few farmers and tradesmen were qualified, but all the landed gentry were. Here attitudes to poaching were usually unequivocal: almost to a

1. For Bailey and Dangerfield, Ridgway to Earl of Uxbridge, 5.1.66 and 23.1.66, and Staffs RO, Q/SR, Q/SO, Q/SM2, all Epiphany 1766. For Marshall and Darlaston, see p. 197, n. 5; the refusal of a prosecution witness to testify may have been the explanation in the latter case. Marshall and Darlaston were successfully prosecuted a year later for killing deer; Staffs. RO, Q/SB 1793 Ep/16.

2. Anon., *Thoughts on the Present Laws for Preserving the Game*, p. 25.

man, squires and peers execrated the 'common poacher'. The very phrase, however, suggests that the game laws not only reflected larger class divisions but also created complex social tensions within the landed class itself. The 'uncommon' poacher, the trespassing gentleman, was also a frequent visitor to Cannock Chase. In one period for which the keeper's accounts seem to be complete, he mentions about a dozen poachers, and the same number of qualified sportsmen.[1] It was usual for gentlemen to extend such courtesies. Most game 'belonged' to all the propertied, although no individual owned it. An action for trespass was usually the only possible restriction on a gentleman's sport, and most neighbours exercised forbearance. For a county to enjoy coursing and shooting a considerable degree of mutual indulgence was necessary; freedom to pursue hares or pheasants onto one another's land, and to allow one's neighbours' servants to do so when the menu required.

This fellow-feeling could disappear, however, in disputes over land, or politics, or special hunting privileges. Both the Pagets became involved in such quarrels over their game. On two occasions the Earl of Uxbridge found his manorial rights in question. Norton parish seemed to nurse deer-poachers, and it became apparent that a local gentleman was encouraging rather than disciplining them. Phineas Hussey owned a third of the manor, as well as that of Wyrley, and he claimed the right to kill all deer straying off the Chase. He supported the right of his tenants to do so as well. Hussey had lost a prized dog to the keepers in 1761, before he owned the manors, but after the purchase his effrontery grew. In 1765 his butler was caught coursing the deer with greyhounds, and two years later the keepers reported that Hussey remained unrepentant about the continuing carnage. Undoubtedly he liked venison, hated the keepers, and sympathized with his tenants, who were exposed to the ravages of the deer in their common and their fields. The issue extended further. Little Wyrley was a barony within the jurisdiction of the Earl of Uxbridge's court leet of Longdon, and Hussey refused to allow his tenants to acknowledge the Longdon court. He may have been interested simply in extending his own manorial rights, but another motive was probably the wish to protect his tenants from pressure, through the manorial court, by Uxbridge's steward.[2] In 1744 a similar dispute had arisen with Richard Dyott of Freeford, who claimed to be lord of the manor there, and hunted

1. D603, financial accounts of 16.1.77 to 5.12.78.

2. Ridgway to Earl of Uxbridge, 3.2.61, 18.2.61, 13.6.61, 21.9.61, 17.11.65, 24.11.67; deposition of William and Henry Cooper, 30.1.61 and 16.2.61; deposition of Coopers and Thomas Brees, 12.11.65; deposition of Joseph Hodgkins, 21.11.67 in D603/C38; William Pitt, *A Topographical History of Staffordshire*, Newcastle, 1817, vol. I, p. 165. See also memo *re Taylor v. Ashmall*, 26.6.83, D603/xxxv, a similar case involving the manor of Farewell.

hares and hanged other men's dogs as his right. But the Earl claimed Freeford also as part of his manor of Longdon; his grandfather had prosecuted Dyott twice, and he had submitted. His abuse of the game laws after Uxbridge inherited in 1743 was another attempt to advance the same claims.

Dyott had other reasons for opposing the Earl of Uxbridge. The politics of the Chase inevitably became involved in county politics as well. Uxbridge was a Tory. His estate stewards were soon active in Tory politics, and when partisan temper sharpened during the 1747 elections they began to use the resources of the estates to further the cause. In 1744 Lord Gower, head of the leading Tory family of the county, had defected to the Bedford Whigs. There were bitter contests for the county representation, and for the seats of Stafford borough and Lichfield. When the Tories organized a demonstration against the Gowerite traitors in September, Uxbridge's Burton steward led a high Tory procession into Lichfield. A Whig witness reported that they all wore plaid waistcoats; he claimed some also had white cockades 'and drank the Pretender's health publicly in the streets, singing treasonable songs'.[1]

At Beaudesert other Gowerites began to feel the Earl's displeasure. The Reverend Richard Congreve, the vicar of Leacroft, wrote to his brother in 1748, 'I am glad you mentioned to Lord Gower the persecutions we meet with on account of the election; it is not to be conceived the malice and knavery they employ to get their revenge.' He accused Nichols of packing a court leet jury to harass one of Gower's supporters; the following year Congreve himself was insulted by a keeper on the Chase. He had always had permission to sport there, and he continued to do so, but in 1755 he was warned never to trespass again. He protested in vain that the keepers indulged unqualified men, that the deer destroyed his estate, that he would not submit quietly. Uxbridge then began a vindictive and costly prosecution against Congreve's servant, who had been shooting on the Chase on his master's orders. The vicar wrote to his brother that he suspected the malevolence of his neighbours:

who cannot forgive ye part I took against em in ye county election, for I never offended em any other way, and I [*sic*. They?] have ever since yt time been making use of the most persecuting malice, with every other mean artifice of this sort to injure me. . . I shall represent these things to my Lord, but expect no redress, as I never could get any when I have been injured, insulted, and perplexed by his agents heretofore.[2]

1. Josiah C. Wedgwood, *Staffordshire Parliamentary History*, vol. II, 1920, pp. 250–53; Ann J. Kettle, 'The Struggle for the Lichfield Interest', in *Essays in Staffordshire History*, ed. M. W. Greenslade, 1970, pp. 115–35.
2. Congreve to Earl of Uxbridge, 8.6.49, 27.9.55, 3.10.55; Ridgway to Earl of Ux-

Congreve's suspicions cannot be proven, but several members of the Chetwynd family also received notice not to trespass in 1749 and again in 1755, and like Congreve they were prominent in Staffordshire Whig circles.

A few years after the Earl of Uxbridge inherited the title and the estates, it also became clear to neighbouring gentlemen that he was not controlling his keepers and warreners. The power of gamekeepers was a necessary but vexatious aspect of the game laws for sporting gentlemen. They could not protect their own game without them, but they had to stay on good terms with those of their neighbours. By statute a keeper had wide discretionary powers, including the right to destroy dogs disturbing the game. In practice these powers were even wider, particularly when an absentee landowner, like the Earl of Uxbridge, gave them great latitude. They were then able to treat gentlemen with a staggering disregard for the conventions of class. William Chetwynd of Haywood received his notice not to trespass after a dispute with a keeper; he protested that 'Gentlemen can't help being a little piqu'd when they are treated with ill manners. . .'[1] Dickin, the chief keeper, trespassed freely into gentlemen's parks in search of straying deer, and in 1762 shot Chetwynd's hound in his own park. When the Earl of Uxbridge refused to make amends, Chetwynd warned the keeper, 'a Mischief-making ungrateful Dog', to stay away.[2] Cope, one of the warreners, was also known for his 'insolent and brutal behaviour': he shot dogs on his warren at sight, and even 'the most substantial Freeholders dog was not safe under his horses Belly from his shot. . .'[3] As Chetwynd's experience showed, by the 1760s gentlemen's dogs were as much at risk as those of farmers. The gentry therefore followed with great interest a dispute that was already before the courts. Cope's son had killed a spaniel belonging to Fisher Littleton, who held an estate not far from Beaudesert. Littleton was furious, particularly when the keeper defended his son, showing none of the respect due a gentleman: 'His behaviour upon the occasion was so uncommonly monstrous, that I imagined he was drunk. . .' But the Earl of Uxbridge

bridge, 10.6.56; John Cooper to Earl of Uxbridge, 13.9.55; examination of John Cooper, 22.9.55; Scott to Earl of Uxbridge, 22.9.55; letter of Ralph Weston, 10.12.81; James Cecil to William Scott, 3.10.55; W S L, Salt MSS 47/21, 47/28/243, 47/28/252, 47/29/253.

1. 'Chetwynd of Haywood Park' (William, later 4th Viscount: D260/M/E/429/31, memo 19.5.50) to Earl of Uxbridge, 12.8.49; and Scott to Earl of Uxbridge, 22.9.55. Members of the Chetwynd family were too useful as JPs to the keepers to be excluded for long; see below, p. 240.

2. Ridgway to Earl of Uxbridge, 21.4.62, 31.5.63; information by Dickin, 28.5.63; William Chetwynd Jr of Haywood Park to Earl of Uxbridge, 27.4.62.

3. D260/M/E/429/31, large vol., p. 207.

refused to discipline the keeper or give any compensation, and warned
Littleton not to go cockshooting on the Chase again. Enraged, Littleton
sued for the dog. Uxbridge defended the action, against the advice of his
lawyers, and lost. A special jury at Stafford Assizes awarded Littleton a
guinea damages and costs, about £40 in all; the Earl's own costs were
probably £150 more. An observer of the trial remarked, 'The gentlemen
on the jury took the guinea offered them for serving which is not usually
done by gentlemen, and they sent it to the Prisoners in the gaol in contempt
of so arbitrary and scandalous a proceeding in Lord Uxbridge.'[1]

The crucial issue for the gentry, however, was not the insolence of the
keepers but the fact that Uxbridge could exclude them from the Chase.
In the eighteenth century, the country gentry were a rude species with an
acute sense of the territorial imperative, and a lively dislike of allowing
others to sport on their land, although they expected the privilege themselves. One pamphleteer suggested that trespassing sportsmen took truly
unpardonable liberties, for

> To many gentlemen of property, I am persuaded that the affection to their
> paternal fields is next in degree to the love of their friends and family, or the
> partner of their bed. What man of sense or sensibility would form a contract of
> copartnery in the article of wives, or allow to every one of his neighbours all
> rights and privileges with his spouse, because he had the same with theirs?[2]

Uxbridge (who had no wife) was more possessive of his lands than most,
and required all gentlemen wishing to enjoy them to obtain his express
permission. Without his cooperation, some of the best sporting country
in the Midlands was closed to the neighbouring gentry, or was at best
hazardous territory for them. Holed up on his Middlesex estates, rarely
venturing into Staffordshire, indulging arrogant and vindictive servants,
the Earl came to be execrated by many of the gentry. Henry Vernon
of Hilton, a neighbouring justice, acidly replied to a steward's complaint
about some heathburners that if Uxbridge 'would not come into this
country it was no matter if it was all burnt'.[3] After his death relations im-

1. Fisher Littleton to Earl of Uxbridge, 27.2.61; Ridgway to Earl of Uxbridge,
14.3.61, 25.12.62, 8.1.63, 26.2.63, 26.3.63, 24.5.63; Whitfield to Earl of Uxbridge,
11.1.63; Henry Wyatt to Earl of Uxbridge, 15.1.63; William Wyatt to Earl of Uxbridge, 15.1.63; Ridgway's accounts (n.d.), June 1763; D260/M/E/429/31, p. 212.
Littleton was Sir Edward's brother (below, p. 218) and held half of the manor and
estate of Pipe Ridware (Pitt, *A Topographical History of Staffordshire*, vol. I, p. 71);
see also M. W. Farr, 'Sir Edward Littleton's Fox-hunting Diary' in Greenslade, ed.,
op. cit., pp. 136–70.
2. *Considerations on the Game Laws in Answer to a Pamphlet Intitled, The Present State
of the Game Law* . . ., Edinburgh, 1772, pp. 35–6.
3. William Cooper to Earl of Uxbridge, 27.9.55; Vernon, who died in 1765, was a

proved. Lord Paget, his cousin and successor, had a proper regard for field sports and the civilities of county life, and resided much of the time at Beaudesert. Congreve and other aggrieved neighbours were welcomed back on the Chase.[1] Paget shared packs of foxhounds with some, and followed the common custom of requesting his keepers to use 'some discretion with respect to persons of credit, tho' unqualified, who are not Porchers'.[2] He had a sharp sense of the social importance of game: in a memorandum shortly after inheriting Cannock he reminded himself that 'nothing his Lordship can do will give him equal eclat amongst the people to that of keeping the buck hounds upon these hills. The old Earls used to do it and it is the talk of the country to this day. . .'[3]

Even Paget, however, soon found himself involved in disputes with his neighbours about the Chase. Choleric sportsmen continued to resent the questions of keepers, however polite.[4] But the resentment of the Stafford-shire gentry had a focus: the claim of the Pagets to full rights of free chase and free warren. The privilege was a royal franchise, inherited with the estates in 1546, and it gave the Pagets more absolute rights over the game than any other gentlemen in the region could claim. Ordinarily the quali-fied were free to shoot or course game anywhere, even on another's land, if they were willing to risk being sued for trespass. But game within chases or warrens or parks or free fisheries belonged to the owner alone. Those possessed of them, Blackstone pointed out, 'are the *only* persons who may acquire any property, however fugitive and transitory, in these animals . . . while living'.[5] Moreover, free chases and free warrens, unlike parks or ordinary warrens did not need to be enclosed. The game there continued to belong to the owner even if it went beyond the boundaries, provided the keepers went after it.[6] This was Dickin's excuse for pursuing the deer into gentlemen's parks, and for prosecuting farmers who killed them in their fields. Finally, franchises of chase and warren were not tied to ownership of the land; the Pagets held exclusive game rights over many acres that were the property of other qualified men. And they claimed

relative and supporter of Lord Gower, and had perhaps been warned off the Chase with Congreve and Chetwynd.

1. Congreve to Paget, 29.9.80; Curzon to Earl of Uxbridge, 11.1.75.

2. Samuel Wyatt to Paget, 20.10.71.

3. Memorandum, n.d., D603/C40.

4. Paget's own sporting soon conflicted with that of others. At first he shared fox-hunting with Lord Donegall of Fisherwick, but the foxes, distracted by two packs of hounds, were unable to sustain their rate of natural increase. Paget ended the arrange-ment, and an acrimonious correspondence ensued. Paget's copy of all the letters is in D603/C40 (November 1770).

5. Blackstone, *Commentaries*, vol. II, p. 419; his emphasis.

6. ibid., vol. IV, p. 408.

these very great privileges through the whole length and breadth of Cannock Chase, some thirty square miles.[1]

Pace Blackstone, many gentlemen could not believe in their bones that such a tyranny really had a basis in law. Men who revered property, who would not dream of touching a neighbour's park deer any more than his silver plate, had no compunctions about the game that roamed on and off the Chase. Sir Edward Littleton of Teddesley Hall, on its western edge, was a knight of the shire and J P, a paternalist, the image of an honourable country gentleman. He was also a keen sportsman and preserved game. As a Member of Parliament he promoted legislation to make the unexplained possession of a rabbit an offence punishable by seven years' transportation, and as a Justice of the Peace he convicted many of the Beaudesert poachers. Yet, like earlier Littletons, he was a bit of a poacher himself. He had no hesitation about killing deer that wandered onto Teddesley and Huntingdon. In his uncle's time and earlier, the Littletons and their servants used red herrings (the originals of the metaphor) to lead their hounds onto the Chase to go after the deer; they could then claim that the dogs had pursued them there from Teddesley. Sir Edward himself kept careful notes on 'How deer may be killed by any person with safety', instructions on avoiding prosecution. And close personal study of the legal opinions surrounding Cannock Chase since the sixteenth century had convinced him that the Pagets' claim to free chase and free warren was doubtful, that the very principle of such a franchise was shaky in law.[2]

Littleton was related by marriage to Lord Parker, Chief Baron of the Exchequer from 1742 to 1772. Parker remembered with affection a glorious chase after the red herring in Littleton's uncle's time. And he assured Sir Edward, doubtless over a good haunch of venison, that lawyers were pretty ignorant of this thing free chase and free warren. 'And he furthermore said, that if a trial, relative to free warren, was to be brought before him, he was far from being certain he should suffer any man to plead his free warren, which he looked upon as a remnant of ancient tyranny, that was now obsolete, and as the forest laws in general now

1. The original grant limited it to the parishes of Cannock and Rugeley, but the Earl of Uxbridge claimed rights throughout by prescription; Ridgway to Earl of Uxbridge, 24.11.67.

2. J. E. Auden, *A Short History of the Albrighton Hunt*, 1905, p. 3, citing Nimrod; Pitt, *A Topographical History of Staffordshire*, vol. II, p. 258; Staffs. R O, D554, bdl 149; Nichols to Earl of Uxbridge, 28.1.54, 2.2.54; Ridgway to Earl of Uxbridge, 18.4.61; Curzon to Paget, 6.7.74; Littleton to Paget, 1.12.75, 11.3.84; W S L, H M, uncatalogued, Box 33. Littleton's records on Cannock Chase were entered in a large manuscript volume in his own hand, D260/M/E/429/31, hereafter Littleton, 'Records'; see memo 19.5.1750 and p. 140.

were'.[1] Finally, Sir Edward knew, by an Exchequer inquiry into common rights in 1595, that certain copyholders in manors about the Chase had had the right to hunt foxes, hares and roes on the great waste.[2] Littleton's opinion, untested in law but held passionately, was therefore that the Pagets probably could not sustain their claims in a court, and had no right to limit his deercoursing. Many of the gentry in the neighbourhood must have shared his belief, and doubtless quoted Chief Baron Parker to one another over their port.[3] More than any other factor, the legal status of the Chase undermined the unanimity which was more usual among gentlemen when they considered the game laws.

The attitudes surrounding game, the social conflicts and alliances that it created in rural society, were thus complex. Although in theory the law created a sharp distinction between qualified and unqualified men, in practice it was a hierarchy of privilege, which gentlemen and peers tried to match to the realities of power as they saw it, and which those excluded from privilege tried to subvert. The broad divisions often were blurred by shifting alliances between classes, and personal friendships and enmities. The poorest men were poachers without scruple and with enormous pride. Some crossed back and forth between other kinds of theft as well, but most stayed with game. The solidarity of the poaching community extended upwards through prosperous artisans and some farmers. Where friendliness and shared exploits stopped, the conspiracy against the keepers was nevertheless respected, although cottagers sometimes used the threat of betrayal to govern their masters and employers. At the upper level of the farming community, the wealthy yet unqualified freeholder or copyholder might be indulged by his landlord in a bit of sport. Where relations were good, 'the qualified and unqualified associate and pursue the pleasure

1. Littleton, 'Records', pp. 141–2. John Turton (d. 1771), who claimed similar rights at Alrewas, admitted to Sir Edward that 'it would be unsafe to hazard a trial on free warren, for that both judge and jury would warp against it'. (ibid., p. 142). Many jurists scorned the game laws as the work of ignorant squires and Norman usurpers, a disturbing anomaly in the laws of property; cf. Blackstone, *Commentaries*, vol. IV, pp. 174ff, 415ff.

2. Littleton, 'Records', p. 116; and below, p 225.

3. Paget sued the Reverend Landor of Rugeley and Pigot of Patshull (an Indian nabob) in 1782, when they ridiculed his claims of free warren; they submitted to prevent a legal finding (Weston, 10.12.81; unsigned memo, 5.3.82; copies Paget to Landor and Pigot, D603/C2; Edward Dickenson to Littleton, 20.7.82 in Littleton, 'Records'.) The claim of free warren was upheld and that of the oldholders finally rejected in *Paget v. Charles Cotterell and Henry Birch* (1810). As late as 1805 Littleton had thought free warren an absurd doctrine, but he testified for Paget, who was a good friend. The judge rejected the 1595 commission because it was an unattested copy, the original still being lost (*Staffs. Advertiser*, 7.4.1810; Littleton to Moreton, 20.6.1805 in Littleton, 'Records'; and below, pp. 225ff).

together with as little distinction as if such laws were as obsolete in *spirit*, as they are in *effect*.'

'Even a brace of pointers in the field has, in all parts of the kingdom, been admitted a qualification equal to a Hundred a year; for the very appearance proclaims the owner too FAIR a SPORTSMAN to fall a victim to the stigma of information.'[1] Finally, among the gentry, as long as feuds or disputes over land or simple bloodymindedness did not mar the harmony of the county oligarchy, mutual forbearance and hospitality was the rule in field sports. These arrangements between gentlemen were never without tensions. The web of relationships was constantly being holed here and there, until renewed through reconciliation, inheritance or the sale of estates. In Cannock Wood, however, these tensions were unusually acute. The Pagets' estates were so large, and their powers over game so absolute, that jealousies could not help but arise. The resentment under Paget was often sharp. Under Uxbridge, a quirky absentee landlord who made very little attempt to honour the conventions, the resentment was sometimes venomous. He therefore had few friends when he began to extend his claims over the Chase in the 1750s. Within a few months the constraints of the game laws and much of the rule of law itself were swept away in a tacit union of virtually all villagers and gentry against him. The issue was rabbits. Rich poachers and poor formed a temporary alliance to slaughter the Earl's gentle conies in one grand assault.

III

The Earl of Uxbridge, like many eighteenth-century landlords, looked to his game as a source not only of prestige but of profit. It was illegal to sell game, as strictly defined, and gentlemen were supposed to find it beneath them to do so. But rabbits, strictly speaking, were not game, and they were a profitable investment. Sandy or rocky waste lands that were useless for any other purpose made excellent warrens, and leading agricultural writers urged that there was no better way to 'improve' such lands.[2] Yet such wastes were very frequently ancient commons, where tenants and cottagers had the right to feed their cattle and sheep. Where both common rights and free warren existed together, as on Cannock Chase, the landlord

1. *Facts, fully established* . . ., pp. 52–3.
2. J. Mordant, *The Complete Steward*, 1761, vol. II, p. 347; Arthur Young, *General View of the Agriculture of Suffolk*, 1813, pp. 220–21. See also the statute 15 Geo. III c. 15 (1775) which penalized the theft of rabbits from lands 'unfit for cultivation, and yet . . . capable of rendering great profit, by the breeding and maintaining conies . . .', and John Sheail, *Rabbits and their History*, 1971.

and the commoners were in direct competition for the use of the land. Sheep in particular competed with hares, rabbits and deer, for all three species cropped closely; countrymen estimated that a brace of hares ate more than two sheep.[1] Rabbits were similarly voracious, and for centuries the Pagets and the commoners of the villages near the Chase had argued about the warrens. In 1595, while the fourth baron was under attainder for treason and his lands seized by the Crown, an inquiry into the customs of the manors showed only one warren in existence, and the jurymen refused to admit that it was a free warren.[2] There had been riots and disputes about other rights in the sixteenth century, and in 1605 these differences were settled in an agreement between lord and copyholders which established their unrestricted right of common within the manors of Rugeley, Haywood, Longdon and Cannock. When the sixth baron considered planting additional warrens after succeeding to the title in 1628, his lawyers' opinion was that the 1605 agreement restricted his rights of warren because overstocking would damage the common.[3]

For sixty years the issue apparently lay dormant. Then, in about 1690, the seventh baron tried again to wring more revenues from the Chase. Perhaps his lawyers sensed that the high courts would be less solicitous for the rights of commoners than they had been under the Stuarts. An enterprising warrener took a tenancy of part of the waste behind the Park and began to dig burrows and cart in conies. He soon found there would be determined opposition:

the . . . freeholders came and dug up the Burroughs and trod them in as he made them, and catched the rabbits what they could, at which . . . Ellis was very much dissatisfied, and upon that took his horse and went to London to Mr Peter Walters who was then my Lords Steward to acquaint him therewith, the said Mr Walters replied, that he would have him go and kill the rabbits, and go back into his own country again (which was Worcestershire) for neither my Lord nor

1. *Some Considerations on the Game Laws and the Present Practice in executing them . . .*, p. 36; and see Pitt's comments on Sutton Coldfield, Pitt, *General View of the Agriculture of Staffordshire*, p. 140.

2. Littleton, 'Records', pp. 109–17, especially p. 110.

3. D1734/2/2/21; D(W)1734/2/3/123; and D1042/15. A list of questions and answers of counsel, including the opinion on conies, is bound in D(W)1734/2/3/123, and refers to 'William Lord Paget deceased', the fifth baron. It is an explanation for his son of the implications of William's agreement with the copyholders, who purchased off their fines, determined their heriots, and established their right of common in exchange for allowing him to enclose coppices for seven years at a time and £1,500. (I am indebted to Mr Chris Harrison of St John's College, Oxford for these references.) An eighteenth-century copy of the 1605–6 decree appears in D603/L1–50. The lawyers' advice was probably based on *Geisel* v. *Leigh*, Jones W. 12, which ruled in 1621 that owners of free warrens could not overstock commons with rabbits to the prejudice of a prior right of common.

he could help him, for if the freeholders etc. had a mind to come and destroy them they might. . .[1]

The commoners' justification was undoubtedly that the rabbits were a private nuisance in law, leaving the commoners insufficient common; and they knew it was legal to remove a nuisance by force.[2] Paget was apparently unsure of his position in law, for there were a number of decisions of the courts which made conies an exception to the rule. Rabbits could not be destroyed, even when they were a nuisance; the commoner had to go to law to get them removed. But if the commoners did go to law, a recent case in the high courts suggested that Paget would have to show that he had left sufficient common for their sheep.[3]

Apparently neither side risked an appeal to the courts at this time. Instead, after 1710 Paget again tried planting new warrens and the commoners again destroyed them as fast as the rabbits appeared. They destroyed the lodge on Haywood warren, and only an armed guard allowed Paget to erect a new one two years later.[4] In 1713 the eighth baron succeeded to the title, and started a fresh attack. The steward harangued the tenants at the court leet, saying that their rights of common for sheep were 'totally subservient to his Lordship's Paramount or original right', and the warreners dug new burrows.[5] On Lamb's warren, where the conies eventually spread over eight fields formerly let by lot among the commoners of Hammerwich, the freeholders and copyholders slaughtered them during three or four years. Gradually, however, the opposition faded. Perhaps all the warreners followed the example of the tenant on Lamb's warren: 'one Benbow who came and lived at the Lodge and behaved civilly to the Neighbours and gave some of them a rabbit or two now and then by which behaviour of Benbow's the neighbours suffered the rabbits to increase upon several hundred acres of ground. . .'[6] They also exacted a promise from the heir, Uxbridge's father, to rout the rabbits when he inherited the estates. Since he was running for a parliamentary seat

1. *Smith* v. *Uxbridge et al.*, Case for the Plaintiff, in Littleton, 'Records', pp. 187, 198. Two leases for warrens in 1635, and another in 1652, are listed in the brief of the defendants' case, D603/L1-50.

2. Coke, *Institutes*, vol. II, p. 88 was cited by their counsel; 1 Burrow 263.

3. The principal cases against destroying conies were Coney's case in 1587 (Godbolt 122), *Bellew* v. *Langdon* in 1601 (Cro. Eliz. 876), *Sir Jerome Horsey* v. *Hagberton* in 1604 (Cro. Jac. 229), *Carrill* v. *Pack and Baker* in 1614 (2 Bulstr. 116). There had been no cases on the question of destroying rabbits in abatement of a nuisance since that of 1614; but *Smith* v. *Feverel* in 1687 (2 Mod. 7) suggested that on surcharge of a common the defendant was obliged to prove that he had left sufficient for the plaintiff.

4. Littleton, 'Records', pp. 187, 195-6.

5. Ralph (?) to Dolphin, 11.10.1715.

6. Littleton, 'Records', pp. 189, 200.

he was willing to agree to anything (his own father had made a similar promise years before).[1] He died before succeeding to the title, and the eventual heir, in 1743, was Uxbridge. And he upheld the honour and the income of the Pagets by extending the warrens.

At mid-century the rabbits occupied about 3,500 acres of the Chase – the stock stood at about 15,000 conies.[2] Prevailing prices gave Uxbridge about 7d. each for the meat, if sold in Stafford or Birmingham; the skins brought £30 a thousand from London furriers.[3] Compared to his other sources of revenue, it was not much; he gave two of the warrens to his keepers in part payment of their wages, and leased the other three to tenants for about £100 a year.[4] He had greater plans, however. Large warrens, veritable megalopolis warrens, could be very profitable: Arthur Young described one in Suffolk that produced 40,000 conies annually, worth some £2,000.[5] Cannock Chase could support at least as many.

By 1750 the commoners of Cannock, Rugeley and Longdon sensed that they were at a crisis. For years they had been losing the initiative by their own inaction and by believing the 'vague promises and fair speeches' of the heirs to the estate. The Earl of Uxbridge had dismissed their protests in the seven years he had held it; he was now ignoring even their letters. There was no heir to whom they could appeal; at the age of thirty, the Earl was a bachelor, with a good life expectancy, and his agents were insisting on his right to turn the whole of Cannock Chase into a warren if he pleased.[6] The commoners were already suffering serious losses from the rabbits, which occupied the best grazing grounds. Some farmers estimated that they could keep only half the sheep they did formerly, that the ewes would not lamb for want of sufficient grass, that the value of the wool had declined.[7] In the sixteenth century there had been 7,000 sheep on the Chase, as well as the deer; now the commoners could foresee the

1. ibid., pp. 189–90.

2. ibid., pp. 188–9; 'Testimony of viewers of Cannock Warrens', 10–11 July 1754, in D603/CE538–68.

3. These figures were calculated for the warrens of Sir Edward Littleton, on the west side of the Chase, in the 1760s; they agree with those of Arthur Young, who put the value of the skins at 7d. and the flesh at 3d., more if sold in the country (WSL, HM uncatalogued, Box 33, and Young, *General View of the Agriculture of Suffolk*, pp. 220–21.)

4. Undated summary of warrens and rioters, D603/E/467; originally enclosed in Ridgway to Earl of Uxbridge, 22.4.54.

5. Young, op. cit., p. 221.

6. Littleton, 'Records', p. 176.

7. Brief relating to John Smith's action, 9.8.53 in D603/L1–50; 'The Case of the Freeholders Oldholders and Copyholders of and in the Manors of Cannock and Rugeley Longdon and Haywood' by Ryder, 2.6.51 (WSL, uncatalogued HM, Box 7, Cannock). These are the claims made by the commoners' witnesses at the trials.

gradual extinction of all their rights.[1] Behind the issue of the warrens was the shadow of another threat – enclosure. It did not reassure them that some of the local gentry who sympathized with their complaints nevertheless refused to promise any legal help, and continued to buy land themselves with common rights. Large landowners notoriously could take care of their own interests when it came to enclosure; it was the small commoner who often lost all. The latter believed 'that by the conduct of the Lords and their agents its manifest that all Endeavours have been to oppress the inferior commoners not only by charging too large rent on enclosing fields but also by planting rabbit warrens, thereby endeavouring to make the common of little or no advantage, that an inclosure of Cannock Wood might in time have been more easily brought about. . .'[2] Meanwhile the sheep near Hammerwich left the destroyed common for neighbouring fields, where they were coursed by dogs. Even on the Chase the warreners' hounds worried them. The ubiquitous rabbits trespassed everywhere into the corn, as did the deer, fleeing before the plague of conies. To add insult to injury, the warreners had the gall to claim that every freeholder or copyholder on the Chase looking for his sheep was a poacher; it did not help that many were. 'The Seven Warreners and Keepers [are] now assuming as absolute a Government in Cannock Wood as the Seven Kings of England in the Time of the Heptarchy in killing the Commoners Sheep-dogs, dogs of no prejudice to Game, and coursing and disturbing their sheep by which many are lost, oft' beating their servants, and threatening their Masters lives.'[3]

In 1751 the villagers decided to take action, and several of the wealthiest villagers began making plans. Henry Brindley of Rugeley and Thomas Birch of Brereton may have been stung into action by Uxbridge's refusal to renew their contract to work his coal mines on the old terms.[4] Other prosperous farmers were concerned solely with the common: John Smith junior, who kept hundreds of sheep and took clay from the Chase for his brickworks, Charles Marshall, a Longdon farmer, and the Avarnes of Rugeley. Thomas Avarne was a cleric, Geoffrey a mercer, and William described himself as 'gentleman'.[5] Even wealthier men may have been

1. Information from Mr Chris Harrison.

2. Littleton, 'Records', p. 190.

3. Littleton, 'Records', pp. 187, 189, 200; Walter Reeve to Earl of Uxbridge, 11.9.53; Parry to Earl of Uxbridge, 16.7.51.

4. Testimony of John Cope in 'Depositions touching Cope's warren, taken 12th January 1754', D603. Brindley and others agreed with the Earl of Uxbridge in 1748 to rent the pits for twenty-one years at £400 per annum, but before the lease was signed the terms were changed to be void on notice at seven years; Nichols to Earl of Uxbridge, 21.11.48 and 10.12.48.

5. Birch of Brewerton and Brindley of Rugeley, apart from their interest in the coal-

involved, but if landed gentry like Littleton were involved they took care to remain in the background. The visible leaders were prosperous farmers and tradesmen, the churchwardens and overseers of the poor, the leaders of village politics. Their allies were the cottagers and villagers who also used the Chase, often believed they had full rights of common there, and hated the keepers. In the pubs someone invented a song, an altered version of 'Charlees Dragoons', a Jacobite ditty:

> Charlees Dragoons, They are jolly Fellows
> When they appear with Broadsword in hand
> And when George he is gone and butcher Bill his son
> We shall have Charlee the Jolly Dragoon.[1]

In their new version 'Charlee' became the commoners' leader, Charles Marshall, and George and William presumably metamorphosed into the Earl and his conies. Neither rabbits nor Hanoverians were very popular in that part of Staffordshire.

The commoners got advice from both a local solicitor and a leading counsel of the Oxford circuit: both advised them not to remove the rabbits by force.[2] Publicly, they threatened to do just that, and when the steward asked Birch and Brindley to curb the loose talk in the villages of attacking the warrens, they declared 'that they had had a great deal of ill usage from my Lord, and if the rest of their neighbours went to dig the Rabbits out, they would join them'.[3] They contented themselves with yet one more respectful letter to Uxbridge.[4] It was scorned. The Earl not only delighted in the fertility of his rabbits; he hoped to prove that sheep were not commonable on the Chase.[5] His steward attended the manor courts with the copyhold agreement of 1605 to convince the commoners that Uxbridge was not exercising all his rights, and thereby 'keep the seditious from credit'. They were not impressed. Their own charter was the Exchequer survey and inquest of customs of 1595: it recorded that they had had common rights from time immemorial, that many of them had rights to take game on the

---

works, were wealthy farmers. Thomas Avarne was vicar of Rugeley from 1736 to 1784; I am indebted to Mr E. C. Toye of Rugeley for this and much other biographical information about inhabitants of the village.

1. Brief *re* Smith's action, 9.8.53, D603/L1–50; 'Depositions touching Cope's warren'; PRO, KB 1/12, affidavit of John Deacle of Banbury, 24.10.55.

2. 'Case of the Freeholders'; opinion of J. Ward, in Littleton, 'Records', p. 175.

3. Nichols to Earl of Uxbridge, 23.9.51.

4. Thomas Avarne *et al.* to Earl of Uxbridge, 25.9.51.

5. Nichols to Earl of Uxbridge, 30.3.54; the argument was not used, but was probably based on the fact that Cannock Chase had once been a royal forest, and sheep were thought not commonable by forest law: see J. Manwood, *A Treatise and Discourse of the Laws of the Forest*, 1598 and later eds., chap. XIV, title 'Common'.

Chase by ancient custom, and that all but one of the Paget warrens were new. The steward, curiously, had never heard of it, yet it was the document which the freeholders believed made their case invincible.[1] The following spring the commoners organized a subscription in the villages and went to law in June, confident of victory.

The law moved with its customary dispatch. After half a year of legal manoeuvring and mounting fees the commoners learned that their case could not be heard for at least another half year.[2] By that time the lascivious conies would be more numerous by two generations. Some of the commoners now decided to take direct action, and on 22 December the Marshall brothers and other men began digging up burrows and killing rabbits in one of the warrens. By Christmas Day the mob had grown, and Nichols beseeched the Earl to send for troops; meanwhile he obtained warrants from the neighbouring magistrates to arrest the ringleaders. Four justices heard the case two days later and made the commoners promise to end their trespass and wait for the issue to be tried in the courts. Nichols did not try to get a conviction on the game laws because he thought it would fail, and the 'riot' was quelled in any case; the Earl began an action against three of the trespassers to establish his rights.[3]

During the early months of 1753 the steward gathered evidence, the lawyers filled briefs and Uxbridge began yet another action, this time suing John Smith junior, the commoners' plaintiff, for himself damaging the waste by making and selling bricks from the clay there.[4] The suits were all to come to trial at the August Assizes, but the commoners were not entirely inactive. John Cope caught ten men in his warrens in June. Two of them, Tipper and Veroe, were familiar poachers, and the keeper seized their rabbits with the violence common on such occasions. He was surprised to be indicted a few days later for assault. Poaching labourers never had the temerity or money to prosecute on such occasions, but Nichols learned that Tipper and Veroe were being supported by Henry Brindley of Rugeley. The wealthy commoners were apparently still hoping to fore-

---

1. Nichols to Earl of Uxbridge, 7.10.51. Before doing so they proposed arbitration rather than litigation; Thomas Avarne *et al.* to Earl of Uxbridge, 1752, in D603/c31/106.

2. Nichols to Earl of Uxbridge, 2.5.52, 12.6.52, 13.6.52; 'Particular transactions relating to the Rabbit Warrens upon Cannock Chace', cited hereafter as 'Particular transactions', D603/CE538–68.

3. Nichols to Earl of Uxbridge, 2.5.52, 12.6.52, 23.12.52, 25.12.51, 27.12.52; 'Particular transactions'; brief *re* John Smith's action, 9.8.53 in D603/L1–50. The action against the trespassers – Stretton, Avrill and Sanders – was brought in the name of John Cope.

4. Nichols to Earl of Uxbridge, 19.6.53, 28.6.53; 'Several queries answered by Mr. Green', D978/20.

stall the courts by encouraging others to remove the rabbits by force.[1] Probably the costs of defending Uxbridge's four actions and prosecuting their own claim to right of common were beginning to worry them, for when the cases all came to trial in August they allowed the Earl victory by default in his actions. Their own, which they tried to win, was greatly weakened by a serious gap in evidence: their solicitors were unable to find the original record in Exchequer of the manorial customs in 1595. As it happened, however, their case was lost on one of the intricate technicalities which made eighteenth-century pleading the delight of lawyers and the despair of all but the wealthiest litigants.[2] To give him final and unquestioned victory, the Earl brought yet another action, suing Charles Marshall for trespass for leading the mob in December. It was to come to trial in April, in eight months' time.[3]

The commoners, however, had had enough of courts. As young men many of them had joined in the successful attacks on the warrens at the beginning of the century. Moreover, very recently they had heard of the success of the commoners of Charnwood Forest in Leicestershire, thirty miles away, where rioters successfully defied troops, keepers, constables and three Lords of the Realm to dig up the warrens in the commons. Their cry had been 'all rabbits are vermin'.[4] Now Brindley, Avarne and

1. Nichols to Earl of Uxbridge, 14.7.53. Cope was found guilty at Easter Sessions, 1754 and fined £1 7s. od. Nichols felt that the chairman, Sir Richard Wrottesley (a Gower Whig) was biased in his instructions to the jury; Nichols to Earl of Uxbridge, 24.4.54. The keepers tried similar tactics: later that month Cooper met a farmer with his dog on the Chase, threatened him, and tried to kill the dog, then prosecuted him for assault. The Grand Jury threw the bill out. Walter Reeves to Earl of Uxbridge, 11.9.53; PRO, Assi 5/73 (Summer 1753).

2. They could provide only an exemplification of the 1605 copyhold decree, whereas the 1595 customary dealt with the rights of all the commoners; Littleton, 'Records', p. 185. (Sir Edward Littleton made a determined search for the original attested copy given to the jurors in 1595, but without success. Paget's agents were still unable to find it in 1809; Littleton, 'Records', pp. 109, 117-19.) The commoners lost because an aged witness defined the bounds of Cannock Chase incorrectly.

3. 'Particular transactions'; D978/20; brief *re* John Smith's action, 9.8.53 in D603/ L1-50; D1511/19/10.

4. The Loughborough riots began in the summer of 1748 and continued for over three years. Dragoons dispersed crowds of two thousand. Eventually litigation established right of common for twenty-six towns and villages within the bounds of the ancient forest, in spite of a landowner's claims to right of free warren. The Leicestershire rioters apparently threatened Cannock, for Nichols wrote to the Earl of Uxbridge that he feared a mob of three hundred. They 'rained triumphant and unmolested all last year,' he wrote, 'but confin'd themselves to their own county, and as they publickly sell the flesh of the rabbits in the neighbouring towns, the profit allures them to continue and extend themselves ... I shall venture upon reading the Riot Act, and hope to attack and defeat.' (Plas Newydd, Box XLVI; the date is probably 1749, but no other mention of the incident appears in the Paget papers.)

Birch decided that shovels might do more for them too than writs, and they began preparing.[1] They sent messengers into Leicestershire to recruit some of its famous rabbit-digging colliers, and paid the town crier of Walsall to announce that any man who joined 'the Free Company on Cannock Wood' would have meat and drink and 1s. 6d. a day, or all the rabbits he could kill. Sixty Walsall men set out on the six-mile walk to the nearest warrens.[2] In Cannock, Rugeley and Longdon the cottagers probably were attracted not only by the wages, but also by the chance for revenge, for the rabbits in two of the warrens were the perks of the keepers who served the Earl of Uxbridge so well. Most important, many cottagers used the waste for common, although not legally entitled to do so, and were probably alarmed by Uxbridge's claim to the right to plant the whole of it with warrens, and by the threat of enclosure.[3] Cannock Chase had played an important part in the economy of the villagers for hundreds of years, just as resisting the pretensions of the Pagets had been a leading theme in their politics.

Most of the men who joined the Cannock diggers were labourers and colliers, but there were also farmers and 'yeomen', innholders, masons, shoemakers, sawyers and weavers. In all, a fairly representative selection of the poor and middling villagers put their hands to the shovels.[4] Their leaders were freehold and copyhold farmers – the Marshall brothers, Henry Jackson, Barnabas Bagshaw, Henry Webb, who recruited and paid the men, and sang 'Marshall's Dragoons', which had been popular in the villages for at least two years. The wealthiest commoners, including Birch and Brindley, and the Avarnes, apparently provided the wages and planned the attack, but prudently stayed away from the battle itself.

Men began gathering in the warrens two days after Christmas, and on

1. A warrener alleged that soon after the assizes Webb warned him to dig up his warrens or the commoners would do it for him. Deposition of John Hodgkins in 'Depositions touching Cope's warren taken 12th January 1754'. Nichols first heard of a subscription 'in order to hire a Mobb' on 24 December; see letter to the Earl of Uxbridge of that date.

2. Nichols to Earl of Uxbridge, 24.12.53; *Case of the Earl of Uxbridge* (printed for submission to the House of Lords) with MS additions, D603/L1–50; 'Depositions touching Cope's warren'.

3. D1511/19/10.

4. In addition to the Walsall colliers, the occupations of twenty-seven other diggers were given in a paper prepared by Ridgway, and in depositions. There were 7 labourers, 6 innholders, 5 'yeomen', 3 farmers, 3 masons, 2 weavers and a shoemaker, sawyer and warrener. The twenty-seven other men whom he names but for whom he does not bother to give occupations are probably labourers and colliers from the neighbourhood. 'Depositions touching Cope's warren'; summary table of trespassers in D603/E467. Most come from Rugeley and Longdon (sixteen and ten); another eight from Hammerwich; but, curiously, only two from Cannock.

the 28th the main assault began. It was conducted with spirit and the ceremony proper to a reclaiming of lost rights. Charles Marshall led 200 of his
'dragoons', spades and clubs at the ready, broom and rushes in their hats,
in a march past Beaudesert Hall. At the gates to the house they halted and
gave three cheers, shaking their hats in the air. The trumpeter blew his
horn, a hat was hoisted on a stick for colours, and they set off for the
warrens. Between two and three hundred men worked steadily for almost
two weeks, killing rabbits with clubs and ferrets, and filling in the burrows.
They left untouched the one warren to which they admitted that Uxbridge
had right, and that of Sir Edward Littleton. Marshall killed an ox and he
and Webb also brought bread, cheese and ale out to the diggers each day.
Other farmers came out to encourage them: 'Well done, lads,' called one,
'God speed you in your honest undertaking,' and casks of beer were
broached in the streets of Rugeley when they returned in the evenings.[1]

Marshall and Webb assured the diggers that no law could touch them
but 'club law', and the keepers and their men were too intimidated to try
it, although they were under orders to beat the trespassers and take their
spades.[2] They found it dangerous to appear at all. One informer retreated
when a discussion began among the diggers on whether he should be
'taken up and hanged for a spy', and when Cooper and Theophilus Bailey
challenged the few men still in the warrens on 10 January they surrounded
the keepers and threatened them with a beating if they did not leave. The
diggers were particularly angry with Bailey, a poacher who had become
an underkeeper.[3] Nichols knew that the keepers would need help and
shortly after the diggers appeared he had written to the Secretary of State.
Within a few days two troops of dragoons were marched over from Stafford
to assist the local magistrates, who met them at Rugeley.[4] 'Marshall's
Dragoons' and George's never met, however, because the justices marched
them back to Stafford instead of onto the Chase and, to Nichols's horror,
'the Ryott & Destruction went on with more fury than before'.[5] The
slaughter was rather astounding. Five of the six warrens on the Chase
were totally destroyed, and ten or fifteen thousand rabbits killed, a loss
estimated by assessors at over £3,000.[6] For good measure the diggers

1. Brief relating to John Smith's action, 9.8.53 (D603/L1-50); 'Depositions touching
Cope's warren'. According to Nichols, Sir Edward's warrener was killing the stock
to prevent the diggers taking it, although they showed no intention of doing so; Nichols
to Earl of Uxbridge, 28.1.54.
2. Nichols to Earl of Uxbridge, 24.12.53, 26.12.53; John Cooper to Earl of Uxbridge,
11.2.54.
3. 'Depositions touching Cope's warren'; above, p. 206.
4. PRO, SP 44/134, p. 242; WO 4/49, p. 356.
5. 'Particular transactions'.
6. 'Testimony of viewers of Cannock warrens', 10-11 July 1754, D603/CE538-68;

stripped a warrener's lodge, taking the doors and all the lead on the building, and when Bailey challenged two men still in the warrens on 21 January, and beat them with his quarter staff, they pinned him to the ground and pummelled him with a stone.[1]

The reluctance of the magistrates to stop the destruction enraged the Earl, his steward and his London attorney, who wrote to him,

> The Law does afford a Remedy to put a Stop to the Violences that are committed daily upon your Lordship's Property, if the Magistrates who are entrusted with the Execution of those Laws would do their Duty; but if your Justices will all act the Part either of professed, avowed Enemies, or treacherous Friends, without Regard to Law or Justice, and become rather the Abettors or Protectors of Violence than Friends or Conservators of the Peace, What are You to expect from such Magistrates?[2]

Undoubtedly the JPs were unwilling to risk a blood-bath on the Chase for the sake of the rabbits. Moreover, one of them, Chetwynd, had already been barred from the Chase; he and Vernon were Gowerite Whigs; and Sir Edward Littleton was certainly delighted to see the commoners contest Uxbridge's claims of free chase and free warren.[3]

Abandoned by the bench, the Earl still had a formidable arsenal of weapons to defend his few remaining conies and to punish the rioters. He first started a complaint to the House of Lords for breach of privilege, for Parliament in the eighteenth century stretched privilege to include the enjoyment of game and the right to try trespassers. The procedure had the advantage of reaching the planners of the riot as well as those who actually used spades, and Uxbridge hoped to be able to force the wealthy commoners to make good the damage.[4] He was apparently prepared to offer them two alternatives: either to rent the warrens from him at a good rent

---

Nichols to Earl of Uxbridge, 22.4.54; 'A case relating to the warrens', 23.5.54, D603/CE538–68.

1. Nichols to Earl of Uxbridge, 2.2.54; information of Theophilus Bailey, 9.2.54 in 'Bills, etc. 1742–9', Plas Newydd; Ridgway to Earl of Uxbridge, 4.5.61.

2. Parry to Earl of Uxbridge, 29.1.54.

3. The claim to free warren was not conceded until April, and the issue of removing rabbits as a nuisance was settled in law only by Mansfield's decision in 1757. In addition to Vernon, Chetwynd and Littleton, the JPs attending the meeting were Sir Walter Wagstaff Bagot, Sir William Wolseley and Brook Boothby; 'Particular transactions'.

4. Nichols to Earl of Uxbridge, 19.6.53, 24.12.53, Parry to Earl of Uxbridge, 29.12.53. The commoners had anticipated the complaint to the Lords, and their apprehensions explain the dates of the riots – the House was not sitting; 'Case of the Freeholders'. Uxbridge's grandfather used the procedure in 1734 in a dispute respecting a water course (*LJ*, vol. xxxiv, p. 327). Kirby, 'The English Game Law System', p. 253, attributes the decline of the use of privilege in poaching cases after 1762 to the growth of private associations.

for many years, during which time they could keep them clear of rabbits, or if they refused, to restock them completely for him and pay him one year's rent in compensation for the slaughtered conies.[1] His lawyers gathered 'a tribe of witnesses' in London, his case was printed for submission to the Lords, but after weeks of preparation he abruptly stopped proceedings. His chief witness from Rugeley, John Trigg, had suddenly refused to testify. Without his evidence the wealthiest commoners could not be touched; and an abortive appeal on privilege would prevent the Earl from taking other, perhaps more rewarding, proceedings in the courts.[2]

Whatever Uxbridge's reasons, his solicitor was appalled: 'Surely Rabbits will hereafter become a very scarce Commodity in the County of Stafford.' And he wondered, 'What will become of Mr. Nicholls?'[3] At Beaudesert, Nichols was preoccupied with precisely the same question. The local outrage that probably frightened Trigg out of turning informer to the House of Lords had also turned against the farmer who had obtained Trigg's evidence in the first place, and his effigy had been hanged from Rugeley maypole, with the placard 'Nichols's Tool'. Now the steward feared that the news from London would 'intoxicate the Rable with an appearance of power beyond imagination'. He soon heard the bells ringing in Rugeley as the commoners celebrated their victory over the Earl and the House of Lords; perhaps he wondered what or who was to be hanged next.[4]

The commoners' remission was brief, however, as the law rose in all its majesty in defence of the rights of conies. Uxbridge proved his grant of free chase and free warren at Stafford Assizes in April, and when the commoners would not admit that this gave his rabbits priority over sheep, sued Marshall and some of the diggers. Nichols was confident this would accomplish 'the total ruin of themselves and their Families'.[5] Another

1. The proposal appears in longhand on a printed copy of the *Case* prepared for the Lords; the parish officers would be required to give bond for £2,000 to fulfil the conditions. There is no record that the proposal was ever made to the commoners. 'Bills etc. 1742–49', Plas Newydd.

2. 'Depositions touching Cope's warren'; *Case* in D603/L1–50. Nichols suggested in August that Trigg could be sued or taken before the Lords for a trespass he had committed in another dispute; Nichols to Earl of Uxbridge, 3.8.54.

3. Parry to Earl of Uxbridge, 25.1.54.

4. Nichols to Earl of Uxbridge, 28.1.54.

5. Nichols to Earl of Uxbridge, 2.4.54, 10.4.54, 20.4.54, 22.4.54, 23.6.54, 29.6.54. The April decision was a special verdict, which was argued in King's Bench in June; 1 Burrow 259. The other defendants in the case were John Howerd, Richard Bee, William Hunt, William Tipper, John Veroe, William Littlewood, Henry Harryman; Ridgway to Earl of Uxbridge, 27.11.57. Great care was taken with the actions. Nichols was pleased to learn that the *nisi prius* judge who was expected to hear them at summer

subscription was made in the village, and the commoners' lawyers delayed the cases, but meanwhile Uxbridge dealt with the rabble; no lawyers could hinder him in that. Many of the diggers were tenants of his own cottages, and in July he embarked on a mass ejection, before their crops were all in, so that their punishment, in the steward's words, would be 'the better proportioned to their offence'. As the steward and sheriff's bailiff served writs of ejectment in the villages there was furious talk of resisting, and old John Deakin made pikes out of scythes and declared he would 'protect his Possession'. But in the end, faced with the threat of greater force, the cottagers left their homes, which were then, in many cases, torn down.[1] Uxbridge was selective, punishing the most active diggers, but also those known for poaching, or who testified against him at the assizes. Probably between one and two dozen families were thrown out: men like Ralph Walker, an elderly day labourer with a large family who lost his cottage because one of his sons had joined the dig. The curate of Longdon and a Justice of the Peace petitioned Uxbridge to take his 'deplorable case' into consideration and forgive him, but the steward advised against it – both sons had been 'constant trespassers'. The offence of Walter Elliots, 'yeoman', was that his mother had testified in court on behalf of the commoners. Robert Wilkinson, another lame and elderly labourer, begged to be readmitted:

Please your Lordship being in Years & almost worne out by hard labour and at times what money I could anyways spare I kept laying it out on the cottage in hopes to reap the benefit of it in my old age (if it please God so to spare me) But since being deprived of it has very much reduced me even to the lowest ebb of fortune having no settled place of aboad but lives at ye pleasure of my friends courtesie And that your poor petitioner thro fretting has been in a very poor state of health which together with ye dearness of provision has reduced me to be very poor.

Wilkinson lost his cottage because his son had been a digger; Thomas Sanders, 'a poor lame Man', because his father had been involved; Thomas Glover's sixty-year-old mother because of her son. Some of these people may have been readmitted. John Deakin was not. The militant old weaver who had prepared to fight the bailiffs with scythes, Deakin, was thrown out because he testified against the Earl and had accompanied the diggers, although at seventy years of age he was scarcely able to dig

---

Assizes in 1754 was 'very remarkable in points of Separate & extensive property. I know your Lordship will have an Eye to everything, & have your rights well considered before Notice of tryall is given by your own Agent ... P.S. please to burn this' 23.6.54.

1. Parry to Earl of Uxbridge, 11.9.54, 13.7.54; Nichols to Earl of Uxbridge, 10.4.54, 15.7.54, 27.7.54; 'A paper re Cottages', n.d., D603/CE569–606; Ridgway to Earl of Uxbridge, 4.5.61.

himself. Reduced to abject poverty, he vainly petitioned to be readmitted. Four years later, destitute, he broke into his nailed-up cottage in Hammerwich and reoccupied it, and appealed to the Earl to pardon him out of his 'great Humanity for the distress'd'. But Uxbridge was still brooding about his conies, and for 'this Piece of insolent, and Assured Behaviour', as the steward called it, prosecuted him at Quarter Sessions for forceable entry and detainer.[1]

As their counsel dragged the case through the labyrinth of the law, the commoners' costs became alarming. In 1754 they offered to make a settlement; the offer was refused. Under the inexorable expense of the law, and the anger of the Earl, the alliance in the villages began to break down. The curate of Longdon stopped supporting the commoners when the keepers raided his house, found a dog, gun and net, and threatened him with a ruinously expensive prosecution. In December 1754, a year after the attack on the warrens, the keeper caught Veroe, Tipper and Steward, well-known poaching labourers, with spades and lurchers on the Chase, and imprisoned them for three months. They expected their fines to be paid by the leading commoners but they were not. Engaged in a desperate legal struggle with the Earl to defend their rights of common, Marshall and the wealthier men backing him had no further interest in the escapades of poachers. When Tipper realized this he swore that Marshall had offered him £5 to set fire to a keeper's house and coppice, but his evidence was useless to Uxbridge because the poacher's own character was so 'infamous' that no jury would believe him.[2]

The Earl's lawsuits against the leaders of the riot ground on slowly through assize hearings in March and July of 1755. With the issue of free warren already decided, the only defence possible was that on a common overrun with rabbits they could be destroyed as a nuisance. Counsel for the commoners may have encouraged them to proceed because the question had not been tried since 1614, but their case was desperate since all

1. 'A paper re Cottages'; Thos Glover's petition, D603/C36; Ralph Walker's petition, n.d., in D603/C33; Thos Saunder's petition in D603/E467; petitions of John Deakin, 14.8.58, 13.12.59, in D603/C34; petition of Robert Wilkinson, 4.11.56; Ridgway to Earl of Uxbridge, 19.12.56, 5.2.59; Staffs. RO, Q/SR and Q/SO Translation 1759 (Deakin confessed, but no sentence is recorded). The estimate of the number ejected is tentative. The 'paper re Cottages' is apparently Ridgway's rough list of some of the victims – six of the thirteen named in it are known to have been expelled (reference above); the other seven were also involved in the riot (D603/E46T summary). But at least one man expelled does not appear in Ridgway's list, suggesting it may be incomplete. A comparison of the presentments at the Rugeley manor courts for November 1753 and November 1754 shows that five more men known to be diggers ceased to hold cottages between those dates; Cannock and Longdon presentments also show such changes in occupants; D603/CE296-400.

2. Nichols to Earl of Uxbridge, 30.10.54, 28.12.54; Parry to Earl of Uxbridge, 28.12.54.

the judgements on the issue before that date were against them. As the final hearings approached, the steward heard that the commoners were trying to influence the prosecution witnesses. He suggested a bigger bribe: a special dinner at the Hall and money 'for their troubles, that they may be kept in good humour, & be more closely attached to your Interest at the . . . assizes'.[1] When some villagers dug out a few more burrows on the Chase in the belief that Uxbridge would drop his actions, they were immediately sued.[2]

Finally, after six years of litigation, and three years after the riot, the cases went before Lord Mansfield in the Court of King's Bench. Interrupting the half-finished arguments of learned counsel, the Chief Justice remarked smoothly, 'I think it so clear a case that I have no difficulty at all about it.' The Earl undoubtedly had the right to put conies on the common, and, His Lordship pointed out with unanswerable logic, 'the conies themselves naturally make the burrows'. If there were too many rabbits, the commoner could not destroy them as a nuisance, for he would be acting as his own judge 'in a complicated question, which may admit of nicety to determine'. Mr Justice Dennison agreed: the commoner could not be allowed 'to destroy the estate of the lord, in order to preserve his own small right of common'.[3]

The words echo the reality of eighteenth-century property relations: the estates of the aristocracy were paramount, and the rights of commoners were beginning the last decline to extinction. After 200 years of conflict the Pagets finally established the pre-eminence of game over the common rights of their tenants. The new temper of the courts, the inexplicable loss of a document crucial to the commoners' case, and the massive financial resources of the family finally brought the Earl of Uxbridge the victory that had eluded his ancestors. The case was enshrined in the law reports and given a full page in the reference books of Justices of the Peace. Its immediate consequence in the villages about Cannock Chase was the disintegration of the alliance against the Earl. The wealthiest commoners, those who had subscribed money to defend Marshall's case in their own interest, now abandoned him, and his attorney sued him for £80 of unpaid fees and prepared to commit him to debtor's prison. His co-defendants were even poorer, and the steward thought it not worthwhile to sue them for damages.[4] The Earl of Uxbridge nevertheless decided to show his

1. Nichols to Earl of Uxbridge, 27.7.54; Ridgway to Earl of Uxbridge, 8.12.55.
2. Testimony of John Seddon, 10.1.56, D603/CE/569–606; Ridgway to Earl of Uxbridge, 21.1.56, 18.2.56.
3. *Cooper* v. *Marshall* and *Cope* v. *Marshall* (1 Burrow 259–68, 2 Wilson KB 51–61, Sayer 234–6 and 285, 2 Kenyon 1–8); Henry Whitfield to Earl of Uxbridge, 11.5.57.
4. Ridgway to Earl of Uxbridge, 27.11.57, 5.12.57.

power and in 1761 got judgement against them. The Stafford Assize jury had the insolence to award damages of only a shilling, but the verdict entitled him to costs, and gave him the power to imprison the men for debt should he choose to make them pay. Apparently he hoped this threat would protect his warrens. During the next two years, however, the keepers surprised several groups of poachers digging up rabbits or taking them with ferrets, and in 1763, ten years after the riot, Uxbridge expressed his anger by punishing the four defendants in the coney cases who still lived near by.

They were all Rugeley labourers, and he had them arrested for debt. Feeling was high in Rugeley, and on the morning of the arrests the steward took care to assemble a posse in order to prevent a rescue attempt. The three men whom the bailiffs managed to seize – John Veroe, Richard Bee and Harry Harriman – were in gaol only six weeks, but it was six weeks of sleeping on straw and a diet of bread and water. Uxbridge released them after extorting what they knew of the planners of the riot, and after petitions from the labourers and their wives to spare them for the sake of their seventeen children, 'begging for a bit of Bread with Tears in their Eyes. . .' Perhaps he was flattered by these appeals to 'the unparalleled tender and compassionate Disposition which your Lordship has the Character of possessing for the Relief of every object or person in distress'; he was, however, probably more moved by the advice of his solicitors. They discovered that the men had been committed to gaol on an erroneous process, and could lay an action for false imprisonment if they found out.[1]

Apart from fights with the keepers about foddering sheep on the Chase, the commoners were quiet for many years.[2] The warrens were restocked, the rabbits bred with enthusiasm, agricultural writers praised progressive landlords like Uxbridge who 'improved' the value of 'useless wastes' by raising conies. But if the villages were quiet it was in the bitterness of defeat. The dozen or so who had testified for the Earl at the trials were never forgiven. Many years later the widow of one of the informers, requesting a new lease, pointed out that her husband had suffered the freeholders' malice to the end of his life, and that she and her daughter

1. Parry to Earl of Uxbridge, 1.7.60; 5.7.60; Ridgway to Earl of Uxbridge, 7.7.60, 11.3.61, 29.3.61, 18.4.61, 13.10.61, 17.10.61, 14.12.61, 13.12.62, 26.2.63, 22.5.63, 31.5.63, 19.6.63, 2.7.63, 12.7.63; 'Case' *re* Quintons in D603/C35; examination of Jeremiah Cope, 8.12.61 in D603/CE569-606; examination of John and Jeremiah Cope, 15.4.61 in D603/C35; Henry Whitfield to Earl of Uxbridge, 27.7.62 in D603, 'Whitfield Miscellaneous 1761-63'; petition of Bee, Veroe, Harriman and petition of their wives, in D603/CE59-114; their statement to Earl of Uxbridge, 28.6.63 D603/C36.

2. Ridgway to Earl of Uxbridge, 18.1.58, 25.1.58, 27.1.58, 18-25.2.58. Paget considered further expansion of the warren in 1774 and 1784; Paget to Harrison, 11.8.74, Harrison to Paget, 31.7.84.

were still hated.[1] Meanwhile the poachers, for whom the exploits of Marshall's dragoons had only been a formal campaign in the midst of a guerrilla war, continued to make their snares and nets, and train their dogs.

IV

The game laws were a complex mass of legislation, even in the middle of the eighteenth century, and gentlemen in Parliament created more and better penalties throughout the reign of George III. The legal armoury of the game-preserver was well stocked. Old statutes were not usually repealed when new ones were enacted, and prosecutors could therefore often make a choice, and hence exercise some influence on the penalty.[2] More important was the choice between a civil action and a criminal conviction. In cases where part of the penalty went to the prosecutor, he could recover it in either way, and if he chose civil proceedings he also recovered double costs.[3] Hence, where a criminal conviction for shooting a partridge might result in a fine of £5, an action could raise the penalty to ten times that much.[4] The Earl of Uxbridge used the method against the servant of Congreve, when he wished to punish the vicar for trespassing. Congreve expected the expense to be well over £20, 'and must have been absolute ruin to my servant and his family, if I had not supported him. . .'[5] In many cases the Pagets saw little in the choice, since most poachers could not hope to pay even £5. They were therefore gaoled: three months for a hare, a year plus the pillory for a deer. Where the offender was wealthier it was worthwhile to sue; on the other hand criminal procedure might still be used if the evidence was shaky, or if a jury was unlikely to give damages. In a case in which a JP suggested an action against a labourer for making nets, the steward disagreed: 'I submit it to your Lordship whether it would not be better as the Man is very poor and the Instruments not compleat to take the Judgement of a Justice of Peace upon the Occasion than that of a Jury if the Man should be able to make a Defence. And if a Conviction can be had before a Justice one would

1. Wm Cope to Earl of Uxbridge, 17.5.62; petition of Margaret Watson, D603/X609.

2. Burn, op. cit., title 'Game', 12th edn, 1772, vol. II, p. 224.

3. 8 Geo. I c. 19 (1722). Double costs were assessed at only half again as much as 'single' ones.

4. Christian, op. cit., p. 215; Purlewent, op. cit., pp. 6–7; *Some Considerations on the Game Laws, and the Present Practice in executing them . . .*, p. 12.

5. WSL, MS 47/28/252; the £20 represented the penalty only, and Congreve's legal fees would be extra.

be in hopes a three Months Imprisonment in the House of Correction would be Sufficient to cure him.'[1]

For the most serious cases the law provided an even more crushing instrument of punishment: an information in the Court of King's Bench, which could bring costs of £50 to £80, or more. This proceeding, wrote one commentator, 'is attended by so heavy an expense, that it is only resorted to in order to gratify a rancourous spirit of malice and revenge. It is not adopted for the preservation of Game, but for the vexation and destruction of a fellow-creature.'[2] In other cases, such as assaults on keepers, it was possible to begin an ordinary prosecution at assizes or Quarter Sessions, then remove it into King's Bench by the writ of *certiorari*. This too was an expensive process, and both procedures had the advantage of taking the case out of the hands of a jury that might be unfriendly to the prosecutor.[3] Most poachers were too poor to make either proceeding worthwhile, although the terror they evoked was gratifying. The Earl of Uxbridge very much wanted to get a King's Bench information against two weavers who had thrashed his head keeper, then prepared to get a *certiorari* when the evidence proved insufficient for an information, and finally decided to prosecute them for assault in the ordinary way at assizes 'which as the Fellows are Scarcely worth Sixpence may sufficiently chastise or drive the country of them'.[4] In at least two other cases, however, he scorned expense and moved King's Bench for an information; the threat of financial ruin was usually enough to bring submission from his victim.[5] The one other legal weapon against poachers, the power enjoyed by Members of Parliament to haul trespassers before the House, failed Uxbridge in 1754, but it was an accepted and often successful practice.

The stewards noted only some of the routine prosecutions, and in only a quarter of those recorded do we know the sentence. But the list gives an idea of the punishments the Pagets exacted. There are thirty fines noted, ranging from £2 to £30 – six of the latter, all for killing deer. Faced with a fine he could not hope to pay, a poacher had the choice of gaol or exile, if he had not yet been seized. 'I have signed Judgement against Dytch', the steward wrote in 1776, 'which has drove him out of the Country, and will be a Rod hanging over his Head that may deter him from visiting

1. Ridgway to Earl of Uxbridge, 25.2.58; Ridgway to Paget, 25.1.72.
2. Christian, op. cit., p. 219; *Some Considerations on the Game Laws . . .*, p. 14.
3. Blackstone, *Commentaries*, vol. IV, p. 320.
4. Ridgway to Earl of Uxbridge, 40.1.59, 24.2.59, 12.3.59, 28.3.59, 12.5.59, 23.5.59. The weavers were fined 10s.; PRO, Assi 5/79, indictment of John and Thomas Wootton of Rugeley.
5. Case of Nott, below p. 244; Harding, above p. 211.

the environs of Beaudesert. I shall keep a look out for him, and carefully watch his motions when the Season of snaring approaches. . .'¹ Many more fines became terms of imprisonment; indeed sometimes the justices did not bother to inquire whether the poacher had enough money to pay before committing him to the House of Correction. We know that a dozen men were gaoled, seven of them for a year, and some with an hour in the pillory; the real numbers were many times that. Life in Stafford's exceedingly unhealthy House of Correction was grim, but imprisonment sometimes caused more suffering to the families of poachers. If there were children they were often left destitute; in other cases wives incurred debts by paying for food for their imprisoned men. Ellen Brown sold most of their few belongings to help feed her husband Tom, who was committed for a year for deer-stealing, because she was convinced that her 'poor miserable old decrepit Object' would starve on the bad fare provided by the county.² Beyond imprisonment was transportation, which three men from the villages suffered. One was sent for seven years on a conviction for stealing geese, though his great crime was poaching; two others had death sentences reduced to fourteen years' transportation for breaking into the Earl's deer barn.³

At the other end of the scale of repression were the dozens of summary executions of dogs by the keepers. After 1722 it was illegal for an unqualified man even to keep a lurcher, whether he used it to kill game or not, and nothing illustrates better the uncompromising nature of the game laws. For dogs were extremely important in rural society. While gentlemen urged the wholesale destruction throughout the country of the 'babbling curs' of labourers, they were extraordinarily concerned to protect their own animals. In the seventeenth century the judges ruled that even assaults in defence of dogs were justified, and in 1770 Parliament passed a very severe act against stealing them. The keepers' lack of respect for gentlemen's dogs was one of the greatest causes of dispute near the Chase. Phineas Hussey, whose spaniel was seized in 1760, swore that he would get it back if it cost him £500. Poachers felt as strongly. Beyond sport and companionship, their trained lurchers guaranteed them success in their trade, and many poachers probably resented their loss as keenly as a three-month spell in gaol.⁴ Another serious blow was the seizure of guns, nets and snares – the 'engines of destruction' which it was illegal for an

1. Weston to Paget, 10.7.76.   2. Ellen Brown to Earl of Uxbridge, 28.4.58.

3. Petition for Gee and Smith, D603/E422–66; Adey to Earl of Uxbridge, 18.6.44, 22.7.44; depositions of Bailey, Bailey and Sleeth, PRO, Assi 5/64, Staffs. Summer 1744 and Assi 2/13, Lent 1745.

4. Ridgway to Earl of Uxbridge, 3.2.61; deposition of William Cooper Jr, 30.1.61, Box 17, Plas Newydd; *King* v. *Filer*, Strange 496, 1 Saunders 84. The lord of the manor

unqualified man even to own. In one unexpected visit a keeper could take away the work of months of winter evenings, to be cut to pieces before a local justice. There were scores of such incidents. Finally, there was a wide range of penalties outside the law altogether. Eviction, the weapon the Earl of Uxbridge used so effectively against the rabbit-diggers in 1754, could be brought to bear on individuals too. When one Clewly was suspected of poisoning the deer, but the case could not be proved, Ridgway pointed out that he occupied a cottage and acre of land at the Earl's pleasure, if he wished to 'make an Example' of him. There were probably others.[1]

Hundreds of prosecutions meant a continuous expense to the Pagets, and employment for many grateful lawyers. Uxbridge was an early subscriber to the national Society of Noblemen and Gentlemen for the Preservation of the Game, founded in 1752, and for five years he regularly forwarded claims for expenses in prosecuting poachers, and requests for legal advice in difficult cases.[2] During the rest of the century the vast majority of prosecutions were initiated and concluded by the stewards, who were attorneys by profession.[3] Difficult cases, however, went to the best London lawyers. Francis Parry, a solicitor in Middle Temple, handled many; Sir Fletcher Norton, alias 'Sir Bull-Face Double-Fee', the former Attorney-General, was consulted on a case in 1769; and in 1776 Lloyd Kenyon, later Lord Chief Justice, advised Paget how best to convict four labourers for deer-killing and tracking hares in the snow.[4] Such briefs were not beneath the notice of great lawyers because the game laws were considered an integral part of the constitution of rural society – and cases on them paid well. Indeed it was not thought strange to consult the most famous judge in England on details of game preservation. In 1771 a conspiracy of deer-poisoners was active on the Chase, and Asshton Curzon, a friend and neighbour, suggested to Paget that he should consult Lord Mansfield on the wisdom of promoting a bill in Parliament to control the sale of poison, and also ask the Lord Chief Justice to approve the wording

---

also had the right to seize dogs for his own use by 22 & 23 Chas II. c. 25, 5 Anne c. 14. The penalties under the dog act were fines of £20 to £30 or imprisonment of six months to a year for the first offences, and larger fines and longer imprisonment, plus whipping, for further ones; 10 Geo. III c. 18.

1. Ridgway to Earl of Uxbridge, 23.11.55.

2. For an outline history of the Society see Kirby, 'The English Game Law System', pp. 254–6; the Earl of Uxbridge subscribed until at least 1759.

3. Nichols and Ridgway were Stafford attorneys. Ralph Weston (d. 1794) of Stone House was a wealthy Rugeley solicitor in partnership with John Hickin (d. 1828); information from Mr E. C. Toye, Rugeley.

4. Fletcher Norton, *DNB*, and Birch's case, above, p. 210: Kenyon's opinions, 2.12.77, 23.12.77 in D603/L51–67 and D1851/5/2; also below, p. 250.

of an advertisement warning the offenders. Legal advice and new penal statutes were the usual reasons why game-preservers went to London; Curzon's third suggestion was more unusual. He advised Paget to approach Sir John Fielding, the famous Bow Street magistrate, to borrow a few of his men. They would come down to Staffordshire 'to mix in the country with the suspected, and by this means bring matters to light'.[1]

Curzon, later Viscount Curzon, was one of the Justices of the Peace who tried poachers caught at Beaudesert. He had good reasons to dislike them too: he leased several warrens and kept a pack of hounds at Hagley Hall for coursing hares and hunting foxes. His relations with the Earl of Uxbridge were good – he promised to do his utmost always to protect the deer and game – and he became a close friend of Paget. 'I have had the smartest days business with offenders against the game laws that I have known since my acting in the commission of the peace,' he wrote in January 1772, and listed with satisfaction the four poachers he had tried for Paget that day.[2] The other magistrates whom the Pagets used most were also sportsmen and preservers. Mr Chetwynd of Haywood Park, later fourth Viscount Chetwynd, apparently made peace with Uxbridge after the rabbit riot, because in 1755 he began to try Beaudesert poachers again and the Earl sent him a doe for his table.[3] Sir William Wolseley, the principal justice in the neighbourhood, kept deer in his own park, a mile beyond Rugeley.[4] So did Sir Edward Littleton, who also had extensive warrens near the Chase. An avid sportsman, he had a pack of hounds and was a frequent visitor at Beaudesert. A jest of Paget's led him to believe, he said, 'that his Majesty means to make me Master of the Fox Hounds. But I would have it understood, that I am, at this time, Huntsman to Lord Paget, & that I like my place too well to quit it.'[5] Justice Dolphin of Shenstone, though not of such high station as the Pagets' other magistrates, and hence without much game of his own to preserve, liked pheasants and venison as much as they did. The Earl of Uxbridge supplied him regularly with a doe, and both Pagets granted him a keeper's deputation, which gave him the right to kill all the game that he might desire.[6]

These five men tried at least three-quarters of the poachers prosecuted

1. Ridgway to Paget, 22.1.72; Curzon to Paget, 25.2.72.
2. Curzon to Earl of Uxbridge, 12.12.57, 18.5.65; Ridgway to Earl of Uxbridge, 4.12.68, 7.2.69; Curzon to Paget, 25.1.72; Walter Noble Landor, ed., *Rugeley Parish Register, part 1, 1569–1722*, 1928, p. xviii.
3. Information of Francis Dickin, 16.10.55, D603/C32; Ridgway to Earl of Uxbridge, 24.12.55.   4. Ridgway to Earl of Uxbridge, 21.2.62.
5. Nichols to Earl of Uxbridge, 28.1.54; note of William Cooper, 12.7.75, E1–46; Littleton to Paget, 11.3.84, Box XL, Plas Newydd; Auden, op. cit., p. 3; *Victoria County History of Staffordshire*, vol. V, p. 110.
6. Ridgway to Earl of Uxbridge, 24.12.55; Dolphin to Earl of Uxbridge, 23.9.54,

by the Pagets.[1] There was no jury in such cases (almost all the game laws provided for summary conviction), and not one poacher in twenty had a lawyer. Contemporary legal theory was that the Justice of the Peace acted simultaneously as counsel for the accused, protecting him from injustice; as the jury, weighing his case impartially; and as the judge, sentencing him majestically. In practice, critics suggested, a sporting JP trying a poacher took the third part of his function – that of sentencing – more seriously than the others. Historians too, in spite of optimistic assessments of the 'judicial impartiality and intellectual integrity' of the JP, have conceded that in game cases he might momentarily abandon those virtues.[2] It is usually difficult to corroborate such a charge. What went on in a justice's study or the local inn was seldom recorded, as we have seen, because no law or court compelled the JP to register all his convictions. Even when he did, the bare record tells us nothing of interest; much of the evidence lies in the unrecorded conversations, even the unexpressed common sentiments of gentlemen dead for 150 years. From the occasional discussion of a case in the Paget correspondence, however, it is possible to see how the strong class loyalties of Staffordshire gentry could take precedence over the impartiality required by 'justice'.

The best legal authorities held that keepers searching for dogs or 'engines' should have proper warrants, since it would give them 'too great a power' to let them search houses at will.[3] Yet the keepers had precisely this power, because the magistrates were often prepared to grant general search warrants which specified no particular suspects: illiterate cottagers were not likely to question such documents in a court of law, and they were unquestionably more convenient. When important men were involved, like the Reverend Muchell, the poaching curate of Longdon, the magistrates made out proper warrants of incontestible validity. In any case, the JPs required no grounds for granting a warrant: the keepers received them for the asking.[4] Evidence, too, was sometimes treated

17.1.56(Box of 'fragment's, Plas Newydd), 19.8.63; Deputations, 31.8.63, D603/CE311–370, and 21.8.70, D603/E255–310. Dolphin was Sheriff in 1760.

1. The remaining cases were tried by ten other JPs: Sir Walter Wagstaff Bagot, Brooke Boothby, William Inge, Fettiplace Nott, Justice Robins, Rev. James Falconer, Rev. Walter Bagot, Willis Kempson, John Sparrow and Fisher Littleton. Lord Talbot, Thomas Anson, the Reverend Walter Bagot and Ralph Sneyd helped to decide the case against Weston's servants (p. 243 n. 1).

2. Sydney James Webb, Baron Passfield and Beatrice Webb, *English Local Government from the Revolution to the Municipal Corporation Act*, vol. I, *The Parish and the County*, 1906, pp. 346–7, 597.

3. Comberbach 183; cited in Burn, 'Game: gamekeepers', 1772 edn, vol. II, p. 223.

4. Nichols to Earl of Uxbridge, 20.10.54; Ridgway to Earl of Uxbridge, 24.2.59; to Paget, 5.1.72, 25.1.72; John Cope to Earl of Uxbridge, 18.8.57; warrants of John Turton, 13.11.50, D603/E143–254, and Fettiplace Nott, 1.10.51, D661/16/1.

rather loosely. In a case Chetwynd heard in 1757 the Earl of Uxbridge's witness contradicted herself on the vital point: whether she had or had not seen the accused carrying a deer into his house. And the man produced three witnesses who swore to his alibi. Deer-stealing was the greatest of crimes against game, however, and the Earl liked convictions. The steward reported the magistrate's dilemma:

Mr. Chetwynd, & Mr. Boothby (whose Thoughts Mr. Chetwynd requested upon the Case) were (upon weighing the Evidence) in Some Doubts, whether Mr. Chetwynd should convict Wiggan; & therefore postponed his Committment for about a fortnight, 'till the Case could be represented to your Lordship, & Mr. Chetwynd hopes (if no further corroborating Evidence can in the Interim be given against Wiggan), That he shall Stand justified in your Lordship's Opinion, as well as his own, (from the loose Manner in which the Woman Seemed to give her Evidence) & upon the Evidence given of Wiggan's being (at the time charged) in another Place, in discharging the Man.

We do not have Uxbridge's reply, but its tenor perhaps may be guessed from the fact that two weeks later, when the witness swore to yet another version of the facts, and 'Some Additional Corroborating Evidence being given, Mr. Chetwynd was pleased to committ him, & he is now in Gaol; Which, I hope, will be agreable to your Lordship, as I look upon him to have been a notorious offender.'[1]

Such requests by JPs to the Pagets for instructions were not uncommon. Besides good neighbourliness, their motives included a desire to protect themselves from being sued by poachers able to afford legal counsel. A JP's best course was to have an understanding with the lawyer that he would not take advantage of him later if he made a mistake. Unfortunately Sir William Wolseley had no such agreement with the solicitor acting for two yeoman whom he tried for digging rabbits in the Earl of Uxbridge's warrens. Wolseley was 'very inclinable to commit them to Prison for three months', but since the case was doubtful and the lawyer unfriendly, he deferred the hearing. The poachers were told he was too busy and preparing to leave for London; in fact he needed time to ask Uxbridge to get him legal advice on the case. The practice of magistrate and prosecutor consulting on how best to convict the accused was not one commended by Blackstone (at least not in print), but there are other instances of it.[2] Because game was a matter of such importance, JPs were often uneasy about prosecuting servants of gentlemen – servants who might be shooting on the Chase on behalf of masters suffering the gout or other passing incapacities. Such cases could start feuds among the gentry; one way in

1. Ridgway to Earl of Uxbridge, 25.9.57, 18.10.57, 13.11.57.
2. Ridgway to Earl of Uxbridge, 26.2.63. See also the case of the hare tracers, referred to Kenyon; below p. 250.

which they were prevented in Staffordshire was to try them by a bench of magistrates instead of a single justice.[1] Justice Dolphin, however, was obliged to try by himself one of Hussey's servants for deer-stealing, and he appealed to Uxbridge to send him the advice of counsel:

> I hope you will my Lord believe that I shall do all in my power that the strictest Justice may be done to your Lordship in this or any other affaire when a Complaint is made to me: but as I am not sure but I may mistake in the Convicting the offender I would not leave it in the power of ill people to take any advantage of me or give them the satisfaction in the guilty person escaping the punishment the Law in such Cases directs for this reason I hope your Lordship will excuse the trouble of the Inclosed which is the Case stated that Your Lordship may give such directions your Lordship shall think proper, and. . . I defer ending the affaire till I receive your Lordship's pleasure and commands. . . I am much obliged in the honour and favour of the veneson by your orders brought to me. . .[2]

The recognition on the part of the magistrates that the Pagets' wishes were at least as important as the letter of the law extended to punishments as well as convictions. When the starving wife and family of an imprisoned poacher petitioned for his release, the steward reported to the Earl of Uxbridge that 'tho the Commitment is for three Months, & the Law I presume Strictly allows of no Mitigation, yet I apprehend, in Case of your Lordship's being Satisfyed, that Sir Walter Bagott would have no Objection to his being Set at Liberty'.[3]

In over fifty years of such complacency and deference in the execution of the game laws, there was one case only in which a justice tried to set his conscience against the power of the Pagets. Mr Fettiplace Nott was an active magistrate in Lichfield, and in 1753 the keepers brought before him John Dewsberry and his fifteen-year-old son for burning the heath on the Chase. Nott agreed that they were guilty, but hesitated to sentence them

1. Congreve's dispute with the Earl of Uxbridge, and a case involving servants of Ralph Weston (later the steward) tried by a meeting of five justices (Ridgway to Paget 8.2.72).

2. John Cooper to Earl of Uxbridge, 7.9.54; Nichols to Earl of Uxbridge, 4.9.54; Dolphin to Earl of Uxbridge, 23.9.54. Dolphin made several applications to the Earl of Uxbridge for advice in difficult cases. See that of Birch, referred to Fletcher Norton (21.1.69, D603/E1–46, and Ridgway to Earl of Uxbridge, 18.2.69, 1.7.69); Lightwood (4.9.54, D603/E1–46); Hopkins (letters of Scott and Hopkins, 13.10.55); Dangerfield (Ridgway to Earl of Uxbridge, 7.9.67).

3. Ridgway to Earl of Uxbridge, 27.1.66. 'By many statutes peculiar punishments are appropriated for several offences, pillory, stocks, imprisonment, and the like; and in all these cases, no room is left for the justices discretion, for they ought to give judgement, and to inflict the punishment in all the circumstances thereof, as such statutes do direct.' Dalton, quoted in Burn, 'Judgements', 1772 edn, vol. II, p. 481.

to the whipping and imprisonment with hard labour demanded by the law. The son, he was convinced, had merely obeyed his father. 'The Father certainly Merited the Punishment the Statute directs', wrote the magistrate, 'but he appeared when before me very Infirm and between 60 and 70 years of Age, and as Whipping is one part of ye Punishment I must confess under his Circumstances, I did not look upon him as a fit Object for such Chastisement . . . an Act of Barbarity rather than of Correction. . .' Neither had ever offended before, and he contented himself with ordering them to apologize to the steward for the bit of burnt heath. The Earl was very displeased, for the steward assured him he had put all possible pressure on Nott to sentence. Within a few weeks Uxbridge had applied for a King's Bench information against the magistrate, for misdemeanour in the conduct of his office. Nott, though he vowed he was guilty of nothing more than 'mistaken compassion', could not afford to fight the case, and he finally agreed to inflict the punishment.[1]

When necessary, as in the case of Nott, the Pagets could use their enormous wealth to compel the magistracy to execute their wishes. What is most striking is the fact that they were very rarely forced to do so. Nor were the frequent grants of game or deputations, or even friendship, necessary. The Earl of Uxbridge was disliked by many of his neighbours, yet as magistrates they willingly sent his poachers to the gaols and the whipping-posts, or released them as he wished. It was the prerogative of his position and in their own interest. Poachers were the common enemy of the landed ruling class, and the solidarity in the villages about Cannock Chase was matched by a similar pact of honour among magistrates. In their minds the game laws had little enough to do with any abstract ideal of justice. Their real meaning lay in the peculiar social connotations of game itself, and of the law.

V

The correspondence of the Pagets casts a curious light on the social role of the eighteenth-century aristocracy. The Earl of Uxbridge and his successor carried out the rational functions attributed to them by economic historians: enclosures, exploitation of mineral deposits, improvement of waste lands, investment in canals. They were also intelligible political

1. Nichols to Earl of Uxbridge, 22.1.53; William Cooper to Earl of Uxbridge (3.2.53), Uppingham Bourne to Parry (27.6.53), John Cooper to Parry (4.6.53, 23.5.53, 10.2.53), and Parry's King's Bench affidavit, all in D603/CE248–359; affidavits of John Cooper (3.7.53, 26.6.53) and Bourne (10.11.53) in D603/X347–50; Parry to Earl of Uxbridge, 28.6.53, 6.11.53; 4 Wm and Mary c. 23.

animals: good Tories both, even if Uxbridge was a bit of a recluse. (Paget performed his historical duties much more ably, as an energetic colonel of the Staffordshire militia, an unswervingly loyal supporter of the Tory cause, and a personal friend of King George III.[1]) And yet throughout the correspondence that records their connections with country life, there runs an extraordinarily strong interest in hares and grouse and deer. In hundreds of letters there is discussion of little else – there is as much correspondence about poachers as about tenants, for example, and certainly far greater concern about deer than about elections. The game laws, on any rational calculation, seem to have occupied a highly disproportionate amount of their energy and their time.

The conventional explanation of lawyers and Members of Parliament, that the game laws were essential to prevent idleness and profligacy, probably had some weight. The eighteenth-century gentry and aristocracy were deeply convinced that the national well-being demanded an industrious poor, and they denounced endlessly the 'immoral economy' of the poacher. Dytch and Wilkins, the non-labouring 'labourers' of Rugeley who slept all day and snared conies all night were not increasing the wealth of Britain, nor the wealth of the Pagets.[2] And poaching certainly made labour discipline more difficult. Many if not most of the colliers worked as readily at digging rabbits as coal, men like Thomas Brown, who throughout his long life in the pits remained 'a rude, disorderly man, & a most notorious Pocher. . .'[3] Material interest, too, is part of the answer. The expansion of the rabbit warrens in 1754 was expected to yield more and more revenue, and the Earl of Uxbridge evidently cherished his conies as a capital resource that bred at compound interest. Paget, in turn, thought seriously of enlarging the warrens again in 1774 and 1784.[4] The other game also represented invested money. Pools had to be stocked, feeding the deer during a hard winter might cost over £150, and the wages of keepers and underkeepers amounted to perhaps four times that much.[5] The gains of the poacher all figured as debits in the steward's yearly accounts. But the importance of the game laws cannot be explained simply by the profits of rabbits and the wish to discipline idle rogues. Game itself and the laws used to protect it served to define and maintain class distinctions in rural society in several distinct ways.

Game was important because, above all else, it symbolized the hunt, the chase, the shoot – the pursuits of country gentlemen and peers – and

---

1. Marquess of Anglesey, op. cit., p. 21, who has a lower opinion of him
2. Above, p. 203.
3. Above, p. 201.
4. D1511(34)/16/5. See above p. 235, n. 2.
5. Joseph Perks's summary of payments, 1789; Box XLIV, Plas Newydd.

because it symbolized land. The qualification reserving game to those with
an income of £100 from land was the only enforceable remnant of the mass
of statutes that had once fixed marks of status among Englishmen, and
was all the more jealously regarded for that reason. It is difficult to exaggerate the importance that qualified gentlemen attached to these prerogatives.
Those barred from shooting in the Pagets' manors burned with resentment: 'This is such Oppression', Congreve wrote to Uxbridge, 'that I am
determined never to submit to it, & if your Lordship will not do me
Justice herein, I hope you will not be offended if I find some way to do it
for myself.'[1] Game could not legally be bought or sold because it was
meant to symbolize the same prerogatives: to show that its owner held
power and position in landed society. (Venison, though not so controlled,
had equal importance because of its expense and its associations with the
hunt.) Legalized sale 'would deprive the sportsman of his highest gratification', observed Lord Londonderry in 1827, '. . . the pleasure of furnishing
his friends with presents of game: nobody would care for a present which
everybody could give.'[2]

Pheasants and hares and sides of venison were, therefore, so many
tokens of social position; game was a special currency of class based on
the solid standard of landed wealth, untainted by the commerce of the
metropolis. It could be spent lavishly at dinners in order to command
esteem, or given to others to mark important relationships: to inferiors as
an indulgence, to superiors as a mark of respect. The significance attached
to it could create long, rancorous disputes over apparent trivialities. The
Earl of Uxbridge owed four bucks a year to Thomas Clifford of Tixall by
the terms of a legal settlement, and Clifford was deeply offended when the
deer arrived in 1767 already butchered instead of whole.[3] More often
exchanges of deer and pheasants created warm fellow feeling among the
rulers of landed society. Lord Ward and Sir William Wolseley presented
bucks and hinds to the Earl of Uxbridge because he was a fellow Staffordshire landowner; Paget sent venison to the Bishop of Lichfield on his
annual visitations because bishops were pillars of the social order.[4]
Similar reasoning excused the regular gifts of game to Justices of the

1. Richard Congreve to Earl of Uxbridge, 3.10.55.

2. *Annual Register*, 1827, p. 184; quoted in J. L. and Barbara Hammond, *The Village
Labourer*, 1966, p. 195.

3. The basis was a 1713 decree in Chancery by which Lord Aston gave up the master-
ship of the game on the Chase in exchange for four bucks a year; see Ridgway to Earl of
Uxbridge, 1.9.67, 7.9.67, 19.1.68, 7.5.68, 11.9.68, 7.10.69; William Cooper and Francis
Dickin, 18.8.67; examination of John Cooper, 4.6.68; William Cooper Jr to Earl of
Uxbridge, 3.9.68; Priest to Harrison, 15.9.74; and WSL, Accessions 45/6/57.

4. Weston to Paget, 3.8.76; Ridgway's accounts, 18.8.59 to 1.9.60 and 5.9.61 to 2.9.62.

Peace and judges on circuit: they sealed the bonds of class.[1] Of course there were a few critics who used harsher words for the practice:

> – Examine well
> His milk white hand; the palm is hardly clean, –
> But here and there an ugly smutch appears.
> Foh! 'twas a bribe that left it: he has touch'd
> Corruption. Whoso seeks an audit here
> Propitious, pays his tribute, game or fish,
> Wild fowl or venison, and his errand speeds.[2]

But the Pagets were guilty of nothing so crude. Gifts of game to magistrates apparently were made on a regular basis, not in particular cases, and if the justices were grateful, was it not right that gentlemen should be on good terms with one another? 'It is too great a liberty for me to take in giveing your Lordship this trouble,' Justice Dolphin wrote to Uxbridge in 1756,

did I not flatter myself your Lordship will be so good to except it, as I thought it my Dutye to own your kind favour of the venison I had the honour to receive from Mr. Cooper one of your Lordships keepers today. I can't pretend to make any other return than by acknowledging of it, and other former favours, but should I be ever honoured in any commands for your Lordships Service they shall with great pleasure punctually be obeyed. . .[3]

Different magistrates had different valuations in the currency of game, of course: Justice Dolphin merited a doe, but when Lord Chief Justice Mansfield came on circuit several years after giving the Earl of Uxbridge victory over the rabbit-diggers, he was pleased to receive from Beaudesert two brace of carp, twenty dozen crawfish, a brace and a half of hares, a couple of wild ducks and a buck from the Park, in addition to the doe traditionally sent to the assize judges from the Burton estate.[4]

Poachers, then, were not only stealing a peculiarly valuable kind of social capital; they were also debasing its coinage. By supplying the black market they allowed tradesmen and Londoners to play the country gentleman at the dinner-table. Worse yet, in coursing and shooting, the poachers themselves aped gentlemen in the field. Where was the power and pleasure in granting venison if your colliers enjoyed it regularly in Rugeley and Longdon? Where was the glory of the chase if navvies on the canal set dogs on the deer, or your labourers ran hallooing after bucks with field forks in

1. Adey to Earl of Uxbridge, 2.7.44; Ridgway to Earl of Uxbridge, 24.12.55.
2. William Cowper, *The Task*, 1785, Book IV.
3. Jonathan Dolphin to Earl of Uxbridge, 17.1.56; box of 'fragments', Plas Newydd.
4. Adey to Earl of Uxbridge, 2.7.44; Ridgway to Earl of Uxbridge, 18.7.62, and August 1762 in D603/CE538–68.

their hands?[1] It was 'abominable assurance', declared the steward, when Harding the maltster hunted hares almost at the door of the Hall,[2] and the keeper at Burton was beside himself with indignation when Henry Pyecroft beat up to the pale of Sainai Park with ten companions and six dogs, shouting that he was a qualified man and vowing death to the keepers if they interfered. The keeper called it 'the most flagrant affront ever offered to nobleman'. For Pyecroft was the poacher for whom the gentlemen and peers writing the game laws had failed to provide. An impoverished hedge carpenter 'that could scarcely get 8d. a day', he had inherited a small estate and was transformed overnight into that new species, a 'qualified person', a transformation too sudden to dissolve his class loyalties.[3]

The peculiar significance of game in rural society helps to explain the Pagets' constant and intimate concern with poachers. But the game laws were important to the gentry not only because they concerned deer and pheasants, but also, quite simply, because they were laws. If sporting was one major prerogative of country gentlemen, the other was the administration of justice. The central role of the Justice of the Peace is well known, and those who had neither time nor interest enough to act as magistrates none the less appeared willingly on the grand jury at assizes. Punishment was both the right and the responsibility of gentry and peers. The game laws, therefore, united the two great preoccupations of the landed ruling class in one knot of emotion. Field sports and justice tended to merge in their minds, and often, in the end, to mean the same thing. A striking expression of the delusion is Somerville's poem celebrating the chase, a work which Surtees suggested was the favourite reading of many country gentlemen. In it the fox hunt becomes the scourge of all who threaten property, and the fox the paradigm of rogues:

> For these nocturnal Thieves, Huntsman, prepare
> Thy sharpest Vengeance. Oh! how glorious 'tis
> To right the oppressed, and bring the Felon vile
> To just Disgrace! . . .
> . . . from his kennel sneaks
> The conscious Villain. See! he skulks along
> Slick at the Shepherd's Cost, and plump with Meals
> Purloin'd. So thrive the Wicked here below.[4]

1. Information of Craddock and Stringer, n.d., D603/E1–56.
2. Above, p. 211.
3. Henry Hayne to Earl of Uxbridge, 7.2.46; John Silvester to Earl of Uxbridge, 30.8.51.
4. William Somerville, *The Chace*, 1735, vol. III, lines 35–60; *Cambridge History of English Literature*, vol. X, pp. 109ff. Somerville's poem is an extraordinary compound of

The Pagets, in dealing personally with the cases of hundreds of poachers, probably followed the practice of a majority of their friends and neighbours. It is not enough, however, to say that the game laws united prejudice, property and the prerogatives of power. The details of the way in which they were used was important in maintaining the tissue of fear and gratitude that we call deference.

As we have seen, the masters of Beaudesert could put the laws into execution, or decide not to; demand penalties, or suspend them at will. Such discretionary power, exercised directly as a prerogative of class, was an integral part of the justice of the eighteenth century: it was used to legitimize power, to tie men in gratitude, to prove the humanity of the English law.[1] At the highest level, royal pardons mitigated the barbarous criminal code by commuting death sentences to transportation or imprisonment; and at the lowest, in rural parishes, the power to intervene in the execution of the laws gave landed gentlemen and peers the opportunity to exercise the same prerogatives of 'mercy' and 'justice'.

This is the significance of the petitions from the gaoled rabbit-diggers to the Earl of Uxbridge's 'unparalleled tender and compassionate Disposition which your Lordship has the Character of possessing for the Relief of every object or person in distress', and to his 'Generosity and Compassion towards the miserable and Indigent' in the case of the men sentenced for breaking into his deer barn.[2] The Pagets, like all great landed proprietors, received dozens of such appeals, and occasional leniency fostered the hopes of petitioners. In game offences their power was virtually absolute. Now and again a boy caught burning the heath was pardoned with a severe reprimand; a poacher was offered the alternative of giving a bond when gaol would bring destitution to his family, and throw them on the parish; and in one case the Earl of Uxbridge returned the £5 fine to a yeoman caught poaching because he had had to sell his horse to pay it.[3] Magnanimity could sometimes command submission

the imagery of the law with that of the hunt. The fox, 'a subtle, pilfering Foe', a 'Felon', when in a trap has often with his limb 'Compounded for his Life'. When caught 'unreprieved he dies, and bleach'd in Air/The Jest of Clowns, his reeking Carcass hangs'. The otter, a 'midnight Pillager', dies like the assize convict, amid the same ceremony; but the hunted stag at Windsor enjoys a royal pardon. The image recurs. Lord Hailsham, arguing that procedural rules allow criminals to escape punishment, said recently 'that we tended to think that the ends of justice were served only when the fox was hunted in accordance with a traditional routine by 12 hounds duly selected by lot, presided over by a red-coated huntsman, and pursued with traditional cries to an uncertain and sometimes surprising conclusion' (*Guardian*, 13 May 1972).

1. See above, Chapter 1.
2. Above, p. 193; 'The Humble Petition of Several Free-holders and Inhabitants of the Parish of Longdon', D603/E422–66.
3. Ridgway to Earl of Uxbridge, 31.5.56, 24.2.59, 17.10.61, 27.2.62, 27.1.66; Harrison

where the use of force might rouse only hatred and a desire for revenge. When the Earl consented to accept a bond for £100, and release William Dangerfield, engineer at the coalworks, from a sentence of a year's imprisonment plus the pillory, the steward reported that 'The Man was quite overjoy'd upon my informing him of your Lordship's Consent to his Enlargement & begged, when I wrote, that I would present to your Lordship his most grateful Thanks upon the Occasion – ' What Dangerfield did not know was that he had been committed to gaol in an illegal fashion, and the J P responsible could be sued for false imprisonment; the magistrate had therefore appealed to Uxbridge to release the man.[1] Impotence masked as mercy was a common tactic of magistrates and landowners on those occasions when they found the law did not meet their needs. Lord Paget too understood the principle. In the bitter winter of 1776 two men were caught tracing hares in the snow. They apologized and seemed contrite, but since Paget knew nothing of 'their characters and common fame' and his game was 'most horridly abused', the steward was instructed to proceed with the prosecution. 'If the Offenders are entitled to any Clemency, however inclined Lord Paget may be to punish with Severity the notorious Poacher', wrote his secretary to the steward, 'I am persuaded there is not alive a Man who would extend his clemency to proper Objects sooner than his Lordship, and from that Quarter, as I apprehend, it should come. . . Lord Paget can easily remit the Fines, if, on proper Representation & Application, it appears to his Lordship a matter of propriety.' But when he learned that a conviction would be very difficult to secure on the evidence, the secretary at once instructed the steward to accept the poachers' apologies and tell them that His Lordship would forgive them: 'for it does not admit of a Doubt, whether, to prosecute *without* Success or not to prosecute at all, is most eligible.' He added,

In cases for the future, where the Magistrate has Doubts, I could Sir wish to recommend the Business may always then take the Turn of Lenity or Favor, and that the Offenders may receive Intimation that on their making proper Concessions & Promises of Amendment in their future Conduct the Justice will for that time interfere and get them excused. But in Cases where the Evidence is full & clear & Conviction can be founded, let no Transgressor escape. Lord Paget can always mitigate or reimburse where the Object proves himself deserving.[2]

---

to Paget, 9.4.74, 16.4.74; examination of Francis Dickin, 29.5.56, 'Bills, etc. 1742–9', Plas Newydd; case of Stanley, Staffs. RO, Q /SB 1785 Ep./25 and Tr/128.

1. Ridgway to Earl of Uxbridge, 7.9.67, 21.2.68; examination of William Dangerfield, 6.9.67, D603/E143–294.

2. Harrison to Weston, 17.1.76; Paget to Harrison, 20.1.76; Weston to Harrison, 20.1.76; Harrison to Paget, 22.1.76; Weston to Paget, 29.1.76.

In this case, as in most, the legal process was a secret between magistrate and landowner. What was an irritating lack of power to Paget could be presented to the poachers and the villagers as magnanimity, the act of a just and merciful ruler, a man who was a credit to his class.

Game offences were particularly important as occasions for such moral lessons. Not only were most cases tried by summary conviction, and hence more accessible to the intervention of the prosecutor; they were also the most common of criminal offences in many parishes. The Hammonds' sketch of the ferocity of the game laws in the early nineteenth century has compelled assent from Professor Mingay and others, but with the corollary that in the eighteenth century the laws were less severe and used far less often.[1] Undoubtedly punishments were milder; frequencies are, however, almost impossible to compare because the vast majority of convictions were never recorded.[2] The Paget papers suggest a darker picture than the optimists present. Against the estimate that one in seven criminal convictions in the late 1820s concerned game can be set the fact that in Cannock, Rugeley and Longdon, the Earl of Uxbridge alone brought at least eighty poaching prosecutions between 1750 and 1765, the years for which the correspondence is most complete. That was *fifteen* times the number of prosecutions in those parishes at Quarter Sessions and assizes, by all prosecutors, for all other thefts in the same years. The figure suggests that the game laws were as common an occasion of class conflict in the eighteenth century as later, even if the penalties, and hence the violence, were milder.

It is difficult to assess how typical the Pagets were in their attitudes to poachers, and whether Staffordshire was a representative county with respect to game. As an area of large estates it may have had more than the average number of large preservers of game, and its substantial areas of waste and forest – notably Cannock Chase and Needwood – perhaps

1. J. L. and B. Hammond, op. cit., pp. 184–97; G. E. Mingay, *English Landed Society in the Eighteenth Century*, 1963, pp. 120, 249.

2. Justices seldom returned formal records of conviction to sessions because they were difficult to draw up, and few of those convicted were ever likely to appeal (Christian, op. cit., p. 200; William Boscawen, *A Treatise on Convictions on Penal Statutes*, 1792, p. 3; William Paley, *Summary Convictions*, 1812, pp. 39, 227). Because of the gaps in Quarter Sessions records before 1770 in Staffordshire, and gaps in the Paget correspondence from the 1780s, it is difficult to assess what proportion of convictions were returned to sessions; it appears to be about one in ten for the 1770s. Most are convictions under 13 Geo. III c. 80 (game), and 16 Geo. III c. 30 (deer), two of the very few acts which specifically required a record of conviction. Between 1740 and 1800 about 200 poaching offences are mentioned in D603; another seventeen appear in the judicial records only. Ten appear in both sources. The Pagets account for four recorded convictions only, out of 47 in the whole county recorded for eight sample years between 1772 and 1802.

made poaching an unusually vigorous tradition. Certainly the common rights on Cannock Chase gave a greater sense of right, a greater independence and better opportunities to poach to the villagers near by. On the other hand, the Earl of Uxbridge's battle for his warrens was minor compared to the similar struggle in Leicestershire during the same years; and early-nineteenth-century statistics on poaching suggest that Staffordshire was in no way exceptional. Nor do Uxbridge and Paget appear exceptional when compared with their contemporaries. There were harsher men, preservers who sought death sentences for deer-poachers under the Black Act fairly frequently; the Earl of Uxbridge did so only once.[1] Even those gentlemen who opposed him on the issue of the Chase concurred heartily in the harsh treatment of labourers who dared to take game. (Phineas Hussey, who coursed deer off the Chase and encouraged his servants to do so as well, prosecuted poachers of his fishponds under the Black Act.)[2] Paget was undoubtedly a more typical peer than Uxbridge, and more of a traditionalist – he revived disused customs such as the annual dinner at the Hall for the servants, tenants and colliers.[3] But he was also more traditional in field sports, and fully as opposed to poachers, urging his stewards to 'hit with spirit' in the war against them.[4] The only real distinction between the two is that Uxbridge, counting his conies in bachelor solitude, thought of his game less as a personal pleasure and more as a commodity. In this, he anticipated the strict preservers of the early nineteenth century, who bred their own game where they could no longer find it wild, and who surrounded their preserves with man traps and spring guns to kill and maim. Paget's son, the first Marquess of Anglesey, began the practice in 1812, the year he inherited the estates.[5]

The villagers about Beaudesert did not ask whether the Pagets were typical. They hated the keepers, the laws and many of the Justices of the Peace. They also hated the Pagets, with a violence that was forced underground by the law and by fear, that was often calmed by charity, but that also surfaced in those isolated, anonymous acts of revenge which were among the few free expressions of the labouring poor. In 1747 several deer were found poisoned, an act of malice since the meat was inedible. Two years later poachers hung a threatening letter at the Park gate, next to a dead partridge hung round with nineteen blown eggs. The hayrick next to the Hall was burnt down the following year, and in 1755 more deer

1. He also once actively pursued a pardon from the Duke of Newcastle for a girl sentenced to transportation for theft at the Berkshire Assizes; PRO, SP 36/123, letter of Francis Parry, 16.8.53; GLCRO (Middx. Div.), Acc. 446/FP.10/1–3.

2. *K.* v. *Sedgwick*, WSL, HM uncatalogued Box 42.

3. Paget to Harrison, 1.8.76; undated memorandum D603/C40.

4. Paget to Harrison, 22.2.76.

5. Printed bill, 'Robbery', 14.9.1812, D603.

were found poisoned. Someone maimed Uxbridge's hound, Beaufort, in 1757, and another unknown man, perhaps a poacher who had lost his dog to the keepers, later killed the beast and threw its body in the horse pool. More deer were poisoned in 1772 after Paget inherited the estate. Two years later one of his finest hounds was killed in the night.[1] As well as prosecuting poachers, he went on to prohibit horse-races on the Chase; they had been a long-standing source of income and amusement for the cottagers. His motive was to protect the game, and his action was deeply resented: 'You have ruined a number of poor familys their exis- tance is as much to them as yours to you,' wrote an anonymous 'Free- holder of Staffordshire',

as Providence has blessed you with affluence you are in duty bound to do good to your fellow creatures, instead of distressing them in the vile manner you have done, I dont wonder your coppice was set on fire neither should I be surprized if your dwelling shared the same fate I have heard several say they hope it will be, and you Burnt to Death as such a wretch and Tryrant is not fit to Exist. . .[2]

In 1793 another angry man wasted no time on words, but set fire to the Park barn and the stable containing all the farm horses.[3] Such acts were the traditional weapons of the powerless against the great. They do not appear in the court records because the offenders were never caught. Few can ever be certainly identified as expressions of wide discontent because their authors spoke to the enemy in a language of symbolism so dependent on personal context that we can rarely recover it. But if we ask whether the Pagets had any enemies we can answer 'hundreds' – and most of them were poachers or commoners who had suffered for their landlord's game. Their acts of revenge, a commonplace of eighteenth-century country life, challenge an historiography that is increasingly complacent about the social harmonies of that society.

1. Adey to Earl of Uxbridge, 31.12.47; *London Gazette*, no. 9044, 26–30 March 1751; Nichols to Earl of Uxbridge, 3.6.49; Ridgway to Earl of Uxbridge, 23.11.55, 8.4.57; Ridgway to Paget, 6.1.72, 22.11.72, 22.2.72; Asshton Curzon to Paget, 25.1.72; Harrison to Paget, 16.4.74. (The threatening letter is not extant, but the context suggests its nature.)

2. Case with Lloyd Kenyon's opinion, 20.3.75, D1511/20; D603/xxxi/93, letter dated 3.7.75.

3. Joseph Perks to Sanderson, 23.5.93. The fires on the Chase in 1755, 1756, 1762, 1772, 1774, 1779 and other years may sometimes have been the result of malice; *Aris's Birmingham Gazette*, 25.5.72.

The Crime of Anonymity

I Wauld Tel you My Name
but My Simplicity Will Not Let Mee.

NEWCASTLE COLLIER, 1765

I

The anonymous threatening letter is a characteristic form of social protest in any society which has crossed a certain threshold of literacy, in which forms of collective organized defence are weak, and in which individuals who can be identified as the organizers of protest are liable to immediate victimization. The same means may, equally, be used in pursuit of private grievance and also as an instrument of extortion: its use, for these purposes, belongs to no particular phase of social development, and it continues today. No tidy line of demarcation can be drawn between these two kinds of action, although the difference between them (in certain contexts) is self-evident. Both kinds will be examined in this essay. From the point of view of the recipient, in any case, the effect of such anonymous menaces upon his peace of mind may be much the same. It can be frightening and disturbing to receive such letters; it can induce extreme anxiety, night-watches, suspicion of friends and neighbours, and justified forms of paranoia.

This study is based in the main upon eighteenth-century evidence. It is best to commence by explaining the nature and limits of the source from which the central evidence is drawn. *The London Gazette: Published by Authority* may seem an unlikely source for the student of plebeian history. The *Gazette*, which appeared twice weekly was, of course, the publication of the most august authority. In its pages appeared the Proclamations of King and Privy Council: arrangements of the Court: announcements of naval and military engagements: promotions and commissions: official notices from Whitehall, the Admiralty, the War Office, the Excise: lists of bankrupts: the prorogation or summoning of Parliaments.[1]

Thus in no. 10752, late August 1767, we have notices for an election of Scottish peers to sit in the House of Lords; of a review in Madrid by the King of Spain of his garrison; of the movements of the Papal Nuncio; while from Berlin it was announced that 'the Marriage of the Princess Louisa-Henrietta Wilhelmina of Brandenbourg with the Reigning Prince of Anhalt Dessau was solemnized in the Royal Chapel at Charlottenbourg by the Reverend Mr. Sack... After which the French Play called Turcaret was acted in the Orangerie...' The gardens were illuminated, and there was a ball, attended by the King of Prussia, which lasted until the next morning. Immediately following, cheek-by-jowl with Princess Louisa-Henrietta Wilhelmina, there appears a rather different notice, addressed to Sir Richard Betenson of Sevenoaks, Kent:

Sr: Your Baily or Steward proper is a black gard sort of fellow to the Workmen and if you dont discharge him You may Look to Your House being sett on fire if Stones will not Burn You damned Sun of a hoare You shall have Your throat cutt from Ear to Ear except You Lay £50 under the Second tree of Staple Nashes from his house at the frunt of the Great Gates near the Rabbit Warrin on Wensdy Morn next...

This was of course, like the preceding one, an official notice, although it was not inserted by the letter's author but by the Secretary of State. It will save much explanation if we cite in full the form of words within which such letters were encapsulated:

Whitehall, August 8, 1767.

Whereas it has been humbly represented to the King, That the following threatening and incendiary letter, was on [date] received by Sir Richard Betenson ... and containing the Words and Letters following [there follows the letter, with its orthography preserved] His Majesty, for the better discovering and bringing to Justice the Persons concerned in Writing the said threatening ... Letter, is hereby pleased to promise His most gracious Pardon to any one of them (except the Person who actually wrote the said Letter) who shall discover his or her Accomplice ... so that he, she, or they may be apprehended and convicted thereof.   SHELBURNE.

And, as a further Encouragement, the said Sir Richard Betenson, Bart, doth hereby promise a Reward of *One Hundred Pounds* to any Person or Persons making such Discovery ... to be paid by him upon the Conviction of ... the Offenders.   Rich. Betenson.

1. For a general history of the *London Gazette* (hereafter *LG*) see P. M. Handover, *A History of the London Gazette, 1665–1965*, 1965.

The critical point here is that the *Gazette* was involved only when an official pardon was offered for information leading to a conviction: and such authority must be obtained from the Secretary of State.[1] In some cases, where a public official or public property was involved, an official reward might also be offered. More commonly, when a private citizen was threatened, he himself found the money for this reward. In order to make it more likely that the author of the letter might be detected, the letter, with its original spelling and its ferocious imprecations, were often published in full.

Hence the *London Gazettes* lie, like so many bi-weekly lobster traps, on the sea-bottom of Namier's England, catching many curious literary creatures which never, in normal circumstances, break the bland surface of the waters of eighteenth-century historiography.[2] It seemed useful to go through the journal systematically from 1750 to 1820, in order both to count these letters and to examine their nature. This is the central evidence drawn upon in this study, supplemented by the use of state papers (especially between 1795 and 1802), the provincial press and other sources.[3]

For various reasons, the picture becomes very confused after 1811. A count of the years 1750–1811 shows about 284 gazetted letters or handbills (anonymous and hand-written), or an average of about 4·7 per year.[4] In fact the incidence is very much more uneven. Taking only those letters which indicate some social or economic grievance of a general character, and excluding those which are evidently the work of private blackmailers, the peak years for gazetted letters are shown overleaf (Table 1).

An attempt has been made, sometimes on slender evidence, to break these 284 letters down into matters of 'private' or 'social' grievance. This attempt may be misguided: as the letter to Sir Richard Betenson shows, a private blackmailing letter may suggest a general grievance ('Your Baily or Steward ... is a black gard sort of fellow to the Workmen'); a blackmailing bankrupt tradesman may have been the victim of another kind

1. For the machinery of rewards and pardons, see Radzinowicz, esp. vol. II, sections 4 and 5.
2. The *Gazette* is, of course, an important source not only for imprecations but also for actions, since rewards for information as to murders, smuggling affrays, arson, industrial riot, and so on also appear in its pages.
3. I am very much indebted to Mr E. E. Dodd for his help in going through the *Gazettes* and to Mr Malcolm Thomas, whose extensive knowledge of the Home Office papers between 1790 and 1803 has been made available to me. I was enabled to draw upon their help with the assistance of a grant in aid of research into food riots from the Nuffield Foundation in 1968–9.
4. No pretence is made as to final accuracy. Gazetted mentions of letters, which give no information as to the occasion or contents of the letters, have been omitted from this count.

Table 1: Gazetted Letters

1800	35	or	1800–1802	49
1766	17		1766–7	27
1796	11			17
1767	10		1795–6	
1801	7			
1802	7			
1771	6			
1792	6			
1795	6			

of extortion; and, equally, social protest may coexist with private grievance. Thus no absolute line of definition is suggested between 'social' and other kinds of grievance. But the distinction may help to further our inquiry:

Table 2: Grievances

Crime-related[1]	13		
Clearly blackmail or private grievance	36	or	49 'private',
Clearly social, economic, political or community grievance	216		
Probably social grievance	19		235 'social'
Total	284		

I have also attempted to list the nature of the dominant threat implied by the letter (see Table 3).[2]

It will be noted that, taking (1) and (2) together, murder was the most common threat in 'private' cases: approximately 71 per cent of all threats, as against 34·5 per cent in 'social' cases. But, taking (3) and (4) together, and again giving approximate figures, arson is a threat most often to be found in 'social' cases: 40 per cent as against 29 per cent in 'private'. The other kinds of threat belong wholly to the former.

In the next table (Table 4) we leave aside (for the time being) the private cases and consider only the social, or putatively social, cases. From

1. By 'crime-related' I mean attempts to influence the course of justice, threats to witnesses, and so on. There are in fact twenty-one such letters, but eight of these I have felt able to allocate to 'social' grievances.

2. In some cases one letter contains several different threats, or threats appropriate to several different persons: for instance, murder to the mayor, destruction of property to the miller, arson to the farmer: this explains discrepancies in figures between Tables 2 and 3, 4 and 5.

Table 3: Nature of Threats

	Social	Private	Totals
1. Murder	60	20	80
2. Undisclosed ('do for you', 'have your blood', etc.), implying murder	25	9	34
3. Arson *and* murder	36	3	39
4. Arson	68	9	77
5. Pulling down or blowing up buildings, attacking machinery, etc.	16	—	16
6. Arming, civil war, rebellion, treason, etc.	31	—	31
7. Mutilation of recipient	3	—	3
8. Maiming of stock, barking or felling of trees, etc.	3	—	3
9. Other	2	—	2
Totals	244	41	285

the inadequate evidence of the *Gazette*s one may identify these recipients of threats:

Table 4: Recipients of Threats

Gentry and nobility	44
Master manufacturers, tradesmen, millers	41
Persons holding some office (excluding mayors and JPs)	27
Mayors	23
Magistrates	18
Farmers	17
Clergy	11
Excisemen	7
Blacklegs	2
General hand-written notices ('To all farmers', 'Gentlemen of . . .', etc.)	39
Others	19
Total	248

* Persons in authority = 68

The final table suggests only the most tentative categorization. Without following each case back through other sources, it is impossible from the evidence of a letter alone to have an exact notion of the grievance at issue; in any case, many letters are expressive of more than one grievance.

However, the number of issues which could provoke men to utter murderous or incendiary threats is itself of interest:

Table 5: Particularization of Grievances

Price of bread, corn, food:	
against forestalling or monopolists	72
Industrial: machines, wages, blacklegs, etc.	34
Attempts to influence course of justice	
(some 'social', some 'private')	21
Politically related (local politics,	
sedition – but excluding most food-and-sedition	
letters of the 1800s)	19
Private grievances (e.g. dismissed servants)	11
Enclosure, common rights	9
Smuggling	7
Poor and poor laws	5
Poaching	5
Turnpikes	4
Press-gang	3
Volunteers	2
Militia ballot	2
Servants' vails (customary gratuities)	2
Licensing of ale-houses	2
Rural labourers' wages	2
Identified grievance, but one case only of each	25
	——
Total	225

Once again, this tabulation (which is based on the dominant grievance in each letter) is at points misleading. Thus, while only two letters are wholly concerned with the low wages of rural labourers, many of the 72 letters arising from the high price of food complain also about the level of labourers' wages. The 25 letters which each voice a distinct grievance range from agrarian protests (against tithes, in support of traditional measures, in defence of gleaning, against threshing-machines), through a scatter of political and religious grievances (anti-Papist, anti-Methodist, Welsh Nationalist) to a grievance against a 'damd horing rogue'.

II

These tables indicate a little. But it is necessary to qualify impressions which they give.

First, the number of letters gazetted gives no constant index to the actual number of letters written. It simply indicates the number of occasions upon which a letter was taken sufficiently seriously both by the recipient and the Secretary of State for an official pardon to be offered. It was never a simple matter to gain this: in general this ensued only if (a) the recipient of the threat was a person who had interest with Government, or (b) evidence was offered to show that there was genuine danger that the threat might be carried out (or was part of a series of threats, one or more of which had already been carried out, as in cases of arson, riot or destruction of machinery), or (c) the seditious nature of the document was very alarming to the authorities.

Second, these variables were given added uncertainty by the dispositions of different Secretaries of State and their underlings under various governments. Not every administration held the same views as to the usefulness of gazetting letters. And only a minority of the recipients of such letters would have bothered to use this method of attempted control. To gazette a letter involved delay, correspondence with the Government, the expense of insertion (£3 3s. 6d. in 1800) and also the offering of a somewhat larger reward than might otherwise seem necessary. The recipients of such letters might more simply advertise immediately in their local press for information and offer a reward directly to informers, although if they acted in this way no pardon could of course be offered.[1] Finally, one may wonder how far the well-tried eighteenth-century system of pardons and rewards was of much use in dealing with an offence which (like arson) could be carried out in secret by one individual and without accomplices.

It is possible to observe some of these variables at work during the years 1795–1805. In 1795 only six letters of social protest were gazetted: but in fact the Home Office papers preserve very many more sent in by anxious correspondents. It is evident that the Government in this year did not wish to give additional publicity to the shocking and seditious sentiments of the letters. In 1796 a few more letters were advertised in the *Gazette* (eleven of social protest) but the Duke of Portland was still counselling caution. In November he wrote to say that he agreed that a handbill sent on to him by the Lord Mayor of London was most inflammatory: 'Yet provided it does not appear to produce any effect, perhaps your Lordship will agree with me, that it is a proof that the prevailing good sense and disposition of the people lead them to treat it precisely in the manner we could wish.'[2] Nothing would be gained by advertising it. When a seditious letter was sent to him from Yeovil in 1799 the Duke was

---

1. For examples of local advertising, see *Aris's Birmingham Gazette*, 11 August 1766, 9 March 1767; *Reading Mercury*, 10 March 1800.

2. PRO, HO 43.8, p. 144.

still not inclined 'to give any notoriety to it, by an advertisement in the Gazette'.[1]

In 1800, however, when widespread riots and arson had made it evident that 'the prevailing good sense and disposition of the people' could no longer be relied upon, and when blood-chilling 'jacobinical' threats became commonplace, no fewer than thirty-five such letters were gazetted. This was still only a small proportion (certainly less than 25 per cent) of the letters sent in to the Home Office.[2] Portland's general advice was to watch, employ informers, and only if this seemed likely to succeed to advertise the letters.[3] This policy was continued through 1800 and into 1801 in cases supposed to affect the public interest.[4] By 1804 the pendulum had swung back to extreme caution. In March 1804 the Home Secretary wrote to one complainant: 'I am doubtful of the expediency of publishing in the Gazette ... the seditious paper ... Perhaps it wd answer the purpose better to insert in the County Newspaper the beginning and end of the paragraph in original, so as sufficiently to identify and point it out, without promulgating the pernicious sentiments which it contains...'[5] Such a compromise had been reached by other authorities rather earlier than this. In October 1800 the Birmingham authorities, who

1. PRO, HO 43.11, p. 131.
2. No exact figure can be given. Home Office out-letter books in 1800 show the receipt of over eighty of such letters acknowledged; but a search of in-letters shows nearly 150 received in the same year. Since some enclosures were returned to the sender, some were sent on to the *Gazette* office, and others appear in War Office papers, 150 must be an underestimate of those brought directly to the Government's attention. In addition many correspondents referred in general terms to the frequency of such letters, but sent on no examples.
3. In February the Birmingham magistrates were advised to 'employ some discreet and confidential agents, to observe, during the night time, in the most suspicious places'; J. King to Birmingham magistrates, 25 February 1800, PRO, HO 43.11, p. 374. Two weeks later Portland appears to have become more anxious: 'I wish an early example could be made of those writing and distributing inflammatory and threatening handbills': Portland to Marquess Townshend, 10 March 1800, HO 43.11.
4. Portland did not consistently advise gazetting: for a contrary example, in this period, see his exchanges with W. Baker, MP, cited below, p. 292. And he consistently resisted gazetting (or offering a pardon and reward) in cases where the letters were of a private and scandalous, rather than public, character. To one recipient (a magistrate) he wrote that advertisement 'would tend to make public the malicious and ill-founded suggestions ... without the smallest chance of bringing the authors of them to justice': see F. Adams, JP to Portland, 2 June 1800, PRO, HO 42.50 and HO 43.11, pp. 511–12. A pardon and reward could not be offered unless the interests of the country at large were involved: J. King to J. Taylor, 11 June 1800, HO 43.11, pp. 518–19.
5. This was, however, a special case, the letter in question being in Welsh, and a translation being proposed for the *Gazette*: clearly this would have afforded to it superfluous publicity: Charles Yorke to C. W. W. Wynne, 5 March 1804, PRO, HO 43.14, pp. 434–5.

found such pernicious sentiments appearing around them daily in hand-bills, placards and wall-chalking, could bear only to publish in the *Gazette* a proclamation commencing: 'Whereas . . . several inflammatory papers (one of which begins with "Countrymen" and another with "Liberty") have been thrown in the streets, and stuck up against the walls. . .'[1] After these years the policy of reticence was confirmed. Only three or four letters were gazetted in 1811, and about five in 1812, yet both years, as the Home Office papers show, saw fecund and ebullient epistolary activity. Thereafter it became usual to publish the fact but not the contents of a letter.

Hence the figures give only an erratic indication as to the extent of this kind of activity. What survives in the *Gazette*s is only what is left after much else has drained through the sieve. And undoubtedly scores of threatening letters were received by persons who never bother to inform the authorities: in 1800 the Lord Mayor of London referred to such letters 'of which by the bye I get a great many and disregard them'.[2] Of those which were sent in, the majority were set aside ungazetted. And, further, there is the unknown and unknowable number of blackmailing or threatening letters which never came to light because the recipients kept them secret and complied with the demands made upon them. The figures which are offered above may certainly not be allowed to enter the intestines of some computer, as the quantity of meditated violence in pre-industrial England.

III

Private blackmailing, like kidnapping and some forms of hijacking, appears to be an epidemic offence which thrives on publicity. It is perhaps possible to date fairly exactly the first occasion when this offence was advertised throughout the whole country.

In the summer and autumn of 1730 threatening letters appeared, in a sensational way, in Bristol. They were thrown into workshops and houses, and dropped in the street, demanding small sums of money on threat of arson. It seems probable that some timid recipients complied. In October Mr George Packer, who had refused several demands to pay six guineas, had his house and part of his ship-building yard fired. His family was lucky to escape with their lives. Within days threatening letters were being reported from many parts of the country. In November a Proclamation was issued, offering a pardon and the very considerable sum of £300

---

1. *Aris's Birmingham Gazette*, 6 October 1800; and ibid., 3 November 1800 for a handbill beginning: 'Vive la Republic!'
2. PRO, HO 42.51, fos. 166–8.

reward for information leading to any conviction: offenders were liable to the punishment of death under a clause in the Black Act of 1723 (see below p. 283). The Proclamation appears only to have afforded further publicity to the offence. The burning of Packer's house, Boyer noted, has 'put it into the head of every abandon'd Wretch through the whole Country to take advantage thereof', and the practice of sending incendiary letters was compared to the fire which they threaten, spreading with equal speed and terror.[1] Some of the letters were clearly extortionary: a Hammersmith farmer, of whom ten guineas were demanded, and who placed some white halfpence in an unsuccessful trap, had his stacks and barn fired.[2] Others suggest the employment of the same form as a means of voicing private grievance: Mr Spragging, a raft merchant at Newark, was warned:

> Spraging, remember thou art but Dust,
> And to thy Neighbour very unjust:
> Thou neither sticks at great nor small,
> Till Vengeance once does on thee fall.
> I think how soon thou wilt be undone;
> In Flames of Fire thy Rafts shall burn. . .[3]

The Bristol offenders were never convicted.[4] But several of their imitators ended on the gallows. Convictions were secured in Lincolnshire, Kent and Hertfordshire, and the rewards of £300 were paid out.[5] Jeremiah Fitch, a joiner, was one of these offenders. He had written to a wealthy farmer, Goodman Jenkyns of Harpenden, a letter commencing:

> This, with my Service to you, and I desire you'l, of all Love, lay me £30 at the Bottom of the Post next to Henry Hudsons . . . a Friday night by Eight of the Clock, or if you do not, I'll burn your House to Ashes God dam your Blood; and God dam you Sir, if you watch, or declare this Secret to any Body dam my Blood if Death shall not be your Portion. . .

---

1. A. Boyer, *Political State of Great Britain*, vol. XL (1730), pp. 439, 497–9, 505–15, 590–93, 600; Samuel Seyer, *Memoirs Historical and Topographical of Bristol and its Neighbourhood*, Bristol, 1823, vol. II, pp. 578–9; J. P. Malcolm, *Anecdotes of the Manners and Customs of London during the Eighteenth Century*, 1810, vol. I, pp. 145–6; *LG*, 17–21 November 1730.

2. Boyer, op. cit., vol. XLI (1731), p. 83.

3. ibid., vol. XXXX, p. 508. A barber and former chandler was taken in custody on suspicion of being the author.

4. Several were tried at Bristol Assizes in March 1731, but all were acquitted for want of evidence. In 1738 the offences in Bristol appear to have resumed: Boyer, op. cit., vol. XLI, pp. 309–10; vol. LV (1738), p. 179.

5. See itemization of reward payments in PRO, T53.36, fos. 58–64, 65–7.

But Goodman Jenkyns did place a watch, of four men, and Fitch was detected.[1]

Contemporaries suggested that 'this is a new crime', although this seems unlikely.[2] The example of executions in several counties appears to have brought this epidemic to an end, although the offence remained in men's memories and a trickle of similar incendiary threats continue thereafter. But – as the case of Fitch shows – it was an offence easy to initiate but very difficult to bring to a successful conclusion. The blackmailer had at all costs to devise means of obtaining his pay-off without fear of detection. The stratagems proposed by some of the letter-writers of 1730 inspired a Norwich satirist:

> If you do not put Six New Halfpence, in Form,
> Into an Old Shoe (we speak for no Harm),
> And place it upon the very Top-Stone
> Of Christ Church high Spire, at Midnight, alone. . .[3]

Since the victim was likely to inform police, or to wait up with friends and servants at the point where money was to be deposited, the blackmailer was likely to succeed only in limited conditions:

(i) If the blackmailer was actually in possession of information as to the criminal record, sexual improprieties, and so on of the victim – information which would be immensely damaging to the victim if it ever came out. These are, of course, the most successful grounds for blackmail; and for exactly the same reasons such offences rarely come to light.[4]

(ii) If blackmail was part of a widespread protection-racket, with effective and well-known means of retaliation against those who failed to comply.

(iii) If the victim could be terrified into compliance and into secrecy, by the very violence of the physical threats.

---

1. ibid. and Boyer, op. cit., vol. XLI, p. 310.

2. ibid., vol. XL, p. 506. Plain blackmail, supported by murderous threats, was of course known previously: indeed, men had been hanged for it in the 1720s (see pp. 286–7). Possibly the incendiary threat was thought to be novel.

3. Boyer, op. cit., vol. XLI, pp. 90–91, reprinted from *Norwich Gazette*. The top of Christ Church spire was 309 feet from the ground: the author further warned the recipient not to station any watch on the weathercock.

4. For an example of such an affair which did come to light, see University of Nottingham, Manvers Coll. B 92. Here the Vicar of Edwinstowe (Notts.), who in 1824 had dismissed a Mrs Clark from his service, appears to have been blackmailed by an associate of Mrs Clark's who wrote: 'i saw Mrs. Clark and you com out of the kitching and both go into the privy together and when you had dun what you whent for come out.' But since the author did not ask for money but only for 'your answer' he could not be prosecuted for felony.

This last point helps to explain the extreme violence of style favoured by such letter-writers. The problem can be seen in a letter received by a gentleman in Ayrshire in 1775:

> There are six of us who being reduced to Misery by Misfortune have pitched upon you for our Relief, Providence has made you able and it is our business to make you willing. You will therefore lay £50 Ster: below the Broad Stone on the Extremity of the South End of the Stone dike on your right hand as you go from Slophouse to Ayr and lett it be in Gold or Silver and lett it . . . ly one Week. . .

But of course the victim was likely to set a watch upon this place, so the author detailed his own arrangements:

> If you are so foolish as attempt to know who we are you are undone. One of us will uplift the Money while three stand on the Watch with a Couple of Good Pistols each and two left at home to take Vengeance on you if you disturb the rest and a Cask of Powder ready to blow up your House – So you see that Silence is equally necessary on both Sides.[1]

This subtle and highly literate letter perhaps failed to command belief: the possessors of at least six good pistols and of a cask of powder were not likely to risk their lives for £50. A more usual style is that which seeks to carry all before it by sheer vigour of style. A Northampton wine merchant received a demand for £800 'by Thursday next' (in January 1763): 'If You do not do as We command You We will put You to the utmost Torture. . . You Villian of a Bitch Yo Theif I will blow out Your Brains. Dam Your Blood You Dog.'[2] Other letters suggest a personal acquaintance between the author and the victim; perhaps the blackmailer had been a tradesman bankrupted by the activities of the recipient. 'I have been your frend Veary Much & I hope Not to go unpade for it I am a Grate Acquintance of yours and by Nesesety is Drove to bad Ways,' a Holborn apothecary was informed in 1760.[3] This correspondent only required a guinea. George Bryant, a Deptford distiller, was formally approached in 1763: 'Sir to aquant you that I am in great Needsesety for a little Mony or otherwise I will be oblidgd to Shut oup Shop or Leave off Busness. . .' £100 would meet the occasion: otherwise Mr Bryant's house would be burnt down.[4] A gentleman in Blackfriars in 1764 was told to bring £50 – 'Under the feet of a verry old Stone Stature with the nose of the statture

1. *LG* 11538 (February 1775). Each *Gazette* was dated over a three- or four-day period, so that it is simpler to identify them by number rather than date. The date given in brackets indicates the month in which the letter was first sent, which was sometimes a few weeks before it was published in the *Gazette*. From 1785 onwards each year of the *Gazette* was paginated consecutively: Handover, op. cit., p. 59.
2. *LG* 10282 (January 1763). 3. *LG* 9971 (January 1760).
4. *LG* 10282 (January 1763).

broke of it is Lying at full lenth Directly Oposite the Entrance of the north door of westminster abbe in the first Ile.' The price for failure was to be the gentleman's 'brains bloud'; 'I am a tradesman well know by you and will return the money to you the 17th of next month.'[1] When we recall the disaster of the debtors' gaol and the cavalier refusal of many gentry to pay their tradesmen's bills, we may perhaps have a context in which to place some of these forcible collections.

Except where a case actually comes to trial, there is little to be learned from such letters. Occasionally there is the suggestion of a protection-racket or general forced levy of money by some group or 'gang'. The smuggling trade involved sudden needs for capital to purchase stocks from an incoming ship; it also required the intimidation of informers.[2]

Suky Boswell, the servant of an Excise officer at Eastbourne, received in 1771 a letter which can have left her in no doubt as to its intention: 'Suky Boswell I hav Ing a few moments to spere I though I Culd not in ploy my self better than send you a Line or to. . .' Boswell's offence was that she had been too officious on behalf of her master: 'Lokeing out for your master that night he . . . went out with the Solgers.' And so to the climax: 'I must and will kill you Dam your blood I will Cut your throat from Ear to Ear Dam Dam and Dubbel Dam you your Liver I will brile . . . God almyty Dam your Soul Dam God Dam y God Dam y. . .'[3] Another excise officer, at Redcar in 1774, was warned to keep off the sands: 'You may as well . . . take what we give you as other officers do, and if you don't we'll sware that you take bribes, you had better take them then not dam you.'[4]

No doubt such letters, in the continuous conflict between smugglers and Excise-men, served their function. They may have been effective in a much wider context than this. The stages by which an offender might be finally brought to (or from) the gallows were, as Douglas Hay shows, open at several points to influence and interest. But, since most prosecutions were privately initiated, they were open at the same points to pressure from the friends of the accused. Anonymous letters can be found which punctuate each stage. Thus, first of all, threats might be issued to intimidate a prosecutor before any action had commenced, or immediately afterwards, in the hope that the action would be withdrawn.[5] And there are

1. *LG* 10392 (February 1764).
2. See Cal Winslow, above, pp. 154–6. A Hackney surgeon received a letter commencing: 'Mr. toulmin this comes from a bloody gang of smuglers being lowe in cash and losing 3 horses within a fortnight therefore by god sir we insist upon your sending us 20 guineas. . .': *LG* 12118 (September 1780).
3. *LG* 11128 (March 1771).   4. *LG* 11521 (December 1774).
5. See e.g. *LG* 12095 (June 1780), 12107 (August 1780).

also many examples of over-officious, over-zealous or avaricious prosecutors (whether public officers or private persons) receiving admonitions. The Chairman of the Surrey Sessions incurred the hostility of debtors sheltering in the sanctuary of the Southwark Mint, and was addressed as 'an old over-grown unparallelled Monster of a Rogue! thou Spawn of fiery Dragons, Hell and Fury!'[1] The Collector of Excise in Bristol was ordered 'to sine no more Warrants' and 'P.S. Dont let Mr. Lion stand in the Pillory'.[2] When in 1776 the Mayor and justices of Norwich launched a campaign to prosecute the embezzlers of yarn they were warned to drop their proceedings or 'you Surtanly will be made to soufer in parson'.[3]

There followed threats to the magistrates, to judges and especially to witnesses: 'by the living eternal Christ I kill you if you appear against me as a witness. . .'[4] If the accused was convicted, threats might ensue directed at the prosecutor (to secure a pardon) or at the authorities (to set the convicted free). In 1810 a London employer received a note: 'I have been in the Country. I had a letter from my Friend that you have transported him and a Nother for 10 lb of Salt Peter. If I had known that you & your Cleark would have prosecuted them I would have put them & you & your Cleark out of the way I am determined on killing you both . . . if you dont Get them Both off.'[5] If prosecutor or informer were the recipients of blood-money they might be expected to be pursued more vigorously. In 1775 a London magistrate received this letter:

Sir we are sorry to be so troublesom but last night Jones was Cast for Death at the old Bayley on the account of generall fitzroys Robery which was brought to Light by Mr. Nickalls who gave the informeation. . . Now Mr. Nickalls is initled to the Reward of sixty guinnies upon that occasion now mr nickalls may Depend upon it for fact that he is not longer live er then the person that is under Sentence of death. . . for we are Determined to putt an end to Nickalls is days if he stays in this metrophelus for he only did it for the Sake of the mony.[6]

Such threats are likely only to have tightened the noose around the condemned's neck since, as Hay shows, the exercise of the prerogative of mercy was supported by an elaborate ideology which might allow mercy only to flow as an act of grace from above to the properly deferential supplicant. Threats at this stage were likely only to hasten execution: and perhaps for this reason they are uncommon. But once the process of law was completed, threats might be resumed. In smaller affairs, like

1 See *CJ*, vol. xx. pp 156–7 (February 1723).
2. *LG* 11793 (August 1776).
3. *LG* 11731 (December 1776).
4. *LG* 16341 (January 1810): see also 15017 (March 1798).
5. *LG* 16341 (February 1810).
6. *LG* 11569 (June 1775).

game prosecutions, this was common. After Rudston Calverley Rudston of Pocklington, East Yorks, had secured the conviction of four poachers in 1793 he was told: 'Rudston our mallis is too great to bear therefore if you don't think proper to Return all the young's men money again we shall fier and destroy everything you have and after that your life shall pay.'[1] In larger affairs, where the condemned was already executed or transported, little could be done. Several letters demand the instant cutting down and burial of a gibbeted felon.[2] And on occasion the prosecutor was followed by threats of revenge. In 1776 one Girdwood, himself at the time a prisoner in Newgate, wrote to the prosecutor of a friend:

Sir, I am sorry to find a gentleman like you would be guilty of taking Mac Allester's Life away for the sake of two or three guineas; but it will not be forgot by one who is but just come home to revenge his cause... I follow the road, though I have been out of London; but on receiving a letter from Mac Allester before he died, for to seek revenge, I am come to town...

Girdwood was detected, since he passed his letter by way of a woman who sold provisions at the prison gates. He was convicted, an appeal was disallowed, and he was executed.[3]

Even small-time blackmailers tried to present themselves as one of a 'gang' or confederacy; those who wrote in support of more general grievances presented themselves as one of a confederacy thirty or ninety or several thousand strong, bound by most solemn oaths to revenge their wrongs. Where smugglers or food rioters or illegal trade combinations were involved, those threats had teeth in them. After food riots in Norwich in 1766, in Halifax in 1770, in Staffordshire and Nottingham in 1800, the authorities were warned to free or respite sentence on their prisoners on pain of retribution. At Norwich sixteen men 'are all sworne by a terrible great Oath' to burn the houses of the great: 'the 16 Men then have gott 80 baggs made of thick paper fill'd with Pitch and Brimstone ty'd up with a Salt Peter match at the mouth of them these we are to cram into Windows houses and Woodstacks the night that any of the Prisoners is hang'd...' But hanged several of the prisoners were. The Staffordshire magistrates received an eloquent letter, threatening them with murder and arson:

... for Wee are determined thay shall not be confined nor no one els for the same cause witch is only bread and that Wee will fight for to the last drop of our

1. PRO, HO 42.27, fo. 722.
2. e.g. *LG* 9327 (October 1753). Archdeacon Robert Oliver of Preston was told that he 'and havery Clergymans that his in this Town' were 'Nothing but Heriticks and damned Souls if William Whittle that Worthy Man Angs up 10 dayes you may fully Expect to be blown to Damnation': *LG* 10616 (April 1766).
3. *R.* v. *Girdwood*, 1 Leach 142.

blood the heads of this Nation in general vialans and cause a famine among the poar whilst they themselves live in plenty. O Bread Bread Bread is the cry of poor Children and you have suffered the prise to go beyond our reach Wee desire printed Hand Bills to be put out concerning this Letter what you intend to do for we are either for War and Peace.[1]

The only reply which the author received was, of course, an advertisement in the *Gazette* offering a pardon for information leading to his apprehension, and £170 reward. Such advertisements were also inserted in the local press and were often circulated additionally as handbills or as placarded proclamations. In matters of general social grievance, this gave publicity to a curious kind of dialogue between the authorities and the crowd. Gazetting was actually courted as a means of publicity, and many authors clearly pondered their best rhetorical flourishes with the care of an author sending his first work to the press. The Mayor of Chester was addressed in 1767: 'God Damn you blood, your house shall be burnt down very soon if you dont look after the Markets better': 'Put this in the News Paper'.[2] A letter from Stourbridge in the same year threatening to have all the gaols and prisons down with a force of upwards of 2,000 armed men concluded: 'Mr. Rabley we Desire you to put in the Birmingham Gazzette . . . if you dwo not gazzette it upon our World we'l have [your house] down.'[3]

In this aim some of the authors succeeded. An interesting example of this dialogue can be seen in an episode of the long struggle over prices conducted by the Spitalfields weavers in the 1760s and 1770s. The 1760s saw a long campaign of threatening notes to non-compliant weavers or masters, the destruction of silk in the looms, and so on. In 1770 several of the silk-cutters were tried at the Old Bailey on capital charges, and were executed.[4] In April 1771 the leading Crown evidence, a pattern-drawer named Daniel Clark, was seen by two weavers in Shoreditch, assaulted, chased from one refuge after another by a growing crowd, dragged and beaten through several streets in Shoreditch and Spitalfields, thrown into a pond in Hare Street Field, and there stoned to death. There followed a campaign of advertisement and counter-advertisement. The King offered a reward of £100 for the conviction of Clark's assailants. In reply David Wilmot, an active Bethnal Green magistrate, received a letter

1. Norwich, *LG* 10690 (December 1766): see also Appendix III (*f*) and (*g*) and *R.* v. *Royce*, 4 Burr. 2073; Halifax, *LG* 11038 (April 1770); Staffordshire and Nottingham, *LG* 1800, p. 475 (May 1800).

2. *LG* 10720 (April 1767).

3. *LG* 10713 (March 1767); WO 1.873; see also Appendix III (*b*).

4. For documents illustrating the long conflict of the Spitalfields silk workers, see *Calendar of Home Office Papers of the Reign of George III*, 1878, vol. I, pp. 312–13, vol. III, pp. 273–4, vol. IV, pp. 39–43.

signed 'One of ten Thousand': 'You Scoundrel the Fellow we kill'd on Tuesday swore away the Life of my dearest friend and if he had had a thousand Lives I would with pleasure have taken them and if you attempt to take his part as you seem to do by your Advertisement you may depend upont that You & Family shall not exist one Month longer. . .' The author had clearly studied the models of such letters which the *Gazette* from time to time published, for he concluded: 'I shall not swear about it as is the usual Stile of these Letters but if you can believe any thing thats True take my word for this'. Wilmot duly advertised this letter and offered a reward for information leading to its author. Thus encouraged the writer sent, four days later, a letter of three times the length, with a fuller defence of those who had lynched Clark, 'that detestable late Object of their revenge who was thirsting after their Blood not thro' any motive of Justice but mearly for Reward': 'We are now satisfied having put an End to the existence of that Monster in human Shape, the fear of whom kept several famillies in a starving Condition by keeping them from their principal Support thro the Apprehension of being Informed against.' 'Know this Busy Villain,' Justice Wilmot was warned, 'that tis not the greatest Reward in the Kings gift that shall either be the means of Detecting or Deterring the writer of these Letters and his Associates in this Affair, from pursuing with insatiable & heart felt Revenge their Designs against You. . . P.S. you may now apply to the King for a larger reward and try to what Purpose it will be.'[1]

It is clear at least that the advertisements in the *Gazette* or the local press found attentive readers among the crowd; and that individuals in the crowd saw in these a possible means of expressing grievances and demands. It is not possible, at this level of analysis, to make much more of the genus. Private blackmail is an offence found in any literate society. While the predominance of private prosecution in the eighteenth century gave some openings to pressure, through menaces, upon prosecutor and witnesses, it cannot be shown that this pressure was generally effective; and threats directed against the courts or against the authorities were likely to defeat their ends. Letters of this kind offer a pathetic and ineffectual counterpoint to the real exchanges of influence and interest passing between the great. It is only in specific contexts of conflict – smuggling, agrarian unrest, illicit trade union activity or massive social protest – that such letters acquire importance. And here they may sometimes be seen as intrinsic to proto-democratic forms of organization, deeply characteristic of eighteenth-century social and economic relations.

1. *LG* 11136 and 11138 (April 1771). The first Spitalfields letter to be gazetted is in no. 10354 (October 1763).

IV

In a prescriptive society which, in myth if not in actuality, rested upon relations of paternalism and deference, domination and subordination, there were very many reasons why men might wish to remain anonymous. It is by no means the case that anonymity was the refuge of the poor alone. Even the gentleman, certainly the professional man, might wish to gain the ear of authority without offending an influential neighbour. Research into eighteenth-century archives gives one a sense of double vision. Among the estate papers of nobility and great gentry there are the obsequious letters of the surveyors, tradesmen, attorneys, petitioners for favour. But in the state papers we seem to meet a society of creeps and informers. Throughout the eighteenth century a percentage of the Secretary of State's in-coming mail was anonymous.

Even highly sophisticated proposals for the public good – relating to taxes, the regulation of markets, the poor laws, the excise – might be unsigned.[1] For even these might imply a criticism of some local figure of influence. More delicate matters – fingering a gentleman who was a papist or suspected Jacobite, exposing corruption in some public office – nearly always came through the post unsigned. Often an elaborate ritual of seeking protection in advance of disclosure then followed. The author, promising information on some racket, would sign his letter with initials; the Secretary of State would then advertise in the *Gazette* that if 'R.S.' would come forward at a definite time and place with further information he would be promised indemnity and perhaps a reward; a meeting might then take place. In the press and the public reviews the same wars of insinuation and character assassination took place under pseudonyms. The free-born Englishman crept about in a mask and folded in a Guy Fawkes cloak.

If this was so even among the higher orders, anonymity was of the essence of any early form of industrial or social protest. The threat of victimization was ever-present; the shelter which the community could afford to the known rebel against the vindictiveness of 'interest' was scanty; the consequences of victimization, over the whole life of the victim, were total. Hence on scores of issues, throughout the eighteenth century and well into the nineteenth, the only protest that can be known is this minatory anonymous 'voice of the poor'. In the earlier decades of the eighteenth century one finds expressions of popular Jacobitism

1. A large parcel of such anonymous communications received by Robert Harley, the Earl of Oxford, in the first decades of the eighteenth century can be found in Brit. Mus. Portland Loan 29.11.

(although this favoured the ballad or the whistled air rather than the articulate letter), or the virulent 'true blues' of Taunton: 'Every damned Wiggish Scoundrel that does not Vote for Popham shall have his Throat cut by Christmas Day next.'[1] By 1811 one finds premature 'Swing' letters such as the one from labourers at Early Court near Reading: 'Blood and Vengeance against Your Life and Your Property for taking away our Labour with Your Threshing Machine . . . if You do not refrain . . . we will Thresh Your Ricks with Fire & Bathe Your Body in Blood. How will the People of Reading Gase To see Early Court all in a Blase.'[2] In between one can sample every grievance of the times: the press-gang, militia ballot, corrupt local courts, electoral scandals, customary rights, the licensing of alehouses.

The letters fall into two groups: those addressed to the rich, the authorities, employers; and those addressed to fellow workmen or to 'the crowd'. Until the 1790s the first group is very much the largest, although perhaps all that we can say is that these were the ones most often preserved and gazetted, since scribbled threats or hieroglyphs wrapped around bricks and thrown into workshops or thrust under the cottage doors of blacklegs were less likely to be advertised or kept in any archive.[3] After 1790 the second group enlarges: but we are now often seeing less a letter than a hand-written placard or a handbill. And those in the first group may be divided in the same way also, some being addressed to the rich or to the gentry of the area and perhaps posted up on a church door or by the market cross, others directed at particular individuals. The great majority of both kinds adopt a similar tone and manner of address, distinguished by the collective pronoun 'we'. What is offered is rarely a personal grievance, but the common sense of injustice of the poor as a whole. And the style appears to impose some controls upon the authors: they do indeed attempt to present not the personal but the collective grievance. It is this which gives exceptional interest to these documents. One can rarely prove that any letter indicates general protest rather than the voice of a

1. *LG* 10724 (April 1767).

2. *LG* 1811, p. 1760 (September 1811).

3. D. J. V. Jones in *Before Rebecca*, 1973, p. 99, quotes excellent examples of these (sometimes decorated with sketches of red bulls etc.) within the context of the 'Scotch Cattle' in the South Wales coal-and-iron 'black domain'; and he comments (p. 100) on their extreme effectiveness in precipitating strikes, intimidating blacklegs, and so on. Very much the same effectiveness probably prevailed in the 1760s in the Spitalfields silk industry and in the West of England woollen industry around 1800. Such warnings (and occasionally those directed to gentry or employers) were sometimes accompanied by the hideous emphasis of blood-smears on the paper, a dead bird or beast on the doorstep, or even the heart of a slaughtered beast: see e.g., Yeovil, 1816, PRO, HO 42.150; E. P. Thompson, 'The Moral Economy of the English Crowd in the Eighteenth Century', *Past and Present*, 50 (February 1971), p. 135.

crank: one is left to judge by the 'feel' of the letter, its style, the particularization of grievances, as well as by the evidence of supporting actions – riot or rattening. Such evidence comes, with regularity, to hand.

With so many grievances to choose among we will limit our concern to three distinct contexts: letters concerned with industrial conflict: those arising within an agrarian context: and finally the largest group of letters and handbills – those concerned with price and food riots, which pass, in 1795 and 1800, into 'jacobinical' sedition.

Letters in the first group arise from many contexts, but most belong clearly to that of early illicit trade unionism, with its summary enforcements: the destruction of the tools or materials of blacklegs or of masters taking unapprenticed men, the intimidation of opponents.[1] The Master Shipwright at Chatham, in 1764, was addressed:

Mr Allen

Blackguard – for Gentleman I cannot call you it have wrote to lett You know without You are beter to the Shipwrights and all the Yard in genurl You will be very soon Nock't out of the Book of Life. . . You are like the rich Man wich refused to give Lazarus the Crums which fell from his tabel. . .[2]

In 1763 London master shoemakers and hosiers were threatened unless they met demands for prices: 'Damn you you are worst than a highwayman for you bete down prises.'[3] In the late 1780s such letters came from London shoemakers, Lancashire calico-printers and weavers in Glasgow, Manchester and Newbury.[4] 'A Good Jurni-man Shoemaker' addressed a master thus: 'You damd Insignificant Proud Impearias Rascal your are detested by every one that Works for you . . . But I hope Soone to put an end to your pride by Eluminateing the Neighbourhood you live in . . . and if possible would Shove your damd Litle Self in to the midst of the Flames. . .'[5] In 1794 the following notice was put under the door of the Blanket Weavers Company's hall at Witney: 'This is to inform you Sirs that here is an agreement made betwene some Men that whoever will not give the gurnimen weavers the two pence . . . take Care of your Selves or you will die and wat a thing to die for opressing the poor.'[6]

Machine-breaking or industrial arson was nearly always accompanied by letters. A group of such letters comes in the 1780s and 1790s, from the

---

1. The letters can be placed in the context defined so clearly by E. J. Hobsbawm in 'The Machine Breakers', *Past and Present*, 1 (1952) and *Labouring Men*, 1963.
2. *LG* 10398 (February 1764).
3. *LG* 10287 and 10288 (February 1763).
4. See Appendix II (*a*), (*b*) and (*c*).
5. *LG* 12854 (May 1787).
6. *LG* 13723 (October 1794).

Lancashire cotton industry, with the calico-printers prominent.[1] The most vigorous series comes, between 1799 and 1803, from the West of England shearmen and clothing workers, in their Luddite resistance to the introduction of gig-mills. The threats were directed equally against employers and against workers who defied the shearmen's regulations: 'The Jurneymen Shearmen of Bradford Trowbridge Melksham Chipinham Calne and Devizes: Have a Greed to Pay you 4 that are at work . . . if you dont leve of you may expect Shearmens Law; that is to be Cuartered. And Your flesh and Bones Burnt and your aishes Blown away with the weend I send this as a frind. . .'[2] Such threats (as in the better-documented Luddism of the Midlands and the North in 1811–13[3]) were given added terror by repeated actions, usually against property rather than person.[4]

The letters from an agrarian context, or from the small market-town, commenced early – the 'Blacks' in the forests of Berkshire and Hampshire were using them in 1723 – and, as a means of mass pressure, continued longest: the 'Swing' letters of 1830 provided one climax, but similar letters accompanied arson in East Anglia in the 1840s and 1850s. They are some of the saddest examples of the genus, especially those written in the nineteenth century – the testimony of men driven to fury by the humiliations of the poor law, low wages, the abuse of charities. The eighteenth-century examples are often more complex, turning upon questions of common right, enclosure, gleaning, local customs. A few are the carefully drawn assertions of the claims of the poor. We cannot prove that these are typical; but since they are among the only surviving articulate testaments of millions of the supposedly inarticulate, they deserve particular attention. The best examples, such as the letter from 'the Combined' of Cheshunt (1799) and that to the 'Gentlemen of Ashill' (1816),[5] rank as important social documents.

Some nine of the gazetted letters bear upon enclosure or common rights.

1. e.g. *LG* 1785, p. 586 (December 1785); 12720 (January 1786); 1786, p. 203 (Glasgow weavers, April 1786); 1792, p. 191 (March 1792).

2. *LG* 1802, p. 386 (April 1802): see also Appendix II (*d*).

3. Good examples of Luddite letters can be found in W. B. Crump, *The Leeds Woollen Industry, 1780–1820*, Leeds, 1931, pp. 229–30 (the West Riding); J. Russell, 'The Luddites', *Transactions of the Thoroton Society*, X (1906), pp. 53–62 (Nottingham); E. P. Thompson, *The Making of the English Working Class*, Harmondsworth (1968), esp. pp. 607–8, 620, 626, 639, 643–4, 658, 784. See also Appendix II (*e*) to (*h*).

4. See e.g. *LG* 1802, p. 1047 (September 1802) listing offences committed in the disturbed district in the summer of 1802, including arson of ricks, interception of carts and cutting up of cloth, firing of guns into houses, armed attacks upon gig-mills, destruction of machinery and arson of buildings.

5. For the Cheshunt letter, see Appendix I (*d*); for the Ashill letter, see A. J. Peacock, *Bread or Blood*, 1965, pp. 65–6.

During resistance to the enclosure of Holland Fen near Boston (Lincs) in 1769 one promoter of enclosure was warned: 'Mr Barlow as you have been one of the Head Injeneyers consarning hollandfen and you used the utmost of your power in geting the Rogish Act of Parleyment to take poors Right from them by Force and fraud ... this is but the Binining of Sorows...' The letters were delivered with gunshot through the windows, accompanied by the destruction of fences, arson of stacks, and shooting at cattle. One was signed: 'An open fen for Ever'.[1]

Any large-scale continuous resistance to enclosure was likely to be accompanied by letters. But, until the nineteenth century when labourers in many areas were reduced to a general level of poverty, the grievances would include those of small-holders or tenant farmers, petty graziers, townsmen with an interest in the local common. A comprehensive letter from Bicester in 1800 attacked the gentry for giving poor pay, the Volunteers, the farmers, millers, bakers, shopkeepers, hog-killers, and concluded with a protest against enclosure and the loss of winter threshing: 'these Justices and Gentlemen have enclosed the Fields and the cause of laying down the flails The Devil will Whip them into Helltails.'[2] A letter from Hungerford in 1763 denounced the misappropriation of moneys which should have come to the poor from the letting of town lands: 'wome You will You kepe alive and whom You will You starve to death and home You will You fatt up and home You will You put dound and now Your harts is Liftied up In Pride and You nowe that thare is no Law for a pore man but If this is not alteard I will Turn Jusstis my salfe...'[3] In 1780 the grievance was still burning: the 'Gentealman Consteable an Free holders' of Hungerford were again accused of taking 'the Pores Wright away' and of failing to pay for the 'dad Comins' (presumably the 'dead' or unused grazing-rights on the common which should have been let for charity).[4]

There were other centres which appear to have had an epistolary tradition of long standing; or perhaps the magistrates in these villages and towns had a tradition of taking notice of letters. At Petworth (Sussex) demonstrations against prices took place in 1790, and copies of an eloquent rhyming manifesto were stuck to the church door, the whipping-post and elsewhere.[5] In 1795 a miller was warned that his mill would be pulled down, for 'you Millers and Fammers one all agreed to starve us poor ... what you can think of yourself we do not know.'[6] And during the 'Swing' riots of 1830, William Stovolt was warned: 'Gentlemen, take care of you cattle and yourselve for we are resolved to burn down the house of Mr. S.

---

1. *LG* 10960 (July 1769); 10964 (July 1769); 11027 (March 1770).
2. See Appendix III (*j*).   3. *LG* 10287 (January 1763).
4. *LG* 12191 (May 1781).   5. See Appendix IV (*a*).
6. *LG* 1795, p. 192 (December 1794).

an perhaps whole of Petwort for when we begin God knows what the end may be for we think Petworth have had it rain long enough. . .'[1]

'When the Spirit of Riot gets into a People,' a pamphleteer noted in 1739, 'No one knows the Consequence. The *Mob* had already got this *Maxim*, "That *Adam* made no *Will*; they are his Sons, and ought to have a Share of their Father's Possessions".'[2] Hence in any general episode of agrarian disturbance or of food riot, a score of grievances come to the surface in these letters, supported upon a general levelling sentiment. This is true of the riot years of 1766, 1795, and 1800–1801; of the East Anglian disturbances of 1816; of the 'Swing' riots of 1830 and their aftermath of arson in the 1840s. One commonly thinks of the 'Rebecca' riots of the 1840s as being directed, in the main, against turnpikes; but in fact Rebecca, in her letters, proposed to settle decades of particular and of general accounts. These might affect the general rights of the tenantry[3] or very particular offences committed by individuals: the spoiling of a salmon river, the failure to maintain illegitimate children, or (in an indictment of the Vicar of Eglwyserow, Cardiganshire), he 'Feeds his sheep in this church yard with the grass growing in the putrifaction of human bodies these sheep are afterwards slaughtered for our Market at Cardigan and we have . . . been made canibals without our knowledge.' His horses grazed over the tombstones and broke them; he was encroaching on common land; and had seized a chapel built by the Methodists.[4]

What marks out the agrarian letter in England, certainly after 1790 (and sometimes before), is its universal resort to the threat of arson. The threat was often carried into effect: indeed, the letter was sometimes found at the scene of the fire. Arson is so terrible and indiscriminate a crime, to the urban mind, that historians have scarcely bothered to consider this tactic of protest: first sympathy and then attention is withdrawn. But in a situation in which the gentry and the employing farmers held a total control over the life of the labourer and his family, and in which (as in 1816 and 1830) open and non-violent manifestations of protest met with executions and transportations, it is difficult to envisage what other forms of protest

1. Letter in QO/EW51, East Sussex RO, cited in Monju Dutt, 'The Agricultural Labourers' Revolt of 1830 in Kent, Surrey and Sussex', PhD Thesis, unpublished, London University, 1966, p. 375.

2. 'Philalethes' [William Temple], *The Case as it now stands between the Clothiers, Weavers, and other Manufacturers, with regard to the late Riot in the County of Wilts*, 1739, p. 37.

3. See Appendix I (*h*).

4. Letter received by E. Lloyd Hall, 25 August 1843, in PRO, HO 45.454 (ii), fo. 468. See also H. T. Evans, *Rebecca and her Daughters*, Cardiff, 1910, pp. 34–5; 68–9; 194–5.

were left.[1] Rural arson was rarely indiscriminate, almost never took human life, and very rarely took the lives of stock. It was directed, first, at the cornstack and the hayrick: next at the outhouse or barn. Since the cornstack represented a substantial part of the farmer's capital, his profit on the year's product, it was the point at which he was most vulnerable. It may be true that arson was a futile and counter-productive act, but the case has been assumed, not submitted to any test of evidence.

A most 'melancholy' letter from the Rector of a Hampshire village terrorized in this way (under peculiar circumstances) in 1729 gives an insight into the 'deplorable condition' into which the inhabitants could be reduced: 'Our farmers, labourers, and servants are all worn out with toil, fear & watching; and as oft as night returns we are all under the dreadful apprehension of having our houses & barns fired . . . of our corn being consumed and . . . of our selves and families perishing in the flames.'[2] Examples of communities or of individuals living in the shadow of such terror were sufficiently numerous in eighteenth- and early-nineteenth-century Britain for a threat to carry conviction. Rural employers, overseers and guardians of the poor, administrators of charities, game-preservers and game-keepers – none of these can have been indifferent to the counter-terror of the poor.

When we turn to the largest group of gazetted letters – those dealing with food prices and marketing practices – a functional explanation may be offered with more confidence. Until we come to the years of Luddism, 'Swing' and of Rebecca, undoubtedly the *annus mirabilis* for threatening letters was 1800. The more than thirty seditious letters gazetted in that year come at the end of an established tradition, which appears in every year of widespread food riot. Only one such letter was gazetted in 1756 (to a mealman in Newbury: 'if you don't stop carrin the Flower to Bristoll we will knock you . . . in the Head'[3]), eleven in 1766, seven in 1767, two in 1772, only one in the great food-riot year of 1795, eight in 1796.

Many of these were less letters than notices or handbills, which served the double purpose of menacing the rich and advertising grievances and intentions to riot among the crowd. The tradition – a notice posted on a

1. Cf. Raymond Williams, *The Country and the City*, 1973, pp. 184–5; on incendiary letters compare A. Abbiateci, 'Les incendiaires dans la France du XVIIIᵉ Siècle', *Annales E.S.C.*, xxv, (i) (January–February 1970), pp. 229–48.

2. PRO, SP 36.14 (i), fo. 125. See E. P. Thompson, *Whigs and Hunters*, Allen Lane, 1975, chap. 10.

3. *LG* 9613 (August 1756). Such letters were certainly being written in the high-price years 1740 and 1753: see e.g. *Newcastle Journal*, 28 June 1740, reporting the committal of a man at Swaffham Bulbeck (Cambridgeshire) for sending an anonymous letter to a miller threatening to fire his mills if the price of flour did not fall; and for an example in 1753 see Newcastle papers, Brit. Mus. Add. MSS 32,732, fo. 353.

church door – goes back until at least the early years of the seventeenth century.[1] Although grievances against particular millers, dealers, and so on, are often mentioned, the notices are addressed either to fellow labourers or to the local rich in general.

The appendix to this chapter includes a sampling of these letters. The production of such letters was so habitual (in times of dearth and high prices), the grievances expressed are so authentic, they are so often accompanied by the action of price-regulation or 'riot', and they appear in so many parts of the country that it would be ludicrous to suggest that they are the work of 'cranks'. I have already discussed their function in the pattern of food riot, where it can sometimes be shown that their appearance was an effective signal to the authorities to attempt to restrain prices, to regulate the markets, to institute subsidies or activate charities, in anticipation of riot.[2] In this sense we may say that the letter or handbill was well understood by both parties in the market conflict, as one element within a regular and ritualized code of behaviour; it was ignored by the authorities at their peril.

Hence it is within this code that the letters must be read. Their intent is serious, but it may not be taken too literally. If on occasion before 1760 the crowd employed Jacobite threat ('we are wishing that our exiled King could . . . send some Officers'[3]), we need not take this as evidence of active Jacobite organization: this is simply the threat thought most likely to send the Whig authorities into a panic. If large boasts are made as to confederacy, thousands of men under oaths, and so on ('there is . . . 3 thousand all ready to fight & I'll be damd if we don't make the King's Army to shite'[4]), we need not suppose such formal confederacy, arming or oath-taking to be true. This is an anonymous literary *genre*: unlike the agrarian letter which often led to the performance of exactly what was threatened (arson), this kind of letter gave rise not to insurrection, mass arson and murder (as promised) but to controlled price-fixing action, or retaliatory action against millers and dealers, in which there was scarcely ever arson or bloodshed.

This is, indeed, one part of the interest and sometimes of the grim and conscious humour of these letters. The authors, evidently, were racking

1. *Calendar State Papers* (*Domestic*), 1630, p. 387.

2. See 'The Moral Economy of the English Crowd in the Eighteenth Century', *Past and Present*, 50 (February 1971), pp. 76–136, esp. the case from Sherborne (Dorset) examined on pp. 125–6.

3. See Appendix III (*a*). For the place of such letters within the 'theatre' and 'counter theatre' of eighteenth-century society, see my 'Patrician Society, Plebeian Culture', *Journal of Social History*, vol. 7, no. 4, Summer 1974, pp. 382–405.

4. Enclosure in PRO, WO 1.873, fos. 505–10; Appendix III (*b*); *LG* 10713 (March 1767).

their brains and embellishing their style in the hope of striking maximum terror into the minds of the great – the great whom they often knew well, and to whom they deferred meekly in the daylight street. The letter from Middleton in 1762 and that from the miners of Clee Hill (Shropshire)[1] give us the mode, as does the paper of 1767 'lately thrown into a Person's House at Kidderminster':

This is to give Notis to badgers and fore Stallers of grain that there as Been sum in perticular a wocheing your Motions and ther whill Be in a wicks time some men Com ought of the Colepits by Nigt to Meak fire brans of all the abitations of the foretallers of grain but the best way to seave your selves seet the Cryer to work hand sell of all your Stock to the Poor at a Reasonable Reat. . .[2]

The demand (to send round the crier and sell off stock to the poor at a reasonable rate) was by no means a utopian one: exactly such measures, to subsidize corn, were a customary response of the authorities to dearth. This letter was very probably the product of some collective, since similar papers 'have lately been stuck up in many parts' of Kidderminster.

Until the 1790s the letters, while often levelling in tone, were directed at the particular marketing and pricing grievances of the time, with reference often to particular dealers or millers. The letters from Norwich and Swansea in 1766 and Carlisle in 1783 are good examples.[3] Norwich had active and eloquent correspondents. The gruff letter cited in the appendix was followed by flowery productions, in which the author represented himself as one of 'a select body' sworn to fire the city:

The City had been of a flame last night . . . but I used all the Eloquence I was Master of and got leave to write to you which is the last time I can intercede on your behalf. . . If you have a mind to save the City and yourself Immediately on Saturday Morning alter the price of most Eatables for the present – in the interim I'll do all I durst to prevail upon them which will be impossible without such an Alteration. . .[4]

Whether the author of this letter correctly judged the psychology of his correspondents may be in question. But there can be little doubt that the authors of a letter affixed to the pillory post in Salisbury market in 1767 judged the mentality of its recipients well (see next page).

The letters of 1795 and afterwards continue to list particular grievances and to threaten identifiable men. But the seditious or levelling threats become more general and, while they remain theatrical, suggest some

1. See Appendix III (*c*) and (*d*).
2. *LG* 10710 (March 1767).
3. See Appendix III (*d*), (*f*) and (*g*); and (for Carlisle) my 'Moral Economy', op. cit., p. 99.
4. *LG* 10671 (October 1766) and 10690 (December 1766); Appendix III (*g*).

Gentleman farmers

Farmers taek nodist form This time be fore It is to let

Be fore Christ mus Day sum of you will be as Poore as we if you Will not seel Cheper

This is two let you no We have stoel a Sheep, For which the resson Was be Cass you sold your Whet so dear and if you Will not loer pries of your Whet we will Com by night and set fiear to your Barns and Reecks gentleman Farm mers we be in Arnest now and That you will find to your sorrow soon.[1]

more serious underground culture of Painites or of 'Jacobins'. Chalking on the walls and pavements, which had certainly been known in London from at least the time of Wilkes, became a far more serious means of propaganda during the French Wars. James Bisset, a Birmingham reformer, noted in his reminiscences that the first chalking which he noticed on the walls of the town were in the 1780s, directed against the brutal flogging of soldiers in the Wiltshire militia. He composed a poem about wall-writing, compiled from 'actual memorandums taken at the time'. In 1791 (at the time of the Priestley Riots) there was 'Church and King', 'No Paine!' and 'Damn the Jacobins'. But by the mid-1790s:

> . . . When trade was quite ruin'd, & ev'rything dead
> The walls teem'd with horror, they wrote 'blood or bread'.
> The tables began to seem turning apace:
> 'Church & King' was rubb'd off & gallows they'd trace,
> Instead of 'No Foxites', 'No Priestley', 'No Paine'
> They next wrote 'No Portland', no damned rogues in grain;
> Fresh inscriptions each day on the buildings were seen:
> 'No Badgers', 'No War', and 'Damn Pitt' too I ween,
> 'No King, Lords or Commons', 'Large Loaves', 'Revolution',
> 'No Taxes', 'No Tythes', but a 'Free Constitution.'[2]

1. *LG* 10784 (November 1767).
2. James Bisset, 'Reminiscences' (Birmingham Reference Library, MS 263924), pp. 74, 153-4. Compare W. Villers and others (Staffordshire magistrates in the neighbourhood of Birmingham) to Portland, 3 October 1800, PRO, HO 42.52, fos. 364-5: 'Inscriptions are constantly making on the Walls and Public buildings exciting to revolt. The King's Proclamation posted up together with the Bills offering rewards for the discovery of the Authors of the seditious papers have been stain'd with a kind of paint resembling Blood. . .'

In the 'underground' years after 1795 the writing of a number of identical handbills was organized in some large reform centres, and the Spenceans adopted the means of propaganda through wall-chalking.[1] But the seditious letters scattered across the whole country in 1800 were almost certainly the work of freelance Painites, supported by a popular ground-swell of food riots and anti-war sentiment. From Hitchin: 'Come forth with courage and reselution if you give way to those Villins you allways be bound under theise changs [chains] . . . our Soupmaker may come with doctrine of fine speecheis as keeping a cleen house and the Wife to give a smile send him to where hee come from. . .'[2] From Clare (Suffolk): 'Gentl men . . . if you do not give the men more wags [wages] for thair time i will Be damd if we do not make france of it.'[3] From Wakefield: 'Damn your old Methodist soul we will bring it down you a Constable damn your eyes . . . if you do stint us to a quartern loaf take care of your life damn King George the third and Billy Pitt . . . damn your Red herrins Potatoes . . . May England fall like dew to the ground and Jacobings ever florish. . .'[4] It is clear enough from the alarmed tone of the covering letters of the magistrates who sent in to the Home Secretary such productions that they had often found their mark. When a clergyman in Ramsbury (Wiltshire) had to copy a paper found affixed to a tree in the centre of his parish and signed 'God Save the Poor & down with George III' he could scarcely keep his hand from trembling: 'Such my Lord are the Contents of a Paper, which chills me with Horror whilst I transcribe it.'[5]

It was against such chilling papers as these that Hannah More and her friends took up their pens. The seditious note which entered in the 1790s was never extinguished: it was to revive in every context in which open agitation brought the danger of persecution and victimization – notably in the Luddite years, in 1816–20, and in a context of agrarian protest. If the anonymous letter and handbill became infrequent in other contexts after 1830, this was because it had been displaced by the Radical or Chartist printing-press.

1. See Thompson, *The Making of the English Working Class*, p. 177.
2. *LG* 1800, p. 202 (February 1800).
3. *LG* 1800, p. 1308 (November 1800).
4. *LG* 1800, p. 1454 (December 1800).
5. Rev. Edward Meyrick to Portland, 12 June 1800 (and enclosure) PRO, HO 42.50. For the letter, see 'Moral Economy', op. cit., p. 128.

V

For most of the period under review the writing of such letters was a capital offence. It was not only a crime but an extremely serious crime, and the gazetting of letters (with attendant pardons and rewards) was an index of the gravity with which they were regarded. Such letters were normally described as 'incendiary', because they commonly threatened arson. Those who wrote them, delivered them, circulated them, or were accomplice to any of these actions risked their lives.

The writing of threatening letters might of course be an offence within common law (as conspiracy), or come within the terms of seditious libel or of defamation.[1] The offence appears to have first come under the particular attention of the legislature in the Black Act (1723), by which any person who 'shall knowingly send any letter without any name' (or with fictitious names) 'demanding money, venison, or other valuable thing' became guilty of felony without benefit of clergy.[2] The terms of this act appear to have led to some uncertainty: were offenders guilty who threatened but who did not demand money or venison?[3] By 27 Geo. II c. 15 (1754) the definition was extended. Corn riots had occurred in 1753, and the preamble to the new act stated: 'Whereas divers letters have been sent to several of his Majesty's subjects threatening their lives or burning their houses, which letters not demanding money, venison, or valuable effects, are not subject to the penalties of the said act . . .' (the Black Act), the authors of letters threatening murder, or the arson of 'houses, out-houses, barns, stacks of corn or grain, hay or straw' became equally guilty. In 1757 a further act was passed, directed against blackmailers, who threatened to accuse any person of crimes with a view to extorting money: but the penalty for this offence was only seven years' transportation. The position remained like this for some seventy years, until 1823, when the capital sentence entailed by the first three acts was reduced to a maximum sentence of transportation for life. This was fortunate for the 'Swing' letter-writers of 1830.[4]

1. See 11 Mod. Rep. 137, for *R.* v. *Woodward* (1707) and the judgement of Holt, C. J.: 'every extortion is an actual trespass'.

2. 9 Geo. I c. 22.

3. Under 12 Geo. I c. 34 (1727) workmen writing threatening letters to masters in the woollen industry were liable to seven years' transportation: this act was extended by 22 Geo. II c. 27 to workmen in the felt, hat, silk, mohair, fur, hemp, flax, linen, cotton, fustian, iron or leather industries.

4. For the state of the law before repeal, see E. H. Hyde, *Treatise of Pleas of the Crown*, 1803, vol. II, pp. 1104–26; for the position at repeal, see Radzinowicz, vol. I, p. 641, and *The Charge of . . . Baron Vaughan . . . at the Special Commission at Winchester*, December 1830, pp. 13–14.

I have no figures which would indicate the number of commitals or convictions for these offences in the eighteenth century. Some figures for the early nineteenth century exist, and these suggest that committals were few and that there was an unusually high rate of acquittals. Thus from 1810 to 1818 – years of industrious letter-writing, which take in Luddism, the East Anglian disturbances of 1816, post-war radical unrest – we have:

	1810	1811	1812	1813	1814	1815	1816	1817	1818[1]
Committals	3	—	5	2	1	2	2	1	1
Acquittals	2	—	2	—	—	1	1	1	1
Convictions	1	—	3	2	1	2	1	—	—

Figures are much the same over the next ten years: 1820 saw 6 committals and 2 convictions (both death sentences), and 1824 (the year after the ending of the death penalty) saw 7 committals and, again, 2 convictions. No other years saw so many committals. The rise in these after 1828 is significant:

	1828	1829	1830	1831	1832	1833	1834	1835	1836	1837[2]
Committals	3	4	4	62	6	12	11	15	7	3
No bills } Acquittals }	2	2	3	38	2	5	6	10	7	1
Convictions	1	2	1	24	4	7	5	5	—	2

While no accurate figure can be offered, there is no evidence from any year of the eighteenth century as to either committals or convictions running at a rate which even approaches that of 1831 – the aftermath of the 'Last Labourers' Revolt'. This is an offence whose incidence evades all quantification: it must remain a 'dark figure'.[3]

What remains is this case or that which research has brought (or will bring) to light from assize records or the press. The very high ratio of offences to committals arises from the extreme difficulty in detecting the offender – a difficulty much greater in letters of social protest than in

1. *PP*, 1819, VIII, pp. 125 *et seq.*

2. *PP*, 1826–7, XIX, pp. 187 *et seq.*; 1831–2, XIX; 1835, XLV. E. J. Hobsbawm and George Rudé, *Captain Swing*, 1969, find (in 1830–31) forty-two names of men and women brought to trial from twenty-two counties for writing 'Swing' letters. Thirteen only of these were convicted, of whom six were transported (p. 241).

3. In 1723, when the Black Act was passed, threatening messages were frequently sent in the disturbed areas of Berkshire and Hampshire: but I have found evidence of only two prosecutions. (See *Whigs and Hunters, passim.*) I have checked both the press and assize records in other periods of peak letter-writing (e.g. 1766–7, 1800) and have found scarcely any prosecutions. But evidence as to a continuing trickle of prosecutions is provided by case law: see East, op. cit., pp. 1104–26: e.g. Jepson and Springett's case (Essex, 1798), John Heming's case (Warwickshire, 1799): also pp. 334–6 below.

blackmail cases, since the blackmailer was vulnerable at the point where he sought to collect his money. And the high ratio of acquittals to convictions suggests the difficulty of bringing the offence to proof.

Even in 1830 there were no accredited 'handwriting experts'. Mr Justice Alderson, notorious for his conduct of the Winchester Special Commission in the winter of 1830–31, was nevertheless at pains to instruct the jury fairly in one case where an attorney, Henry Pollexfen, was accused of writing a threatening letter to a magistrate: 'Evidence as to handwriting was in general most vague and unsatisfactory, and there was no subject on which men could be more easily deceived.' He suggested that strong additional proof was required, such as the circumstances of two matching half sheets of paper.[1]

The defendant in this case was found not guilty. One wonders whether Mr Justice Alderson remembered his own warning when, two weeks later at Salisbury, he sentenced a prosperous farmer, Isaac Looker, to transportation for life for writing to a neighbouring farmer: 'Hif you goes to sware against or a man in prisson, you have here farm burnt down to ground, and thy bluddy head chopt off.' Witnesses swore that Isaac Looker had said in a pub that the labourers were doing the right thing in going round to raise wages and to reduce tithes and rents, and that it was not they but the magistrates and soldiers who were creating disturbance. If the people were left alone they would do what they had to do peaceably. This evidence must have filled the minds of judges and of special jury with a strong presumption of Looker's guilt. It was then proved that the letter did in fact fit exactly to a half sheet in Looker's bureau, and that the water-mark had been divided. Several prosecution witnesses affirmed with the greatest confidence that this was Looker's handwriting, although witnesses for the defence denied this. The jury found the accused guilty. Alderson made no bones of the fact that this was also his direction. Isaac Looker's vehement protestations of innocence met with this remark: 'We all know that a man who can be guilty of such an offence as that of which you have been convicted, will not hesitate to deny it as you now do. I would rather trust to such evidence as has been given in your case, than to the most solemn declarations even on the scaffold.' The mention of the scaffold brought a surge of nostalgia into the judge's mind; had the death penalty still been available for this offence, he informed the farmer, he had little doubt that he would have used it. Transporting Looker for life he added: 'You will be sent to a country where you will find very few worse than yourself.'

Exhausted by this exercise of disciplinary rhetoric the judge retired for

1. *The Times*, 24 December 1830.

refreshment. In the interval the farmer's eighteen-year-old son, Edward, came forward and confessed that he had written the letter. His father had been away that day and knew nothing of it. Two of his cousins were then in prison awaiting trial for their part in the 'Swing' disturbances: 'I heard people talk that it would get my cousins off if threatening letters were written.' Slightly discomforted, Mr Justice Alderson immediately put Isaac Looker on trial *again*, for either writing the letters or for aiding and abetting his son. But the case could not stand up and he was acquitted. This time all the handwriting experts could see that the letter was undoubtedly in a better hand than the old farmer could command. Edward, the son, was then sentenced to seven years' transportation.[1]

This episode serves to emphasize the difficulty in securing a conviction – a difficulty perhaps increased by the reluctance of eighteenth-century juries to send a man to death for committing a few lines to paper. Since there were few convictions, it follows that there is little information as to the authors of the letters. Several examples of death were made shortly after the passage of the Black Act. The cases are pathetic ones – bungling amateurs trying their hands at blackmail. The first to be executed for the offence was probably Bryan Smith, an Irish Catholic, at Tyburn in 1725. A friend of his lay under sentence of transportation for stealing a silver spoon from a tavern: ordering a gill of Rhenish and a little sugar, the sugar was brought in a silver spoon which he had taken away. Smith wrote to the prosecutor, threatening his life if his friend was transported. As it happened, his friend's transportation was held over. A witness testified: 'There was no persuading Smith but that his letter was the occasion of it. He became strangely elevated, and mightily admired his ingenuity and contrivance, as if no body but himself was able to do the like.' He was encouraged to attempt his hand a second time. He set up an accomplice, who was a tailor, to whom he pretended to be in debt for £27. He then wrote to 'Baron' Antonio Lopez Suaffo a letter threatening murder and arson, signed 'John Brown', demanding that Suaffo should pay off his debt to the tailor. It was a foolish contrivance. The tailor was of course arrested and held in Newgate until he turned evidence against Smith. This evidence was corroborated by 'the hand-writing, spelling, imprecations and Irish blunders' of the letter. Smith was one of the first to adopt the fashion of riding in the cart to Tyburn in his shroud, which turned out to be an even greater blunder than any he had committed before. As his fellow sufferers were being attended to by the hangman, Smith slipped his head through the noose and jumped over the cart into the crowd;

1. J. L. and B. Hammond, *The Village Labourer*, 1920 edn, pp. 271–2; *The Times*, 7 January 1831.

hopping around like a pantomime ghost in his shroud he was easily re-taken.[1]

Jepthah Big, hanged at Tyburn in 1729, had tried his hand at equally silly means of extortion with equal lack of success. According to the Ordinary of Newgate he was twenty-five years old, an apprenticed gun-stock-maker out of employment (given of course, in the usual ritual terms, to 'drinking, swearing, whoring, &c.'), whose parents had given him a good education in reading and writing. His exit at Tyburn was little more decorous than that of Smith, since he got hold of the rope and hung by his hands for a minute or two after the cart was driven away. This may have provided drama for the crowd. Both Smith and Big appear to have complained that they did not know that their offence was capital, although Big admitted that he had heard of two or three who had suffered upon the same law.[2] And, on occasion, others were to suffer upon it.[3]

What kind of men wrote the letters of social protest? Until the 1830s and 1840s convictions are so rare that the faces as well as the figures must remain dark. One would like to offer, as the type of one kind of letter-writer, William Tillotson, found guilty of sedition in 1804. Tillotson was an elderly man who, in the notion of the Crown brief, for a great part of his life had

rambled about the country to cock fights, rush bearings, and amusements of that description, affecting to collect hare and rabbit skins and to sell trinkets, rings, and other suchlike small articles usually vended by pedlars. . . He has been always deservedly considered a blasphemous, seditious and disaffected character, and suspected of obtaining his means of livelihood and dissipation in other ways than those which he appeared to pursue.

Tillotson, a native of Colne (Lancashire), spent the day of 6 August 1803 drinking in an inn in Grindleton, among the Clitheroe moors on the Yorkshire–Lancashire border, and 'sotted all or great part of the day, singing and talking in the most blasphemous, seditious, and licentious way that can be imagined'. The boggling imagination finds that his ribald and bloodthirsty jests were aimed at King George, Mr Pitt, and the country gentry generally.[4]

1. *Select Trials for Murder &c at the Old Bailey*, 1734-5, vol. II, pp. 31-4; the Ordinary's *Account*, 30 April 1725.
2. *Select Trials for Murder &c at the Old Bailey*, vol. II, pp. 292-5.
3. For convictions in 1730-31, see above, p. 264; for the case of Girdler, above, p. 269. Peter Linebaugh notes a less amateurish blackmailer in Robert Brownjohn, for ten years a sailor, who boasted of having successfully sent a number of extortionary letters: he was executed in 1738: the Ordinary's *Account*, 8 March 1738 and *The Proceedings*, 13-16 January 1738.
4. Crown brief in PRO, TS 11.1070.5025.

But this traitorous old man – this scandalous antithesis to the high-minded and moralistic pedlar of Wordsworth's 'Excursion' – was, so far as the evidence allows us to see, no letter-writer. He belongs to an older, oral tradition of sedition, whose expression took the form of riddling rhymes, songs, prophecies and elaborate patter.[1] A more likely candidate for the 'type' might be Charles Alderson, a journeyman saddler of Lowestoft, who did indeed write three seditious letters to a magistrate in 1793. The first two letters were full of passionate hostility towards the war against revolutionary France. Alderson claimed to have discovered some great secret weapon which would overthrow the Duke of York's army and enforce peace upon Britain; he was willing to reveal his secret to the magistrate if he could be assured of the latter's cooperation. When he failed to receive this reassurance he wrote a further letter, in the usual terms, threatening to lie in wait for him and punish him.

Identified, Alderson was fetched by the recipient of the letters before the Quarter Sessions at Beccles. But the threatened magistrate refused to press the case against him, on the grounds that Alderson was of 'disturbed imagination'. His fellow magistrates, however, would not let off the saddler so lightly and they committed him again, this time for sedition. They could certainly not tolerate leniency towards a man who had written: 'I am . . . well perswaded that the life of aney man in the world even the most opresed african is and ought to be of more value in the sight of one and other than all the revenues of King George the third and all his familey. . .' A former employer was brought forward to testify that Alderson showed no signs of insanity, except that he 'used to spend much of his time and particularly Sundays in reading old Books of History'.[2] It is a dangerous complaint, fully justifying any man's committal.

Alderson is not wholly untypical: his learning, his quotations from Pope, his attempts at a high literary style, can be matched in other letters; and these become rather more frequent in Luddite and post-war years, when eccentric enthusiasts and odd-balls turned their hands to elaborate

---

1. See Keith Thomas, *Religion and the Decline of Magic*, 1971, esp. ch. 13, 'Ancient Prophecies'. This kind of 'patter' continued well into the nineteenth century, as Mayhew testifies. Its adaptation to seditious purposes can be illustrated in a case from Bath, in 1797, when some journeymen shoemakers and a journeyman smith got into trouble for delivering inflammatory handbills at alehouses, accompanied by the 'parole' (verbal patter): 'that there was a Flat (meaning the King) between Two Sharps, who was Pitt and Dundas, and that the Rogue was taken in, for he had lost all his Money in the Bank of Venice': see J. Jeffreys to Portland, 11 August 1797, in PRO, HO 42.41. See also Birmingham handbill headed: 'To Arms Countrymen To Arms' (September 1800) and continuing: 'Let the deep Pitt be made Level and all his bandette Beheaded. . .': HO 42.52, fo. 363.

2. Crown brief in PRO, TS 11.460.1544.

epistolary menaces.[1] Although his productions were briefer, one such man can be identified in 1830 – Joseph Saville, a straw-plait manufacturer, who rattled about Cambridgeshire in a gig in which were found between 600 and 700 inflammatory letters. He was a man used to putting out work to the cottagers, and no doubt he put out some copying work as well. Letters manufactured on this scale were of necessity brief:

> Oh ye church of England Parsins, who strain at a knot
> and swallor a cammell, woe woe woe be unto you, ye
> shall one day have you reward   Swing

> If you dont behave better and give the Poor Man his
> due I will visit you or my name is not   Swing

> You clergy, ye Vipers, you love Tithes, Cummin, and
> Mint; ye are men-eaters and not soul savers, but Blind
> leaders of the Blind, twice dead, plucked up by the
> Roots   Swing

Saville was described as some kind of Methodist ranter, and he made no attempt to deny that he had distributed the letters. What he did deny, vigorously, was that he had any interest in politics. The officers of his parish came loyally to his defence in the local newspapers, deploring his 'folly' but describing him as the author of a Sick Society and a Sunday School:

> About Christmas he provides a good dinner for the poor widows; has given a large quantity of potatoes to the poor; has been the means of distributing some hundreds of bushels of coals in winter; has made a proposition for the poor to dig up the waste ground . . . for their benefit; has been one of the first to lower his tenants' rents; is a warm advocate and supporter of Bible and Missionary Societies. . .

In his defence Saville said he was actuated simply by the words of Scripture, especially such as commenced: 'Woe unto you Scribes and Pharisees. . .' He was not the first or last to come under the notice of a Christian judiciary for taking Christian texts too literally, although, as a Scribe in some kind himself, he might have suspected that woe would be coming to him also. He was, nevertheless, most fortunate not to have come under the notice of Mr Justice Alderson, to have had the loyal backing of his parish (it could scarcely be possible to receive a better character than that which they gave to him), and to have been tried in a county in which the disturbances had been comparatively light. He was fined £50 and imprisoned for twelve months.[2]

1. See e.g. Appendix I (g) and II (g).
2. 'F. Singleton' (but in fact A. J. Peacock), 'Captain Swing in East Anglia', *Bulletin of the Society for the Study of Labour History*, 8 (Spring 1964), pp. 13–15; *The Times* (citing *Suffolk Herald*), 23 December 1830.

This was indeed a light sentence. Other 'Swing' authors received transportation (for seven or fourteen years, or for life); the same sentences were handed out in East Anglia in the 1840s; and even in the 1850s (although by now there is more evidence of clemency) two years' hard labour could be expected.[1] Such sentences fell, in the main, upon labourers – young men like Edward Looker – or, on occasion, men in some clerical occupation.[2] By the 1830s it might be possible to show that in rural England the march of intellect and the march of incendiarism went hand-in-hand. When the epidemic of 'Swing' letters was at its height, a York newspaper reported that 'some boys belonging to the Skidby school have been detected as the writers of the letters to the neighbouring farmers'.[3] Thomas Brown, a seventeen-year-old labourer, transported for life at Lewes Assizes for the offence, pleaded that old and young Miller (both labourers) had put him up to it, since they could not write themselves.[4] For the illiterate, the fact of writing sometimes seems to carry magical powers.[5]

---

1. I have had the advantage of seeing two excellent studies both of which deal with threatening letters in association with arson in East Anglia: A. J. Peacock, 'Village Radicalism in East Anglia, 1800–1850', in J. P. D. Dunbadin, ed., *Rural Discontent in Nineteenth Century Britain*, 1974, and Julian Harber on incendiarism in Suffolk in the 1840s (unpublished). William Cornish of Gelderstone, who pleaded guilty to sending a threatening letter to a farmer who employed machinery in 1853, was recommended to mercy by the prosecution and received only two years' hard labour: *Norfolk Chronicle*, 23 July 1853.

2. Hobsbawm and Rudé, op. cit., pp. 131–2, 241, identify among accused 'Swing' writers four labourers, a gardener, two schoolmasters, an attorney's clerk and a journeyman tailor said to be a 'ranting' preacher. (The tailor was transported, but the schoolmasters and the attorney's clerk were acquitted: *The Times*, 22, 24 December 1830.) Peacock's letter-writers were mainly young labourers: Josiah How, a seventeen-year-old Huntingdonshire labourer, earning 5s. 1d. a week threatened his employer with arson in 1835 if he did not 'behave better' to his labourers, and in 1844 Edmund Botwright, aged twenty-two, left a letter by the scene of a fire: 'You bluddy farmers could not live if it was not for the poore, tis them that keeps you bluddy raskells alive.' Harber identifies Samuel Stow, a thirty-one-year-old labourer (and poacher) of Polestead, Suffolk, transported for ten years (in 1845) for a threatening letter. Hobsbawm and Rudé (op. cit., p. 241) identify five women indicted for the offence in 1830–31; I have noted only two cases of female offenders prosecuted in the eighteenth century.

3. *The Times*, 21 December 1830. During the Cardiganshire 'War of the Little Englishman' against enclosure in the 1820s, the authorities suspected that the author of anonymous letters was James Morris 'formerly a Clergyman of the Established Church, but deprived of that dignity, thro' ill conduct; he keeps a School for the education of Children in the Neighborhood, and wanders from Cottage to Cottage for his Meals: he is one of the most troublesome Trespassers': D. J. V. Jones, 'More Light on "Rhyfel y Sais Bach" ', *Ceredigion*, IV (1965), pp. 88–9.

4. *The Times*, 22 December 1830; J. L. and B. Hammond, op. cit., p. 286.

5. See J. R. Goody, ed., *Literacy in Traditional Societies*, Cambridge, 1968, pp. 13–17.

We are still very little closer to the authors of the letters of social protest
and sedition of the eighteenth century. But when a face appears, which is
rarely enough, it does not appear to be that of a crank; it is simply that of
a member of the working community suffering under common grievances,
perhaps set a little apart by his literary aptitude. Thomas Bannister, a
yeoman farmer in Windsor Forest, who thrust some furious threatening
letters through a hole in a neighbour's stable door early one January
morning in 1724 – an action which had been supported by window-
breaking, the cutting of cart-leathers, breaking of fences and maiming of
cattle – appears to have been a typical yeoman of the area, of long-settled
family; and his neighbour appears to have given offence by giving
evidence leading to the conviction of other local men.[1]

On occasion the correspondence of the authorities indicates a possible
author, although the evidence may not have been firm enough to lead
to a prosecution. In the high noon of anti-Jacobinism this kind of source
must be used with extreme caution. As Wordsworth learned at Alfoxden
and William Blake at Felpham, any stranger, especially one often closeted
with books and paper, could easily be suspected as a revolutionary or a
French spy. In 1795 the Mayor of Hastings wrote to Portland to assure
him that the seditious handbills and threatening letters circulated in the
town could not possibly have come from the hand of any citizens of
Hastings, who had 'ever been distinguished' for their attachment to the
King and Constitution. But he was happy to be able to disclose the true
author, a Mr Leigh, a stranger recently settled in lodgings in the town.
This man, 'of middle stature, dark hair without powder tied in a queue
behind, black coat and waistcoat, nankeen breeches' and a 'down-cast look',
may perhaps not have been a conspirator, but he was certainly the object
of a conspiracy. The Mayor, the officers of the militia, the master of his
lodgings, the servant-girl – all were watching his least motion. The
directions on his letters were closely observed, and when the eighteen-
year-old girl at his lodgings was asked to post a letter, 'The girl . . . seeing
one of his letters directed to *Lord Stanhope* had the curiosity to open a
corner of the letter but cou'd only read the following part of a line:
"News, you know I am here for that purpose". . .' The master of his
lodgings kept back the next letter, with a view to its examination. The
man 'is employ'd generally in reading Paine's "Rights of Man", Brother's
"Prophecies" . . . his conversation is extremely indecent in speaking of
the King or Government and . . . he has taken infinite pains to mix with
the soldiers . . . giving them money to drink &c.' The Mayor added, with
seeming self-contradiction, that the master of his lodgings 'has got a vast

1. PRO, Assi 5.44 (ii); *Whigs and Hunters*, ch. 3.

deal of his writing which exactly resembles the threatening letters which I have receiv'd, but as he can easily disguise his natural hand, and seldom writes twice alike, it is impossible for me to take him up with a chance of conviction.' He admitted the want of evidence, but had 'not a moment's doubt of his being the Man'. As he was writing this essay in criminal detection a message was brought to the Mayor indicating that the mysterious stranger had announced that he was about to leave Hastings, and on foot. No doubt he had his reasons.[1]

We may hesitate to convict this stranger in his absence. But a clerical magistrate in Gloucestershire did follow up a series of measures of detection which were more thorough. The whole episode, which illustrates the kind of 'dialogue' which took place between authorities and the crowd through this medium, is worth recording in detail. On 16 July 1795, a gentleman in Uley, Gloucestershire found this note in his garden:

O remember ye poor in distress by ye high pr^s of provison if not the consiquens will be fatall to a great many in all parishis round a bout here how do ye think a man can suport a fam^{ly} by a quartern [?] flour for a shillin and here is a man in this parish do say the poore was never beter of as they be now a fatel blow for him and his hous and all his property we have all redy 5000 sworn to be true to the last & we have 510000 of ball redy and can have pouder at a word & every think fitin for ye purpose no King but a constitution down down down o fatall dow high caps & proud hats for ever dow down we all.

Another gentleman received a similar note on the same day, and a further note was found at another house a few days later. The three gentlemen conferred with the magistrate and agreed to keep the notes secret, while making inquiries. But this proved to be impossible, since two of the notes had been first picked up by labourers in the cloth manufactory, who had spread their contents abroad. The JP (the Reverend William Lloyd Baker) then issued a public statement that 'some exertions which we had intention to have brought forward for the relief of the poor should be suspended for a week' in consequence of the letters. This is a nice moment in the contest for 'face' in the paternalism–deference equilibrium: that is, these 'exertions' for charitable relief had not yet been made – and were perhaps prompted by the letters and the fear of riot – but they must on no account seem to be hastened in response to duress. The Reverend Baker understood this game of threat and counter-threat only too well. He lived in a district in which more than one clothier's house had been

1. Edward Milward, Mayor of Hastings, to Portland, 1 May 1795, PRO, HO 42.34. The letter is annotated: 'Leigh is a member of L.C.S. [London Corresponding Society] & was distributing the publications of Eaton &c &c.' See also HO 43.6, pp. 344, 402 and HO 42.52, fos. 304–5.

burned to the ground, and his own house was provided with an alarm bell which, on a calm day, could be heard by 6,000 people.[1]

At this point subsidized food for the poor was provided in Uley. But the disgruntled correspondent was still unsatisfied, and some time afterwards left a further bulletin near the workhouse where 'we distributed our provisions'. This alleged that the gentlemen's subsidized bread, at 5½ lb for 1s., compared poorly with the bread provided by a baker in the parish at 6 lb for 13d. for bread 'as white as snow'. It compared unfavourably also with Cambridge, where the poor have a bushel of wheat for 10s.: 'You blood thirsty crew . . . remember Dives and Lazerus.'

The gentlemen ignored this piece of ingratitude and went on as before, ending their subsidies on 3 September: 'we had great reason to imagine every one was pleased with what had been done till the fifteenth of September when the following note was found. . .':

> The distress of the industerous people through the dearnes of provisions calls aloud for an immediate consultation therefore a meeting is desired next Munday morning 21 in[t] by nine o clock in the morning on hampton coman to consult what steps to take for an immediate alteration. Be pl[d] to let more know it further. With it make no delay or else we all must starve immediately.

Troops were alerted, and a magistrate in the neighbourhood of Minchinhampton Common rode over the field on the day. He saw nothing; but the time had been altered, and in the afternoon some three hundred assembled, but without any leader or concerted plan. They reassembled again, with fewer numbers, on 5 October: once again they were observed by troops.

Baker and his friends now conducted a systematic investigation. Individuals from Uley who were present at the meetings were interrogated. The search was narrowed to three men, who had been especially active in recruiting attendance. Suspicion fell upon one of these, and the train of evidence was rather more convincing than in the case of the Hastings stranger. The man was known to have attended the meetings and to have solicited attendance; alehouse gossip among 'the lower class of people' nominated him as the author; samples of his handwriting ('a number of bills') were collected and compared closely with that in the notes, 'some of the letters being very particularly shaped'. The suspect was a tailor who was born and had lived all his life in Uley: 'an obscure individual' and those with whom he is connected 'each is alike obscure'.

But although the evidence might convince a jury, Baker and his fellow

1. For Baker, see E. Moir, *Local Government in Gloucestershire, 1775–1800: a study of the justices of the peace*, Bristol and Gloucestershire Archaeological Society Records, vol. VIII, 1969, pp. 145, 150–51.

magistrates were uncertain as to how to proceed. They had at first thought
of giving the tailor a severe reprimand and a warning that he was being
watched, since 'we were afraid that his offence did not make him actually
liable to such a punishment as we wished'. This was, presumably, because
the letters were directed to no particular person, and they did not extort
money or threaten arson or the murder of any individual, although one
had warned unnamed persons to 'expect to loase y^r heads without any
ado' and others, which referred to arming and warfare, were clearly
seditious. The fact of the two assemblies eventually decided the magistrates to refer the whole case to Portland for his opinion. In his reply
Portland commended the magistrates for their vigilance, but counselled
caution:

> The person in question is in so low a situation of life, and his endeavours
> appear to have produced so little effect in the Country that I am inclined to
> think it may perhaps be the best way of preventing disturbance in future to let
> him know that the Magistrates are well informed of his attempts & that they
> have it in contemplation to proceed against him, which may possibly induce him
> to quit the Country. . .[1]

In any case, this should deter him from repeating the practice; and, if he
should do so, then 'proper measures' should be taken to bring him to
justice. What such proper measures would be the Home Secretary did not
propose; presumably a charge of sedition would be the most likely to
stick.[2]

This case shows the whole process of 'dialogue' at work and illuminates
the functions of the letters. It also shows that self-reliant magistrates
would not inform the Government of such letters for many weeks, if at all,
if they thought they could handle the matter on their own. Finally, it may
point to an additional reason why the numerous letters of 1795 were
given no publicity and kept out of the *Gazette*. Government was still
adopting the traditional posture that serious political or seditious threat
could come, not from 'obscure individuals' in 'low' situations of life,
but from men in higher stations. A stranger with books, a portman-
teau, a black coat and nankeen breeches was likely to draw more attention
than a tailor in a Gloucestershire village; the information that Wordsworth and his sister were taking 'views' of the Somerset coast was sufficient to send a Government agent hurrying down to Stowey. If the

1. Portland's endorsement of the letter from Baker is more terse: 'If the Writer of
the Hand Bill can be *frightened* out of the Country the best way of preventing disturbance
then almost seems to be . . . [rest illegible].'

2. Baker to Portland, n.d. (October 1795), PRO, HO 42.36; Portland to Baker
22 October 1795, HO 43.7, pp. 219-20.

anonymous productions of the obscure were not accompanied by acts of arson, gunshot or riot, then as late as 1795 Government was willing to pass them by. In 1800, when a plebeian Painite underground culture had become manifest, Portland himself was to change his stance.

One other case of such a letter-writer is fairly well documented, although in this case it is by no means so probable that the author was correctly identified. In the Somerset parish of Stogursey a letter-writer was busy between 1794 and 1800. In 1794 notices were posted on behalf of the poor of six parishes, demanding an advance of wages: if not, 360 men would 'take arms'. In 1795 a similar notice was stuck upon Stogursey church door. In 1800 a longer letter was thrust under the door of a market room where local gentlemen were supervising the sale of subsidized barley. What is peculiar about this letter is that, while literate and forceful, its spelling was erratic ('deturmed' for 'determined', 'genearel' for 'general'), and yet it closed with four well-presented lines of Latin verse. Suspicion fell upon one Joseph Brown, a labourer of the parish, who was known to be a literate man. He had served briefly (1797–8) as a sergeant in the Somerset Volunteers, and one of his officers, a lieutenant-surgeon, claimed to identify his handwriting by comparing it with lists of the sick drawn up by Brown during his volunteer service. An indictment was drawn against Brown, which exists in draft, but the case rested only upon the evidence of handwriting. Moreover, while the letter was cited in full in the indictment, the lines of Latin were omitted: this suggests that no proof could be adduced that Brown knew Latin, and that, if he had a hand in the letter at all, he must have had a classically minded accomplice.[1] Unfortunately Coleridge had left Nether Stowey (some three miles from Stogursey) two years before, so that we cannot pin the Latin on him. But there were certainly other aspirants to literary honours around in the Somerset villages, as was illustrated by the handbill stuck up in the small market town of Wellington (Somerset) in 1801:

> Then raise yr drooping spirits up
> Nor starve by Pitt's decree
> Fix up the sacred Guillotine
> Proclaim – French Liberty![2]

Hundreds of such productions never found their way as far as the Home Office. Nevertheless, it remains something of a puzzle to know

---

1. Informations and draft indictment exist in a transcript copy of 'papers relating to the Stogursey riots 1794–1801 in the possession of Lord St. Audries'. This transcript is kept by the Vicar of Stogursey, to whom I am indebted for permission to quote from it. For the letter see Appendix III (*n*).
2. See Appendix IV (*e*).

what Government thought it was doing, in 1800, in gazetting and thereby giving further publicity to so many examples of sedition. For Portland informed one correspondent that: 'I must admit that I do not recollect an instance of any discovery having been effected by the offer of reward and pardon, any more than of the threats contained in incendiary letters having been carried into effect.' He was, however, 'persuaded ... that advertisement ... operated by way of prevention'.[1] On one count this evidence is important: it confirms the impression that very few successful prosecutions were carried through in these years. But on another count Portland, who was writing in confidence to a friend, was making a directly misleading statement. It may be true that cases of murder rarely, if ever, eventuated from such threats. But cases of riot and of arson in direct association with threatening letters were passing through his hands every month.

Indeed, this very correspondent, W. Baker, the county MP for Hertfordshire, was in a position to contradict Portland's statement. On 15 July 1800, barns, hovels and a quantity of grain belonging to Robert Young of Holwells, near Bishop's Hatfield, Hertfordshire, were fired. The offence was gazetted on 19 July. On the same day Farmer Young was sent a letter signed 'Dr Steady', commencing:

I am sorry your Corn was destroyed it was what I was against but the next step will not be to destroy the Corn but you may tell all Farmers that with-hold it as you have done that their lives will be weary shorte if they do not sell their Corn much cheaper immediately and likewise the lives of that damned sett of Salesmen and forestallers of Mark Lane that keep the price up as they have done shall soon go to pott.

We are more than 1000 strong in Harford Essex and London ... we have many friends in Arms you little think of, but its Committee Night I am obliged to attend but at no public house...

This letter was sent from London and could of course have come from anyone who had noted Young's address in the *Gazette*. Baker forwarded the letter to Portland and pressed for it to be gazetted. Portland, as we have seen, was reluctant. But on 11 September the farmer suffered the firing of a further stack of oats in his yard. Farmer Young, Baker reported, was 'much distracted by agitation of mind', less, it would seem, on account of his losses, which were insured, than on account of the hostility surrounding him and the reputation which he had gained for avarice. Reports had been 'most maliciously circulated' as to the quantity of corn which he was holding – reports which he 'means to contradict in the most solemn

1. Baker to Portland, 17 August 1800, PRO, HO 42.50; Portland to Baker, 24 August 1800, HO 43.12, p. 78.

and formal manner'. 'The poor man ... is so affected ... that his life is made truly miserable.'[1]

In this case the arsonist and the author were not necessarily accomplices. But in these same months Portland must have noted cases where the two must have been directly related. Thus in Whiteparish, Wiltshire, this letter was found in February 1800:

> He that finds
> it open it and
> read it & set the
> news all over
> White-Parish
>
> If all the Farmers in White-Parish Dont sink their
> Wheat their Barns shall be burn'd and they shall be
> in the middle of it, it is no use to offer no reward
> for I have nobody but myself Amen.

Beneath the gazetted letter there followed the further announcement (over Portland's signature): 'And whereas the above Threat (in Part) has been put in Execution by some evil-minded Person or Persons unknown, in the wilfully setting Fire on the Evening of ... the 12th Instant to Two Barns, a Cow-House, a Quantity of Hay and Straw, a Fatting Calf...' and other articles on a gentleman's farm in Whiteparish, the customary offer of pardon and reward was published.[2] Such letters could never be taken only as acts of theatre. As young Thomas Brown was to write to Lord Sheffield in 1830, 'My writing is bad, but my firing is good my Lord.'[3]

1. *LG*, 1800, pp. 814, 1120–21; W. Baker to Portland, 12, 18 September 1800, PRO, HO 42.51.

2. *LG*, 1800, p. 202 (February 1800); G. J. Fort to W. Hussey, Esq., MP, 19 February 1800, PRO, HO 42.49. Another case which had been before Portland was that of barns etc. fired at Odiham (Hants), on the land of a tenant of Sir H. P. St John Mildmay, followed a week later by a furious letter claiming responsibility and threatening further actions: the Vicar of Odiham suspected (on the evidence of handwriting) 'a man of a very fair character – employed by most of the farmers, & sufficiantly opulent not to feel the pressure of the present scarcity very severely': *LG*, 1800, p. 248; letters of Mildmay and of the Rev. J. W. Beadon in HO 42.49. Other examples of letters directly associated with arson or riot include Wedmore (Somerset) 2 April, Lewes, 17 April, Nottingham, 25 April 1800 (all in HO 42.49); Wimborne (Dorset), 19 June, Taunton district, 31 July 1800 (HO 42.50); Blandford, 9 September 1800 (HO 42.51); Haverfordwest (HO 42.53), and others.

3. J. L. and B. Hammond, op. cit., p. 286.

VI

If the authors of these letters were various, we must expect the styles to be various also. Generalization does not take us far. The orthography of the letters is interesting, although at times it may have been deliberately disguised. Very often the dialect or lilt of regional speech can be detected beneath the letters – West Country, or Irish, or East Anglian; these are written by men who knew their letters, but whose writing was guided by their ear rather than by the standards of memory and eye. There are letters as roughly hewn in the 1820s and 1830s as in the 1760s, although when we come into the nineteenth century there are more letters which suggest the 'intellectuals' of the movement: schoolmasters, tradesmen, clerks, artisans with a shelf of books.

One might perhaps find evidence in the letters for a footnote to the history of popular literacy. Clearly, the arrival of a method of mass agitation which involves notices in the market square, handbills and chalking implies a mass audience of whom many could read these signs. A rapid review of the letters suggests that there is a movement outwards from the larger towns (in the 1760s, London, Taunton, Tiverton, Plymouth, Chester, Nottingham, Norwich, and so on) to the village or smaller market town (in the 1790s, Whiteparish, several Essex villages, Newport (Isle of Wight), Petworth, Odiham, Bideford, Stogursey, Uley, Crediton, and others). But we have noted a letter from Clee Hill colliers in 1767; there is another from the colliers of the north-east in 1765, and Berkshire yeomen farmers were employing them in the 1720s. Scotland vindicates its reputation for educational advancement by providing some of the earliest examples of highly polished literary production; and the pawkiness of the Presbyterian end of Scottish culture peeps out even amidst the unkirklike imprecations, as when Lieutenant-Colonel John Crawfurd of Crawfurdland, Ayrshire was warned not to 'hurt the Countrey bay the Advise of one abonible Hure ane Adoltres woman'.[1] Until the arrival of the often highly literate Rebecca, the common Welsh production showed no educational advance upon the English (but letters in the Welsh language might provide different evidence).[2] From the evidence of the *Gazette*, until 1790 the north and north Midlands were backward areas compared with the south and south Midlands, the east and, especially, the west.

Although most of the authors were guided in their spelling by ear, most also fell into that formal, mimetic style required by epistolary address.

1. *LG* 12084 (April 1780).
2. See an early Welsh Nationalist letter in *LG* 11368 (July 1773).

The recipient was warned that the author proposed to burn down, not his 'house', but his 'abitation'; blackmail pay-off must be laid in a hole in a tree on the such-and-such 'inst.'; the murderers promised to perform at 'the first opertuerty'. Such phrases, in elevating the style, seemed somehow to elevate the threat. So also did the literary flourishes which no doubt gave the authors much satisfaction. A Devon gentleman received in 1779 a letter describing him as: 'A Narrow Back, Lowsey, false, Little forswareing, Little Rogue. I don't look upon thee no more than the Leaf of an Asp for he Whivers and is gone. . .'[1] The literary flourishes of the Painites of the 1790s fell too often into cliché, with 'sons of liberty', 'monarchical fetters', or warnings couched in the high style of a letter to the Mayor of Plymouth (1792) to 'dread to come within the reach of a well pointed Poignard'.[2]

The most polished letters probably belong to the last years of the tradition, at least in the towns, from 1800 to the 1830s. A Manchester cotton-master received one in 1812 which commenced: 'Sir, We begin with the Language of the Prophet of old, in saying that your Destruction is at Hand, and why? because we the Cotton Spinners of this Town have been the means of raising you from the Dunghill to Independency.'[3] But such writers could, on occasion, be equalled by their eighteenth-century forebears, such as one in Norwich in 1766 who, after threatening to raze the city by fire and sword, ended with a 'noble Sentence of Horace' in the Latin.[4] In their form also, some of the letters followed the forms of authority or of the counting-house. A number of the hand-written bills posted in market squares adopted the 'Wheareases' and flourishes of official proclamations. Others included touching epistolary formalities. A letter (Ayrshire, 1775) which went on to utter the most bloodcurdling blackmailing threats commenced: 'Sir, This is perhaps the most interesting Letter you ever received as Your Life depends on your abaying its

1. *LG* 11956 (January 1779).

2. *LG* 1792, p. 953 (December 1792).

3. Letter to Mr Kirkby, Cotton Master, Ancoats, enclosed in Holt, 22 February 1812, PRO, HO 42.120.

4. *LG* 10671 (October 1766). In 1840 a Chartist in Gloucester sent a letter to the Marquess of Normanby which must have given the author much satisfaction: the letter threatened retaliation against all those involved in the trial of John Frost and his fellow insurgents at Monmouth: 'Depend on it there shall be a glorious cor-de-main-come-e-fo it shall be a proper Chef-d'oeuvre with ec-la, depend on it ye are all number'd and mark'd out – are not the poor suffering beyond anything through your damnable poor laws and going to marry your rapacious Vic to a German rat to give him 100,000 a year . . . If you stand Versus us it shall be such a time as those of ye whom may have the chance to escape to say its Sui-gen-e-vis. Can Miss Vic think she will ever prosper to Consummate her cannubialis state by shedding the blood of those poor creatures at Monmouth . . .?' PRO, HO 40.57, fo. 13.

demands.'[1] The Mayor of Nottingham received a letter in 1800 drawn up with impeccable attention to proprieties:

Sir,

If the Men who were taken last Saturday be not set at liberty by tomorrow night, the Shambles the Change and all the whole Square shall be set on Fire, if you have an Army of Constables they can't prevent it for the greasy boards will burn well –
Hoping that you will take this into consideration.

I am, your hble Servt.
Will. Johnston.[2]

Until Ned Ludd, Captain Swing and Rebecca, there were no favoured pseudonyms. Those chosen range from 'Probono Publico' to THE MONSTER. When the chief magistrate of Tewkesbury was called upon to convene a meeting in 1795 to petition for peace, on pain of getting a bullet through his brains, the signatories were: 'Revenge, Force, Mallice, Determination'.[3] The tinners of Polgooth, Cornwall, signed their letter: 'Captins Audacious, Fortitude, Presumption and dread not'.[4] A Sussex complaint about small measures (1793) was signed: 'from the old devle that will have you all if you dont alter'.[5] Bloodcurdling threats in a Somerset village were over the signature:

Pull grip Pull Devel
Devel take Both
Now lets Drink
My Jovel
Soles[6]

Letters in two Northamptonshire villages in 1800 were addressed to farmers and dealers: 'If you dornt Lower the greain whe will destroy all your Farm with Fire . . . whe will destroy all your sheep and . . . whe will pull all your turnips up. . .' On the envelope, beside the addressee's name, was written: 'Walentine'.[7] A letter from Newport (Isle of Wight) against the press-gang, in 1793, signed itself simply 'we ham For the rights of Tom Paine you Bouger'.[8]

There is no doubt that some of the authors enjoyed their stylistic extravaganzas. Months and perhaps years of pent-up resentment and of assumed deference were released in a few lines. From Bideford (1812):

1. *LG* 11538 (January 1775).   2. *LG* 1800, p. 475 (May 1800).
3. *LG* 13805 (July 1795).   4. *LG* 1796, p. 45 (December 1795).
5. PRO, HO 42.27 cited in 'Moral Economy', op. cit., p. 102.
6. *LG* 1800, p. 1093 (September 1800).   7. *LG* 1800, p. 1455 (December 1800).
8. *LG* 1793, p. 292 (March 1793).

'Your Carkase if any such should be found will be given to the Dogs if it Contains any Moisture for the Annimals to devour it.'[1] Possibly it was the same author who had warned a Bideford miller ten years previously that 'the Devil will grind your head in powder as the mill grinds Corn'.[2] A Dumfries notice of 1771, which is an excellent example of the popular 'proclamation', warned forestallers, engrossers and dealers (and those 'aiding or assisting to any that have hitherto engrossed', etc.) –

To the great Hurt and Prejudice of the Country, the Poor in particular, to the Violation of the Laws of God and Nature; Public Notice is hereby given, that they from the Date hereof, desist from such sinful Practices, under Penalty of having their Houses burnt to the Ground, and punished in their Persons in Proportion to the Office they bear, viz. if a Magistrat with Mutilation, and if a Tradesman to have his Ears cut off at the Cross.[3]

A Bridgnorth writer remarked, less formally, of the farmers and millers: 'we will cut off their Ears and slit their Noses as a mark that the country may know them.'[4]

The highest literary style to which most authors wished to attain was not that of John Locke nor even of Tom Paine but of the Bible. The abundance of biblical reference must have been evident throughout this essay. The Old Testament lent itself easily to imprecations; and if the authors appealed to morality, as they commonly did, it was with reference to biblical text and style. Authors recalled Dives and Lazarus, compared employers or foremen to Herod, or recalled the sermons preached in church. A common posting-place was the church door; other letters were sent to clergy with the demand that they be read in church. In a Suffolk village in 1800 what appears to be verse was nailed to the church door:

> ... the first that mix his Grain shall forfit his heid,
> For your entent is to starve us to ded ...
> But the lord have [Raised?] our Curage so hie
> That soner than starve we fight till we die
> For the poor against the rich through out the land
> Will Conker the rich and have them at Command.
> So repent of your sins do not take it amiss
> It is your Cruelty the Cause of all this
> The day is epointed & that you will find
> The poor will have all this to share mind.

To be red in the Church by the Clargeman after surmon.[5]

1. PRO, HO 42.121, cited in Thompson, op. cit., p. 68.
2. *LG* 15540 (December 1802).   3. *LG* 11133 (March 1771).
4. *LG* 15327 (January 1801).   5. *LG* 1801, p. 56 (December 1800).

This might perhaps have sounded oddly among the banns and parish notices. So also would have a letter sent round to several Essex parishes in 1800 which concluded:

We will kill burn and destroy every thing we Come at spesely the greate land-hldrs and the most sevear men in every parish to the poor. . .

We mean to behave well to every minester that will read this in the Church if not he is a ded man by night or by day by means we will distroay the king and his famealy and likewise the Parlerment.[1]

What is surprising about this letter is that we know that in at least one case (a dissenting meeting-house) the request was complied with.[2]

Most often the biblical reference comes through as echo or allusion. On occasion the aid of the God of Battles is summoned, as at Exeter (1801): 'Fire and Sword is the word, and by the Almighty God they shall not escape our vengeance, we have cried unto Man in vain, we have now appealed unto God. . .'[3] More often there is an appeal to a moral code of charity, grounded upon the Gospels. A gentleman, probably a mealman, in High Wycombe was warned in 1800 that it was likely that he would

be sent to hell before the time god opinted you to live on all the Luxearys of Life and your poor nabour Clothed in Rags and starved for want of food his Children Crieing for Bread and none to give them I have yoy to Read the 12 Chapter of luke and the 8 Chapter of Amos. But you are as great a Stranger to the Gospel as you are to him that sent itt. . .[4]

Few letters carry such explicit reference: one would imagine that in the seventeenth century citations of texts would have been more frequent. Nor does it seem, on the evidence at present to hand, that this manner of expression was often employed by the ranting or millenarial writers; although if such letters were received, the magistrates could have put them aside as the productions of cranks. The expression of faith in a hereafter, when the rich will be chastened in hell and the poor meet their reward, is met more often. The Surgeon of the *Sandwich* who had been an evidence against Richard Parker, the naval mutineer of 1797, was informed:

1. *LG* 1800, p. 814 (July 1800). These letters were found in the parishes of Finching-field, Old Samford, New Samford and Great Bardfield.
2. The minister excused his reading through 'personal fear': see Thos Ruggles to Portland, 24 June 1800, PRO, HO 42.50. When the letter was gazetted Ruggles asked for extra copies of the journal to put on the church doors in the disaffected villages: it was felt that the official *Gazette* would have more effect than the notices of the local authorities: Ruggles to Portland, 6 July 1800, ibid.
3. *LG* 15349 (March 1801).
4. *LG* 15302 (October 1800).

Mr. Parker . . . is we hope where such infernal villains as you can never enter for hell is made for such base abominable miscreants and such as . . . yourself are vessels of wrath fitted to everlasting destruction o how will it gall your souls thro' all Eternity to See Blessed Parker full of Joy and happiness and Glory in the blissful presence of God and Christ and Holly Angels, when you will be company to devils and damned Souls, and full of wrath, Misery and Woe for ever and ever.[1]

One further stylistic device is of interest; it will already have been noticed that a number of the letters fall, at one point or another, into rough rhyming verse or doggerel. In some cases – addressed to a public at large rather than an individual – this is the ultimate in elevated style. In other cases – the examples from Wellington (Somerset) or from Maldon[2] – we have a genuine propaganda by poetry. But in other cases one suspects that one is seeing late examples of an older mnemonic tradition. This had been seen on a church door in Kent in 1603:

> The poor there is more
> Than goes from dore to dore
> You that are set in place
> See that youre profesion you doe not disgrace[3]

These rhymes have a magical quality, like the riddle rhymes of Merlin, those of Mother Shipton, and 'the late prophecy of a Cumberland cow' –

> Two hard winters, a wet spring
> A bloody summer and no king

which were circulating throughout the eighteenth century, were still alive in the 1790s, and which take us back to the rhyming riddles of the Fool in *Lear*. Joanna Southcott's writings are one corrupted end of that tradition, and they carry the incantatory quality of even bad verse. A rhymed threat at the foot of a letter carried some additional magical force:

> You will think it hard when you this reed
> But your Life must pay for it in Deed

Or, at the conclusion to an incendiary letter sent to a Newbury brewer in 1810:

> Wee will be gin at the Bell and so we will
> Contunu till you all goes to hell.[4]

1. *LG* 14033 (August 1797).   2. See Appendix, IV (*c*) and (*e*).
3. *Calendar State Papers* (*Domestic*), 1630, p. 387.
4. *LG* 1810, p. 632 (April 1810).

VII

The anonymous threatening letter was an intrinsic component of social and individual protest in that complex society of manufacturing industry and of capitalist agricultural improvement which scholars persist in calling a 'pre-industrial' society. In rural society it sometimes accompanied, punctuated and illuminated the reasons for arson, fence-breaking, houghing of cattle, and so on. In mines, workshops, dockyards and the clothing industry it accompanied illicit trade union organization and rattening.[1] In years of high prices its function in intimidating some practices in dealing and marketing, and in stimulating charity or subsidized food, is clear. In such circumstances it sometimes performed the role of a channel of 'negotiation' within the paternalist–plebeian equilibrium.

These generalizations do not take us far. Nor could we go far if we confined our examination to the forms of a subsequent phase of organization – the strike or the small printing-press – since each serves so many functions and carries so many voices. To learn more we must re-place each letter or group of letters within the specificity of its own context.

In the end, the form as such can be bound together only by two uniting themes. First, the act of sending such letters, for whatever purpose, constituted a crime; in the eyes of the law all literary styles, elevated or semiliterate, and all grievances, were reduced to a common level. And their authors were criminals, over whom hung the threat of the gallows or transportation. Second, these letters are, in many cases – and over many decades – the *only* literate expression of the 'inarticulate' which has survived. The 'dark figure' of the crime itself is dwarfed by the even darker figure of the plebeian consciousness through much of the eighteenth century and, in rural areas, well into the nineteenth. How did a society whose manifest ideology was that of paternalism feel from below?

Had these letters never been written we might suppose, although we would find it difficult to prove, that England between 1750 and 1810 was always a land of moderate consensus, within which the lower orders showed their gratitude towards a humane paternalism by a due measure of deference; or, if not quite this, then a society in which until the 1790s

1. As late as 1869 or 1870 John Wilson, the Primitive Methodist pitman who was to become an MP and leader of the Durham miners, found it necessary to conduct an anonymous underground propaganda in the attempt to organize the Haswell colliery. 'Mysterious notes began to appear on the pulley frames and waggons . . . on pieces of paper about three inches square'; but according to Wilson's memory his notes incited to organization ('Arise and assert your manhood!') and carried no threats: John Wilson, *Memories of a Labour Leader*, 1910, p. 223.

the gentry attained to such an overwhelming hegemony that their order appeared to be as unquestionable as the overarching sky. At least it has been possible to show that here and there something a little less than deference was to be found. 'Lord Buckingham,' a Norwich handbill writer remarked in 1793, 'who died the other Day had Thirty Thousand Pounds, yeerly For setting his Arse in the House of Lords and doing nothing.'[1] This sentence should perhaps be included in a footnote to the *History of Parliament.* Or, again, regimental histories sometimes overlook aspects of their subject which were apparent to observers at the time. 'We fear not the Soldiers,' remarked an Exeter author (1801), 'neither the Volunteers (vulgarly termed the Farmers Bull-Dogs).'[2]

Or, if we go back earlier in the century with expectations conditioned by much eighteenth-century historiography, it will be only with difficulty that we will recognize in 'that Bich oud Clifton', Lady Clifton of Clifton Hall, Nottingham.[3] Nor will expectations as to the impartial workings of the law prepare us for such an account as that of the Southall Court of Requests (1757): 'For Them Prespetrenc that You set as Comishenors have no regard of Conscienc in Them for They will swear a black Cro is whit for a Six peny Peic.'[4] Or, again, a Hampshire villager sent, in 1798, a letter to Henry Chichley Plowden, which perhaps may modify orthodox views as to the ways in which commercial wealth, brought back to England, fertilized the agrarian and industrial revolutions: 'You are a Damd Rogue and Damd Roguish you got your Money and a Damd Rogue you are in not paying it where it is owing you thinks to do as you did in the Indies but I am damd mistaken if you do for you killed thousands of poor Souls for to get their Wealth and now you makes a god of it.'[5]

We now know enough about the actions of the eighteenth-century crowd to distrust the rather comfortable historiography dominant until recently. According to such accounts the English country gentleman was 'close to the common life of the common people' and 'never far from ordinary humanity': and 'honour, dignity, integrity, considerateness, courtesy and chivalry were all virtues essential to the character of a gentleman, and they all derived in part from the nature of country life'.[6] A writer from Witney (1767) displayed country life in a different nature: 'Do not suffer such damned wheesing fat guted Rogues to Starve the

1. *LG* 1793, p. 926 (October 1793).
2. *LG* 15349 (March 1801). See also Appendix III (*k*).
3. *LG* 10366 (November 1763).
4. *LG* 9754 (October 1757). For 'Prespetrenc' I read 'Presbyterians'.
5. *LG* 1798, p. 76 (January 1798).
6. R. J. White, *Waterloo to Peterloo*, 1957, pp. 40–41; F. M. L. Thompson, *English Landed Society in the Nineteenth Century*, 1963, p. 16.

Poor by such Hellish Ways on purpose that they may follow hunting horse-racing &c and to maintain their familys in Pride and extravagence.'[1] And in 1800 an inhabitant of Henley-on-Thames, who had had the benefit of seeing the Volunteers in action against the crowd, offered to historians an alternative framework of analysis: 'You gentleman as you are please to call Yourselves – Altho that is your Mistakes – for you are a sett of the most Damnable Roughs that Ever Existed.'[2]

No doubt an author who had been ridden over by the Yeomanry wrote from a biased position. But the voices remain in one's inner ear. And they prompt one last, and important, reflection. The very vehemence of style should not mislead one to another extreme in which plebeian England in the eighteenth century is seen as made up of impotent revolutionaries, a few articulate (in the *Gazette*), the rest incoherent with wrath. For the imprecations and the vehemence are the other side to the medal of deference. They are those who come from a religious culture for whom the oath and the blasphemy carry most magical power. And they are those who cannot articulate their grievances openly, who cannot form their own organizations or circulate their own pamphlets and press, whose voices break out anonymously with intemperate force.

But we should not be misled by this. *Given the opportunity*, such insurrectionary voices could be followed by insurrectionary actions. Revolutionaries may indeed come on the streets, as in Paris by 1791, with voices like these. But *without the opportunity*, the voices could switch back once again, with remarkable suddenness, to silence or to abject dependency. This is apparent in many of the letters, especially those written before the influence of Tom Paine. It can be seen in the oscillatory tone of the letter from the commoners of Cheshunt in 1799: on the one hand, the unmeasured violence of language – 'Whe like birds of pray will prively lie in wait to spil the bloud' of those preparing enclosure, 'whose names and places of abode are as prutrified sores in our Nostrils'; on the other hand, if instead of enclosure the same gentlemen had effected a fair regulation of common rights, then 'thou instead of being contempabel whould thy Name been as Oderriferous Ointment pour'd fourth to us'.

Whe leave it for thy consideration Wheather thou would like to be sorted out from the land of the liveing or would like to have the poors hearts and there all if required for if thou proceeds to inclose our blood will boil like a pot if thou goest to regulate it then . . . will whe come and give our hearts and voices to it and to you for ever. . .[3]

1. *LG* 10779 (November 1767).   2. *LG* 1800, pp. 346-7 (March 1800).
3. See Appendix I (*d*).

And, behind this again, there is a resignation in the inevitability of the given social order: the poor, by threat or even by violence, are recalling the rich to certain notional duties. What the letters show is not the absence of deference in this kind of society, but something of its character and limitations. This deference has no inwardness: these writers do not love their masters, but, in the end, they must be reconciled to the fact that for the duration of their lives these are likely to remain their masters. It is like this in smaller institutions which profess paternalist values; the NCO may despise or hate his officers, the servant in the great house, or college, may despise those whom he serves, but dependence demands that certain dues of conduct and speech be paid.[1]

Hence the historian who encounters such letters as these, and then turns back to the licensed press or to the papers of the great, has a sense of double vision. On the surface all is consensus, deference, accommodation; the dependants petition abjectly for favour; every hind is touching his forelock; not a word against the Illustrious House of Hanover or the Glorious Constitution breaks the agreeable waters of illusion. Then, from an anonymous and obscure level, there leaps to view for a moment violent Jacobite or Levelling abuse. We should take neither the obeisances nor the imprecations as indications of final truth; both could flow from the same mind, as circumstance and calculation of advantage allowed. It would now seem, Richard Cobb tells us, that half the valets of pre-Revolutionary Paris, who followed the nobility servilely through the suave *salons*, were nourishing in their reveries anticipations of the guillotine falling upon the white and powdered necks about them.[2] But, if the

1. It is exactly in servant–master relations of dependency, in which personal contacts are frequent and personal injustices are suffered against which protest is futile, that feelings of resentment or of hatred can be most violent and most personal. Even the prospering tradesman whose prosperity depends upon concealing his true feelings from his arrogant and time-wasting customers can suffer such feelings: Francis Place testifies to this in his autobiography, which is perhaps warmer on this point than on any point of general political rights: 'I knew . . . that the most profitable part for me to follow was dancing attendance on silly people, to make myself acceptable to coxcombs, to please their whims, to have no opinion of my own . . . I knew well that to enable me to make money I must consent to submit to much indignity, and insolence, to tyranny and injustice. I had no choice between doing this and being a beggar, and I was resolved not to be a beggar . . . In short, a man to be a good tailor, should be either a philosopher or a mean cringing slave whose feelings had never been excited to the pitch of manhood': *The Autobiography of Francis Place*, ed. Mary Thale, Cambridge, 1972, pp. 216–17.

2. The managing director of the County Fire Office (who had much experience to draw upon) also found that the intimate dependants of the propertied were those most likely to commit acts of arson and incendiary letter-writing. He advised his agents; during the 'Swing' episode: 'The *servants of the sufferer*, people in his employ and even confidence, and living on his land, and near the spot fired, are very frequently found to

guillotine had never been set up, the reveries of these valets would remain unknown. And historians would be able to write of the deference, or even consensus, of the *ancien régime*. The deference of eighteenth-century England may have been something like that, and these letters its reveries.

---

be capable of committing these acts. A slight, a refusal, a supposed harshness, nay, even the gratification of an envious and malicious feeling are sufficient motives with some people of this class to do these acts. Some of the most persevering attempts at house burning that we have on record have been committed by servant girls.' Circular headed 'To Discover an Incendiary in the Country', 24 December 1830, PRO, HO 40.25 cited in Radzinowicz, vol. II, pp. 450–54.

Appendix: A Sampler of Letters

This sampler illustrates anonymous letter-writing from complete examples rather than from selective quotation. It has not been easy to select characteristic examples from so wide a field. I have therefore concentrated upon three major groups: (1) rural labourers, as far as the 'Swing' riots of 1830 and the Rebecca riots; (2) industrial protest, as far as the Luddite years; (3) protests against high prices, as far as the years of 'seditious' letters, 1800–1801. Seditious letters of course continued for more decades, but I have not followed them into the different post-war context.

The orthography of these letters follows that of the originals which I have used: but these 'originals', especially those in the *London Gazette*, were often based on copies made by gentlemen or parish clerks of the true originals; and sometimes, when I have been able to compare the two, it is evident that they were poorly transcribed. Hence a phrase which seems meaningless may simply be the clerk's (and not the author's) error.

   I   Rural Grievances
  I I Industrial Grievances
I I I Prices, Riot and Sedition
I V The Anonymous Muse

a. Gleaning

Ms orpen i am informd that you and your family whent before last year and glent up what the pore should have had but if you do this year it is our desire as soon as your corn is in the barn we will have a fire for it is a shame you should rob the pore as you have done for years so you may depend upon thes lines to be trwe for we will sartainly do it we have suffered so long that we are detarmied that sun shall suffere as well we you are not alone by night or day we will seek revenge.

Received by Mrs Sarah Orpin in Bradwell, near Coggeshall, Essex. Gleaning was regarded not as a favour but as the right of the village labourers and poor.
Source: London Gazette, *no. 11383 (August 1773)*

b. Crediton: 1795

To the Gentlemen of This Parish Greeting

Know ye not that the Lord of Life Liveth and that he will come again at the Last Day to judge the world in Righteousness to Give unto every man according as his work shall be some to Life Eternal and some to Everlasting punishment would ye not therefore Joyfully receive Mercy and forgiveness for your manifold sins and wickedness at the hand of our most Graceous Lord and Saviour at that Great trybunual Day. Should ye not Likewise therefore have Mercy Upon your poor Destresst Brethren who are Drove into the Greatest Destress of Poverty and to Extreem want at the highest Degree alarming under which Great Opression and heavy

Burden can no Longer be born for the advanced Price of every Individual
thing from this thirty years past are advanced some things to one third
some Half and many things are at a Double rate both of Provisions and
Wareing apparel and our wages are no more than at that time was therefore we hope that you will take this in Consideration how the poor man
Is to Live and how he is to support himself and his poor Destressed Family
under which Burden these have Long unhapply felt it is not to be supported any Longer an for which occassion there will be a General meeting
held at that Feild Belonging to Sir John Davey joining hard by the fir
wood Laying Between Barnstable Cross and Crediton forkes on monday
the 13th Day of this Instant April 1795 by Eight O Clock in the morn
Directly the thing that we Do ask is no more than Nature Doth Crave and
not so much as things are advanced upon us which is for Every man to
have one shilling and sixpence per Day or to be Settled according to the
price of wheat Every man to have the value of one Peck of wheat per day
supposing from 11 shills to 9 shills the Bushel hours to Labour and
Lyqour as used at which time this Great assembly will upon the Period
of Death Gain or perish at the atempt to the End that our Little ones for
want perish not – all such Gentlemen who are of a Remorse Conscience
as have an Eye of pity upon the Destressed which is an object truly
Deserving Compassion would be Desired to Meet us there are the Place
above mentioned to settle with us in amity Peace an Concord which we
shall Gratefully receive but the refusal of such will Return your Recom-
pence Upon your own head and your Reward be given you which may
soon Unhappily come Upon you.

> God Bless our Gracious King and Send
> Health and Prosperity may his Days attend
> May his Ruleing Subjects Humanity then show
> And Pay unto the Poor what they to them do owe.

This letter was found on the church door and copies in other parts of Crediton.

Source: enclosure in the Reverend George Bent of Sandford, near Crediton, to Portland, PRO, HO 42.34.

c. Berkshire, 1795: A Call to Strike

This is to give Notis all the poor Men in this parish to ly still and meake
the Farmers give us more Monny for our Labour for our provicion is so

very dear that we cant liv without starving to Dearth Wone and all to lye still and that Man goes to Worke without more monny his house shall be set one fier uppon his head.

> God save the King.

And if the Beakers ont let us have bread we will take every loaf that the have and Faney Pather shall have hur House set on fier if shee sink not her bread in three Days. 1795.

> God save the King.

And if the Farmers ont give us more monny a good Fier shall be without anny Delay a tall within 10 Days and your riks bournd to the Ground.

This notice was stuck on the church door at East Hagborne, Berks, on 21 March 1795. There is as yet no evidence as to whether the call to 'lye still' (or to strike) met with a response. Rather than give higher wages, the farmers and landowners preferred to subsidize wages out of the poor rates in relation to the ruling price of bread, and the famous 'Speenhamland' decision of the Berkshire justices was taken six weeks later (6 May 1795).

Source: Reading Mercury, *30 March 1795.*

d. Enclosure: Cheshunt, 1799

Feb[y] 27/99

Sir,

Whe right these lines to you who are the Combin'd of the Parish of Cheshunt in the Defence of our Parrish rights which you unlawfully are about to disinherit us of the Same   Resolutions is maid by the aforesaid Combind that if you intend of incloseing Our Commond Commond fields Lammas Meads Marshes &c Whe Resolve before you shall say & the rest of the heads of that bloudy and unlawful act it is finished to have your hearts bloud if you proceede in the aforesaid bloudy act Whe like horse leaches will cry give, give untill whe have spilt the bloud of every one that wishes to rob the Inosent unborn it shall not be in your power to say I am safe from the hands of the Enemy for Whe like birds of pray will prively lye in wait to spil the bloud of the aforesaid Charicters whose names and plaices of above are as prutrified sores in our Nostrils   Whe declair that thou shalt not say I am safe when thou goest to thy bead for beware that

thou liftest not thine eyes up in the mist of flames and when thou goest
out be shour if you can that thou returns in safety the bloud of every
one that wishes the distruction of this parrish in the aforesaid bloudy act
Whe are deturmined to have if at the expence of ours Whe cannot but say
that there is plenty of room for Alterations for Whe cannot see why that
Ruskins and a few more of them should run our Common over while
there is no room for another to put any thing on [If] thou hadst made an
Alteration in the rights of Commoning thou instead of being contempable
whould thy Name been as Oderriferous Ointment pour'd fourth to us the
voice of Us and the maguor part of the parrish is for a regulation of commons rights is in the follow manner that Every one to turn on the Com-
monds in proportion to what they hold which to be deturmined by our
superiours so that every one may have his alotment to do as he pleases to
keep annerkey from our parrish so that if he dose not wish to keep anything let him or hur let those proportions to whome they like so that it
may be an easement to them in the poors rates if thou had took this step
then would thou had our hearts and our all at they survise Whe leave it
for thy consideration Wheather thou would like to be sorted out from the
land of the liveing or would like to have the poors hearts and there all if
required for if thou proceeds to inclose our blood will boil like a pot if
thou goist to regulate it then as aforesaid then will whe come and give our
hearts and voices to it and to you for ever but no inclosure will whe agree
to

Sir you may let Mr. George Prescott and Mr. Russell and the rest of our
Nobility know our Resolutions for as there was only thy Name in the
papers

Whe only right to you if agree to our proposals from your well wishers the
Combind in the defence of the rights of the parrish of Cheshunt

This letter was received by Oliver Cromwell, Esq., of Cheshunt Park.

Source: PRO, HO 42.46; Copy (with minor differences in transcription) in
London Gazette, *1799, p. 267.*

e. Isle of Wight: 1800

The Farmers friends and the Pasens enemy Wee have taken the liberty
of riting this few lines to you to inform you of our intention and that is to
let you know our determanation is to live or Die. For this last 20 years

Wee have been in a Starving Condition to maintain your Dam Pride. So now jintelmen if you Dont advans our wages Wee will See what can be don. So now jintelman wee should be fery sorry to burn any Corn for wee have not half bred a nof now. For what we have done now is Soar against our Will but your harts is so hard as the hart of Pharo but wee will see if it cant bee Broken. So now as far as your Constables wee dont care a dam for wee have four to one Jent. and three out of four of them will turn to bee of our Sides. And insted of making Constables Staves thare shall bee more Need of Coffens. So now as for this fire you must not take it as a front. For if you hadent been Deserving it wee should not have dont. As for you my Ould frend you dident hapen to be hear. If that you had been rosted i feer. And if it had a been so how the farmers would lagh to see the ould Pasen rosted at last. As for you Mr. Hicks Wee have been informed that you have got some dam bad tricks and as for Admorell Hamond he seems to talk like a Man and wee are in hopes that he will do somthing for us if he can. And as for Mr Crozier tho' he is hapst up in with bricks wee will get at him if he don't leave of his bad tricks. So now if you acts like jintelmen it shall be all fery well.

But if you dont you will Shurley go to Hell and as for this litel fire Don't be alarmed it will be a damd deal wors when we Burn down your barn. So no I hope that you will stand a poor felow frend or els in a Midel of a fier you shall Stand.

Wee should be glad if you would show this to all the jintlemen in Freshwater.

This letter was found on the premises of the Very Reverend Dean Wood, Rector of Freshwater, Isle of Wight, on the morning after a fire, 29 November 1830.

Source: copy in PRO, HO 52.7.

f. Swing and Tithes

Sir,

We have inquired into your tithes, and we have determined to set fire to you in your bed if you do not lower them. You receive from Fletching £500 a year, and give your curate only £100 a year, and you starve your labourers that works for you, you old canibal. You parsons have fleeced the country long enough. Strain, if you dare. You and your daughter shall be burned in your beds if you do. We shall tell all the people in the parish not to pay you, for we are determined and our names are legions of liberty.

Deem this as friendly, and consider that we would not burn you up without notice.

Y.Z.X.

[Drawing of penknife, with drop of red ink]

William and Henry Bish, brothers and both schoolmasters, 'respectably dressed young men', were tried at Lewes Assizes for sending this letter to the Reverend George Woodward of Maresfield: both were found not guilty.

Source: The Times, *22 December 1830.*

g. The Fruits of Literacy: 1839

A PROCLAMATION OF BLOOD AND FIRE!

To all Churches, States and People, on the Sea Sand

O Remember

Samson sent 300 foxes with firebrands into the Philistine's corn fields, because they robbed him of his natural rights, and God declares Samson more justifiable than them – so now the Gentiles and Heathen starve the poor, why marvel ye if every man turns after Samson, 'for these are the days of vengeance, when all shall be fulfilled' under

> MAHERSHALALHASHBAZ, Sec.,
> and
> JESUS CHRIST
> CHOLERA, BLOOD, FIRE, and Co.
> Extra Executors.
> Earthquakes, Panics and Co., Witnesses.

Source: Salisbury Herald, *copied in* London Dispatch, *6 January 1839.*

h. A Rebecca Letter

To William Peel, Esq., High Sheriff of Carmarthenshire

Monachlogddu
June 14th, 1843

Sir,

Being aware of the scrutenizing system of most of the gentry and

316

nobility of the County of Carmarthen in my journey of doing good to the poor and distressed farmers I took notice of *you as one* who not careful enough of your tenantry do by your oppressing and arbitrary power make them to languish under your hand. You know very well I dare say that every article the farmer has to sell is of a very low price in this county and you know too well that your rent is as high as ever therefore if you will not consider in time and at your next Rent day make a considerable allowance to your Tenantry I do hereby warn you in time to mind yourself for as sure as this letter will come to your hand I and my dutiful daughters from 5 to 10 hundred of us will visit your habitation at Taliarris in a few days and you will do well to prepare a secure place for your soul we will do well with your body your flesh we will give to the Glausevin hounds and your bones we will burn with those of Sir James Williams and Lewis Gilfach in Tophet unless you and them will make more good to the poor farmer than you do. Down with the Rent all will be good. It seems now that you are Sheriff for the County you better to behave like a man then not like Phillips Aberglasnen and some fools of his sort we will be there waiting your coming. Not many days again we will visit Dynevor & Gelliawr palaces to see what they do there this bad time. Tell that Lloyd Tanyrallt that he is a mortal man very soon not long ago he displeased me.

[A ring of crosses]

If you will not try in the course of this week to take off the tolls paid at Gurreyfach gate on your road we will be there make our visitation very soon take the hint in time, lo, I tell you fairly.

> I remain your faithful Servant,
> Rebecka Dogood.

Source: Enclosed in Lord Dynefor to Barrington, 27 June 1843, PRO, HO 45.454 (i).

a. Manchester Calico-Printers, 1786

Mr. Taylor If you dont discharge James Hobson from the House of Correction we will burn your House about your Ears for we have sworn to stand by one another and you must immediately give over any more Mashen Work for we are determined there shall be no more of them made use of in the Trade and it will be madness for you to contend with the Trade as we are combined by Oath to fix Prices we can afford to pay him a Guinea Week and not hurt the fund if you was to keep him there till Dumsday therefore mind you comply with the above or by God we will keep our Words with you we will make some rare Bunfires in this Countey and at your Peril to call any more Meetings mind that we will make the Mosney Pepel shake in their Shoes we are determined to destroy all Sorts of Masheens for Printing in the Kingdom for there is more hands then is work for so no more from the ingerd Gurnemen Rember we are a great number sworn nor you must not advertise the Men that you say run away from you when your il Usage was the Cause of their going we will punish you for that our Meetings are legal for we want nothing but what is honest and to work for selvs and familers and you want to starve us but it is better for you and a few more which we have marked to die then such a Number of Pore Men and there famerles to be starved.

Addressed to Mr Charles Taylor, a Manchester master calico-printer, as part of a general organized resistance to the introduction of machinery.

Source: London Gazette, *1786, p. 36 (January 1786).*

b. Glasgow Weavers, 1786

Glasgow April 14 1786

Sir,

We take this Opportunity to give You this warning of Your danger for

Your behaviour in breaking the prices of the poors work and if You do not amend Your ways and put on what You have unjustly taken of the wages, we are determined that within the Space of One Month upwards of One hundred of us have made an Oath and entred into a Bond that if you do not retrac from what You have done that we will set Your warehouse in fire about your ears and for Yourself wherever we can find You and Your Accomplices we shall make you suffer for what You have done and likeways we hear in the Newspapers that You and Your combined begerly Crew are designed to oppose the opperative Weavers but because You think if that pass into a Law Youl be prevented from breaking the Prices by reson the workmen will not be so plenty, likeways we hear whenever any person Complaens of his prices to his Master they will tell him to go to Mulrie sword or Bartholemews Warehouse and see there regulations that they are less by this we learn that You Damn'd Rascalls are always the first to break the prices so by this if You have any regard for Your safety You will take Warning both Your and Your Accomplices You Lousy Rougues that comes from nothing and wants to make rich but we will soon deprieve You of that for we are desgned to put in execution what what we have sworn so take warning Mulrie Sword Bartholemew Sweet Dennisloan Crum and all You that has the most active hand in so doing.

Addressed to David Mulrie, Manufacturer, 'Head of the Havannah-street', Glasgow.
Source: London Gazette, *1786, p. 203 (April 1786).*

c. Newbury Weavers, 1787

Gentlemen Clotheiers I A Weaver Am Determined Except This Combination Is Quite Void, And The Weavers Have Work As Usual, Without Working Under Price, in One Thing or the Other. As For Shalloons We are agreeable To work Them At the Usual Price Or Any Thing Else You May Find Us To do. Gentlemen would you Think It a Crime in any one Liveing, To stand In His Own Defence Against His Enemy, You Gentlemen Are Agreed To Beat Down The Price of the Weavers Work, The Price of the weavers Work is already so Low They Cannot Get A livelywood like Almost any Other Trade, why should you wish To starve Us Quite, Yours Lives As well as Ours are Not Insured One Moment, Neither Can You Carry Your Ill Got Treasure with you

Into The Next Life, As For This life I Look upon It as Nothing in
Respect of The life To Come, If you, with Starveing The Poor, Could
Gain The whole world And at the same Time Greatly Indanger Your
Precious soul's, In what Point Have You The Advantage let me Desire
of you Gentlemen To Take This Wicked Device Into Consideration, Or
Else Prepare your selves For A Good Bonfire at Both Ends At Each Your
Dwellings, which Thing is Fully Determined Without An Alteration
within This Month, was I sure To Dey For standing For My Right, I
would Dey Willingly, But Trust Me In That, I will Trust My self, and
not another I May As well Dey with a Houlter, As Be starved To Death,
with Wicked Men's Devices, Gentlemen I am determined To Execute
The Contents of These lines In Every Degree.

Found under the door of Mr Thomas Brown, Clothier of Newbury.

Source: London Gazette, *12846 (April 1787).*

d. West of England Shearmen, 1799

I send you this to inform you That wee the Clothworkers of Trowbridge
Bradford Chippinham and Melkshom are allmost or the greatest part of
Us Oute of work and Wee are fully Convinst that the gretests of the Cause
is your dressing work by Machinery And wee are determind if you
follow this Practice any longer that wee will keep som People to watch
you Abought with loaded Blunderbuss or Pistols And will Certainly Blow
your Brains out it is no use to Destroy the Factorys But put you Damd
Villions to death And that you may depend up on will be don the County
then but make up your lost when your soul is blown into Hellfire And
this shall be done as sure as you are Alive give your Brother Brown a
Caution of this as hee will shear the same fate and Cook and Bamford
Allso there is every thing gott in readyness for the Busness now you know
what you have to Trust to it will be no use For you to cry out when to
Late when you be in hell I mean you was better perswade your mother
from her evill Ways in it or shee will share The same fate do Consider and
put a stop to it in Time or Death and Damnation will be your Fate.

We are yours the Clothworkers of the afforsaid Towns
Apreil 7th 1799

Source: London Gazette, *1799, p. 507 (May 1799).*

320

e. Nottinghamshire Luddism

DECLARATION; EXTRAORDINARY
JUSTICE
DEATH, OR REVENGE

To our well-beloved Brother, and Captain in Chief, Edward Ludd

WHEREAS, it hath been represented to us: the General Agitators, for the Northern Counties, assembled to redress the Grievances of the Operative Mechanics, That Charles Lacy, of the Town of Nottingham, British Lace Manufacturer, has been guilty of diverse fraudulent, and oppressive, Acts – whereby he has reduced ⁀o poverty and Misery Seven Hundred of our beloved Brethren; moreover, it hath been represented to us that the said Charles Lacy, by making fraudulent Cotton Point Nett, of One Thread Stuff, has obtain'd the Sum of Fifteen Thousand Pounds, whereby he has ruin'd the Cotton-Lace Trade, and consequently our worthy and well-belov'd Brethren; whose support and comfort depended on the continuance of that manufacture.

IT appeareth to us that the said Charles Lacy, was actuated by the most diabolical motives. We therefore wishing to make an example of the said Charles Lacy, do adjudge the said Fifteen Thousand Pounds to be forfeited, and we do hereby authorise, impower, and injoin you, to command Charles Lacy to disburse the said sum, in equal shares among the Workmen, who made Cotton Nett in the year 1807, within Six Days from the Date hereof.

IN default whereof, we do command that you inflict the Punishment of Death on the said Charles Lacy, and we do authorise you to distribute among the Party you may employ for that purpose the Sum of Fifty Pounds, we enjoin you to cause this our Order to be presented to the said Charles Lacy without Delay, November 1811.

BY ORDER

This declaration, in beautiful copper-plate, might perhaps be considered as an 'official' Luddite document, in the Nottinghamshire war of nerves.

Source : *Facsimile in John Russell, 'The Luddites',* Transactions of the Thoroton Society, x (*1906*).

f. Yorkshire Luddism

To General Ludd Juner

Nottingham, 1812

By Order of Genral Ludd . . .

I am reqested to express the hye sence of honer entertaned of the meretoreous movments you and your forses have so gallently mad in the neberood of Hudersfeld to secure the rites of our pour starving fellow creturs.

I am also desired to say that they lament with extrem regret the fate of the two *brave boys* who galantly spilt theire blod in a lodible cose at Rawfolds. They further learn with pleser that a noble attempt was made about a mile from Huddersfeld though without suckses [two words illegible] the Hytown *machenry man*.

The Genral further auhtorises me to say that he trusts to the attachment of his subjects for the avenging of the death of the two brav youths who fell at the sege of Rawfolds. He also wishes me to state that though his troops heare are not at present making any ostensable movments that it is not for want of force – as the orgenisation is quite as strong as in Yorkshire – but that they are at present only devising the best means for a grand attack and that at present thay are dispatching a few indeviduals by pistol shot on of which fel last nite.

I am further otherised to say that it is the opinion of our general and men that as long as that blackgard drunken whoreing fellow, called Prince Regent and his servants have anything to do with government that nothing but distres will befale us there foot-stooles.

I am further desired to say that it is expected that you will remember that you are mad of the same stuf as Gorg Guelps Juner and corn and wine are sent for you as wel as him.

Peter Plush
Secretary to General Ludd

This letter was addressed to 'Mr Edward Ludd, Market Place, Huddersfield'. Perhaps it was the effort of a freelance Nottinghamshire Luddite, and was intended more to alarm the authorities than to communicate with Yorkshire Luddites. It is dated 1 May 1812.

Source: Radcliffe MSS, *126/46*.

g. Lancashire Luddism

Sir,

This would be an error that our very blood could not expiate, if these lines were stuffed with nothing but mere malice and injustice, for conscious we are you must at first think so, but if you will take a little advice from a few friends, you will then immediately become an Apostate to your principles. The Fable of the 'Plague amongst the Beasts' is well worth a Coroner's reading. Had some poor man murder'd two or three rich ones in cool blood, Nat. Milnes would then have buss'd in their ears a 'Packed Jury' loaded with Contagion, these Words: 'Willful Murder', instead of 'Justifiable Homicide', but know thou cursed insinuator, if Burton's infamous action was 'justifiable' the Laws of Tyrants are Reasons Dictates.

Beware, Beware! A month's bathing in the Stygian Lake would not wash this sanguinary deed from our minds, it but augments the heritable cause, that stirs us up in indignation.

Milnes if you really are not a Friend to the great Oppressors, forgive us this – but if you are – 'the rest remains behind'.

Ludd finis est.

This letter was sent to Milne, the Clerk to the Manchester magistrates and the Salford Coroner, following upon the attack on Daniel Burton's power-loom mill on 20 and 21 April 1812. On the first day Burton defended his mill with musket-fire, killing three of the attackers: more were killed by the military on the next day. This letter is protesting at the subsequent verdict of 'justifiable homicide', and is an example of the freelance high-flown radical style becoming more common in the early nineteenth century.

Source: PRO, HO 40.1.

h. Freelance Luddism

If you keep that Rouge in you house Ned shall visit you and we shall be acpt too give you a little could led and you cattle too if you dont get shoot ove [shut of] im very soon and Need will send them too Hell and Hall ove you too and you sheep Ned will ham string And ef you don thay will send me word in the course ove a day.

March the 12.   J. Genrall Lud.

This letter was thrown in at the door of Richard Dennis, a Nottinghamshire farmer who also owned some knitting-frames, and who had once been visited by Luddites. The 'Rouge' (rogue) in his house was one Twist, a journeyman framework-knitter, and the letter was written by Adam Wagstaff, also a framework-knitter, who lived close to Dennis and who had once been employed in one of Dennis's frames. Twist had informed against Wagstaff for poaching and, as a consequence, Wagstaff had demanded that Dennis dismiss Twist. When Dennis refused, this letter followed. Wagstaff was seen throwing the letter in at the door and was convicted.

Source: Rex v. Adam Wagstaff (*Nottinghamshire Summer Assizes, 1819*), *Russ. & Ry. 398* (English Reports, *vol. 168, p. 865*).

i. Industrial Wales, 1816

The Poor Workmen of Tredega to prepare Yourself with Musquets, Pistols, Pikes, Spears and all kinds of Weapons to join the Nattion and put down like torrent all Kings, Regents, Tyreants of all description and banish out of the Country every Traitor to this Common Cause and to Beuray famine and distress in the same grave.

Notice posted in Tredegar Iron Works, 22 December 1816.

Source: PRO, HO 40.4.

a. Jacobite Threat, 1766

Dear [torn]

We are all consulting about destroying the workhouses, and so Crush it in the Budd, and likewise the Butter Warehouses at Woodbridge as the Soldiers are agoing from thence next week and the Mills, & some Gentlemans Houses, and we hear they are ready about Shobisham, and all along those Towns, & we will join [illegible] at first notice, we are wishing our exiled King could come over or send some Officers with a few [illegible] Troops and that would do as we are all sold for the National Debt & give my love to Sisters and Brother Will.

This letter was found, in October 1766, 'fixt upon a signpost in the public marketplace' of Woodbridge, Suffolk, and was taken down by the Clerk of the Market, and brought to Thomas Cardhew, a local magistrate, who found it 'peculiarly bold and seditious and of high and delicate import'.

Source: PRO, WO 1.873 fo. 495.

b. Levelling Threat, 1767

This comes to let you know that there is a small Army of us
Upwards of 3 thousand all ready to fight
& I'll be damd if we don't make the Kings Army to shite,
If so be the King & Parliment dont order better
We will turn England into a Litter
& if so be as things dont get cheaper
I'll be damd if we dont burn down the Parliment House & make

325

all better Think of poor People makes my Heart to ake
Bakers Millers Farmers Badgers also
Get all in their Clutches when nobody knows
But as for them we'll make them tremble
We'll fetch all they have & make them to humble.

Mr Kettley we desire you to put it in the News Paper immediately or
we will burn down your House. I'll be damd if we dont but if you put it
in the Paper we shall be greatly obliged to you.

> So no more from your most humble Ser^vt
> N.B. Kidderminster & Stourbridge.

This letter was addressed to Mr Kettley at the Golden Cross on Snow Hill, Birming-
ham, in March 1767.

Source: PRO, WO 1. 873 fos. 505–10. (I have transcribed parts of the letter as
verse.)

c. Manchester, 1762

> Rosandale August 21. 1762.

This his to asquaint you that We poor of Rosendale Rochdale Oldham
Saddleworth Ashton have all mutaly and firmly agreed by Word and
Covinent and Oath to Fight and Stand by Each Other as long as Life doth
last for We may as well all be hanged as starved to Death and to see ower
Children weep for Bread and none to give Them nor no liklyness of ever
mending wile You all take Part with Brommal and Markits drops at all the
princable Markits elceware but take This for a shure Maxon, That if You
dont put those good Laws in Execution against all Those Canables or
Men Slayers That have the Curse of God and all honest Men both by
Gods Laws and Mens Laws so take Notice Bradshaw Bailey and Lloyd
the biggest Rogue of all Three I know You all have Power to stop such
vilonas Proceedings if You please and if You dont amaidatley put a Stopp
and let hus feel it the next Saturday We will murder You all that We have
down in Ower List and Wee will all bring a Faggot and burn down Your
Houses and Wait Houses and make Your Wifes Widdows and Your
Children Fatherless for the Blood of Shul de hill lyes cloose at Ower Harts
and Blood for Blood We Require.

> Take Care. Middleton.

This letter was addressed to Mr James Bailey, a JP, and followed upon the extensive riots of 12 July 1762 in Manchester. The 'Blood of Shul de hill' refers to the 'Shude Hill Fight' of 1757, in which several were killed: see F. Michelson and E. Axon, 'The Hatfield Family of Manchester, and the Food Riots of 1757 and 1812', Transactions of Lancashire and Cheshire Antiquarian Society, XXVII (*1910–11*) *pp. 83–90.*

Source: London Gazette, *no. 10242 (August 1762).*

d. Swansea, 1766

To the Honnered Magistrates & Elders of Swanze

This is the Generall Complaint of the Poor and Distressed.

First, That the farmers doth aske for the korn that We Can harly get Bread for our Starving familise.

Secondly; That the Millarts doth take a Quarter which is the fourth of a Peck for Towel.

Therdly; That the Molsters doth agree with the farmers for the Bearly Ho bring three bushel to the Market and open One and Caring the Rest to Theiar houses Instant for One John Vos and others and Likewise, the Bakers takeing in the Wheat In the Week Comming to Meet them in Mylls.

Now Sirs We hope that Wisdom will teach You that have Authority to order these Things

Or Else we cannot Perrish without – Reveng we dwo intend two Meet together on the Borough of Crynlyn on the 29th Day of November 1766.

God Save the King

This notice was stuck up on the door of Mr William Davies, the Portreeve of Swansea. The second grievance relates to the toll which the millers took for grinding other people's corn. The third (relating to the maltsters) concerns market practices and offences against the regulations against forestalling and regrating. A further notice was fixed to the Market House, calling upon 'all Sorts of Tradesmen Colliers and all Distressed Labourers' to attend a meeting in Crynlyn 'to ask Mercy of God and to Consult one with the Other what Method to Take to get Bread for Our Starving familise'.

Source: London Gazette. *no. 10681 (November 1766).*

e. Clee Hill Miners (Shropshire), 1767

To John Child at the Clee Town
near the Brown Clee Hill

This is to Lett you know our Design that wee will put to death all that have united their Farms & cutt the years of them that occupy them & allso them that have staken up their Corn, The Parliament for our relief to help to Clem us Thay are going to lesson our Measure and Wait to the Lower Standard We are about Ten Thousand sworn and ready at any time And we wou'd have you get Arms and Cutlasses and swear one another to be true and we will Joyn you We have but one Life to Loose and we will not clem We desire you to send to the Fur Hill no more from your Brother Sufferers at present

Industrial Shropshire was a riot-prone district: the miner's grievances extend to the enclosure or consolidation of small farms, and to the introduction of new standard measures. To 'clem' means to starve.

Source: London Gazette, *no. 10710 (March 1767).*

f. Norwich, 1766

For Mr. Pooll Grocher in Norwich

Mr. Pooll

This is to Latt you to know and the Rest of you Justes of the Pace that if Bakers and the Buchers and market peopel if thay do not fall thar Commorits at a reasnabell rate as thay do at other Markets thare will be such Raysen as never was known for your vinegar hoses and your Taller Chandler and fine House will be sat on fire all on one Night for we are detarmed we will have our Minds as wall you have your minds ant you all grand Rouges for to suffer the Bakers to him the flower as deare as to was before but tis to Lat you all know that we will Rise 9 hundred Men and no Boyes for we will clare all before us and if we have not a now we will rais twise 9 hundred

This and the following letter illustrate widely differing modes and styles of threat from the same city.

Source: London Gazette, *no. 10671 (October 1766).*

g. Norwich, 1766

Sir,

The party w^h whom I am their Cheif. and was an Eye Witness to your generosity and lenity to which cheifly you owe your Protection amidst the Variety of Passions that have Inflamed the breast of an Injured and Inraged people they have launched frequently upon Incomiums of you and hope you will further merit their good Will – the Subsequent discours is particularly adapted to you and the Corporation which is in brief, as follows, – We are a select body which are determined at all Events to chastise monopolizers and those particular Gentleman whose distinguished bravery was Evident in defeating a few miserable wretches? The City had been of a flame last night, which was Thursday, but I used all the Eloquence I was Master of and got leave to write to you which is the last time I can intercede in your behalf the time draw near If you have a mind to save the City and yourself. Immediately on Saturday Morning alter the price of most Eatables for the present – in the interim I'll do all I durst to prevail upon them which will be impossible without such an Alteration – therefore for God Sake if you have any regard for your own Safety do what is commanded or expect the dire Event, as for the poor Soldiers I pity them for by God we neither give nor receive Quarter but are determined to perish by the Sword as death will be a deliverance – The land is fertile and bring forth well cultivated fruits in due Season but knavery on one hand and pollicy on the other we have made things thus artificially dear but woe to Mr. Pool – the attack will begin in four different parts and those that do not fall by the Sword shall by the flames – You will be out of danger for you can look of this noble Sentence of Horace without any check. Hic murus ahenous esto nil concere fibi nulla pallescere culpa.

The letter was addressed to Jonathan Gleed, Esq., but was left on a tobacco-dish at the Rose Tavern.

Source: London Gazette, *no. 10761 (October 1766).*

h. Colchester, 1772

This is to give notice to all farmers Mellers and Butchers and Shopkeepers and Corn merchoants that the poor of this nation are brought so low that they must all come to the parishes If there beant an Alterration made in the provisons you are a damd Rogue ashwell so your brick front or your life we will have.

First for the Candle and Soap butter and Cheeslses and let the farmers and all the damd Rogues like your self take Care for this is november – and we have about two or three hundred bum shells a getting in Readiness for the Mellers and all no king no parliment nothing but a powder plot all over the nation.

Found under the gate of James Ashwell, Grocer in Colchester.

Source: London Gazette, *no. 11304 (November 1772).*

i. Essex Villages: 1800

I

June 18, 1800

  this will all com true
this is to give notis that you millers and shop keeper all
  kill the over Seeer
had best to take keare of youer selves and mind that you
arnt kild and if you dont sink with your folower [flour] we will make
  tom Nottage is a dam Rouge
you sink for we have rob your Mill seavel [several] Times and we
  kill him for one   there is 4 more we will kill
will rob it again if you doant look dam sharp we
  sink your Flour to 2 and 6 a peck
set fier tu it and burn it down.
  Burn up all the Mills
and du all the Mischife as we can and weare every you la weete up we set
fier tu it, and burn up every thing here is 10 of us in this Gan [gang] and
we had least di as live for we ar all most stavrd i my Sealfe hast got a Wilfe
and 6 Chirildren and tha low me 4 and 6 a weak. Ther shall be the most
fiers in this Town betwen now and 5 of November then ever was none in
this wold and morst murder done it shall never mis a weeake with out a fier
we will set fier to that god dam Meller and all the pepel that is thear in for
that doth [illegible] and the Church doth fale and that is the R of ingling
for ever.
  Burn up all ever thing an set fier tu the Gurnray

330

This is my copy of a contemporary copy in which some words may have been wrongly transcribed. Part of the letter remains unintelligible. 'Weare every you la weete up we set fier to it' I suggest means 'wherever you lay wheat up we set fire to it'. Presumably on the original letter the first few lines of the letter alternated with interjections such as 'Kill the Overseer!' In any case, the intention of the letter is clear enough.

II

Now Jantleman this is to let you know in all Parts that we have suffered hungary for sumtime and we have bore it paceantly but you still keep starfing us more and more but with great reaserlusen we will not bear it no longer for we live in a Land a planty and if you do not chuse for to lower things so eveary wone may live and in a shoart Time for all warking Hands are sworn true to each other the hole Kingdom through and the first Nobleman in engelin for we have seaveal Nobleman will in cearuges us for the damd Farmers and Factors an like wise mellers an Shopkeepers for thay are worse then the head Jantleman and we mean to set out with a grate reaserlusen to destroy all them kind of men for we will kill burn and disstroay eveary thing we come at spesely the great Landholders and the most searvear men them and there famealys and now Jantlemen you have brought all this on yourselves. We mean to behave well to eveary minester that will read this in the church if not he is a ded man by night or by day we by all means disstroay the King and Parlement.

These two letters appear to be part of a letter-writing campaign in several neighbouring Essex villages. The first was addressed to Mr Joseph Colling at Clavering; the second to 'Mister', Deanes Church, Minster. These two letters come from copies in the Essex RO Q/SBb 380/66/1–2: a letter nearly identical to the second (but differing at a few points) is referred to above in my text (p. 302) and was gazetted in LG, 1800, p. 814, where it was said that such letters had been received in the parishes of Finchingfield, Old Samford, New Samford and Great Bardfield.

j. Bicester, 1800

Here is to all Bicester Gentlemen as calls themselves clever Gentlemen if they dont rise Poor Mens pay as they can live better we will rise and Fight for our Lives better fight and be killed nor be starved an inch at a time. As for your Association Beggar Boys we dont mind no more nor a parcel of Old Women for if we dont have more Bread in short time we will have more Blood for the Farmers and Millers and Bakers are all Damned Rogues but they shall go to rack in short time for we will slaughter them and set Wheat Ricks on Fire. As for our Town Bakers we will choke them and make them up like their Cakes in their Ovens and Burn their Premises down all round this Neighbourhood that Birmingham Waggon has Carried a deal a Wheat away but for the future they shall be looked into as for the Shopkeepers pinch the poor of their Weight and Hogkillers be Rascals they buy their Hogs at 12 shillings a Score and sells them after the Rate of 20 Shillings but the Justices should look into those things but they rather all them Starving but rather than starve we will rise and Fight for our Lives and they will not we will Burn them alive as for these Justices and Gentlemen have enclosed the Fields and the cause of laying down the flails The Devil will Whip them into Helltails.

Affixed to a sign-post in Bicester town (Oxon.).

Source: London Gazette, *1800, p. 347.*

k. *Odiham, 1800*

To The Damd Eternal Fire Brands of Hell Belonging to Odiham and its Vicinity. In other Words to the Damd Villans of Farmers that with hold the Corn that please God to send for the Poeple of the Earth away from them.

This is to inform you all that me, and my Companions have Unanamously agreed and Likewise made Oath to Each other that If Thare is not a speedy Alteration made for the Good of the poore that you that have corn thinking to make your fortunes of shall have it burnt to the Ground whether It Be in Stacks or Barns for the fire that took Place Last Week was But the begining of your Trouble, we know Every Stack of Corn about this Country, and Every Barn that have Corn concealed in it for the Purpos of starving the Poore But we are Determind if thare is to Be Starvation it shall Be a General thing not a parcial one for Both Gentle, and Simple shall Starve if any Do we dont care a Dam for them fellows that Call Themselves Gentlemen Soldiers But in our opinion the Look moore like Monkeys Riding on Bears Whe Can and will take opportunities to Execute our Business thare is 21 of us in number But wee are now

Divided about the Country to in Different Countys to take account of what Wheat Stacks wee can and the poore in Every place is very willing to tell us the Farmers that ask the most Money and Likewise the Millers that Bid the most But Beware of your Dwelling Houses as well as your corn for thare will be something take place Very soon that will Bee a Suden alarm to the County att

Large

for we Can Soon Increace our number & wee have got some Gentlemen that will back us, and they Determined to Se the poore Righted, and for Every fire wee have a *Bounty*.

This letter was picked up in Odiham, Hants, one week after the barns and outhouses of a farmer, containing grain and hay, were burnt.

Source: London Gazette, *1800, p. 248.*

l. Soldiers, 1800

General,

This Note Does Signify that if Provisions Does not fall Down to the old Price as it was In the year 1790 we are Determin'd to a man to Lay Down our arms, and to Scour the Country, & hang up a farmer In Every Parish for an Example to others, that is the only Method to get Provisions Reasonable and if Parliament will not agree to these Proposals there shall not a Parliament Exist on this Island, we are Determin'd one and all, not to see our Familes and the People at Large Starve In a Plentiful Country, through a tyrant and a Dam'd Infernal Imposing Lords & Commons, a Republic must Ensue, and we will fight for our rights & Liberties to the Last moment. France has succeeded In her grand undertaking, and got every Article Cheap and Reasonable and we will follow her Example, so we wid advise you to communicate it so soon as possible ere it be to Late.

We are yours &c
Brother Soldiers

Let the mob Do as the please   Peace & Large Loafs
    We will not interfere

Addressed to Lieutenant-General Rookes, in Bristol.
Source: PRO, HO 42.61.

m. Dorset, 1800: A Prosecution

Blandford

July ye 27, 1800

Tom Compton, I am just going to give thee a friendly Caution if thee dos Nat Looer thy wheat that thee has in thy Stoore house by Monday Next thee mayest Ashure thy Self that thy house and meel Shalt Come flat to ye Ground it shall Be don at one Blow thou Shalt not know it till the moment I Approach for it. Now if thee does mean to Save thy Life thy family and wife Let me hear of the thing I now Request Necesity Calls a Loud for It you Bought your Ship of wheat in a wrong time I say once more Loore it their is plentey in ye Land we must have it down and a Little drop will not do you Raskel down wilth it down with it or down you shall come and Bowdich must down with his Bread are his house Shall Be seet on fire Tom; Cosider All this must Be don in A Short time are thou wilt have But A Short time to Live.

P S depend on it you will Not give me ye trouble to write aney more.

This letter was sent to Thomas Compton, on 29 July 1800, and John Whittle, a gardener, of Upway (Dorset) was committed in August 1800 and tried at the Lent Assizes, 1801.

Source: PRO, Assi 25/1/2.

n. Somerset, 1800: Preparations for Prosecution

To the Honourable John Acland Esqr

We labourers do desire that your Honour will tack it into concideration concerning the high price of provisions & the low rate that we are oblige to work at every artical is dubbeled as dear as it was formly how can you think or imagine that we can suport nature it is inbareable so to do much longer. For if you labour 12 Hours you shall Recd. but 1s 2d for it & you must give 1s 1d for one small lofe of Bread which a man that labours hard can eat it him self in one Day and not to much for him & what is to be com of his Family starve. We are deturmed not to live so much longer the farmers sells their wheat to you for 14s pr Bushell & give you 14d for a Days Work We whants to know ware the fiealings of such dam Rascals can be as to your Barly Market it is of no use to us for that will starve us to death & the usuarping farmers parts with it allredy like drops of Blood from their Hart.

If you do not think proper to call a mitting so as the farmers to give us something for hour labour in proposhon to the times we will fire their wheat ricks for if you mentions anything to the farmers that as Ricks of wheat by them that wheat is dear their answer is ameaditly the do not care the as none to sell.

We whant to know how could the light of thy reason be so darkened how couldst thou be so grosly seduced to think of having but one publick House in this place which is of the greatest hurt imaginable to the people in genearel. I will show you reasons for it first short meashure sould to you & the ale not worth one penny pr pint 2^{ly} was you to drop down for one pint of small beer you could not gate it 3^{ly} if you hadd a mind to keep a small pig you cannot gate one peck of grains from their hands 4^{ly} the will sell you Barm for 2s 6d pr Quart.

Now I leave you to judge if it was not better for every one when their was three publick Houses in this place then if you hadd money you could be suplied with either of the above articals but now if you do carrey money in your hand you cannot gate it.

Now we should be glad to know if it is Bareable or no. But we are deturmed to alter it. For if you do not think proper to liccon a nother House we are deturmed to pull that that is now standing to the ground. It will be to late for you to think of it when houtrages is commited & your house is Burned to the ground.

I only writes this to you as a caution for you to alter it and a publick House to be licconed a meditly above all things.

> Queis patrice pretiosa, finite dolores
> Consilio nostros, & si spes ulla supersit
> Propitias adhibete manus: sis Cadwaladeri
> Dum clarescat honos, vestra hic quoque gloria vivet.

This letter was thrust under the door of the market house in Stogursey, a large village in West Somerset. John Acland, Esq., JP, was a local landowner and had taken part in supervising the sale every Monday in the market house of barley and other goods at reduced prices (subsidized from the poor rates) to the local labourers. Joseph Brown, a local labourer and former sergeant in the Volunteers, was suspected of being the author of this and other letters, on the evidence of handwriting only. Informations and a draft indictment survive (see p. 295 above), but I have not found that the case was brought to trial. Possibly there was no proof that Brown knew Latin.

Source: Papers relating to riots in Stogursey, 1749–1801, in the possession of the Lord St Audries: this copy is taken from a transcript in the keeping of the Vicar of Stogursey.

a. Petworth, 1790

An Address from the Poor to the Wheat Hoarders, Farmers, Butchers, Brewers, Bakers, &c. on the present High Price of Provisions.

> We hope, that the Bread in the price will abate
> And Bakers remember to sell us full Weight,
> To stop our Proceedings in M*bs for the Wheat
> Likewise that the Butcher do give some Relief
> In the present high Price of Mutton and Beef
> One Penny less in a Gallon of small Beer,
> Fall Butter and Cheese for this Shamefully dear
> We hope these few Lines will afford us some ease
> Or we will *rise* a M*b & do as We please

We had better be *lanchd* into Eternity at Once than submit to your Diabolical Imposition and starve by Inches.

N.B. Any Person who shall take down this Paper may depend on being particularly Noticed, when We are assembled.

Copies of this paper were put on the church door, the whipping-post and other places in Petworth, Sussex.

Source: London Gazette, *1790, p. 299 (May 1790).*

b. Lewes, 1795

> Soldiers to arms, arise and revenge your Cause
> On those bloody numskulls, Pitt and George.
> For since they no longer can send you to France
> To be murdered like Swine, or pierc'd by the Lance
> You are sent for by Express to make a speedy Return
> To be shot like a Crow, or hang'd in your Turn;

Ye Britons can you hear this and dauntless stand?
Arise with thoughtful Heads, and nervous Hands.
Let Prudence guide, and patriotic Valor give the Blow
And whelm in Ruin the Aristocratic Foe.
You have of Chiefs and Patriots a matchless Train
To end a Pitt and bloody George's Reign.
Haste Soldiers now, and with intrepid Hand
Grasp Sword and Gun to save thy native Land
For see your Comrades murder'd, ye with Resentments swell
And join the Rage, the Aristocrat to quell
Let undaunted Ardor each bold Bosom warm
To down with George and Pitt, and England call to Arms.

Copy of a paper stuck up at two different places in Lewes on Sunday night, 14 June 1795. Earlier on that day the Oxford regiment of militia had been forced to attend the execution of two of their own soldiers, who had been condemned to death for taking part in price-fixing riots and in a raid on a flour mill in Sussex villages in the previous April.

Source: PRO, HO 42.35.

c. Maldon, 1800

To the Broth Makers & Flower Risers

On Swill & Grains you wish the poor to be fed
And underneath the Gullintine we could wish to see your heads
For I think it is a great shame to serve the poor so –
And I think a few of your heads will make a pretty show

1

We would tye them to a string to make a little fun
There is so many of you wish us to eat Bran
& with these pretty things we would lose many an hour
Intile the rest Consented half a crown a peck the flour

2

The hogs Rise up in Jugment for eating of their food
While you Puffed up Gentry eat the Best of that is good
But we will make your windows fly likewise your Doors indeed
Unless half a crown a peck the flour our poor Children for to feed

3

Here's a hint upon a many you all know very well
I mean your Brothscribers for you'l sur:ey go to hell
Had you But Consented to let us had the flour
We should all a Reason to have Blessd you every hour

4

So now to conclude we shant at this time say any more
For our Determination is that we will have the flour
Our Children Cry for Whitebread there Bellys for to feed
Se we'l have you all beware for this is truth indeed.

Charity Broth one penny a Quart

Migges Maggot & Quids of Tobbacco

& All for one penny per Qt

A magistrate wrote directly to the Secretary of War from Maldon, describing 'much discontent' among 'the lower orders of the people' and 'various inflamatory letters':he sent on the poem from amongst a 'number of papers' to 'shew the ideas of [the] Mob'. A 'great number of Women & Children were excited yesterday to open Riot and threating [sic] to pull down Mills &c and carrying Flags & poles with bread stuck thereon.' The magistrate asked for a Company of Foot to be sent to his aid: the annotation to his letter shows that his request was met.

Source: J. Lee to War Office, 6 February 1800, PRO, WO 40.17.

d. North Shields, 1800

No more ye Britons vainly boast your freedom of a Nation,
When Laws are only made for those Miscreants of Creation,
A Proclamation from the King for Men to cease complaining.
Such Vengefull threats will surely bring an end to unjust reigning.
When Kings neglect the peoples good with reason we complain
Ower allegiance then is understood to be absolved again.
To curse the King or wish their fall is language bad to use
Compassion in their breast were small when they Prclame such News.
Then cease to hope in Tyrants reign with Averace in the rear
The Language now speaks very plain no better times are near.

I have once more ventured to oppose oppressions wicked breast
And Violate the Laws of those who starve the poor to Death
Then rise ye Britons claim your right your children call for Bread
O'erthrow the savage Monsters meight or mingle with the Dead.

These verses were posted up in North Shields on a market day in October 1800. There had been similar verses posted before – the Duke of Portland's informant took down the paper 'when a Number of Men was reading it, they were very quiet sayd nothing. . .'

Source: Robert Laing to Portland, 11 October 1800, PRO, HO 42.52, pp. 339–40.

e. *Somerset, 1801*

Let half starv'd Britons all unite
To tread oppression down
Nor fear the rage of red or blue
Those despots of the Crown.

Then raise yr drooping spirits up
Nor starve by Pitt's decree
Pull down the tyrant from his throne
Proclaim French liberty.

On cursed statesmen and their crew
Let bolts of vengeance fly
Let farmers & engrossers too
Like Brutes be doom'd to die.

Then shall we live as heaven designed
On Finest Flour of Wheat
When all the knaves are put to death
Our joys will be complete.

Then raise yr drooping spirits up
Nor starve by Pitt's decree
Fix up the sacred Guillotine
Proclaim – French liberty!

This handbill was stuck up in Wellington (Somerset) in March 1801.

Source: Papers relating to riots in Stogursey (Somerset) in the possession of the Lord St Audries: transcript in the keeping of the Vicar of Stogursey.

Stratton April 2.

To all the labouring Men and Tradesmen in the Hundred of Stratton that are willing to save their Wifes and Children from the Dreadfull condition of being Starved to Death by the unfeeling and Griping Farmer,

My fellow Sufferers and Country Men, now is the time to exert yourselves and show yourselves Men and true born English Men, not to be inslaved by any Nation or Power of men on Earth, now is the time to come forward and take Vengeance on your Oppressors, Assemble all emeadiately and march in Dreadfull Array to the Habitations of the Griping Farmer, and Compell them to sell their Corn in the Market, at a fair and reasonable Price, and if any refuse and will not comply with our just demands, we must make them feel the Punishmet due to their Oppression and Extortion

Therefore you are desird to meet at Stratton next Monday by 2 of the Clock in the afternoon and march one and all with determind Hearts and Hands to have redress or Vengeance ———>

Cato

A poster from Stratton (north-east Cornwall) in 1801 (PRO, HO 42.61).

Our Liberties are assailed, — but shall we not resist the attack?

We are deprived of our Rights, — shall we not strive to regain them?

We are an Oppressed People, — and shall we not complain? &c. &c &c

"This being the case, we are desirous that our Wants and Conditions should be laid before Parliament, and at same time, that they should be informed, that we (the inhabitants of Birmingham) do not carry our Zeal and Loyalty, so far as to rest silently and submissively under the present Seat of Corruption.

We command attention! — Then through whom shall we make known such complaints? — And upon whom should we call to assemble the inhabitants for such purpose? — We conceive this is a duty which appertains to your Office, and therefore we entreat you will maturely consider this important subject, and use your utmost power and influence in forwarding our views. It is with eagerness and anxiety, we wait the result of a third application.

NB for your further information our
last meeting was held on the 2nd Decr.

"The voice of the Multitude! —

Birmingham, 8th Decr 1818.

342

A contrast in styles. 'The Monster' is the signature to a threatening letter sent to Captain Russell of Dronfield in May 1794 (PRO, HO 42.30). The British lion, holding a cap of liberty on a staff, is executed with the care of Bewick: it is at the head of a carefully-handwritten poster (opposite) of some Birmingham radicals, signed 'The voice of the Multitude' and dated 11 December 1816 (PRO, HO 40.3).

ONE HUNDRED
Guineas Reward.

WHEREAS some wicked and evil disposed Person or Persons, did write a Letter, addressed to JOSEPH BULMER, threatening to take his Life, and to burn his Premises, unless he would advance the Shipwright's Wages—and did put the same Letter under the Door of the Compting-House of Messrs. R. BULMER and Co. in *South Shields*, where the same was found on the Morning of the 14th Inst.

Whoever will give Information so that he, she, or they, may be convicted thereof, will be paid a Reward of ONE HUNDRED GUINEAS by the said Messrs. BULMER, on the Conviction of such Offenders or any of them :—

And his Majesty's Pardon will be applied for, to be extended to any Person or Persons concerned in the above, giving such Information, except to the Person who *actually* sent the said threatening Letter.

15*th December,* 1801.

Printed by PAXTON, Market Place.

Dialogue by advertisement. A cut in wages provoked a strike of shipwrights at Messrs Bulmers, followed by this letter : 'You Bulmer if you do not give the Carpenters a Gunea a Week as sure as Hell is hot O before Winter is done you may be shot O and worse than that a blease [blaze] about your Ears for that O you have been the worst Friend to us that ever cam here and we will take care of some more you may depend.' Bulmer's advertisement followed. (PRO, HO 42.62).

344

Index of Persons and Places

345

Index of Subjects

349

About the Authors

Douglas Hay, a graduate of the University of Toronto, is now lecturing at the Memorial University, St. John's, Newfoundland. Peter Linebaugh, a graduate of Swarthmore College, lectures at the University of Rochester, New York. John G. Rule, a graduate of Cambridge University, lectures at the University of Southampton and will shortly publish a book on the Cornish tin miners in the eighteenth and nineteenth centuries. E. P. Thompson, author of *The Making of the English Working Class* and founder of the Centre for the Study of Social History at Warwick University, is now writing full-time. Calvin Winslow lives in Detroit and is a journalist specializing in the labor movement in the Midwest.